Accident Management and Investigation

John Norton-Doyle

THOMSON

™

GEE

RoSPA's mission is to enhance the quality of life by exercising a powerful influence for accident prevention. We campaign for safety issues, and offer a wide range of services to organisations such as Occupational Health & Safety Training (including Accident Investigation), Audits, Consultancy, posters and other information products. Show your commitment to Health & Safety by becoming a member of RoSPA. See our website for further details: www.rospa.org.uk or ring 0870 777 2171.

© 2003 GEE

ISBN 1 86089 8254

Published by:
GEE Publishing Ltd
100 Avenue Road
Swiss Cottage
London NW3 3PG
Tel: 020 7393 7400
Fax: 020 7393 7462
Website: www.gee.co.uk

Typeset by Multiplex Medway Ltd, Walderslade, Kent.

Printed by Ashford Colour Press Ltd, Fareham Road, Gosport, Hampshire.

Contents

Chapter 1:   Introduction – the Principles of Accident Management and Investigation

i

Contents

Chapter 3:   Procedures and Arrangements for Investigating Accidents

Contents

Chapter 6:   Collating and Analysing Evidence, and Reporting Findings

Contents

Chapter 8:   Further Action

Chapter 9:   Legal Processes

Contents

Contents

Chapter 12:   Reporting to Senior Management

Contents

Appendices

About the author

John Norton-Doyle, BSc, MSc, MCIEH,
FIOSH, FRSH

John has 30 years' experience of public health and safety both in the UK and overseas. After obtaining a first-class honours degree in 1972 John joined the then Leeds City Corporation and qualified as a Registered Environmental Health Officer. Several years of enforcing legislation – largely in the commercial sector – were followed by a five-year spell overseas in the Middle and Far East, including working on the then world's largest construction site and later as the disaster plan administrator for emergency medical services at Riyadh International Airport.

On his return to the UK, John spent some time in the local authority enforcement sector developing expertise in the field of legionella control, before moving into private consultancy work, specialising mainly in health and safety in the health service. In 1990 he took up an appointment as health and safety manager for the London Fire Brigade. As a Health Education Council Fellow at Manchester Medical School, his thesis for submission for his MSc degree was on accident prevention. He remains an active member of both the Institution of Occupational Safety and Health and the Chartered Institute of Environmental Health.

The author would like to thank the people who, over many years, have provided him with the advice and support necessary for this publication to reach fruition. He would like to thank the editorial staff at GEE for staying with this project and his fellow contributors; he would also especially like to acknowledge the support, foresight and integrity of Frank David QSFM, who, many years ago, sowed the seeds for what is now in your hands.

Other contributors

Chris Staples

Chris Staples is an associate in the London Environmental Law Group of Allen & Overy. He specialises in advising businesses on the large number of complex environmental and health and safety issues that face them today. He has advised clients on these issues in a wide range of corporate, property and banking transactions. He regularly advises employers in respect of non-compliance with health, safety and environmental law and has given practical legal advice to clients on establishing and improving their health and safety and environmental management systems. In addition, he has advised clients under caution and in relation to criminal liability for workplace accidents. In the world of publishing, Chris is the legal editor of GEE's *Health & Safety Training Toolkit*.

Len Wilkins

Len Wilkins began his career first as a broker and then as an underwriter at Lloyd's of London. He was the senior tutor at the Chartered Insurance Institute's College of Insurance from 1976 to 1997 and then joined the Institute's marketing department running their team of education advisers. He is currently an assistant manager at the General Insurance Standards Council where he runs their compliance training scheme. Len qualified as an ACII in 1976 and as an FCII in 1992.

Dedication

This book is dedicated firstly to the memory of my brother Ernest Norton MM and my cousin Walter Norton (M Inst Linguists), both of whom sadly I knew for only a short time and who I would have liked to have shared this with, and secondly to all emergency services personnel who have lost their lives in the course of their duties.

List of figures

List of figures

List of abbreviations

ABI	Association of British Insurers
ACOP	Approved Code of Practice
ADR	alternative dispute resolution
BIBA	British Insurance Brokers' Association
BSI	British Standards Institute
CEN	European Committee for Standardisation
COSHH	Control of Substances Hazardous to Health Regulations 2002
CPA	Consumer Protection Act 1987
CPI	Criminal Procedure and Investigation Act 1996
CPR	Civil Procedure Rules
CPS	Crown Prosecution Service
EA	Environment Agency
EHO	environmental health officer
FAA	Fatal Accidents Act 1976
GISC	General Insurance Services Council
HAZOP	hazard analysis and operability study
HEMS	helicopter emergency medical services
HSC	Health and Safety Commission
HSE	Health and Safety Executive
HSWA	Health and Safety at Work etc. Act 1974
IBRC	Insurance Brokers' Regulation Council

ISO	International Organisation for Standardisation
LSE	London Stock Exchange
MHSWR	Management of Health and Safety at Work Regulations 1999
OH&S	occupational health and safety
OHSAS	Occupational Health and Safety Assessment System
PACE	Police and Criminal Evidence Act 1984
PPE	personal protective equipment
PTW	Permit to Work
PUWER	Provision and Use of Work Equipment Regulations 1998
RIDDOR	Reporting of Injuries, Diseases and Dangerous Occurrences Regulations 1995

1 | Introduction – Principles of Accident Management and Investigation

Issues discussed in this chapter:

- What is an accident?
  - Events and outcomes
- The legal requirements when investigating the cause of accidents
  - The effects on corporate governance
  - Influence of the Turnbull Report
  - The differing needs of insurers
- What are the principal causes of accidents?
- The influences on accident investigation
  - Cultural factors
  - Individual factors
  - Human factors
    - Ergonomics
    - Psychology
    - Errors

1:1 Why an organisation needs to be aware of the nature/definition of accident

1:1.1 What is an accident?

There is no one precise meaning of the term 'accident'. The dictionary defines 'accident' as:

> an event without apparent cause or is unexpected – an unfortunate event (especially causing harm or damage) brought about unintentionally – occurrence of things by chance

> (*Concise Oxford Dictionary*, 9th edition)

This definition provides only a limited reference for the application of duties with regard to health and safety in the workplace.

The law in itself is generally not explicit about the term 'accident', although there is specific reference in some legislation to 'accidents' (*see also* **Chapter 10**).

In most situations people do, however, have an idea of what is meant by the term 'accident'. These ideas are often a reflection of personal experience, understanding and the society and culture in which the person has developed. In many cases what are now described as accidents would in earlier times be regarded as Acts of God. In primitive societies most of life is regarded as being controlled by the 'spirit world'. What these societies regard as misfortune brought about by their gods, advanced societies regard as events explainable by science. This particularly applies to illness. Advanced societies can identify the micro-organisms which cause recognisable diseases, an explanation not available to primitive societies. The term 'Acts of God' is still something that is familiar in the context of insurance contracts (*see* **Chapter 11**), where it is used to describe events and occurrences which cannot be controlled by humans – such as earthquakes.

1:1.2 Separating event and outcome

The separation of event and outcome has to be made most strongly; otherwise the point of accident investigation can be missed. When accidents are considered in law it is generally to stress the extent of damage; as such, it has led to the idea that the greater the damage or injury sustained the greater the accident. When it comes to examining and managing 'accidents' within an organisation this idea is not helpful.

Accidents are generally identified because there has been an **outcome**, rather than because there has been an event. An **event** refers to what is happening or has happened, for example a passenger falling out of a lorry cab, whereas **outcome** describes the result of the event, for example the passenger being severely injured.

The predominant outcome is often injury or death, although it may (also) be physical damage to property, including equipment. An injury caused on the road is referred to as a road traffic accident; an injury caused at work is referred to as a workplace accident.

This can cause difficulty when determining what has to be investigated. For example, a lorry turns on its side whilst moving along a road (i.e. a road traffic accident), the door comes open and a passenger falls out. The lorry falls onto the passenger who dies as a direct result of the injuries sustained by the lorry crushing him. The driver and another occupant of the cab are uninjured. What should be investigated? Should it be:

- the road traffic accident, i.e. the lorry turning over and injury to the occupants (the **outcome**)?

or

- the door coming open and the passenger falling out (the **event**)?

In this case the answer is both. However, if the passenger falls out and is uninjured then it is very likely that *only* the road traffic accident will be investigated (i.e. the reasons why the lorry overturned and was damaged).

However, to protect the passenger in the event of a road traffic collision it is important to ensure that the cab doors stay firmly shut. If the doors fly open on impact or during the course of an unusual movement, such as a skid, then there is a risk of the occupants being thrown out, exposing them to injury. It is therefore important to investigate events – like lorry doors coming open – so that lessons can be learned and corrective action taken before any injuries occur.

In **Figures 1:1** and **1:2**, the idea of separating *events* and *outcomes* is considered in more detail. Two scenarios are presented which challenge how most people generally see events and their outcomes (adapted from Arbous, A. G. 1951 in Arbous, A. G. and Kerrick, J. E. J. *Biometric*, Vol. 7, 340).

In the first scenario (*see* **Figure 1:1**) a worker on a high scaffold drops a brick over the side which plummets 40 feet to the ground. The question is whether there has been an accident. If challenged, the worker would say the brick was dropped accidentally. Most people would accept this, without question.

Now take a second scenario (*see* **Figure 1:2**). This shows the same situation – a worker on a high scaffold dropping a brick over the side which plummets 40 feet to the ground. This time, however, the brick strikes a passer-by who happens to be on the pavement immediately underneath the worker. The passer-by, of course, goes to hospital, where the event is recorded as an accident.

The passer-by would say that they had had an accident. Most people, if asked, would also say the passer-by – not the worker – had had the accident.

The reporting procedures that exist in UK law under the Reporting of Injuries, Diseases and Dangerous Occurrences Regulations 1995 (RIDDOR) (S.I. 1995, No. 3163) would also require the event to be classified as an accident to the passer-by. The report, therefore, requires details of the injured person, *not* the person dropping the brick. In the first scenario the event would not even be required to be reported under current law, as nobody was injured (i.e. there was no outcome) and the event itself does not qualify as a dangerous occurrence (*see* **Chapter 4, section 4:4**).

FIGURE 1:1 SCENARIO 1

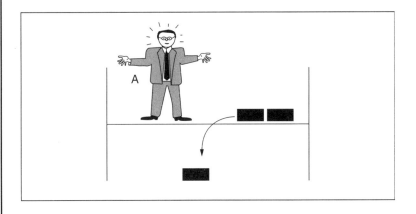

FIGURE 1:2 SCENARIO 2

So who had the accident: the worker or the passer-by?

This is a question that has to be answered if lessons are to be learnt from accident investigation. If these lessons are about how to prevent bricks falling from the scaffold, then all such events should be investigated, regardless of outcome. This is especially so if the system of work was designed to prevent bricks falling. In general, the failure in the system of work will only be identified when somebody is injured. The problem of who has had the accident – the worker or the passer-by – arises because the majority of people do not distinguish between event and outcome. When undertaking accident investigations it is important to make this distinction in order that the right information can be gathered and examined.

Clearly the thing to prevent is the dropping of the brick. It could be argued that strategies to keep passers-by away from the area or to get them to wear hard hats would also be successful, but then these are only mitigation measures. In an organisational sense it is better to prevent all items dropping from the scaffold than it is to hope that people will keep away or wear their hard hats.

1:1.3 The 'near miss'

The concept of a 'near miss' is often used to describe events that do not lead to any significant outcome, such as injury or property damage. A useful definition is:

> *Any situation in which an ongoing sequence of events was prevented from developing further and hence preventing the occurrence of potentially serious [safety related] consequences.*

> (Van Der Schaaf, Lucas and Hale, (eds), 1991. *Near miss reporting as a safety tool* Butterworth–Heinemann)

A well-known type of near miss is when two aircraft unintentionally come very close together in mid-air. Frequently, in such circumstances the pilots take avoiding action to prevent a mid-air collision. This situation should not arise because arrangements for controlling air traffic are designed to keep aircraft a safe distance apart. By reporting and collecting information on aircraft near misses, the air industry is able to examine how well the control system is working and take corrective action, as necessary.

However, it is not necessarily the case that near misses are indicative of a serious incident being averted. The accident triangle is frequently quoted as showing such a relationship between near-miss events, minor injury and major injury accidents. This relationship may be open to question – as is discussed in **Figure 1:3**.

FIGURE 1:3 THE ACCIDENT TRIANGLE

Two typical accident triangles are shown. The first of these (figure A) was derived by Frank Bird, the acknowledged founder of loss control.

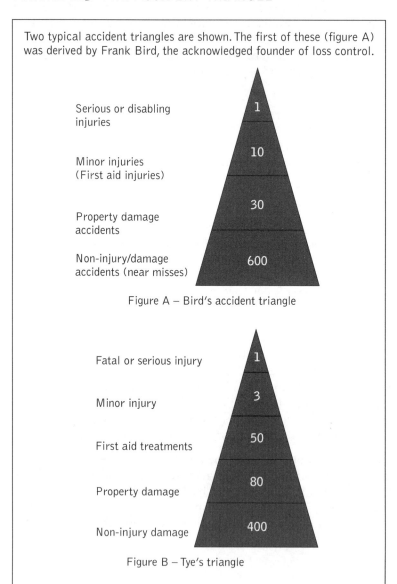

Serious or disabling injuries — 1

Minor injuries (First aid injuries) — 10

Property damage accidents — 30

Non-injury/damage accidents (near misses) — 600

Figure A – Bird's accident triangle

Fatal or serious injury — 1

Minor injury — 3

First aid treatments — 50

Property damage — 80

Non-injury damage — 400

Figure B – Tye's triangle

Bird derived his triangle from a detailed study of insurance accident report claims. The triangle purports to show that for every certain number of accidents that result in damage there will be a proportionate number that involve injury or fatality. This idea was picked up subsequently by several others and the second triangle (figure B) developed by James Tye (the late founder of the British Safety Council and acknowledged catalyst of the Robens Report which led to the Health and Safety at Work etc. Act 1974) is a development of Bird's original ideas.

Utility of accident triangles

Accident triangles have been used in an attempt to illustrate that the prevention of minor accidents is a useful approach to preventing major accidents and that the prevention of events described as 'near misses' could be effective in preventing accidents resulting in fatality or serious injury. The investigation and control of near misses or accidents resulting in minor injuries can provide both an indication of the potential for accidents involving major injuries and fatalities, as well as indicate strategies for prevention.

The problems with accident triangles

Accident triangles only show a descriptive relationship between the various events and outcomes described, i.e. the ratio of major accidents to fatal and minor accidents. They do *not* show a direct and implied relationship between the causes of events leading to minor injury and the causes of events that have fatal consequences; neither do they show that because there have been minor accidents there will always be serious ones. Imagine a snooker table with a mixture of different coloured balls in the triangle. The red balls represent serious accidents, the other colours minor accidents. Take away the coloured balls and the red balls still remain. The red balls will always be there, no matter what you do with the other coloured balls.

Indeed the evidence from the research made in this area suggests that whilst part of the outcomes of accidents are down to chance, the causative factors in relatively minor events can be distinguished from those which result in more serious outcomes. Thus considerable effort can be spent in examining and then preventing situations resulting in minor accidents which do not have the capacity to cause major injury, death or illness.

1:1.3.1 Gaining information from near misses

Events described as near misses may provide useful information. This is because they may indicate how risk control systems are *actually* working. Where an unexpected event happens it may be the result of a variety of circumstances. To illustrate this consider the scenario of a crane dropping a load unexpectedly. The dropping of the load would represent a dangerous occurrence because all the crane's design features, operating systems and methods of work should stop this from happening. One outcome of the load falling could be that it hits and injures or kills somebody standing beneath it. Such an event would normally be described as an accident and would be investigated. However, if nobody is standing under it at the time the event *may* be considered a near miss and probably would not be investigated. (For further information see Van Der Schaaf, Lucas and Hale, (eds), 1991. *Near miss reporting as a safety tool* Butterworth–Heinemann). In this case investigating the near miss would provide information on how well the crane operation control systems were working, even though no injuries resulted from the incident because nobody was underneath the crane.

A further example is provided by goods moving on a conveyer belt. The goods travel on a roller bed designed so the path and direction of travel is pre-determined. If some of the goods fall off during the process, this may often be seen as inevitable and indeed in some processes acceptable. On occasions the goods may fall off near people working around the conveyer belt. Should these goods be reasonably heavy and land very close to somebody this may be seen as a *near miss*. Should they fall and injure somebody the event will be an accident. If the process of conveying the goods has been designed to ensure that accidents do not occur, then examination of a near miss will be useful. Such an examination may find, for example, that:

- the design of the conveyer and its associated equipment is inadequate;

- there has been a change in the size or weight of goods being carried;

- new staff have not understood the correct means of putting goods on the conveyer belt;

- the conveyer belt has been speeded up in response to increased production rates;

- guarding around the conveyer belt is inadequate.

In such cases the investigation of a near miss may lead to actions that will prevent more serious outcomes from occurring, such as an injury. Notably it will also lead to measures that will reduce and even prevent damage to the goods falling from the conveyer belt – a form of 'loss' not generally considered in accident investigations.

1:1.3.2 The legal requirement to report near misses

Dangerous occurrences, as defined by the reporting duties required by RIDDOR 1995, represent a special class of near miss. Employers have a legal duty to report defined dangerous occurrences to the enforcement authority (*see* **Chapter 4, section 4:4.1.6**). These dangerous occurrences represent serious failures in control measures, which indicate that safety has not been correctly managed.

The RIDDOR requirements are related to events that happen relatively infrequently. The aim of RIDDOR is to provide information on accidents and trends to the Health and Safety Executive (HSE) that can be used to prevent accidents (RIDDOR 1995, ACOP page 36, para 102). The HSE will use the information when revising or issuing regulations, approved codes of practice and guidance notes.

This supports the general assumption that near misses provide information on failures in safety performance before a serious loss occurs (*see* **section 1:2.3**).

1:2 The reasons for investigating accidents

There are a number of reasons why accidents need to be investigated. These include:

- legal requirements;

- corporate governance;

- loss control;

- management systems;

- organisational learning;

- insurance requirements.

1:2.1 Legal requirements

The legal framework in the UK requires accidents to be considered in respect to both criminal and civil law. The legal aspects are discussed more fully in **Chapter 10**.

1:2.1.1 Criminal actions

1:2.1.1.1 The implicit requirement to conduct an accident investigation under the Management of Health and Safety at Work Regulations 1999

Under current UK legislation there is a general requirement for employers to assess the significant risk to their employees arising from or involved in their work activity.

Regulation 3(1) of the Management of Health and Safety at Work Regulations 1999 (MHSWR) requires every employer to make:

a suitable and sufficient assessment of –

(a) the risks to health and safety of his employers to which they are exposed whilst they are at work; and

(b) the risk to the health and safety of persons not in his employment arising out of or connection with the conduct by him of his undertaking.

A similar requirement applies to self-employed persons (Reg. 3(2)).

Of particular importance is that the risk assessment needs to be reviewed if:

there has been a significant change in the matters to which it relates; and where as a result of any such review changes to an assessment are required, the employer or self-employed person concerned shall make them. (MHSWR Reg. 3(b))

Whilst the MHSWR do not indicate a specific duty to undertake accident investigation, such a duty is implicit. The occurrence of an accident indicates a number of possibilities including:

- an inadequacy in the risk assessment undertaken prior to the accident, for example hazards being underestimated or overlooked;

- a deficiency in the control measures applied as a result of the pre-accident risk assessment. Such deficiency may include a range of factors, for example design and specification of equipment, human errors or the impracticality of the control measures;

- the confirmation that a risk exists, but which previously has been assessed as being acceptable. The law does not require the total elimination of danger and it is to be expected that sometimes exposure to risk will occur. However, it may need to be acknowledged that the severity of an accident may be unacceptable;

- a change in the conditions of work or the products being used since the original risk assessment was undertaken and control measures put in place.

In all such cases an adequate accident investigation will provide the information that is required to review the risk assessment.

1:2.1.1.2 The explicit legal requirement to conduct an accident investigation

A number of statutory instruments place duties on certain sectors of industry to undertake accident investigations. These include:

- the Ionising Radiation Regulations 1985 (S.I. 1985, No. 1333);

- the Railways (Safety Case) Regulations 1994 (S.I. 1994, No. 237);

- the Control of Major Accident Hazard Regulations 1999 (S.I. 1999, No. 743);

- the Reporting of Injuries, Diseases and Dangerous Occurrences Regulations 1995 (S.I. 1995, No. 3163) as applicable to railways and mines and quarries;

- the Nuclear Installations Act 1965;

- the Transport of Dangerous Goods (Safety Advisers) Regulations 1999 (S.I. 1999, No. 257);

- the Safety Representatives and Safety Committees Regulations 1977 (S.I. 1977, No. 500).

Where no special provision is made, any requirement to investigate accidents is therefore implicit under the MHSWR 1999 and relies upon a proper examination and review of the pre-accident risk assessment.

1:2.1.1.3 The proposed new duty to investigate accidents

In 2001 the HSE consulted on a proposal for legislation to create a specific new duty to investigate accidents (Consultative Document CD169). The main thrust of the proposed law would be to investigate all accidents currently reportable under RIDDOR, and re-visit risk assessments as a result of the investigation. Two options for locating the new legislation are being considered: one is to include it in the RIDDOR regulations themselves, whilst the other option is to incorporate it into the MHSWR. A good deal of support has been forthcoming from safety specialists, although concern has been expressed over the limited remit of the new duty. It is quite likely that the new legislation will be brought in over the next one to two years.

1:2.1.2 Civil actions

The civil procedure rules set out a list of requirements for the disclosure of information. These have a particular bearing on accident investigation where there has been personal injury. The pre-action personal injury protocol consists of a standard list of matters that should be disclosed. For workplace accidents this list is extensive and includes all information relating to the pre-accident risk assessments as well as a range of other matters (*see* **Chapter 9, section 9:6.1**). Within this list is an assumption that the review of risk assessment or control provisions, which are implicit in many regulations, should also be provided. The regulations in which these are implicit include:

- the Management of Health and Safety at Work Regulations 1999;
- the Control of Substances Hazardous to Health Regulations 2002;
- the Noise at Work Regulations 1989;
- the Health and Safety (Display Screen Equipment) Regulations 1992;
- the Manual Handling Operations Regulations 1992;
- the Personal Protective Equipment Regulations 1992.

The specific mention of pre- and post-accident assessments in the protocol suggest most strongly that accident investigation will need to be undertaken.

1:2.2 Corporate governance

Corporate governance is the process by which corporate bodies are controlled, managed, directed and developed – in essence, how they govern themselves. The aim of corporate governance is to ensure the viability of the company and investment reward for shareholders. In the UK, companies that are listed on the London Stock Exchange (LSE) must comply with the rule book of the LSE, which requires them to demonstrate that they have processes in place that effectively control both financial and operational risks.

These requirements follow the corporate governance code (otherwise known as the Combined Code) that was established as a result of enquiries and reports during the 1990s led by Sir Adrian Cadbury (December 1992) and later by Sir Ronald Hempel (June 1995). The Combined Code requires companies to address the following in a Director's Statement:

- a formal schedule of board matters;

- the business is a going concern;

- the effectiveness of internal controls.

The Turnbull Report or *Internal Control: Guidance for Directors on the Combined Code* (chair Nigel Turnbull, 1999, Institute of Chartered Accounts in England and Wales, London) provided additional guidance on the application of the combined code to LSE-listed companies. This guidance is predominantly directed at financial aspects of internal control and focusses on strategic issues. The Turnbull Report places responsibility for internal controls at board level. As such the boards of listed companies should be receiving information on the effectiveness of controls for health and safety risks, especially where these may have an impact on the companys' strategic objectives.

Some additional guidance has also been provided by the British Standards Institute (BSI), in the form of a 'published document' (PD 6668 – *Managing Risk for Corporate Governance: 2000*, which covers subjects such as risk assessment and the management of change in more detail than Turnbull (BSI website: www.bsi-global.co.uk).

1:2.2.1 A formal schedule of board matters

The board of a listed company must take responsibility for identifying issues that could potentially expose the company to risk and that therefore need to be controlled. Both health and safety and environmental protection are included as such issues by the Accounting Standards Board.

1:2.2.2 The business as a going concern

Of primary importance for any business is that it is a viable trading concern. A business which is not making money or which cannot cover its debts, etc., should not be trading.

The process of corporate governance places a requirement on companies to identify the risks to their business. These risks include safety, health and environment issues. Where such risks are not controlled a company can rapidly become non-viable. There is a distinction to be made here between 'pure' risks and 'speculative' risks. The former refers to issues such as health and safety risks, whereas the latter refers to the types of risks entered into as part of competitive business ventures.

1:2.2.3 The effectiveness of internal controls

This is about ensuring that those with responsibilities and obligations within a company can exercise control. It is the duty of directors to provide the board with timely, quality information. This includes identifying when things are going wrong. Five aspects need to be considered:

1. the environment in which the controls operate;

2. information and communication;

3. the nature of control activities;

4. the undertaking of monitoring and corrective action;

5. risk identification, and the setting of objectives and priorities for action.

1:2.2.4 The relationship between corporate governance and accident investigation

The occurrence of health and safety-related accidents forms part of the overall losses of any business. Such losses need to be examined and investigated so that corrective action can be taken. Accident investigation thus forms an important tool. It is one means for providing the sort of information that directors of companies will need to enable them to respond to the requirements of corporate governance and forms an important aspect of the monitoring and corrective action requirements of corporate governance.

Accident investigation is also important as a means of highlighting risks to an organisation. The principles of corporate governance require boards to be concerned with both the financial and *operational* risks, which include safety, health and environmental risks.

1:2.2.5 The impact of corporate governance

The regulatory requirement for corporate governance in the UK applies only to those UK companies listed on the LSE. These companies, however, will be suppliers to and be supplied by many other businesses. As such the requirements placed on them to ensure all risks are controlled are likely to affect a much wider range of business. Losses in supply chains or customers suffering business losses (such as lost production, extreme financial penalties and loss of public confidence) (*see* **section 1:2.3**) represent a risk to a listed company's business. Similar requirements exist or are being introduced for companies registered on stock exchanges in other countries.

It is also likely that the principles of corporate governance will be transferred to the public sector (*see* **Chapter 12, section 12:2.1**).

1:2.3 Loss control

The concept of loss control laid the foundations of the Health and Safety at Work etc. Act 1974 (HSWA). Lord Robens pointed to the link between efficiency, damage and physical injury. In his report he stated:

> *the essential import of this approach is that the employer who wants to prevent injuries in the future, to reduce loss or damage, and to increase efficiency, must look systematically at the total pattern of accidental happenings – whether or not they caused injury or damage (to property) – and must plan a comprehensive system of prevention, rather than rely on the ad hoc patching up of deficiencies which injury accidents have brought to light.*

Accident investigation is thus a requirement for organisations that wish to understand how losses occur.

The control of loss involves a managed approach to evaluate the potential for losses and to create systems through procedures and physical controls to reduce or eliminate them. It is as applicable in the public sector as it is in profit-making businesses. Loss control is part of the general business management of any organisation.

Therefore, any loss which can affect profitability should be considered, including:

- the security of premises, services and products;
- the reliability of supply and materials;

- public and product liability;

- public confidence in brand name (which will affect whether or not customers continue to buy products/services);

- business confidence in brand name (which will affect whether or not other business continue to supply or work with the organisation, or banks continue to invest);

- confidence in the management (*see* **section 1:2.2**);

- financial controls, including protection from fraud;

- environmental impact (including waste management);

- plant and equipment;

- fire protection;

- human resources;

- health and safety.

1:2.4 Management systems

Regulation 5 of the MHSWR 1999 requires every employer to put in place arrangements for:

> ... *the effective planning, organisation, control, monitoring and review of the preventive and protective measures.*

This, in effect, is a duty to take a systematic approach to the management of health and safety and is supported by the HSE guidance given in *Successful health and safety management* (HSG65) (HSE Books, tel: 01787 881165; website: www.hsebooks.co.uk) (*see* **Chapter 2, section 2:3.1**).

An effective management system will have accident investigation provisions in place. Information from this will assist in the monitoring and review arrangements of the health and safety system by ensuring that deficiencies and failures are adequately picked up and acted upon.

The role of accident investigation in management systems is discussed more fully in **Chapter 2**.

1:2.5 Organisational learning

Organisational learning refers to the ability of an organisation to develop and improve. It is a complex area, but of interest here is the role of accident investigation. Successful organisations are those that learn from their mistakes. Accidents in the workplace represent a special class of mistakes. Accident investigation is the means by which the core information is obtained so that lessons can be learnt and corrective action undertaken.

If an adequate and effective accident investigation system is not in place then the lessons will not be learnt and organisational learning will not take place.

1:2.6 Insurance requirements

Insurance is a means by which an organisation or an individual can be safeguarded against financial loss. By taking out insurance an organisation is paying a premium and effectively gambling that this will buy sufficient cover to offset any losses that occur. The setting of the premium is linked to the likelihood of loss. Where the losses involve a workplace accident an investigation will be made of the circumstances and this will determine the liability of the insurer to pay for the losses incurred.

A thorough accident investigation system will assist an organisation to meet the demands of the insurance company for information. It will also highlight areas where the organisation may be under-insured (i.e. where unpredicted losses have occurred which are not insured for) or where better control measures are required to satisfy the demands of the insurer.

This relationship between insurance requirements and accident investigation is covered more fully in **Chapter 11**.

1:3 The causes of accidents

There are a number of factors and conditions that may be involved in the causes of accidents.

Factors are facts or circumstances that can influence the way an accident can develop. They tend to be 'givens' which cannot be easily changed or influenced. For example, human beings will be less vigilant when tired and hence make mistakes. The state of tiredness cannot be altered once it exists, unless the person stops work and sleeps.

Factors include:

- the nature of human behaviour;

- the way that management systems work;

- the complexity of the organisation;

- the nature of work tasks and activities and processes.

Conditions refer to the physical state or attributes that may exist in the workplace. They tend to be situations that can be changed. For example, insufficient light may mean that gauges are difficult to read and this causes someone to undertake the wrong actions during a process.

Conditions include:

- the working environment;

- the social and cultural environment;

- normal working or maintenance working.

In accident investigation it is important to have an understanding of the factors and conditions involved. This helps to ensure that the *cause(s)* of the events can be identified and the extent of their contribution understood. For example, in the investigation of a failure of machine guarding, a simple approach would be to consider only the engineering of the guard, examining only the mechanical failure issues. However, by adopting this approach, the investigation would overlook a number of other possible contributing factors and conditions, such as:

- the way that the operator uses the machinery;

- the decisions made by designers and/or management in developing and installing the machine;

- ergonomic factors involved, such as work space, access to the machinery and ease of use;

- whether the guarding failed during normal working, during maintenance or as a result of production pressures;

- whether the machine complies with all relevant legislation and standards.

1:3.1 Interacting factors in accident causation

Figure 1:4 illustrates how accidents are caused by a variety of interacting factors. These include:

- the working environment;

- the human factors (the types and causes of human errors);

- the management system which is responsible for designing, regulating and monitoring the controls that prevent exposure to risk;

- the risks involved (and how they have been identified and assessed).

FIGURE 1:4 THE INTERACTING FACTORS CAUSING ACCIDENTS

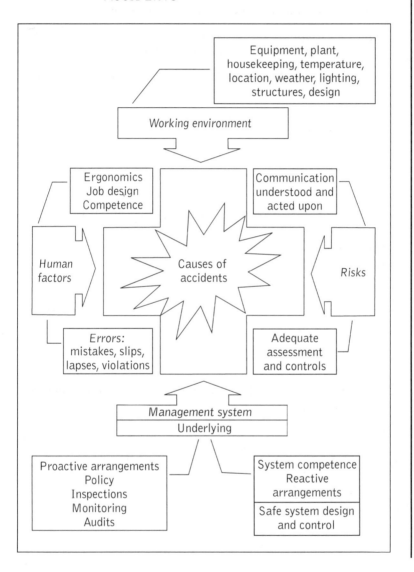

1:3.1.1 The working environment

Conditions in the working environment can play their part in accidents. For example, where there is insufficient lighting people will be unable to spot hazards and may trip up. Extremes of temperature (whether working inside or out) can cause hypothermia or heat exhaustion, conditions which can lead to errors being made or short cuts being taken (*see* **section 1:3.1.4**).

Working outside may also be affected by elements of the weather other than just temperature. For example, wet, windy and icy conditions increase the risk of slips and falls, as well as hypothermia.

1:3.1.2 Human factors

Attention must be given to the way the workstation is designed because if insufficient attention has been given to the way human beings respond in different circumstances, then operators will make errors or find short cuts. Both increase the risk of accident. For example, if a supermarket checkout is not properly designed the cashier may suffer from upper limb disorders, such as stiff shoulders. A control room which is poorly laid out may cause an operator to mistake one dial or control for another.

1:3.1.3 Management systems

If adequate management systems are not in place, inspections and other monitoring processes (for example) will not identify when control systems are not working. As a result, poor systems of work may develop which eventually lead to accidents. Inspections and monitoring need to take into account the human factors and the working environment. The necessary risk assessments will need to be reviewed to take these factors into account.

1:3.1.4 Risks

The risk assessment process should take into account all the factors involved – the working environment, work processes, human factors and management systems, etc. If the risks are not known or communicated to the workforce, then people may take dangerous actions or operate controls in a way that is not intended, for example driving a fork-lift truck with the forks raised. Changes in environmental conditions during the execution of any work task, for example the loss of natural light whilst working outside, may affect work. Repetitive work actions/tasks may lead to boredom and inattention, leading to an increased risk of accidents. Therefore, human factors and ergonomic considerations should be taken into account when assessing the risks (*see also* **section 1:5.2.2** on human factors).

1:3.2 The complexity of accident causation

In practice, accidents do not occur because of a single factor. A combination of two or more factors will usually be involved in the immediate cause, and the underlying causes can be quite complex. The nature and detail of these complexities are discussed in more detail in **Appendix 1** and are illustrated with a number of models.

1:4 The relationship between risk assessment and accident investigation

The purpose of the arrangements for preventive and protective measures required by reg. 5 of the MHSWR – as well as the general duties required by s.2 of the HSWA – is to ensure exposure to risk is avoided as far as is reasonably practicable.

An important aspect to consider in accident investigations is the nature of the provision made for the identification and management of risk. This is a key factor in determining if an organisation has adequate measures in place to prevent or control exposure to risk. An accident arises when there has been an exposure to risk. The occurrence of an accident is in itself a strong indication that the preventive and protective control measures are inadequate or missing.

The investigation approach must therefore look at the nature of the risk or risks involved in the work or activity being undertaken when the accident occurred. In effect an accident investigation forms part of the resilience mechanism of an organisation (*see* **Figure 1:5**). The investigation will question whether the risk had previously been identified as part of a risk assessment and whether adequate precautions had been put in place to eliminate or control it.

An accident investigation will need to consider:

- the risk to which there has been exposure;
- whether or not the risk had been previously identified (as part of the risk assessment required by reg. 3 of the MHSWR);
- the nature of the preventive and protective measures.

There will be situations where the accident reveals a risk which had not previously been considered or which had been assessed as being minimal or acceptable (*see* **Figure 1:5**).

In some circumstances events may occur which represent exposure to a known risk at an acceptable level. Such situations will be rare but may occur in well-managed organisations, especially where there is a higher degree of hazard. The accident may be one which has been predicted and for which reasonable and practicable measures are in place to control it. Nevertheless the accident has occurred and can be adjudged as being 'unavoidable'. In other words, it would not be reasonably practicable to remove this danger, but the chance of it happening is very rare and the circumstances are known about. For example, launching a lifeboat into stormy seas requires an understanding of the extreme risks involved. Whilst all practicable measures will be taken to minimise and control these risks, the nature of the environment will mean that in order to attempt a rescue certain dangers must be accepted. Occasionally these dangers will give rise to an accident that may involve loss of life at sea. This would not stop the work of the lifeboat service and would not necessarily cause a change to procedures and equipment unless the nature of the event was entirely unexpected.

Accident investigation thus provides a means of identifying 'new' risks and re-categorising known risks.

When completed, the investigation should be used to improve the preventive and protective arrangements required by the MHSWR (*see* **section 1:5.3** and **Chapter 8, section 8:6.1**).

FIGURE 1:5 TERMINOLOGY FOR RISK

An accident investigation should lead to a clear description of the risk(s) involved in the accident. This will require consideration of the processes and methods that should have been used to identify the risk and eliminate or control it. The identification and response to risks has a number of stages. There are a number of ways in which these stages can be represented. The following is a suggested approach:

- **Risk analysis:** this is the process of describing risk, its size, shape and form, and this will include hazard identification and analysis. For example, what are the hazards when working over open water and what risks exist? An example of a hazard is the depth of the water and the rate of the current. An example of a risk is falling in the water and drowning.

- **Risk assessment:** this is the process by which decisions are made about risks. It involves considering such questions as:

  - are they too high?

  - are they tolerable or acceptable?

  - are they important or not?

  By using this process, a boundary around the risks, based on what is acceptable and what is unacceptable, can be defined. For example, it would be unacceptable for someone working on a bridge over water to fall into the water – under any circumstances.

- **Risk management:** this process is concerned with the controls exercised over risk, in other words how a particular risk is kept inside the risk boundary described in the risk assessment. Stepping outside this boundary would be unacceptable, i.e. it may lead to an accident. For example, providing guarding and fall protection and a described safe system of work when maintaining a bridge over water in order to reduce the likelihood of the person falling into the water makes the risk acceptable.

- **Resilience:** some flexibility or resilience needs to be built into systems to ensure that they can cope with a breakdown in either one or all of the other processes, i.e. analysis, assessment and management. Most organisations are familiar with this, at least in part. It is called emergency preparedness, a typical example being a fire evacuation plan for a building. More importantly, an organisation needs to be able to respond to the lessons provided by examining accidents. These should be used to inform the management process and the system of controls.

1:5 The influences on accident investigation

There are a number of influences that need to be taken into account when dealing with workplace accidents. These are:

- cultural factors;

- individual factors;

- organisational factors;

- the law (*see* **Chapter 10**);

- insurance (*see* **Chapter 11**);

- society.

1:5.1 Cultural factors

The cultural factors involve:

- the wider culture in which we live;
- the culture of the organisation in which we work.

1:5.1.1 Wider culture

Culture reflects the values, beliefs, behaviours and expectations that people share. An event attributed as an Act of God is seen differently to an event in which human intervention is involved. Traditionally, events such as floods, earthquakes and landslides were described as Acts of God. In some societies everyday events, such as a load falling off the back of a cart, are still perceived as Acts of God. Such events are considered as 'fate' and beyond the control of humans. That there are Acts of God is a reflection of the religious nature of a culture. Each culture has its own religious connotations and these can be powerful forces in ordering society and the response of people to calamity. This applies to how people (as groups and as individuals) identify and react to accidents.

1:5.1.2 Organisational culture

Each organisation has its own 'culture'. The relevance of the culture of an organisation to health and safety is now well established. The expression 'safety culture' reflects the nature of the shared beliefs, expectations, values and behaviours of people within an organisation. Safety should be seen as an important and essential part of the way the organisation works.

The HSE describes culture in guidance HSG65 *Successful health and safety management* as:

> *the product of individual and group values, attitudes, perceptions, competencies and patterns of behaviour that determine the commitment to, and the style or proficiency of, an organisation's health and safety management.*

An organisation may be described as having a 'blame' or 'no-blame' culture. A 'blame' culture is one where individuals are blamed if something goes wrong and an accident occurs. In this type of culture it is very difficult to find the true causes of accidents. In a 'no-blame' culture people are open to discovering the true cause of an accident. As a result of this, the event is easier to investigate and it is more likely that prevention of future accidents will result from actions taken.

1:5.2 Individual factors

Two aspects of individual factors are important here:

1. how individuals understand accidents;
2. individuals' roles in causation, i.e. human factors.

1:5.2.1 The meaning of accidents to individuals

Individuals tend only to refer to events as being accidents when there is some tangible outcome, such as damage and/or injury.

Individuals can have different perceptions of an event. If somebody is injured, the individual may attribute the cause as being 'accidental', whilst another person may *not* consider the cause of the injury (or the event) to be an accident. An individual may not report an event if they did not think it was an accident, whilst another will report virtually everything that happens to them. This has implications for accident investigation, especially near-miss reporting, because events have to be reported before they can be investigated.

There are a number of factors that affect whether an individual perceives an event to be an accident:

- the amount of control they have over a situation;
- the degree to which they have voluntarily chosen to enter the situation;
- the amount of risk they expected to take;
- whether they expect to be disciplined for their acts or omissions.

As part of the perception of events, people will react to accident situations in different ways and this includes a need to consider aspects of blame.

An individual may regard themselves as blameless and seek to avoid blame by laying the fault elsewhere. They may accuse others of not taking enough care or of deliberately exposing them to risk. In some cases individuals may regard an accident as an act of malice.

In an organisation with a 'blame' culture, individuals may seek to cover up the causes of accidents or, at the very least, attempt to apportion blame elsewhere. In a more open and 'no-blame' culture, individuals are more likely to give an open and honest account of the circumstances involved in the accident.

How an individual views an accident will reflect their attitudes and the general culture that exists. If somebody has an accident, others may regard it as a result of 'not taking enough care'. The reality may be that the person involved was distracted at the time or was not sufficiently knowledgeable or skilful to do the tasks involved. It is very important when dealing with accidents to consider the perceptions and attitudes of individuals towards the accident.

1:5.2.2 Human factors

The part that individuals may play in accidents is generally considered under the heading 'human factors'. The study of human factors considers both the attitudes and behaviours of individuals and groups and the underlying psychology. It also embraces the study of how people and their work environment interact.

Humans factors are an important consideration when dealing with accidents – especially in accident investigation. They should, however, be taken account of in the wider context of organisational management (*see* **section 1:6** and **Chapter 2, section 2:3.3**).

1:5.3 Organisational factors

Responsibility for accident prevention is mainly a requirement for employers. This is set out in s.2 of the HSWA and is supported by a number of regulations, particularly the MHSWR.

Section 2 of the HSWA states:

(1) It shall be the duty of every employer to ensure, so far as is reasonably practicable, the health, safety and welfare at work of all his employees.

This duty is further explained by the succeeding requirements in the Act and regulations made under the Act.

Under the MHSWR, employers have a duty to conduct a risk assessment of all health and safety hazards their employees and anyone else on the premises may be exposed to. Furthermore, employers must have suitable arrangements in place for the effective planning, organisation, monitoring and review of prevention and protective measures that are set up to eliminate or control the identified risk (*see* **Chapter 2, section 2:2.2**). These arrangements need to be based on the risk involved in the work.

An accident can therefore be regarded as a failure or deficiency in these arrangements. The employer is responsible for the selection, recruitment and training of employees, the provision of working procedures (i.e. safe systems of work) and ensuring that these are supervised. Section 2(c) of the HSWA requires an employer to provide:

> ... *such information, instruction, training and supervision as is necessary to ensure, as far as is reasonably practicable, the health and safety at work of his employees.*

An organisation therefore needs to be well organised and have a systematic approach to the management of health and safety. Accidents are more likely to occur when these fundamental duties are ignored or poorly exercised.

The way in which any organisation operates and the effectiveness of the arrangements made to identify risk and prevent accidents will affect the way accidents are identified and investigated. It is therefore useful to regard an accident as being some indication of a failure or deficiency in an organisation's management system.

The effectiveness of management arrangements will be reflected in the culture of the organisation. In one which has a good safety culture it will be recognised that it is hardly fair to blame individuals if there are deficiencies in any of these important aspects and duties.

1:5.4 The law

The HSWA makes absolute the duty employers have to protect, as far as is reasonably practicable, the health and safety of their workforce and others affected by their business. When an accident occurs in the workplace, the duty of care between the employer and employees comes into question and claims for damages and negligence can result (covered in detail in **Chapter 10**).

The legal definition of what constitutes an accident can be quite difficult. Sometimes fault (i.e. liability) cannot be assigned to an individual or organisation. This causes difficulty when dealing with an accident with regards to the law.

The law requires certain outcomes, be they to put someone behind bars or to decide upon a claim of damages. An accident investigation is therefore seen as a way of apportioning blame and defining retribution, the latter either by way of a payment of damages awarded against the organisation or for substantiating early retirement on the grounds of work-related debility and the consequential award of added pension, and sometimes both. This can be a hindrance when seeking to make accident investigation a tool for the improvement of management systems.

Managing an accident requires an understanding of the balance between the legal requirements and the need for an organisation to learn. Such organisational learning may be directed at improving the safety culture in general or specific safety procedures or practices. Very often both are required.

1:5.5 Insurance

A contract of insurance is a particular area of law (*see* **Chapters 10** and **11**). It is possible for an event to be discounted as being an 'accident' for the purposes of the insurance contract whilst at the same time being regarded as an 'accident' by those involved.

1:5.6 Society

Society responds to accidents in a number of different ways. This has the effect of both describing accidents in terms of who happens to be involved and in terms of where the accident takes place. Societal influences in the way accidents are perceived and considered have a bearing on accident management and investigation. This involves both society at large and the social functioning and structure of organisations.

1:5.6.1 Society at large

The requirement in law is not to entirely eliminate danger. This is because it is recognised that in order to have a functioning society some risk must be taken. Some jobs, such as those of the emergency services, flying aircraft, deep-sea fishing, mining, etc., have, in real terms, a high degree of inherent risk and exposure to hazardous circumstances. Society expects workers in such jobs to face the hazards and overcome them in order to do the tasks which society expects them to carry out.

However, the societal response to this varies. Emergency services' workers are expected to be exposed to real hazards. This is what society pays them to do. This expectation is supported by the pension scheme arrangements, which are designed to account for the dangerous nature of the job and the possibility of being killed or injured at work.

The same is not true, however, of other occupations where a similar (or sometimes perhaps greater) level of hazard exists. Aeroplanes are expected to stay in the air and there is no societal provision for the fact that flying at 35,000 feet represents exposure to a very real hazard. Thus, society views accident events differently depending on context and situation. This difference in the way accidents are seen in some part reflects the degree of enterprise involved. Fishermen are exposed to severe hazards, but do so voluntarily to earn a living whereas emergency services operate to provide a public service and there is a degree of perceived altruism in the way they are exposed to danger.

One consequence of how society treats accidents is the division made between the various places where accidents happen. The law tends to reflect this. Thus society has different responses and perceptions of accidents that happen in the home, on the road and in the workplace.

1:5.6.2 At home

Accidents in the home tend to involve children and the elderly. This is not surprising as these two groups spend most of their time in the home. Children are exploring their environment and learning about risk and generally being exposed to the hazards of growing up. The elderly are frail and perhaps less able to cope with the home environment than when they were younger.

However, what is of importance to the workplace accident investigator is the part that home life can play in contributing to the causes of accidents at work. Many of the stress factors of life, such as the death of a close relative, moving house and divorce, arise in and around the home.

An accident might happen at work, but its causation may lie partly at home. For example, somebody who has had an argument with their spouse before coming to work may not be in the right frame of mind to give their full attention to work.

1:5.6.3 On the road

A road traffic accident investigation will have different implications compared to an at-work accident precisely because of the societal context in which it takes place. In law, for the most part, a road traffic accident is not a workplace accident – although many people in fact are at work when driving.

The exposure of employees to the hazards and risks of driving on the road may currently lie outside the duty of care of the employer. Employers may therefore have or take no responsibility for the behaviour of their drivers or time pressures and other stresses to which the employees are exposed whilst driving. This is a subject currently being examined by a task force, to decide on the extent that occupational health and safety law and practice should be extended to driving in the course of employment.

A court will have little (or no) interest in the fact that a company may not have trained its drivers to drive to a high standard when a driver is being prosecuted for driving without due care and attention. The fact that the driver was driving fast or using a mobile phone to meet the interests of the company has no bearing on the fact that the driving itself was being done without due care and attention. However, the losses and impact on the company may be significant when such a road traffic accident occurs as a result of such driving.

Therefore, the management and investigation of road traffic accidents is different, but the employer will need to be prepared and take action when they occur.

1:5.6.4 The workplace

The structure and functioning of society is also reflected in the workplace. Work represents one of the social structures that are fundamental in society. As such it is to be expected that the societal context of the workplace will have its own impact on accidents. For example, the beliefs of a group of workers, the relationship between workers and managers and the pressures that exist between members of a team – or those pressures that are exerted by others – will all have an effect on the way accidents are perceived and dealt with (*see also* **section 1:5.1**).

The way that workers and managers and different groups of workers relate to each other may affect the way accidents are perceived and dealt with. For example, the death or serious injury of a close colleague will have a profound effect on immediate colleagues, but may have less of an effect on managers, especially if the organisation is large and the senior management is remote from the site. There is the possibility that the workforce will see management as to blame for the incident. Managers, on the other hand, may regard the incident as due to carelessness or self-inflicted – the person did not obey the rules or did something when it was common sense to avoid the situation or not undertake the actions.

Again it is possible that accidents that result in death or serious injury will be seen as important, but near-miss events will be disregarded. This can be a direct result of how the society of the workplace is organised and how it functions. There may be tacit or even explicit acceptance of poor safety behaviour because of the way the relationships between people in the workplace are structured. It is very much related to the culture of the organisation: the beliefs, attitudes and behaviours that shape the way people see and respond to accidents (*see* **section 1:5.1**).

Who does what, when, where and how can all give insights into the understanding of management systems and the root causes of accidents (*see* **Chapter 2** and **Appendix 1**).

The impact of a fatality or serious injury in the workplace will be greater than that in society as a whole. Society as a whole may be relatively unaffected by such an event, especially if it receives scant media attention. On the other hand, in the smaller society of the workplace the event may have profound implications. People may be traumatised, put under stress or generally be unable to cope with the situation. The perception of an accident in the workplace will to a large extent be different from that of the general public.

1:5.6.5 Public perception

Society has a different perception of separate, individual accidents and those that involve numbers of people or certain situations. Aircraft accidents, for example, always attract a considerable degree of attention and concern. In the UK the recent history of major rail accidents has received significant attention and dramatic responses, both in the media and in Parliament. A similar amount of concern is not expressed for those road traffic accident victims who die regularly and in relative obscurity.

Society is not consistent and those dealing with accidents need to be aware of this fact. In the public mind there is a difference between the low-frequency, high-severity events such as the Paddington train and Concorde aircraft crashes and the high-frequency, lower-severity events (in terms of number of people injured or killed at one time) such as road traffic accidents. This difference in public perception is often seen as a lower social acceptability of high consequence events. Society is said to be more risk averse when it comes to the number of people dying together as a result of a single accident.

Organisations and their managers need to be prepared to deal with major events as well as the events which result in less serious consequences. They especially need to be aware of the differing pressures that arise when a major incident − i.e. one attracting public attention − occurs and those when the event is more or less contained in house. The organisation and functions of management need to be such that the lesser events are taken seriously. If an organisation waits for the socially unacceptable accidents to occur before it responds then significant opportunities to learn will be missed (*see* **section 1:2.5**).

1:6 Human factors in accident investigation

Many workplaces, work activities and procedures are designed and developed on the basis that humans are infallible. This is despite the fact that there is a vast body of evidence that indicates that humans are quite the opposite.

It has been known for many years that some 95–98% of road accidents are caused by human error. The actions and decisions of drivers generally contribute in some way to the causes of accidents, with engineering causes − such as road layout and street furniture − being the sole cause in less than 2% of accidents. However, emphasis has been placed on engineering measures rather than human behaviour measures because approaches to modify human behaviour have been singly unsuccessful.

The introduction of mini-roundabouts was a direct response to drivers exhibiting poor driving behaviour at road junctions, resulting in head-on impacts with serious consequences. The mini-roundabout causes drivers to alter the position of their car on the road and, even if they exhibit bad behaviour, the resulting accident will be a sideswipe with less serious consequences than a head-on collision. In a similar way speed bumps restrict traffic speed in built-up areas and contribute to the reduction of road accidents involving susceptible pedestrians, such as children and the elderly. This is despite the fact that socially responsible drivers would be expected to be aware of the risks to pedestrians when driving on urban roads. Both these measures change the behaviour of the car on the road. Even if the human continues to drive recklessly in the majority of situations it is their car that gets damaged and not people.

Similarly in the workplace, human behaviour and decision-making has a major part to play in the causes of accidents. This is true both for individuals and for organisations as a whole. In the Clapham rail disaster the inquiry found that short cuts were taken by signalling engineers to save time (they had long working hours) and because no immediate danger was foreseen. Cables were cut and left in place. This was not just a single human failure but reported in the inquiry as generally poor management practice. In the case of the roll-on/roll-off passenger car ferry the *Herald of Free Enterprise*, which capsized in the approaches to the Belgian port of Zeebrugge en route to Dover in England on 6 March 1987, it soon became apparent that the vessel had left the port of Zeebrugge with her bow doors open. The inquiry referred to the company as being 'infected with the disease of sloppiness'.

1:6.1 The HSE's definition of human factors

The HSE defines human factors in their guidance *Reducing error and influencing behaviour* (HSG48) as:

> … *environmental, organisational and job factors and human and individual characteristics, which influence behaviour at work in a way which can affect health and safety. A simple way to view human factors is to think about three aspects, the job, the individual*

41

and the organisation and how they impact upon people's health and safety and safety related behaviour.

The HSE approach is to divide the human factors into consideration of:

- **the job** – this includes the tasks and activities that need to be performed, the workload, environmental conditions, the use of controls and equipment, the display of signals, process information and the procedures to be used;

- **the organisation** – this is about the culture, leadership and management style, allocation of resources, patterns of work, communication and organisational arrangements, particularly those for health and safety;

- **the individual** – this considers an individual's capabilities (i.e. physical abilities, age and sex), competence (i.e. skills, knowledge and experience), personality, attitudes, behaviours and perception of risk.

1:6.2 Approaches to human factors

The study of human factors has been approached from two basic angles:

1. ergonomics;

2. psychology.

Both ergonomics and the application of psychology in the workplace are sometimes referred to separately. This confusion arises from the two different routes that the subjects have followed as they have developed. However, they should be considered together when looking at human factors.

1:6.2.1 Ergonomics

Ergonomics has developed from the integration of a range of sciences, mainly biological sciences such as physiology, bio-mechanics and anatomy, with engineering. Ergonomics is not a discrete subject as it involves the application of both technology and science. It is concerned with the study of the interaction of humans with their work and workplace.

Ergonomics has largely been to do with improving the design of equipment and workstations so that the work can be designed to match the human doing the job, rather than the other way round. The application of ergonomic principles in job design is to ensure that the health and safety of the individual is safeguarded.

A simple job, such as checking goods at a supermarket checkout, can be particularly harmful to the cashier. The job involves a series of repetitive small movements, involving the lifting or handling of goods from one side of a till to another, passing them over automatic readers and at the same time using the cash register to input information. If not properly designed the work can produce severe upper limb disorders and musculo-skeletal problems for the back. An ergonomically well-designed supermarket checkout will minimise or totally eradicate any risk of musculo-skeletal problems from occurring.

More recently ergonomic principles have been applied to the design and operation of whole organisations. This involves applying ergonomic principles to the design of the organisation as a whole with a view to improving productivity and increasing job satisfaction as well as safety.

1:6.2.2 Psychology

The application of psychology in the workplace has generally been concerned with identifying the nature of human errors and how they can be prevented.

Approaches to human error have been classified as follows:

- the commissions/omissions approach;
- the task-specific approach;
- the detection and recognition approach;
- the skills, rules and knowledge approach.

1:6.2.2.1 The commissions/omissions approach

The commissions/omissions approach is to consider errors in terms of acts of commission and omission, selection, sequence, time and quality. These are defined as:

- errors of commission – this is doing something that should not be done, such as adding or including a step in a process that is not supposed to be done;
- omission – this is *not* doing something that should be done;
- selection – this is about making a wrong choice from a range of options;
- sequencing – following steps (i.e. actions or events) out of sequence;
- timing – doing the right thing but too early or too late;
- quality – not doing something properly.

1:6.2.2.2 The task-specific approach

The task-specific approach involves looking at specific aspects of work such as:

- substitution – wrongly selecting an activity or task due to habit (i.e. driving to work at a weekend instead of the shops because the habitual route is familiar);

- selection – making the wrong choice from a number of options;

- reading – making a mistake in collecting information, for example reading a gauge incorrectly;

- forgetfulness – cognitive failure (but the use of checklists can overcome this);

- reversal – doing the opposite of what is intended. This is often associated with stress and related to design, for example a tap set in such a way that you cannot tell when it is on or off;

- unintentional activation – turning something on unintentionally, such as a valve, engine, etc. (but positive controls can prevent this action by locking off);

- mental overload – becoming unable to think properly, for example when suffering from fatigue (the design of tasks and the length of time on the job have an affect on this);

- physical limitations – individual perception, the layout of workstations, the design of the working area, the physique of the individual.

1:6.2.2.3 The detection and recognition approach

The detection and recognition approach, developed in the rail industry, involves the following categories of error:

- detection errors – not detecting danger or not noticing that something is wrong;

- perceptual errors – not understanding or misunderstanding the characteristics of signals;

- recognition errors – not recognising a signal and giving it the wrong meaning or interpretation.

1:6.2.2.4 The skills, rules and knowledge approach

The skills, rules and knowledge approach is the most useful categorisation of errors. Developed by Rasmussen and Reason ('Reasons, causes and human error' in Rasmussen, J., Duncan, K. and Leplat, J. (eds), 1987. *New Technology and Human Error* Wiley) it considers the *levels of control* at which people operate and the *types of errors* that they make involving each level.

There are three levels of behaviour that show an increasing level of conscious control:

1. skill-based behaviour in which people carry out routines on 'automatic pilot' with built-in checking loops;

2. rule-based behaviour in which people select those routines, at a more or less conscious level, out of a very large inventory of possible routines built up over many years of experience;

3. knowledge-based behaviour where people have to cope with situations which are new to them and for which they have no routines. This is a fully conscious process of interaction with the situation to solve a problem.

Errors in these three categories arise as:

- skill-based errors arising during the execution of a routine task, e.g. operating an incorrect control;

- rule-based errors occurring when using a set of operating instructions to guide a sequence of actions, e.g. the correct diagnosis of a problem followed by the right operations to correct it but in the wrong sequence;

- knowledge-based errors happening when a choice has to be made between alternative courses of action, for example an incorrect diagnosis based on scientific knowledge and the conscious formation of a judgement about what will happen.

As a working principle humans try to delegate control of behaviour to the most routine level at any given time. Only when they pick up signals that the more routine level is not coping do they switch over to the next level. This provides an efficient use of the limited resources of attention which humans have at their disposal and allows them to operate to a limited extent as 'parallel processors', i.e. doing several things at once, for example talking and driving. The crucial feature in achieving error-free operation is to ensure that the right level of operation is used at the right time. It can be just as disastrous to operate at too high a level of conscious control as at too routine a level.

1:6.2.2.5 Categorising errors

A critical distinction has been made between **mistakes**, such as selecting the wrong plan of action, and **slips**, which are errors in the implementation of an otherwise appropriate plan:

- slips (unintended actions) – unconscious automatic reactions (observable when made) not intended by the doer which lead to a task-execution failure;

- lapses (unintended actions) – unconscious mental errors, possibly later recalled, related to memory failures;

- mistakes (intended actions) – can be rule-based or knowledge-based, and involve applying good rules incorrectly or applying bad rules;

- violations, deliberate acts, decisions deviating from standard practices (intended actions) – can be made to continue or bring about safe operation as well as failures. These occur when a human deliberately carries out an action contrary to a rule, such as an operating procedure, or maliciously tampers with or disrupts a work process or product. Violations involve complex issues of conformity, communications, morale and discipline.

It is the skill-based errors which are amenable to prediction. The rule-based errors are more dependent on time, the mind-set and state of the human being concerned, and thus are harder to predict. The knowledge-based errors are even more difficult to predict, as they arise from a detailed knowledge of the process possessed by an individual. It is at this end of the spectrum that mistakes are found.

1:6.2.2.6 Error detection

Detecting human error is a difficult and poorly-refined process. The probability of human error is often expressed as:

$$\frac{\text{number of errors}}{\text{number of opportunities for error (exposure)}}$$

Figure 1:6 illustrates the relative contribution of the different types of error.

FIGURE 1:6 PREDICTING TYPES OF ERROR RATES

Error type	Probability of occurrence	Proportion of all occurrences (%)	Detection rate (%)	Recovery rate (%)
Skill-based	< 1 in 10,000 > 1 in 100	61	86	69
Rule-based	< 1 in 1,000 > 1 in 10	27	73	35
Knowledge-based	< 1 in 100 ~ 1 (certain)	12	71	23

Detection rate indicates the percentage of times when the error is actually detected; if the error is not discovered there is no opportunity to do anything about it. Recovery refers to the percentage of times the error does not lead to an accident or failure because steps have been taken (after detection) to control the consequences of the actions.

1:6.2.2.7 Stages when errors 'kick in'

The following three stages can be recognised when errors happen:

1. the planning stage – rule-based mistakes tend to arise during the planning stage of any action;

2. the storage stage – lapses are made at this stage which reflect the degree to which memory is accessible at the time when the action or decision is being made;

3. the execution stage – slips occur at this stage, i.e. when the action is being made.

1:6.2.2.8 Additional types of error

It is useful to think of active and latent errors. **Active errors** are errors that have an immediate effect. **Latent errors** tend to be hidden in systems and indicate that the accident will occur sometime after the error has been made, for example making incorrect calculations in a design that then fails once the item is built (*see* **Appendix 1, section A1:3.1**).

1:6.2.3 Mind set

Psychologists have recognised that people perpetually persist in making the facts of a situation fit their view of the situation in preference to adjusting their view to fit the facts. This is usually referred to as their 'mind set'. The incident at the nuclear reactor at Chernobyl in April 1986 is a classic example of this. The people operating the plant convinced themselves that all the warning signs that something was going wrong were expected to happen and were the direct result of the experimentation they were performing and which they believed they had under control. Several of the most serious nuclear accidents had similar causes – people making the wrong decisions based on what was happening and then implementing the wrong actions as a result of these bad decisions – despite the fact that warning signs were still evident.

1:6.2.3.1 Group think

When people work in groups, consensus can be achieved but the actual problem is often not identified and/or resolved. In 'group think' everybody believes that everything is alright when in fact it is not. The group works together to confuse the reality. Again, the events at Chernobyl are a good example of this.

The idea of group think is particularly important in the understanding of the latency of management failures and solutions (*see* **Appendix 1, section A1:3.1**).

2 | Systems and Procedures to be in Place Before an Accident Occurs

Issues discussed in this chapter:

- What systems should be in place?
- Effective safety management systems
  - HSG65
  - BS 8800
- The properties of a safety management system
- The purpose of accident investigations
- The procedures and arrangements needed to manage accidents
- What first aid arrangements should be in place?
- What procedures and arrangements are needed to manage major incidents/disasters?

2:1 Introduction

The management and investigation of accidents should form a part of an organisation's systematic arrangements for health and safety. This will ensure that every foreseeable eventuality has been prepared for and that procedures can be carried out effectively and with the minimum delay in order to reduce the stress and suffering experienced by any casualties. It will also enable the organisation to respond efficiently and effectively to any impact on its business.

This chapter provides an overview of the nature of system requirements and sets out the basic facilities, systems and procedures that should be in place. It guides the choice and training of persons who will be able to manage an accident, and shows what support will be needed. Guidance is given on providing first aid personnel and facilities.

To ensure that the systems and procedures are effective and practical, regular review should take place. The procedures should be rehearsed in a realistic situation. Revisions of the systems and procedures will need incorporating into the lessons learnt from the reviews and rehearsals.

2:2 A systematic approach to accident management

Regulation 5 of the Management of Health and Safety at Work Regulations 1999 (MHSWR) requires all employers (and the self-employed) to make arrangements for the:

> *effective planning, organisation, control and monitoring of the preventive and protective measures*

to ensure the health and safety of people whilst at work. This duty is explicit and is designed to promote a systematic approach to the management of health and safety in the workplace.

Regulation 3 of the MHSWR requires an assessment to be made of the significant risks arising out of the work activities and processes so that adequate control can be achieved.

This requirement to have a systematic approach supports the more general duties in the Health and Safety at Work etc. Act 1974 (HSWA). These duties are designed to create and maintain workplaces to be free, so far as is 'reasonably practicable', from any risks to health and safety to employees and others, such as the general public and visitors.

Ensuring a safe place of work and safe working practices can be quite complex. It involves the understanding of a wide range of subjects including human behaviour, engineering principles, ergonomics, etc. A systematic approach is required to ensure that these complexities can be dealt with in a timely and cost-effective way.

It has been known for some time that effective management equates to good health and safety performance. Studies by the Health and Safety Executive (HSE) as long ago as 1976 (*Success and Failure in Accident Prevention* (out of print)) revealed that well-run businesses also had good accident records. Current wisdom is that safe and healthy organisations are also successful and well-run organisations. The main driver for success in health and safety is ensuring that the management of any organisation is systematic and focussed on continuing improvement.

Disasters such as the Piper Alpha production platform explosion in July 1988 have led to the idea of a safety management system. Several industries, including the offshore extraction and railway industries, are now required by specific legislation to demonstrate that they have a safety management system in place (through the development of a safety case) before they are allowed to operate.

2:3 Management systems

A number of guides to the formal creation of a systematic approach to the management of health and safety have been published. These formal approaches are more likely to be taken up by larger organisations. However, smaller employers can also benefit from paying attention to their general principles.

2:3.1 *Successful Health and Safety Management –* HSG65 1997

This guidance was originally issued by the HSE in 1991 and has been subsequently updated to include simple guidance on accident investigation. HSG65 describes the main principles of the systematic approach to managing safety. Enforcement agencies (i.e. the HSE and local authorities) use it as a source of reference when undertaking their duties, such as doing an investigation following a report of an accident or dangerous occurrence (*see* **Chapter 4, section 4:4**), inspecting workplaces and providing advice. Increasingly the enforcement approach focusses on the nature of the management processes adopted by the employer.

The guidance in HSG65 is thus extremely relevant, if only to understand what an enforcement officer may be looking for after an accident has occurred. It is based around five defined steps or activities: policy, organising, planning and implementing, measuring performance and reviewing performance. These processes should be combined together in such a way that they can be audited. They are explained in **section 2:3.2** in the consideration of the BS 8800 standard.

2:3.2 *Guide to Occupational Health and Safety Management Systems* – BS 8800

BS 8800 was developed by the British Standards Institute (BSI) in 1996 to provide guidance on occupational health and safety management systems. It draws on a number of other systems 'standards', including the HSE's HSG65 approach and BS:EN:ISO 14001 on environmental management systems. This standard introduces no actual new system, but offers a way of integrating the existing system standards into general business operations to create an overall management system.

The standard makes the point that:

> *many of the features of effective occupational health and safety management are indistinguishable from the sound management practices advocated by proponents of quality and business excellence.*

This approach is used by organisations that have already commenced developing health and safety systems and do not perceive benefits in significant change (*see* **section 2:3.2**) and is illustrated in **Figure 2:1**.

FIGURE 2:1 THE BS 8800 MANAGEMENT SYSTEM MODEL

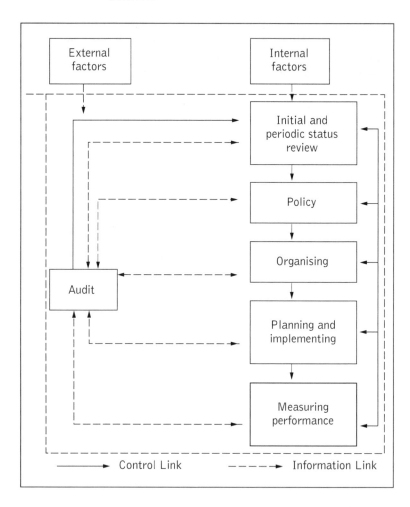

An organisation has both external and internal factors that it has to respond to, such as political and legal pressures from outside and space, financial planning and personnel on the inside.

In order to put a safety management system in place, the organisation needs to build a framework, comprising the elements shown in the model. An **initial status review** is undertaken which should consider legal requirements and make a comparison with best practice, both within the industry and elsewhere. A **policy** should be developed which ensures that health and safety is recognised as a prime part of the organisation's business and is integral to all its decisions and actions.

The organisation should **organise** responsibilities for health and safety and make arrangements for the management of health and safety. Health and safety requirements should be identified in a **planning** approach that also allows targets to be set, and provides for and is based on risk assessment. The plan should then be **implemented** and monitored to ensure that it is being met. **Performance should be measured** to ensure that the effectiveness of the management system can be known. Accident investigation is a key part of this performance measurement. Finally, there should be a process of **periodic review**, so that all the factors about health and safety can be analysed and improvements made, including the actual system itself. The whole system should be subject to an **audit process**. The model shows that there are several control links (the arrows with the heavy lines) which work together to drive the system. The system also has a number of information processes, shown by arrows with dotted lines. It should be noted that there is a great deal of overlap between parts of the system and what the model seeks to point out is the key areas that should be in place.

The initial status review element has been put into the description of the HSG65 model in BS 8800 to allow continuity with the other models set out in the BSI standard. The original HSE version does not have this element.

2:3.2.2 Environmental management system BS:EN:ISO 14001

This method is suggested for organisations wishing to base their arrangements on an environmental management systems standard. Like HSG65, BS:EN:ISO 14001 describes a process in a number of steps. These are shown in **Figure 2:2**.

FIGURE 2:2 THE BS:EN:ISO 14001 APPROACH

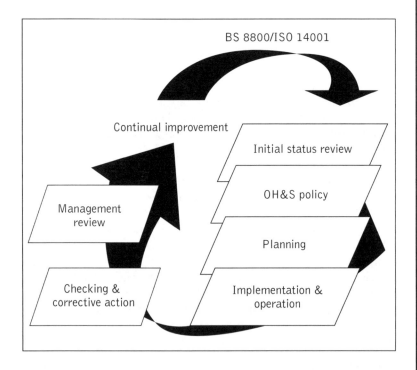

BS 8800/ISO 14001

Continual improvement

Initial status review

OH&S policy

Management review

Planning

Checking & corrective action

Implementation & operation

There are no major differences between this model and the approaches outlined in the BS 8800 model. The BS:EN:ISO 14001 model has an initial status review which is a key feature for environmental purposes. The model suggests that this approach ought also to be applied to health and safety management. Like HSG65 there is a policy element that fulfils the same general requirements. Planning is similarly set out as for HSG65. It should be noted that the organising part of the HSG65 model is subsumed into the implementation and operation elements of the model. This makes sense, as organisations generally plan what they have to do and then organise themselves to do it. Checking and making corrective action is the same as the measuring performance aspect of HSG65. Management review similarly takes the place of the review aspect of HSG65. The main difference is that the BS:EN:ISO 14001 approach has continuing improvement as a key driver for the whole system, the idea being that as the system develops and is operated, improvement will be an overall goal.

2:3.3 Quality management system BS:EN:ISO 9000:2000

In 2000 the quality management system BS 9001 was updated: the standard BS:EN:ISO 9001(2):1994 was replaced with BS:EN:ISO 9000:2000. A three-year grace period has been given to organisations currently certified to the 1994 standard to allow them to upgrade to the 2000 standard. The new standard is 'process based', and requires organisations to identify the various processes within their business and to consider these from 'input' to 'output'. One of the 'value added' inputs to the process control is stated as being health and safety.

There are benefits in having an overall management system to cover every aspect of an organisation's operations. The general quality management system standard as set out in BS:EN:ISO 9000 can be used for this. The BS 8800 standard sets out the various elements required to achieve certification in management systems.

BS 8800 illustrates the links between the various system approaches, showing how the various elements correspond to the quality management system standard. This is useful for organisations that have or are introducing a quality management system, as safety and environment issues can be integrated. However, it is up to each organisation to achieve the integration and develop the links.

2:3.4 Occupational Health and Safety Assessment System OHSAS 18001

BS 8800 was never intended for certification purposes. Certification against a standard (BS or ISO) provides independent verification that an organisation has taken all reasonable measures to minimise risks and prevent accidents. A number of bodies independently attempted to put together a scheme that could be certified. This culminated with the coming together of a committee formed in November 1998 consisting of the British Standards Institution, the major UK certification bodies and other national standards organisations known to be active in health and safety, with the remit of creating a single standard. The Occupational Health and Safety Assessment System (OHSAS) 18001 unifies existing schemes to create an auditable standard. One of the purposes of this was to put pressure on the ISO and CEN committees to produce a certifiable standard. OHSAS 18001 is the specification against which certification is awarded. OHSAS 18002 provides guidance on implementing an occupational health and safety management system and corresponds directly to the specification.

The structure of OHSAS 18001 is virtually identical to the current models for management systems set out in BS 8800 and consists of six sections:

1. General requirements – this section stipulates that the organisation must establish and maintain an occupational health and safety (OH&S) management system.

2. OH&S policy – an OH&S policy statement must be produced. It must be appropriate to the organisation and specify a commitment to health and safety.

3. Planning – the organisation must formulate an action plan, with clearly documented procedures to fulfil its OH&S policy.

4. Implementation and operation – necessary capabilities and support mechanisms must be developed to achieve the objectives and targets within the organisation's OH&S policy.

5. Checking and corrective action – OH&S performance must be measured, monitored and evaluated.

6. Management review – the standard requires the organisation to review and continually improve its OH&S management system, with the objective of improving its overall safety performance.

2:4 System properties

There are some common features of these systems that can be simplified making it easier for the purposes of accident investigation. This simplification also more generally reflects the duties in reg. 5 of the MHSWR.

Each system has the common basic elements of:

- policy-making;
- planning;
- organising;
- implementing;
- monitoring;
- reviewing.

These elements describe the various functions of the management of the organisation that are required to demonstrate that a system is in place.

2:4.1 Policy-making

Policy-making provides both the direction and the motivation for what happens in the organisation. In simple terms it is a description of 'the way we do things around here'. Large organisations may have well-defined and well-documented policies, whereas many small organisations may have less formalised written policies. In either case, it must be clear to all employees what the policy of the organisation is. Policy is both the driving force and the standard for the management of the organisation. In effect, policies set out the expectations of the organisation, what is to be achieved and how. The approach to systemic management of health and safety should, ideally, be expressed in an organisation's policy.

The HSWA places a requirement on all employers with five or more employees to have a written health and safety policy.

Although it is not a requirement of current legislation to specifically address accident investigation in the policy documentation, except for certain industries, a fundamentally sound safety management approach will include the arrangements for, and policy on, accident management and investigation.

The requirements for such a policy are outlined in **Chapter 3**.

2:4.2 Planning

Planning is the process of setting priorities by deciding on what needs to be done, what resources are to be set aside and when specific health and safety issues are to be addressed. Large organisations may achieve this by developing a programme of work. This programme will be linked to hazard identification, risk assessments, and control measures required to ensure a safe place of work. Finances have to be arranged and built into budgetary mechanisms to pay for things like training, provision of protective equipment, assessing and updating control measures, etc. Whether an organisation is large or small, a systematic approach will involve some degree of planning.

The results of any accident or incident investigation will need to be fed into the planning processes so that correction to control measures or review of risk assessment can be properly resourced and undertaken in a timely manner.

2:4.3 Organising

Organising is the process of assigning specific roles, responsibilities and duties to people within the organisation to ensure the policy and plan objectives can be achieved. The management structure should be such that support and arrangements are in place so that the plan can be delivered. In small organisations where everybody knows everybody else, the need for a structured organisation may be less apparent than in larger organisations. However, there is a need to ensure that roles and responsibilities are adequately identified and all foreseeable eventualities, as well as statutory duties, are catered for. The objectives in policy and procedures must be shared (i.e. communicated) and people must be competent to do the tasks assigned to them.

2:4.4 Implementing

Put simply, this is doing what the organisation has set out to do. It is about people doing the actions and tasks assigned to them at the planning and organising stages. In effect, this is about ensuring that the control measures identified by risk assessment and other means in the planning stage are in place and are working.

2:4.5 Monitoring

The objectives and tasks set out by the management system may often not be achieved. A monitoring system should therefore be designed to identify when standards and objectives are not being met so that corrective action can be taken. Monitoring can be either proactive or reactive. Proactive monitoring is about ensuring standards are being maintained; a variety of measures can be used, such as inspection of plant and premises, performance appraisals and auditing. Reactive monitoring involves the investigation of incidents, accidents and safety events (*see* **Chapter 1**) so that lessons can be learnt and corrective action taken to prevent recurrence or in many cases more serious consequences arising.

2:4.6 Reviewing

Reviewing is a process of standing back and assessing whether the previous five elements are actually correct. It involves using accident reports and incident data, the results of monitoring, and key indicators. One way of developing key indicators is by adopting (or examining) industry 'best practice'; another way is to undertake benchmarking. This process involves comparing certain aspects of the organisation with those in another business – not necessarily in the same industry sector. For smaller organisations it may be a much simpler process of determining how well they are doing against standards. Standards can be derived from best industry practice by comparing the organisation with the requirements spelt out in HSE Approved Codes of Practice and Guidance or as set out in management standards such as BS 8800 and OHSAS 18001. The minimum standard would be compliance with relevant legislation.

2:5 The purpose of accident investigation in safety management systems

2:5.1 Monitoring

As a monitoring and corrective process, accident/safety event investigation provides information on how well the organisation is doing. Accident investigation provides the main reactive part of the monitoring system.

A good investigation will highlight the areas where planning and implementation have been lacking. In particular, the outcomes of the investigation will direct attention to the nature of existing control measures and risk assessments.

2:5.2 Control measure verification

Once an accident has happened the most central question will be 'why'? In a well-managed organisation, where safety is afforded a high priority, accidents are not supposed to happen. The purpose of the safety management system and the preventive and protective measures it gives rise to is to prevent accidents.

Whatever the nature of the outcome (*see* **Chapter 1**) the identification of an event as being unexpected or unplanned will call into question the nature and effectiveness of control measures. It could be that control measures:

- existed but were not applied;
- did not take into account this type of event;
- were inadequate;
- were disregarded.

The outcome of the investigation will, therefore, highlight:

- where the plan did not take into account certain types of events;

- where the implementation of control measures was ineffective.

2:5.3 Risk assessment

Reflecting on risk assessment will be a key post-event task. The risk assessments required by reg. 3 of the MHSWR or by specific legislation, e.g. the Electricity at Work Regulations 1989 and the Control of Substances Hazardous to Health Regulations 2002, should have identified all appropriate hazards and the necessary control measures.

The accident/event investigation provides the opportunity to review the risk assessment by:

- determining if the risk assessment was appropriate given the nature and outcomes of the accident;

- increasing the priority given to the risk assessment in the planning part of the safety management system (reg. 5 of the MHSWR).

2:5.3.1 Appropriate assessment

The fact that an incident or event has occurred does not necessarily mean that the risk assessment carried out prior to the event was incorrect. Often, it will be found that control measures were inadequate or not properly applied. However, the nature of risk assessment is such that it should:

- be applied to significant risks;

- enable control of risks to be within the 'as low as reasonably practicable' boundary, i.e. all that can be done is being done without involving excessive costs that negate the benefit being gained from the risk control measure.

Consideration after the event will take into account whether the situation that has been examined indicates that:

- the actual risk is significant;

- all that was 'reasonably practicable' to do had been done.

In some cases it may be that an event has occurred, which, although regrettable, is still acceptable or tolerable. One measure of this is the amount of effort, resources and time required to bring about corrective action. This is the principle (in part) on which the measure of 'as low as reasonably practicable' as defined in law is assessed. 'As low as reasonably practicable' has been defined in a case where the court had to decide if what an employer had done, in terms of safety precautions, was sufficient to show that it had exercised all the care that could reasonably be expected in the circumstances. Although the expression 'reasonably practicable' is provided in s.2 of the HSWA, it has come to take on a more general meaning as a test of whether an organisation has demonstrated that it has put enough effort into safety. The 'test' measures the degree of harm that may be caused on the one hand and the cost of the effort, in terms of both time and money, that has to be expended to prevent the harm from occurring on the other. Obviously, the greater the degree of harm that might result, the greater the effort expended.

In this sense, the HSE describes risk as being negligible, broadly acceptable or intolerable. An intolerable risk is one that has to be reduced, i.e. no further work should continue until the risk has been reduced. An acceptable (or tolerable) risk is one where it is recognised that there is a possibility of harm, but that the benefits to be gained from the activities being undertaken generally outweigh the disadvantages that the harm might cause, both in terms of its likelihood and its severity. There may be times when harm does occur (e.g. in an accident), and therefore the risk has been realised. However, on balance it was right to take those risks as all that was reasonably practicable was being done to prevent an accident. An accident investigation of such a situation should identify that the risks being taken were acceptable in the circumstances, even though there was in fact harm.

It may be, therefore, that effort put into dealing with a risk that has been highlighted as a result of an investigation may detract resources from more important areas, such as dealing with a more significant risk which has not yet been properly controlled, or even, perhaps, identified.

The accident investigation process must therefore have a very strong link to the planning mechanisms and processes required for compliance with reg. 5 of the MHSWR.

2:5.4 Culture

A very important aspect for achieving good performance in health and safety matters is the development of a supportive culture. In short, this means everybody in the organisation (however large or small the business is) sharing the same values, beliefs, attitudes, behaviours, commitment and responses to health and safety.

An accident investigation system can assist in the development and maintenance of a supportive safety culture in a number of ways:

- an open and non-blame approach to event investigation (*see* **Chapter 1, section 1:5.1.2** and **Chapter 5, section 5:2.2.4**) will persuade the managers and employees alike that safety failure does not necessarily mean blame for the person or persons involved. This makes it more likely that evidence will be forthcoming and the true reason for the failure identified. People then begin to respect safety and share in the need to be positive about finding why things went wrong;

- this also promotes a learning attitude so that more care is taken in the future as people begin to recognise the true impact of an accident;

- managers and supervisors come to recognise the worth of having a systematic approach to the management of safety as evidence builds up to show that the underlying causes are in fact management issues (*see* **Chapter 8**).

2:5.5 Learning organisations

Organisations that prosper tend to be those that have the ability to learn from their own mistakes and successes, and from those of others. The systematic accident investigation provides one means by which information can be obtained about how well the organisation is doing. It also puts information into a format that enables the lessons to be readily shared within an organisation. This is supported by a culture that promotes learning rather than blame.

2:5.6 Training issues

One crucial factor that frequently arises from investigations is that training has been neglected or overlooked in some areas. Regulation 13 of the MHSWR 1999 requires employers to ensure that their employees are capable of doing the tasks and jobs assigned to them. The investigation of a wide range of events (and not just those with serious outcomes) is a tool that can aid the identification of training needs (i.e. where the skills and knowledge are lacking). It also assists in providing a measure of the amount of training required to ensure that the outcomes of risk assessments and the implementation of control measures can be successful.

2:5.7 System development

Accidents tend not to have a single cause. The multi-factorial nature of accidents has been long appreciated (*see* **Appendix 1**). Because of this, the systematic approach to accident investigation frequently raises information that is useful in developing and maintaining management systems. This is especially so if the underlying or root causes are identified. Frequently the system for ensuring control measures are implemented is deficient. Information from a good investigation will provide the evidence required to ensure the gaps are plugged.

2:6 Procedures and arrangements required for managing accidents

A number of arrangements need to be in place so that accidents can be effectively managed. These include:

- contracts of employment;
- welfare and counselling support;
- employee next-of-kin details;
- attendance records;
- evacuation procedures;
- accident reporting and recording procedures;
- how to deal with the media;
- medical referral procedures;
- insurance and legal advisers;
- emergency services arrangements.

This also includes policies relating to:

- visitors;
- drug and alcohol use and abuse;
- stress;
- first aid.

2:6.1 Contracts of employment

It is a legal requirement that employers provide their employees with a contract of employment and/or letter of employment. These documents set out the rights of each party during the period of employment. In some instances, these rights may also be extended for a period beyond the termination of the contract.

Following an accident it is often useful for the employer to obtain a medical opinion on the nature of injuries sustained (*see* **section 2:6.8**). This can only be demanded as a right if it is included in the contract of employment. Effectively the employee agrees to a contract which allows the employer to request a medical examination be carried out or access to medical records be allowed.

Employers should consider including a suitable clause in the documents stating that the employer has the right to require the employee to undergo a medical examination and provide agreement for access to medical records. The contract should also include requirements for compliance with the organisation's drug and alcohol policy (*see* **section 2:6.11.2**), in particular to including statements, allow random sampling, and permit sampling following involvement in an accident.

2:6.1.1 Employers' access to an employee's medical records

The Access to Medical Reports Act 1990 restricts the employer's right to access an employee's medical records held by their general practitioner. The employer requires written permission from the employee before applying to a general practitioner for a general medical report.

2:6.2 Welfare and counselling support

The majority of accidents and some near misses will give rise to emotions and feeling of stress amongst many of those involved. This includes onlookers and helpers, as well as casualties.

Ideally employers should have a programme in place to manage the stress (and other reactions – such as grief, helplessness and mental trauma) resulting from witnessing and being involved in traumatic events.

Best practice for dealing with the psychological trauma of incidents includes the pre-incident (or emergency) arrangements made by the organisation. These arrangements should include the education of staff and management in what to expect should an incident occur. Developing the 'coping skills' of people is generally found to be beneficial. Whilst this is mostly applied to major incidents – as would be considered in an emergency plan – it is also of benefit for smaller scale accidents. It has been shown that staff who are prepared for the effects of the trauma of an incident, particularly serious injuries and death, are more able to cope with the situation. This in turn reduces the likelihood of psychological damage.

Specialist assistance should be obtained when establishing programmes to introduce and maintain the coping skills, preferably from occupational physicians with psychiatric training or from psychiatrists with counselling services support.

Additional welfare support will include the provision of food and drink, clothing and other facilities such as showers likely to be required in the event of certain types of incident, including evacuations.

2:6.3 Employee next-of-kin details

When people are involved in an accident, especially when someone is seriously injured or killed, it is absolutely essential that immediate access can be made to relevant personal details in order to notify the next of kin. Those people tasked with informing the next of kin will need to be able to obtain contact addresses and to find out any other relevant information (*see* **Chapter 4, section 4:3.2**).

Contacting the next of kin is therefore only possible if the organisation actually maintains an up-to-date register of next-of-kin details for its employees and has this available for easy access by authorised managers. Smaller organisations may have managers who actually do know everyone who is employed, their addresses and family, but larger organisations will need to formalise this arrangement. It is therefore important to have a list available of employees' personal details for this eventuality.

Occasionally next of kin have found out about the involvement of a relative in an accident from the press or another party before the company or the police have been able to inform them. This naturally creates stress and anxieties that can be avoided. The administrative procedures put into place will depend upon a company's size, structure and culture, but the systems should ensure that the next of kin can be contacted quickly and sensitively.

Communicating with the injured person's family is not an easy task and preferably all those senior managers likely to have to undertake this role should be prepared for such an eventuality. They should receive training in counselling and understand how to deal with such situations. Basic first aid training would also be an advantage.

In the case of a fatality the role of the police and coroner's officer (*see* **Chapter 4, section 4:3.1.2**) will need to be taken into account. It will always be the case that a police officer and/or coroner's officer will attend the scene of the incident at some point to ascertain details and undertake a preliminary investigation into the cause of death.

After the next of kin have been contacted, work colleagues should also be informed by line managers and/or human resource personnel. This should be defined in the company's procedures, and will depend upon the nature and size of the organisation and the action taken for those colleagues identified as being close to the injured or dead.

It will almost certainly be the case that the police will take on the responsibility of informing the next of kin, members of the public, visitors and contractors involved in a fatality at a workplace or arising from work.

2:6.3.1 Setting up a system to collect next of kin records

It is likely that the best person to establish and maintain a register of next-of-kin details for employees is the personnel manager. Once established, the register must be regularly updated to ensure that the records it contains are current. The records kept for next-of-kin purposes need to contain only the information necessary for the purposes described.

Records may be on the personal record file, or as part of a separate register kept by senior managers party to the organisational arrangements, or as part of a password-activated computer database. They should include the following:

- address and telephone number;

- legal name;

- name of the next of kin/nominated beneficiary;

- emergency contact details including telephone number(s) and address(es);

- marital status.

Care should be taken to ensure that the database and other records are backed up so that they are not lost or made unavailable by likely accident scenarios, such as a major fire.

Employers will need to ensure that the records, whether held manually or in a computer system, comply with the Data Protection Act 1998, which came into force in March 2000. The Act applies to information 'recorded as part of a relevant filing system or with the intention that it should form part of a relevant filing system' (Data Protection Act 1998, s.1(1)(c)). The Act defines a 'relevant filing system' as:

any set of information relating to individuals to the extent that, although the information is not processed by means of equipment operating automatically in response to instructions given for that purpose, the set is structured, either by reference to individuals or by reference to criteria relating to individuals, in such a way that particular information relating to a particular individual is readily accessible.

If an employee has had an industrial accident, records for personal liability claims may need to be kept for 12 years.

2:6.3.2 Availability of records

The record of next-of-kin details needs to be kept in a secure place and be immediately available when required as part of the organisation's arrangements for dealing with accidents. In determining the storage location, companies need to ensure that the records remain accessible in any likely accident scenario.

Employers should note that the Data Protection Act 1998 requires that where personal records are kept, a 'data controller' is appointed to understand the scope and content of records and the use to which they are put. The data controller will be responsible for any breaches of the legislation. Under the Act employees will be able to gain access to data stored about them by making a request to the data controller. The employer must comply with the request within 40 days.

2:6.4 Attendance records

The employer should have in place systems which record who is in attendance on any particular day. The type of system adopted will vary depending on the size and structure of the organisation. Systems can range from simple attendance registers to sophisticated time capture and access systems. The system chosen should be able to take account of movements during the working day. Employers should also take steps to ensure that they have the details (including company name and telephone number) of any contractors and other business visitors, so that they can inform the appropriate office of any serious accidents/incidents.

They should ensure that the names of their employees are known by any organisations that they are visiting on a contract, supply or delivery basis, so that the employer can be informed should anything occur to their staff whilst away from the organisation's premises.

The records must be readily available so that a roll call can be carried out following any accident so that all those present may be accounted for. The manner in which this can be achieved will depend upon the recording system chosen, and the facilities it offers. The emergency services will also need the information.

2:6.5 Evacuation procedures

Regulation 8 of the MHSWR require employees to be provided with the means to effect their immediate removal from any place of danger in an emergency. Employers are also required to nominate a 'sufficient number of competent persons' to implement the procedures for evacuation of premises (reg. 8(1)(b)). To avoid confusion and ensure co-operation, a hierarchy should be established between the competent persons. The appointed competent persons will need to be trained in the execution of the procedures, and named individuals (with deputies were necessary) given specific tasks to perform.

A typical evacuation procedure will include the following requirements:

- calling the appropriate emergency services (usually the fire brigade);

- helping disabled people to evacuate or relocate to a place of safety;

- checking that their area of the premises is empty;

- making sure the visitors' book and all lists of who was present on site are to hand;

- keeping order at the assembly points;

- giving a roll call at the assembly points to make sure everyone is there;

- co-ordinating the roll calls if there are several assembly points;

- liaising with the emergency services;

- co-ordinating a return to the building when it is safe to return.

A common evacuation procedure is that developed for the event of fire (*see* **Figure 2:3**). These arrangements are generally well understood, if not always well executed. Similar arrangements are made for bomb and other terrorist threats where these are likely, athough it must be noted that the procedures in case of a terrorist or other threat may not be the same as those required for a fire.

Drills to test the effectiveness of the evacuation procedures (in conjunction with the local fire authority) should be carried out regularly. The fire certificate should cover frequency of fire drills, which is likely to be at least once a year.

Everyone on the premises, for example staff, contractors and visitors, must receive instruction on evacuation procedures. These should include arrangements for the evacuation of disabled people. In the case of fire, this may include relocation to a place of safety, for example a fire-protected lobby on a stairwell.

FIGURE 2:3 MODEL FIRE SAFETY INSTRUCTION NOTICE

By law staff must be instructed as to what to do should a fire break out. The example 'Fire Safety Instruction' below can be tailored to the details of the company, and posted on a notice board and/or included in an induction information pack.

WHAT TO DO IN CASE OF EMERGENCY

FIRE ALARM

The fire alarm system is activated by:

- voice
- break-glass call point
- automatic detectors

IF YOU DISCOVER A FIRE:

1. Shout FIRE, ensuring that the warning has been heard by other occupants. Operate the nearest fire alarm.

2. If it is SAFE to do so, attack the fire with the nearest appropriate fire extinguisher.

3. Always ensure there is a safe exit route before attempting to extinguish any fire.

4. If not attacking the fire, immediately vacate the premises by the nearest available exit and proceed to the assembly point indicated below.

WHEN INFORMED OF A FIRE:

1. Immediately vacate the premises by the nearest available exit.

2. Proceed to the assembly point indicated and await the roll call.

ASSEMBLY POINTS:

- car park
- main thoroughfare
- other location

FOLLOWING EVACUATION DO NOT RE-ENTER THE BUILDING TO COLLECT PERSONAL BELONGINGS UNTIL TOLD TO DO SO BY MANAGEMENT, ACTING UNDER INSTRUCTION BY THE SENIOR FIRE OFFICER AT THE SCENE.

In many other situations a risk assessment will show that there may be circumstances when it is necessary to undertake evacuation. For example, the release of a gas cloud from industrial process plant following some form of accidental (or deliberate) failure will necessitate employees and others in the immediate vicinity vacating the premises and its environs. Other examples where evacuation might be needed are where adjoining buildings are a risk or where lighting has failed. It is important to ensure that the evacuation plan is realistic and can be put into effect immediately. The on-site supervisor or senior manager should initiate the evacuation plan as soon as the identified events occur.

An accident investigation may need to examine the effectiveness and suitability of evacuation arrangements.

2:6.5.1 Decision to evacuate

In several situations it may not be possible for the on-site supervisor or manager to be able to identify and initiate the procedure. In such cases, identified through risk assessment, a system will need to be in place to ensure that evacuation occurs automatically. To illustrate this, consider the example of 'confined-space' working. The permit to work and safe system of work developed for any confined-space working needs to be correct, reliable and effective. However, if during the course of work a situation develops which is not in accordance with the documented work process, then evacuation should be undertaken. For example, the release of a gas into the working space when the safe system of work should have 'locked off' the routes by which this could happen would act as a trigger to evacuate the confined space. The crew working in the confined space need to have the ability to identify such deviations and take evasive action. Human factors (*see* **Chapter 1, section 1:6**) will play a significant role here. Should somebody collapse or become trapped by an unplanned occurrence then colleagues will inevitably be tempted to assist, attempt rescue or stay with the person affected. This, however, is not the correct action as it puts further lives at risk. Workers must be able to take the appropriate action in such circumstances. This demands a high degree of competence, especially that relating to the understanding and recognition of dangerous situations.

2:6.5.2 Communication

Once a decision has been made to evacuate, it must be communicated to those affected without delay. The employer must have appropriate procedures and alarm systems in place to enable this to be carried out.

Various types of alarm systems are available. They range from the simplest form, such as a whistle or hand-operated bell, to sophisticated fire alarms or voice alarms. Employers should seek the advice of their local fire brigade or a reputable supplier if they require information or if they believe that their system is inadequate.

Procedures, whilst being concise, must be flexible and take into account, for instance, environmental factors and/or the site of the danger. It would be foolhardy to direct employees to an assembly point in the path of a gas cloud or to evacuate past a suspect package!

2:6.5.3 Welfare of evacuees

Organisations need to have pre-planned welfare arrangements for their staff and visitors following an evacuation. Consideration should be given to ensuring that a roll call is carried out, and that first aid is available. If the evacuation is likely to be for an extended period, then consideration should be given to being able to provide refreshments (particularly hot drinks). Some means of transport to ensure staff can reach home safely may also be needed as it may be unsafe to go to the car park.

2:6.5.4 Training

No evacuation procedure can be carried out swiftly and safely without all those involved being aware of what is expected of them.

Training must be provided to:

- competent persons – the training provided to competent persons needs to ensure that in the event of an accident they are able to act positively and without hesitation;

- other staff – the level of training required by other staff will depend upon the nature of the risk inherent in the business.

The ultimate objective of the training is to ensure that in the event of an evacuation being needed, it is carried out safely and in a controlled manner.

It is worth bearing in mind that a disorganised or panicked evacuation is likely to result in more-severe injuries and/or a higher casualty list.

2:6.6 Accident reporting and recording procedures

Procedures should be in place to both identify all accidents which have occurred and to ensure the appropriate authorities are notified, where relevant (*see* **Chapter 4, section 4:4**). In the case of a fatality it will be necessary to inform both the police and the relevant enforcement authority immediately in accordance with the HSWA.

In addition, key personnel, including senior managers, safety advisers and those with legal or insurance responsibilities, should be informed. Those responsible for undertaking the reporting of accidents to the authorities should have received sufficient training so that they are both aware of the legal implications of reporting (and failing to report) and are conversant with the relevant in-house arrangements for reporting and investigating accidents.

A formal system must be in place to record accidents, and to comply with social security legislation and RIDDOR requirements (*see* **Chapter 4, section 4:4.1**).

2:6.7 How to deal with the media

The majority of accidents within an organisation do not attract much attention. Most will be contained within the organisation and be of only limited interest to others. However, when the outcomes are serious, such as a fatality or the collapse of a structure, the media will often show an interest. This has an impact in a number of ways:

- it highlights the organisation – its name, location, business and the problem;

- a story must be generated with some interest for the readership/viewers;

- the story will often be a human-interest one;

- enquiries can be intrusive and personnel may be bothered by unwelcome approaches for interviews;

- the facts will never be clear immediately after the event (that is why there is an investigation) – but this will not hold back speculation;

- there can be a knock-on effect on customers and suppliers, especially if the journalists have been adventurous in their reporting;

- the bigger the event the greater the media intrusion.

Dealing with the media requires some training and knowledge of how to control such situations. Although the effect is often transitory with interest waning in a matter of days, there can be a longer-term impact. It is therefore important when something happens to be in a position to be able to deal with the media. This could be direct contact through a company spokesman, PR agency or press release. How this is handled will depend upon a number of factors, including the culture of the company and the nature of the accident.

Clear procedures for dealing with the media should be established with professional advice from both legal and public relations experts.

2:6.8 Medical referral procedures

Establishing an occupational health service (easier for a larger organisation) or obtaining occupational health services with a suitably qualified medical practitioner should form part of the accident management system. It is sometimes useful to refer injured personnel to an appropriate medical practitioner. This will normally be one qualified in occupational medicine and often may be the organisation's own occupational health service provider (either in-house or contracted). By doing so the employer is able to easily assess the nature and extent of injuries and in certain cases may obtain useful information relating to the cause of injuries. Perhaps more importantly, suitable medical intervention – for example, the early application of physiotherapy in the case of musculo-skeletal injury – can have desirable effects in terms of an earlier return to work. Although currently uncommon in the UK, the utilisation of rehabilitation practices (such as physiotherapy) following occupational injury is likely to grow in the future with benefits for both employer and employee alike.

An occupational health adviser may also be able to assist in obtaining information from other medical personnel, for example accident and emergency departments where injured employees have been sent following an accident at work. In some cases this can be vital to ensure that specific and accurate information is given where immediate action is required, for example in a situation where there has been exposure to a respiratory agent.

The procedures established with the occupational health adviser may also include:

- providing advice to the workforce following an incident (such as exposure to asbestos);

- acting as both an adviser and a gateway to psychiatric services (where people have been exposed to mental trauma);

- assessing injured employees in relation to fitness for work, pension scheme requirements and contracts of employment;

- assisting in the formulation of drug and alcohol, stress and first aid policies.

In some cases, insurers may also undertake medical examinations of a company's employees where accidental injury has occurred.

2:6.9 Insurance and legal advisers

The employer should have a procedure in place to ensure that in the event of an accident the organisation's insurance provider (either broker or insurance company) is immediately notified. The procedure should identify who will make the contact. If the company does not have an in-house insurance department, this responsibility will usually fall to a senior manager.

Similarly the organisation's legal advisers should be informed. During the process of the investigation there may be evidence that is discarded or regarded as irrelevant. Such evidence may be of use to the lawyers and insurers, and, as such, someone will need to keep track of it. Again, treatment of this aspect needs to be considered at the planning stage, and incorporated into the organisation's safety policy.

2:6.10 Emergency services arrangements

Under reg. 9 of the Management of Health and Safety at Work Regulations 1999 (MHSWR), employers have a duty to inform the emergency services of any specific site requirements, such as access, escape routes and location of particular hazards, so that safety is ensured:

> *Every employer shall ensure that any necessary contacts with external services are arranged, particularly as regards first-aid, emergency medical care and rescue work.*

The local fire brigade may have some information on the site and its facilities from inspections they have carried out previously (as part of their duties under the Fire Services Act 1947, s.1(1)(d)). The police and ambulance services do not have such a facility and employers need to make direct contact with them to discuss their requirements. However, it is important to ensure that as much pre-planning is undertaken with the emergency services as possible, and is commensurate with the risks and foreseeable emergencies on the site.

2:6.10.1 Pre-planning with the emergency services

The fire brigade and ambulance service will need to know of any particular hazards and be informed that they will be involved in rescues from confined spaces and other difficult areas, such as those requiring high-line rescues or rescues in or from water. In some circumstances it may be necessary to provide the fire brigade with emergency equipment on site and arrange for them to be familiarised or trained in its use. Nationally, fire brigades vary in the extent of their rescue capabilities, but in all cases the capability of the fire service is limited to the extent of their resources and the physical limits on firefighters. It is important, therefore, that any organisation that has assessed particularly hazardous or difficult emergency scenarios discusses these at a local level with fire brigade personnel.

Prior arrangements with the emergency services (usually but not always led by the fire brigade) will include forms of notification detailing the information to be given, the locations involved and the access to the site or premises concerned.

Where the premises are remote from the nearest ambulance station, employers may need to have pre-arranged transportation arrangements, such as using their own facilities or by having standby arrangements with a local transport provider.

2:6.11 Policies

A number of policies ancillary to the health and safety system need to be in place to enable the effective management of accidents. Principal among these are policies relating to:

- visitors;

- drug and alcohol use and abuse;

- stress;

- first aid.

2:6.11.1 Visitor policy

Visitors are anyone on site who is a non-employee. Visitors include temporary workers and contractors, as well as people only on site for a few hours or minutes, such as friends of employees, members of the public and associates touring the site.

An organisation should have a safety policy for visitors. A model policy is given in **Appendix 2**.

In the event of the visitor being involved in an accident on the premises, the arrangements detailed in the accident reporting/investigating procedure should be followed.

2:6.11.2 Drug and alcohol policy

Employers are recommended to formulate and introduce a drugs and alcohol policy into their company.

Working under the influence of drugs and alcohol can significantly increase the risk of an accident occurring. The extent to which the risk increases will depend upon the extent of the drugs and/or alcohol abuse and the nature of the task being undertaken. In obvious cases the consideration of an event which has resulted mainly or entirely because of drug or alcohol misuse/abuse should not ordinarily be treated as being an 'accident'. The development of a sound policy can assist in clarifying this within an organisation. Where the abuse is obvious the matter is more aptly dealt with as a disciplinary or contract-of-employment matter rather than as a safety issue, although there are clearly health and safety implications.

The Misuse of Drugs Act 1991 classifies controlled drugs into three categories:

Class:	Drugs include:
A	heroin, cocaine, LSD and methadone
B	amphetamines, barbiturates and cannabis
C	tranquillisers such as valium

Note: Consideration is currently being given to reclassifying some of these drugs, particularly cannabis. Not all drugs and substances that are abused are 'controlled' drugs. Solvents and butane gas are purchased quite legally. The misuse and abuse of steroids for body development is not uncommon.

Abuse of drugs can be a deliberate act, but may also on occasions be an accident. Drugs prescribed by a medical practitioner may also have similar effects on an individual's safety performance. Where this effect is inadvertent, it may be appropriate to treat any event as an accident until or unless there is evidence to the contrary.

Alcohol even in moderate amounts affects performance. As little as one pint of beer is said to reduce efficiency by as much as five to ten per cent.

Drugs and alcohol are frequently abused together, making the risk of an accident even greater.

A guidance document entitled *Drugs and the Workplace – a Guide to Policy Development and Training* is available from CPD, Station House, Manningtree, Essex CO11 2LH (fax: 01206 391467). The guidance recommends that any drug policy should:

- ensure equality of treatment and consistency;

- promote educational awareness at all levels;

- focus primarily on employee welfare rather than discipline;

- incorporate alcohol abuse as part of a wider occupational health strategy;

- encourage networking with other agencies who can offer support;

- be monitored and reviewed regularly.

The policy should be included in the contract of employment and/or letter of appointment.

A model drugs and alcohol policy is provided in **Appendix 3**.

In preparing the policy, consideration should be given to providing statements, allowing random sampling and permitting sampling following involvement in an accident.

Specialist legal advice should normally be sought where there is an intention to undertake blood or other invasive sampling for drugs or alcohol. The issue of actually obtaining evidence of drug and/or alcohol use after an accident from an individual can be quite complex and subject to stringent legal requirements.

2:6.11.3 Stress policy

The management of stress arising from traumatic events depends upon a number of factors. Good-practice principles include:

- a way of dealing with the subject that is suitable for the organisation and adapted to its needs. There is no off-the-shelf solution or programme for this;

- a defined policy which explains who is responsible for the processes, what actions should be taken and the type of support expected from the management of the organisation. The policy should cover the provisions outlined in sections on defusing and debriefing (*see* **Chapter 4, sections 4:1.3.1** and **4:1.3.2**);

- critical incident procedures that provide an immediate response after a critical incident (one likely to give rise to mental trauma) has been identified;

- short- and long-term measures. In the short term there is a need for immediate support, comfort and management of those affected. In the longer term there may be need for counselling or psychiatric support (*see* **Chapter 4, section 4:1.3.2**);

- information and training/education support to provide general awareness and specific assistance both about the processes used by the organisation and the way people can access them, for example the provision of counselling/psychiatry services.

2:6.11.4 First aid policy

The provision of first aid in the workplace is a legal requirement. The extent of provision is dependant on a number of factors, but clearly the treatment of any injuries resulting from accidents must be a priority and covered by suitable policy arrangements. The requirements for first aid are discussed in **section 2:7**.

2:7 First aid requirements

2:7.1 Legal requirements to provide first aid care

The Health and Safety (First Aid) Regulations 1981 (S.I. 1981, No. 917), as amended by the Health and Safety (Miscellaneous Amendments) Regulations 2002, require all employers to make adequate provision for first aid treatment of their employees. The Approved Code of Practice (ACOP) and Guidance *First Aid at Work (The Health and Safety (First Aid) Regulations 1981) Approved Code of Practice* advise that the extent of the provision made for first aid should be relevant to the risks to which the workforce may be exposed.

The Health and Safety (First Aid) Regulations 1981 do not place any obligation on employers to provide first aid for the public. However, where the public regularly visits an employer's premises, for example shops, or where some other activity of the employer brings the company into contact with the public, it is recommended that the public is included in the organisation's arrangements and adequate additional first aid provision is made.

2:7.1.1 Adequate and appropriate first aid provision

The purpose of first aid is to preserve life and minimise the consequence of injury and illness until help from a medical practitioner or nurse arrives, and to treat minor injuries which would not otherwise receive treatment.

The arrangements made for first aid must be suitable for the workplace and the hazards and risks it contains. An employer must determine, by carrying out a risk assessment, the need for the provision of first aid. Where the hazards and risks vary significantly between areas of a business, or where there are multiple buildings or floors, then different assessments must be made for each area, building or floor. The employer must appoint trained first aiders where this is necessary on the basis of the assessment made of the hazards and associated risks. The assessment may indicate the need for a rest room or first aid treatment room with or without qualified nursing or medical staff.

The risk assessment should consider the type of work being carried out, the number of people involved, and the hazards and risks associated with the activities. Where the risks are small, only a few trained persons may be required. Where the risks are great, a number of first aiders will be needed.

Sufficient first aiders/approved persons must be provided to ensure adequate cover is available at all times. For guidance, the following minimum numbers of first aiders/appointed persons listed in **Figure 2:4** should be provided. However, the employer must take into account shift/evening work and leave/sickness, etc. to ensure that sufficient first aiders are available to provide cover whenever work activities are being carried out.

FIGURE 2:4 A GUIDE TO THE MINIMUM NUMBERS OF FIRST AIDERS/APPOINTED PERSONS

Category of risk	Numbers employed at any location	Suggested number of first aid personnel
Low risk (e.g. shops, offices, libraries)	• Fewer than 50 • 50–100 • More than 100	• At least one appointed person • At least one first aider • One additional first aider for every 100 employed
Medium risk (e.g. light engineering and assembly work, food processing, warehousing)	• Fewer than 20 • 20–100 • More than 100	• At least one appointed person • At least one first aider for every 50 employed (or part thereof) • One additional first aider for every 100 employed
High risk (e.g. most construction sites, slaughterhouses, chemical plants, extensive work with dangerous machinery or sharp instruments)	• Fewer than 5 • 5–50 • More than 50 • Where there are hazards for which additional first aid skills are necessary	• At least one appointed person • At least one first aider • One additional first aider for every 50 employed • At least one additional first aider trained in the specific emergency action

Particular consideration must be given to workers who may be particularly at risk. These will include:

- staff moving from site to site who usually work on their own, for instance service engineers, salespersons, surveyors) – these may spend most of their time away from the main site and may require to carry their own first aid kits. Training is also important. A means of communication to their base should also be considered;

- young and/or inexperienced workers;

- the disabled – consideration should be given to any specific first aid needs they may have.

It is recommended that a procedure is established to enable appointed persons and first aiders to record any first aid given to a casualty. A typical record form is provided in **Figure 2:5**.

FIGURE 2:5 EXAMPLE FIRST AID RECORD SHEET

RECORD OF FIRST AID GIVEN					
Company name:					
Death		Injury		Disease	
PERSONAL INFORMATION					
Name and address of injured person					
Occupation or status					
Nature of injury or disease					
Name of person entering details					

THE INCIDENT	
Date and time of accident	
Or Date of diagnosis of disease	
Location of accident	
Circumstances of accident, including cause of injury (if known):	
Details of first aid administered:	
Administered by:	

Where employees of a number of employers are working on one site, for example a construction site, it would often be preferable for one employer to make the necessary provision for first aid. This is best done through a written agreement involving all the employers. A typical letter of agreement is provided in **Figure 2:6**.

FIGURE 2:6 EXAMPLE FIRST AID AGREEMENT

FIRST AID AGREEMENT	
From:	Date:
To:	
Site:	
As the person responsible for the above site, we advise you that we will provide first aid facilities for all parties working at the site. The following facilities will be provided:	
Facilities will be provided at:	
Please acknowledge these arrangements by returning a signed copy of this agreement.	
Signature of provider: Signature of tenant/contractor:	

2:7.1.2 Medical assistance

The risk assessments for some sites may indicate the need for the full-time presence of qualified medical staff. These sites will have high risks associated with them, for example chemical works, steel works, nuclear facilities, etc. The assessment may indicate the need for a first aid room to be provided (*see also* **section 2:7.3.2**).

Exposure to certain chemical products may require the application of special antidotes and the use of special equipment. Many of the antidotes need to be applied without delay and may only be administered by qualified medical staff.

It is unlikely that medical staff will be required in an office environment.

2:7.2 First aiders/appointed persons

2:7.2.1 Minimum requirements

Employers must make suitable arrangements for the provision of first aid in workplaces. The minimum requirements set out in the Health and Safety (First Aid) Regulations 1981 are that an employer must:

- appoint a person to be available at all times to take responsibility for first aid in the workplace;

- provide a suitably stocked first aid box (container) with first aid material relevant to the risks in the workplace. All establishments must have at least one first aid kit placed in a clearly identified and readily accessible location such as the main office, or workshop office (*see* **section 2:7.3**);

- inform the workforce of the arrangements made for first aid (*see* **section 2:7.2.3**).

Employers are advised to obtain insurance (*see* **Chapter 11**) to cover the actions of any first aider/appointed person whilst giving first aid to staff and visitors.

2:7.2.1.1 Appointed persons

In circumstances where the risk of injury is negligible, such as in offices, it may only be necessary to provide an appointed person. The number of appointed persons needed will depend on the number of employees at any given time and the category of risk (*see* **Figure 2:4**).

This person does not need to be trained in first aid but should be conversant with the identification of injuries and the appropriate actions to be taken to obtain assistance. In the majority of cases the action will be summoning either an ambulance, a doctor (on site or off site) or a suitably trained first aider. This person will be responsible for the first aid facilities, such as maintaining a first aid box.

2:7.2.1.2 First aiders

Where the risks of injury are identified as being more serious as a result of the hazards in the workplace it will be necessary to appoint one or more persons as first aiders.

A first aider is a person trained to a standard approved by the HSE. A person appointed as a first aider will have to pass an examination to obtain a qualification in first aid (*see* **section 2:7.2.2**).

Where qualified first aiders have been provided, an appointed person can cover temporary and exceptional absence (e.g. sickness) but not annual leave. The employer must take into account foreseeable absences, such as holidays, when deciding how many first aiders to appoint.

2:7.2.2 Training

Training for appointed persons and first aiders must be provided by training establishments approved by the HSE. Lists of approved training providers are held at local HSE offices.

The course content and the knowledge required is established by the HSE. The basic level of training required by the Health and Safety (First Aid) Regulations 1981 for an appointed person is acquired on a half-day course.

The training course for a first aider normally lasts four days. On satisfactory completion of the course the training provider awards a certificate, valid for three years. Refresher training will need to be undertaken to maintain competence in first aid and this may be required more frequently than the three-year period between examinations. Refresher training in any case must be carried out before the expiry of the three-year certificate; otherwise a full re-certification must be undertaken.

Amongst the approved training establishments are the:

- British Red Cross (tel: 020 7235 5454);
- St Johns Ambulance Association (tel: 020 7235 5231).

2:7.2.3 Communication

Employers must have in place arrangements to ensure that staff and visitors are aware of how to contact a first aider in an emergency. They must also be made aware of the location of first aid equipment and facilities. This will normally be by publishing names, contact arrangements and the locations of equipment on notice boards, etc. It is advised that all notices and signs follow the form shown in the Health and Safety (Safety Signs and Signals) Regulations 1996, i.e. green background with white writing. Additionally, first aiders may be provided with an appropriate badge identifying the wearer as a first aider. This may take the form of a pin badge or logo on work wear.

2:7.3 First aid equipment

2:7.3.1 Minimum requirements

Minimum requirements for the contents of first aid boxes is set by the Health and Safety (First Aid) Regulations 1981. These are shown in **section 2:7.3.1.1**.

First aid kits should contain appropriate first aid materials and should not contain things like aspirins, creams or sprays. They must be suitably designed and identified (usually a white cross on a green background) to meet the Health and Safety (Safety Signs and Signals) Regulations 1996.

A water supply is required for eye irrigation. If mains tap water is not readily available, then sterile water or sterile normal saline (0.9%) solution should be provided in sealed disposable containers. Once opened, the containers should not be re-used.

The organisation must have in place a system to regularly inspect and replenish the contents of all first aid kits. The inspection should check:

- that the contents are complete;

- that sealed sterile items are within their 'shelf life';

- that there are no aspirin, creams, sprays or other items of medication in the kit.

Special antidotes and equipment for specific hazards may be included in or near first aid boxes, but only where the first aiders have been specifically trained in their use.

2:7.3.1.1 First aid kit

The minimum quantities to be held within a first aid kit as specified by the Health and Safety (First Aid) Regulations 1981 are:

Guidance card★	1
Individually wrapped sterile adhesive dressings (assorted sizes)	20
Sterile eye pads with attachment	2
Individually wrapped triangular bandages	6
Safety pins	6
Medium sized individually wrapped sterile unmedicated wound dressings (approx. 10cm x 8cm)	6
Large sterile individually wrapped unmedicated wound dressings (approx. 13cm x 9cm)	2
Extra large sterile individually wrapped unmedicated wound dressings (approx. 18cm x 17.5cm)	3
Disposable gloves	1 pr

★Leaflet INDG215RV2 provides basic guidance for first aid at work. This should be included in first aid boxes. Copies can be obtained from HSE Books (website: www.hsebooks.co.uk).

2:7.3.1.2 Travelling first aid kit

Travelling workers who spend most of their time away from the main site may require their own first aid kits. If they work alone a form of communication with their base should be provided. Training is also important.

The minimum quantities to be held within a 'travelling' first aid kit as specified by the Health and Safety (First Aid) Regulations 1981 are:

Guidance card★	1
Individually wrapped sterile adhesive dressings (assorted sizes)	6
Individually wrapped triangular bandages	2
Safety pins	2
Extra large sterile individually wrapped unmedicated wound dressings (approx. 18cm x 17.5cm)	1
Individually wrapped moist cleaning wipes	6

★Leaflet INDG215RV2 provides basic guidance for first aid at work. This should be included in first aid boxes. Copies can be obtained from HSE Books (website: www.hsebooks.co.uk).

2:7.3.2 First aid rooms

The risk assessment may show a need for a first aid room. These sites will have high risks associated with them. They may also be required on large sites remote from accident and emergency facilities.

It is recommended that first aid rooms:

- contain the first aid equipment and facilities appropriate to the nature of the site and its hazards;

- be easy to find (i.e. clearly and appropriately signposted)★;

- be readily accessible to stretchers★;

- ideally be used solely for giving first aid.

★In accordance with reg. 2 of the Health and Safety (Miscellaneous Amendments) Regulations 2002, which added to reg. 3 of the Health and Safety (First Aid) Regulations 1981, these are now legal requirements.

2:7.4 Basic start-up/review procedure for first aid and accident reporting

The checklist in **Figure 2:7** is a guide for the person with responsibility for establishing the first aid facilities and accident procedures. It can be used when considering the procedure for required annual checks (or more frequently, if stated in specific assessment) or when auditing the arrangements already in place in order to evaluate the need for amendment and development. It can also be used as part of the job description for the appointed first aider.

If the guidelines in the checklist are to be implemented within an organisation that has been dealing with such matters for a period of time, the annual check is an audit tool. For organisations without a history of providing such facilities, the annual check represents a starting point for getting a system going.

FIGURE 2:7 BASIC START-UP/REVIEW PROCEDURE CHECKLIST FOR FIRST AID AND ACCIDENT REPORTING

1. Review the work activities undertaken on the premises to establish whether any are of high or medium risk. If all activities are low risk, typical of an office environment, the recommendation is to have a first aider for every 50 staff members.

2. Review the appointment of first aiders. It is good practice to have a first aider on site most of the working time, and to have one per floor of a large office, etc.

3. Review the training of first aiders. They are required to attend an HSE-approved course or have a recognised medical qualification. Where first aiders are not required, consider appropriate training for appointed persons and other staff, e.g. a one-day training course.

4. Check that there are sufficient first aid boxes, that they are accessible and that the system for replenishing them is functioning.

5. Whatever medical room/rest facilities are provided, check that they are in a clean and usable condition and that any equipment in them is in good condition.

6. Check that staff generally are aware of the availability of first aid, the location of first aid boxes and the identity of first aiders.

7. In the light of the above, amend the first aid policy as necessary and ensure relevant information is disseminated to staff and those responsible for training and management.

8. Review the accident reporting procedure.

9. Review accident investigation and follow-up procedures.

2:8 Procedures and arrangements for major incidents and disasters

Major incidents and disasters, that is incidents which are viewed as catastrophic, require additional management arrangements to be in place. The identification of the probable nature of catastrophic events requires the application of a more global risk assessment and the envisaging of worst-case scenarios. The more common catastrophic event is that of total loss of business premises by fire. However, a range of other events can be equally damaging to a business. Insurers may offer assistance in the preparation of arrangements and procedures, as it is in their interest to avoid large losses. These arrangements are often referred to as business continuity plans, as they are intended not only to cope with the emergency but to ensure that the business is capable of getting back on its feet as soon as possible after the major event has occurred.

2:8.1 Disaster planning and business continuity

Planning to limit the damage caused to an organisation by an accident or major incident is good business practice. In some establishments there is a specific legal requirement to prepare a plan showing how a company will respond to an emergency.

The Control of Major Accidents Hazards Regulations 1999 (COMAH) apply to operators of establishments where dangerous substances (as defined in the Regulations) are present in quantities that could cause a major incident or accident. There is a general duty to take all measures necessary to prevent major accidents and to limit the consequences to persons and the environment. Operators must have a documented safety policy with respect to the prevention of major accidents and must notify the relevant authority of various matters, send them safety reports, provide information when required to do so, make certain information public and establish emergency plans. The Regulations also provide for inspections and investigations by the relevant authority.

Guidance on preparing an on-site emergency plan is available in the Health and Safety Executive (HSE) publication *Emergency planning for major accidents: Control of Major Accident Hazards Regulations 1999* (HSG191, available from HSE Books, website: www.hsebooks.co.uk). Whilst this guidance is primarily intended for major industrial hazard sites, it is nevertheless a useful source of reference for other enterprises.

In other organisations where there is no legal requirement for a business continuity plan, one may still be required by insurers as part of business continuity cover. A plan will also comfort shareholders, particularly those of a company quoted on the London Stock Exchange, that the company will survive any incident. More general advice for businesses is provided in the Home Office document *How resilient is your business to disaster?* available online at www.ukresilience.info/contingencies/business/resilient1.htm).

Business continuity planning generally has two phases: the contingency plan and the recovery plan. The contingency plan is concerned with the identification of what might go wrong and the methods by which the foreseeable contingencies are managed. The recovery plan is concerned with the procedures and methods that are required to maintain or re-establish the business both during the course of the emergency and immediate aftermath to it. The recovery plan may be further divided into plans dealing with:

- premises and working areas;

- technology.

What can be achieved obviously depends on the extent of the consequences of the disaster.

2:8.1.1 The contingency plan

This plan should be devised by examining all the possible threats to the business and the worst-case scenarios that could occur. This examination is rather like a global risk assessment and the methodologies used for risk assessment can be applied for this purpose. Reference to the costs of safety outlined in **Chapter 12, section 12:5** may be especially useful when considering the types of losses that can be envisaged.

The use of logic trees, similar to those outlined in **Chapter 6**, can also be helpful when examining the nature of the risks and contingencies which may be involved. Dependency analysis is one way of revealing the extent of any disasters that might occur. In this type of analysis the head event of the fault tree is expressed in terms of a key organisational function and then the logic tree approach (as explained in **Chapter 6**) is used to determine what the key function depends upon. Event trees may also be constructed to examine contingencies, as in the example given in **Chapter 6, section 6:12**.

The contingency plan should focus very much on crisis management and the people, procedures and communications that will be necessary.

2:8.1.2 The recovery plan

This part of the plan deals with all the work that needs to be carried out to ensure that the business can either continue operating or can get back to work in the shortest time possible. The main risks to the organisation will determine the functions and procedures required in the recovery process (*see* **section 2:8.2.1.3**).

2:8.2 What to put in a business continuity plan

The plan should include as a minimum:

- evacuation procedures;
- means of contacting emergency services;
- means of contacting insurers and legal advisers;
- means of contacting and replacing communication systems;
- means of controlling likely incidents.

The steps to developing a business continuity plan are outlined in **section 2:8.2.1**.

2:8.2.1 Developing the business continuity plan

2:8.2.1.1 Identifying responsibility

It is important to appoint someone who is to be the responsible person (plus a deputy if they are absent) for:

- developing a business continuity plan;
- organising and co-ordinating events at the time of the emergency.

The co-ordinator will need to bring together a team which will be responsible for the co-ordination of certain aspects.

2:8.2.1.2 Setting objectives

Simple objectives then need to be set:

- for reducing the effects of an emergency;
- for recovering from the effects of an emergency.

Examples may be:

- 'In the event that the telephone system is irreparably damaged, an alternative system needs to operating by the start of the next working day.'

- 'In the event that the premises can no longer be occupied, alternative facilities providing the same service must be operating within 48 hours.'

A broad plan needs to be prepared to overcome each eventuality.

2:8.2.1.3 The main risks to cover

A list should be compiled of those aspects of the business which would be most damaged if an emergency occurred and what form that emergency might take.

Examples of parts of the business which might be at risk are:

- computer systems;
- other company records;
- communications systems;
- utilities;
- stores;
- manufacturing and warehouse facilities.

Serious emergencies may arise because of:

- fire;
- natural causes (such as flooding or wind damage);

- computer viruses/hacking;

- power cuts or other utility failure;

- physical damage to premises or services due to civil unrest, terrorist attacks, etc.

Steps should be taken to reduce the effects of emergencies by:

- backing up all computer systems at least daily and storing records off the premises overnight;

- storing all short-term, hard-copy records in fireproof cabinets or safes;

- storing all long-term records in properly protected archive storage facilities;

- if necessary, microfiching/microfilming or electronically storing all documents and keeping them in secure premises.

2:8.3 Rehearsal and review

Disaster plans should be rehearsed. The frequency of the rehearsal will depend upon the nature of the company, the inherent hazards, and the success of previous rehearsals. The scenarios tested should be as realistic as possible in order to fully test the plan.

Employers will need to review their plan to respond to changes in their companys' circumstances and the results of their rehearsals.

3 | Procedures and Arrangements for Investigating Accidents

Issues discussed in this chapter:

- Accident management and investigation policy and procedures
  - Organisational commitment
  - Scope
  - Triggers for and extents of investigations
  - Roles and responsibilities
  - Training investigators
  - Management support and resources
  - Expert assistance
  - Administration

3:1 Introduction

The need for accident investigation should be identified in an organisation's general policy on health and safety (required under the HSWA s.2(3) and the MHSWR reg. 5) and planning processes.

Like all parts of a safety management system the various aspects of policy making, planning, organising, implementing, monitoring and reviewing can be applied to the accident investigation process.

A policy for accident management and investigation is not a legal requirement for the majority of organisations. However, it is very useful to any systematic approach to safety management as it provides support and direction to an accident investigation.

The policy for accident investigation and management should form part of the general policy required by the HSWA and provide for the arrangements for both the management of accident situations and their investigation. It may also extend beyond matters generally considered with respect to the HSWA, for example preparing for litigation and other claims as a part of civil justice procedures (*see* **Chapter 9, section 9:6**) or other claims (*see* **Chapter 11**).

Naturally the extent of the accident management and investigation policy should be considered and supported by the senior management of the organisation. It is also necessary to include the workforce in this process, to provide both confidence in the management and investigation of safety events and to ensure general compliance with the requirements of the Safety Representatives and Safety Committees Regulations 1977 (S.I. 1977, No. 500) and the MHSWR (*see* **section 3:2.5.5.4**).

An effective approach to involving the workforce and their representatives in accident investigation will give commitment to examining underlying systems failures and deficiencies, rather than just superficial reasons or apportioning blame to the individual or individuals involved.

3:2 Accident management and investigation policy and procedures

When formulating a policy on accident management and investigation, consideration should be given to:

- organisational commitment and culture;

- what should be done (scope and nature of events to be managed and investigated);

- when to initiate an investigation;

- the extent of the investigation;

- what people are required to do;

- these people's training requirements;

- how they should be supported;

- what resources are required;

- practical matters.

A simple outline accident management and investigation policy is shown in **Figure 3:1**.

FIGURE 3:1 SAMPLE SAFETY POLICY FOR ACCIDENT MANAGEMENT AND INVESTIGATION

ABC Company

Date:

Accident management and investigation policy

Statement of intent

The ABC Company is committed to the thorough and open investigation of accidents appropriate to the level of harm and lessons to be learnt. The Company will support the investigation of accidents to discover how the management systems for health and safety have failed and what lessons can be learnt.

Communications

The lessons learnt from any accident investigation will be shared widely across the company and managers will be supported in seeking to improve safety performance as a result of the lessons learnt.

Training

Accident investigation training will be provided to selected managers and supervisors.

Events to be investigated

- All RIDDOR-reportable injuries and dangerous occurrences.

- All events which might have resulted in a RIDDOR-reportable injury or dangerous occurrence if the circumstances were different.

- Any safety event (occurrence of a situation which was not intended) which the Director responsible for safety or any departmental manager wants to be investigated.

Responsibilities

The production director is responsible to the board for ensuring that a system is in place to manage and investigate accidents. All employees of the company, including line managers, supervisors and directors will be expected to co-operate fully with any accident investigator assigned by the director of production.

Reports

Regular reports of accident trends and patterns will be brought to the board.

All major accidents will be reported to the board.

Employee representatives

Employee representatives will be invited to undertake joint accident investigations with the company.

No blame

No manager or employee will be disciplined as a result of being open and honest during the course of any investigation, unless it can be shown that they were wilfully negligent or deliberately disobeyed a clear order or instruction. If information is subsequently found to have been withheld, then disciplinary action may be taken against that individual.

Support for investigations

Resources, both financial and human, will be made available to accident investigators to ensure detailed and thorough investigations can be undertaken. Heads of departments and senior supervisors have the authority to expend finances during the course of an investigation if it is necessary to do so. If expenses are to be incurred outside of the limits set for their budgetary control, the approval of the finance director should be obtained.

Confidentiality

All information collected and used in an accident investigation will be held as confidential until such times as the investigators final report is presented.

3:2.1 Organisational commitment

The process of creating an accident management and investigation policy will not work unless the organisation is behind it. Everybody needs to co-operate and will probably need to respond to the outcomes generated. If the commitment of the staff is not gained early on, it is likely that accident investigations and the investigators themselves will be seen as a secondary consideration to mainstream management work. This is, of course, counter-productive if the policy has made the commitment to organisational learning.

3:2.1.1 Culture and expectations

Even where the prime purpose of any investigation is to expose a management system's failures (*see* **Chapter 2**), it is a natural human reaction to be defensive. The accident management and investigation policy needs to protect both the investigators from this attitude so that they are not blamed for what has happened. Accident investigation should be about the reasons for failure and not personal blame; it is about identifying failures in the management system. Developing a blame-free culture through the use of sensitive and competent investigators can avoid problems of people being defensive. Offering support for everybody involved when something has gone wrong can be a great motivator for a successful investigation.

However, a balance has to be struck between support for individuals and the need for discipline and sanction. Where negligence on an individual level could be considered criminal or wilful, then it is better to resort to other methods of investigation such as following the organisation's disciplinary and personnel management processes rather than considering the matter as an accident or safety issue. Dealing sensitively with the balance between sanction and discipline (which may need to be resolved in a court) and having an open and frank approach to learning from mistakes should be spelt out in the policy.

3:2.2 Scope

The accident management and investigation policy should spell out the scope of any accident investigation. Ideally, investigation is about finding organisational system failures in response to risk exposures.

The need to find someone to blame and apportion individual responsibility is less important than establishing how the management structure as a whole has failed or has been deficient. The crucial question is often whether the organisation is concerned about changing itself to prevent recurrence or is more concerned with protecting itself. The balance between protecting the organisation in the short term and learning from mistakes in an open and frank manner may sometimes be a difficult choice. Experience and research has shown that many organisations have been galvanised into substantial change after a serious incident has occurred. A clear example of this is the substantial management changes that took place at London Underground after the Kings Cross fire. If a commitment can be given to being open about the less serious issues, it is highly probable that the more serious issues will never arise. Learning from mistakes does not necessarily mean unwarranted exposure to severe legal sanction (*see* **Chapter 9**).

3:2.2.1 The nature and type of events to be investigated

Which events are to be examined as part of an investigation and how the investigation is to be managed should be covered by the policy. A minimum requirement of any policy will be the investigation of events falling under RIDDOR (*see* **Chapter 4, section 4:4**). However, organisations, as part of their review of the safety management system, must be prepared to amend the minimum requirements to reflect changes in legislation.

Whilst it might be useful to apply the same approach of accident investigation to every reported incident, it is likely that (especially in the early days of introducing an accident management and investigation policy) this will simply overwhelm the process. The events which are likely to be investigated in some detail, in addition to those reported under RIDDOR, will include certain near-miss events such as:

- those that might have resulted in serious injury or death, for example a near miss involving the reversing of a fork-lift truck in a warehouse;

- substantial technical failures;

- matters related specifically to the nature of the business.

The policy is likely to be extended to those accidents and events where there may be a need to prepare reports in response to the new Civil Procedure Rules (the Woolf Reforms). This will happen where an injury to an employee, visitor or member of the public is likely to lead to a claim for damages in a civil court.

3:2.3 Triggers for initiating an investigation

An accident investigation should be initiated as soon as possible after the accident has occurred. The extent and type of investigation to be undertaken will depend on a number of factors, all of which need to be considered together to form a judgement on whether any particular event should be investigated.

A number of useful triggers may be used for deciding if an event is to be investigated:

- any RIDDOR-reportable event (including those immediately reportable and three-day injuries and dangerous occurrences) (*see* **section 3:2.4.4.1** and **Chapter 4, section 4:4**);

- any injury requiring first aid treatment;

- any near miss with serious loss potential;

- any event where the risk(s) appear to be unknown or underestimated. This trigger is identified by people saying 'we did not expect that to happen' or 'we can't believe someone could be so stupid' and similar comments, which indicate that there is a distinct possibility that the risk was not in fact identified before the event happened. These events may also be better know as near misses;

- any event resulting in damage to equipment or property;

- any potential or actual release of an environmentally damaging substance;
- the likelihood of any insurance claim being made;
- the likelihood of any litigious action being taken. This is, of course, linked to the degree and nature of any damage to either person or property that has occurred.

When identifying the events to be investigated in the policy, it is important to bear in mind the need to separate events from outcomes. Although using outcomes as a means of identifying events is a pragmatic way of prioritising the investigator's role, it is important that people know that events need to be identified, not just outcomes. Once the list is made it will need to be kept under review to ensure it remains valid. The process for reviewing the list will need to be put in the policy so that the investigation process can be properly communicated. A general caveat is to ensure that important events that do not have serious outcomes are not excluded from investigation. Many important lessons can be learnt from examining apparently harmless events.

3:2.4 The extent of an investigation

Most accidents will be investigated to some extent. There is a need to ensure sufficient information is obtained to complete both internal and external reporting requirements. It is also necessary to determine the extent of benefit to the organisation for establishing an accident investigation and the degree of resources and time allowed for this.

In many circumstances it will not be possible to decide on the extent of the investigation required until the investigation process has itself commenced. It is only after preliminary enquires have been made that the extent of the investigation required will be understood. For example, an apparently simple incident in which an item of equipment suffers minor damage may reveal more serious problems and indicate that a detailed investigation is required. Had this approach been adopted with regard to the 'minor' fires on the escalators at London Underground stations, the events of Kings Cross may well have been avoided. By only reporting apparently minor fires and not undertaking detailed investigations, the extent of the risk to London Underground was overlooked – until the Kings Cross fire all too vividly pointed out the risks and dangers.

As the extent of any accident investigation – how much effort is put into it and how detailed it is – cannot always be decided at the point where the investigation is itself initiated (*see* **section 3:2.3**), it is important therefore to ensure that:

- all accidents are recorded;

- the process for ensuring line management is immediately informed of accidents is robust;

- all accidents are reported internally.

The effort and time put into an investigation will depend on a number of factors. Principal among these are:

- the extent to which the organisation is likely to learn anything;

- the extent of potential (or actual) loss;

- the likelihood of recurrence;

- conflicts/problems that may arise.

3:2.4.1 The extent to which the organisation is likely to learn anything from investigating the event

This will include the nature of any risk assessment and the information to be gained about the management of safety.

3:2.4.1.1 Risk assessment

Following an accident, information may come to light which will require a risk assessment to be reviewed and altered. For example, battery acid splashing into the eye of a mechanic when moving a battery powered generator may identify the fact that eye protection is insufficient or that there is a problem with using wet cell batteries. This will indicate that the risk assessment originally undertaken was inadequate and needs to be amended.

3:2.4.1.2 Safety management

An accident may identify weakness or inadequacies in the safety management system. For example, battery acid splashing into the eye of an operator using a battery powered generator may identify that a wet cell battery has been supplied instead of the required dry cell battery as a result of a failure to recognise a change in the supply of batteries. The failure to recognise the change and to ensure that only the correct type of battery is supplied is essentially a safety management system matter. It is likely that this failure to identify a change in supply could affect other items of equipment, such as high pressure hoses, 'o' rings, lubricating oils, etc.

3:2.4.2 The extent of potential (or actual) loss

The extent of actual loss will be a major factor in deciding whether or not to investigate and in determining the extent of the investigation. Clearly the occurrence of a severe injury fatality or major damage to property or equipment will indicate that an investigation must be undertaken. Minor injuries and damage may not warrant a full or detailed investigation. For example, people frequently cut their fingers on the edge of paper. Such paper cuts are more of a nuisance than an actual injury and are rarely if ever worth reporting or recording; therefore one would not expect these to be investigated. However, were such cuts to be incurred in a sterile environment such as a laboratory or hospital where there is the possibility of areas becoming contaminated with human blood or the person with the cut becoming infected, an investigation may well be warranted.

Potential loss is often more difficult to determine. Clearly any event which gives rise to a requirement to report a dangerous occurrence under the provisions of RIDDOR (*see* **Chapter 4, Figure 4:4**) should be investigated. Other near miss events will need to be examined very carefully to judge the likely extent and nature of any consequences. This is only something that can be gained through experience and with a knowledge of the risks involved. For example, the dropping of an object from a height may not have injured anyone or even caused any damage, but the potential for more serious loss is clearly obvious and this would indicate an investigation should be undertaken.

3:2.4.3 The likelihood of recurrence

If an event is so rare or so unlikely to occur, then there may be a case for not carrying out a detailed investigation on the basis that nothing of great importance or usefulness will be gained. Such situations are relatively rare in themselves and there are often other pressing matters which will result in the event being investigated anyway. An example is the Selby rail crash, where a vehicle left the road and fell into the path of an oncoming train, which derailed hitting a goods train coming in the opposite direction. This event is very unlikely to happen again, especially with this unusual and coincidental set of circumstances: the risk of a car falling into the path of a train was estimated at one in a million (a fairly low risk), and therefore the chance of another train hitting it in the way that occurred at Selby must be even less. However, no one suggested that the Selby train crash should not be investigated. In addition to learning about safety, matters of responsibility, liability and public perception need to be taken into account, all of which really lie outside of the health and safety framework. By comparison, the likelihood of another train crash like the Hatfield derailment was extremely high at the time. The derailment was found to be the result of poor quality metal in the track. Immediate action was required as a result of the early findings of the investigation, with vast resources having to be expended to identify and replace poor quality track elsewhere in the rail network.

3:2.4.4 Conflicts/problems

A number of problems can arise when deciding if and to what extent an event needs to be investigated. Most of these problems have to do with timing.

3:2.4.4.1 RIDDOR-reportable events

Immediately reportable RIDDOR events do not present a problem. Providing the chain of management responsibility is working, it should be fairly easy to identify that these events need investigating and for the accident investigation to be started. However, in the case of those events where injury has resulted in a three-day sickness absence it is obvious that the RIDDOR report itself cannot be the trigger for the investigation. If a company waits three days (or possibly four or five if a weekend break intervenes in the information flow) before deciding that the event is to be investigated, then much of the evidence may have been lost and some if not all of the impetus will have gone from the investigation process itself.

It is therefore important to ensure that any event which could become RIDDOR-reportable is in fact investigated as soon as it happens, without waiting to see if a person is in fact off work for three days or more.

3:2.4.4.2 Hospital-treated injuries

Under RIDDOR (*see* **Chapter 4, section 4:4**) an injury is reportable if it requires a 24-hour (or longer) stay in hospital. It is again obvious that a full 24 hours (but generally more) can be lost in initiating the investigation if the RIDDOR reporting process is relied upon to initiate an investigation. A useful addition to the triggers described in **section 3:2.3** is to ensure that any situation where someone has been taken or referred to hospital for treatment is seen as an event for which an investigation should be undertaken.

3:2.4.4.3 Near-miss events

The main problem with near-miss events is that very often those involved and those managing the situation do not see the events as near misses. This means that the events go un-remarked as people tend to respond to the degree of damage or injury that occurs and not to the events themselves (*see* **Chapter 1**). An important part of the accident investigation initiating process is to ensure that staff and managers understand the importance of identifying near-miss events and report them.

3:2.5 Roles and responsibilities

The accident management and investigation policy needs to define who carries out the investigation, who is responsible for its direction and who is responsible for implementing its outcomes.

In an ideal world all line managers, at an appropriate level, should have the knowledge, skills and competence to be able to carry out investigations. In the real world, a degree of expertise takes time and practice to develop. The greater the perception of an event as serious, and the greater the opportunity to bring about change as a result, the higher the degree of competence required.

Many organisations will not have the time and resources to develop competence in their line managers in one go. In such cases, a small cadre of trained investigators can be created. Smaller organisations will have no choice but to give investigation duties to line managers/supervisors, there being no other suitably located personnel. The need to ensure competence in the investigation process then becomes an early imperative for smaller organisations.

A balance needs to be drawn between creating specific and specialised investigation roles and the needs of the organisation and the personnel available. Line managers and supervisors are often best placed to conduct investigations. Wherever possible, however, it should be a matter of policy that they do not investigate incidents or situations where their own role could be called into question.

The policy needs to be bold on this point. The final decision about who does the investigation will very much reflect an organisation's needs and culture.

It is often better for the investigator to report to a senior manager: if not the chief executive then at least somebody on the board. In smaller enterprises the owner or managing director will take this role. This not only gives the investigator credibility and independence but also protects them from the fear of having a conflict of interest. This arises where the investigator fears that their future promotion or their working conditions can be adversely influenced (real or perceived) by the person or group they are investigating. This is clearly a cultural issue and one that can apply to both small and large workplaces.

3:2.5.1 Moral hazards

In preparing and implementing policy it is important to be explicit about moral-hazard issues. This may be reflected in fears about promotion, having to work in a climate of mistrust after the investigation or being subject to victimisation. For example, an investigator should be confident that they are empowered to stop production in the event of an accident occurring that may place others at risk. This, of course, requires the development of both guidelines and training to ensure that they are competent to make such decisions. Safety will not be provided for if such supervisors are confused or concerned that they will suffer some detriment if their decision is subsequently shown to be unjustified or if, even when justified, it is criticised for other business reasons.

Persons appointed to manage and investigate accidents should be assured by the policy that their approach and findings will not expose them personally to criticism. This is a difficult area as they may be commenting on the actions of their peers or more senior company personnel as well as leaving themselves open to criticism from all parts of the workforce. Careful selection and training of investigators can overcome some of this, but explicit policy will provide a standard for the whole organisation to work to.

In smaller businesses and workplaces the management and investigation of accidents is likely to be undertaken by the supervisors or senior managers. Moral hazards may still exist but be more evident, especially if the investigation is undertaken by the person(s) actually responsible for ensuring the event should not have taken place. This requires a high degree of commitment to learning from failures and deficiencies and a lot of support from others, principally legal and insurance advisers.

Those undertaking investigations need to be supported and championed. In an open, blame-free business culture this is seldom a problem. In more defensive organisations an investigator is unlikely to pursue the real reasons for an accident if they are fearful (real or imagined) of being placed in some sort of jeopardy. External investigators are not of course hampered by such fears.

3:2.5.2 Management authority

Someone at senior management level (director, proprietor or a senior manager with a suitable budget) needs to have the authority to undertake the required actions during the investigation. Such actions could include the obtaining of expert advice, organising the expert examination of equipment and producing documentary evidence. Assigning authority to deal with these issues should be part of the accident management plan. The authorised person will also require access to financial resources. Experience dictates that such resourcing must be forthcoming as a matter of urgency. A delay can be crucial, especially where the preservation of physical evidence is in doubt. Again, adequate planning should address this issue and therefore help to avoid problems.

In addition, authority to speak on behalf of the organisation, particularly to enforcement agencies and representatives of claimants, and (to some extent) on product liability matters should be decided in advance. The process of handling outside agencies requires particular care (*see* **Chapter 10**).

3:2.5.3 Investigators' authority

The people assigned to carry out the investigation need access to individuals, documentation and work sites. They need to be assured of the co-operation from colleagues and employees at all levels, as well as senior managers. They should have access to resources or the means to get resources. They also need the ability to make quick decisions in prescribed circumstances, for example preventing the use of machinery or processes where there is a danger of recurrence.

In addition to these requirements, the investigators also require more wide-ranging authority.

On many occasions there is a risk to others which is not altogether obvious. For example, a failure in one piece of equipment may be indicative that similar pieces of equipment may fail and cause injury, perhaps at different sites or locations. This, of course, is part of the argument for investigating all accidents and not just those which give rise to injury (*see* **section 3:2.3**).

People on the spot need to be able to recognise such circumstances and have the authority, or access to the authority, to take immediate preventive action. They also need to be protected from the effects of competing priorities – safety first has to be the rule. This can happen, for example, when there is a conflict between ensuring safety and continuing production.

In other circumstances it is absolutely necessary to continue working even though to continue with normal working procedures and activities is in itself unsafe. This is a situation frequently encountered by the emergency services. For example, if somebody collapses in a confined space it may be necessary to continue normal operations to effect rescue even when the situation has become more hazardous and safe working procedures no longer apply.

3:2.5.4 Confidentiality and status

A key feature of the policy should be to give status to the investigators and the investigations they undertake. During the course of investigations rumours can circulate, evidence can be damaged by false assumptions and people who should know better can meddle. The policy needs to be clear about confidentiality of information so as to protect the innocent and support the sensitivity that can be required, especially in the case of serious injuries and death.

There are other reasons for being careful with information. The protection of the organisation needs to be considered: not the protection from the cover-up syndrome, but rather protection in the sense that the outcome from the investigation should be about organisational learning. To promote this learning, a degree of trust and valid communication needs to be established. This will not happen if the world is exposed to the deliberations of the investigators. Sifting evidence and cross checking with witnesses can often be a lengthy process and it needs to be done quietly and discreetly. An open-house approach will also possibly pollute the evidence obtained by witnesses, whose recollections become based on rumour rather than what they saw or did.

3:2.5.5 The appointment of investigators

3:2.5.5.1 The selection of investigators

The selection of investigators must be planned. Not everyone has the right attributes to succeed in investigation. Competence needs to be developed and maintained. Attributes that a suitable investigator should have include an enquiring mind, determination, sensitivity and often stamina. A knowledge of safety legislation and of the technical processes involved in the business will also be an advantage.

For routine investigations the investigator is likely to be drawn from the first or second level of line management such as a foreperson or supervisor. Managers and supervisors would be expected to have knowledge of the work processes. Care needs to be taken to ensure that the role of the supervisor undertaking accident investigation is not compromised. For example, in some cases their duties may have been to ensure the appropriate control measures were in place before the incident even though they weren't. The use or support of an independent competent person, such as an appointed safety adviser, will overcome difficulties in this area (*see* **section 3:2.10.1**).

3:2.5.5.2 One investigator or a team of investigators?

The number of investigators required will depend on organisational size, their availability and the number of accidents to be investigated. Larger investigations will require at least two investigators and a back-up administration team.

Organisations with high risks may require a greater degree of care in the selection of investigators and the support and training they receive. This is largely because the lessons to be learnt following any investigation may have a significant impact on the way risk is considered by the organisation.

3:2.5.5.3 The availability of investigators

It is important to ensure that the right balance is maintained between:

- knowledge of the work activities, processes and hazards involved in the accident;

- accident investigation skills.

The success of an investigation depends on the plans being put into action. It is essential to have competent investigators available around the clock, or as appropriate for the operational schedule of the organisation. The investigators need to have easy access to the workplace.

Where there is likely to be a high workload it is essential that the investigators have no other operational or business commitments whilst they are carrying out the investigation. This can be arranged in a number of ways, but it is important to resolve any conflict between operational duties and the need to investigate an accident, especially a serious one, before any accident occurs.

3:2.5.5.4 Trade union representatives

An important policy consideration will be the involvement of the representatives of the employees. These may be duly elected and appointed trades union representatives. (The HSWA s.2(4) provides for the appointment of safety representatives by recognised trade unions from amongst the employees, as provided for in the Safety Representatives and Safety Committees Regulations 1977 (S.I. 1977, No. 500).) Under s.2(6) of the HSWA, employers have a duty to consult safety representatives, members of trade or professional bodies or representatives of employee safety on health and safety matters. Under reg. 3 of the Health and Safety (Consultation with Employees) Regulations 1996 (S.I. 1996, No. 1513), as amended by the MHSWR, employers have a duty to consult on health and safety matters with employees who are not represented by safety representatives under the Safety Representatives and Safety Committees Regulations 1977.

It could be argued that the extent of consultation with employees should include the procedure and outcome of any accident investigation. Where safety committees exist, accidents will inevitably come onto the committee's agenda.

Provision should be made for keeping staff and trade union representatives updated on the investigation. Inevitably both groups will have questions to ask and will expect a response from management. The role and responsibility for responding to employee groups needs to be decided and a record needs to be kept of any questions raised and the answers given. The safety committee is a good conduit for these questions and answers.

The best approach is to invite the employee representatives into the accident investigation process. This will depend upon the organisational culture and reflects the relationship between employees and management. However, wherever possible, joint working and collaboration in the accident investigation process should be encouraged.

The benefit of involving employee representatives in the accident investigation process is that they can assist both in the understanding of the situation and the undertaking of any remedial work required. In addition, involving employees in the investigation process encourages the development of an open culture and acceptance of the outcomes of the investigation (*see* **Chapter 1, section 1:5.1**). However, where safety representatives are to be involved in the investigation team, it will be necessary for them to adhere to the confidentiality and communication rules of the investigation process.

3:2.6 Training investigators

An organisation's safety policy should cover the selection and training of investigators and designate responsibilities for those involved in the management process. How this should be achieved and the precise nature of the policy direction will be a matter for individual organisations. It is therefore likely to vary depending on the size of the organisation, the nature of the business (and therefore risks) and the skills in and competence of the workforce, including the availability of a competent adviser or trained safety specialist.

Investigators should be competent, with the necessary skills, knowledge and experience to undertake the task in hand. The training will need to be planned and kept up to date. At best, planning needs to be flexible as it is not possible to predict when an accident could happen.

The range of competencies and skills which the investigators requires will reflect:

- the extent to which the organisation wishes to undertake an investigation;

- the relative risks involved in the day-to-day work processes.

Whatever decision is taken on the selection of personnel and allocation of resources for accident investigation some level of training will be required.

3:2.6.1 Training requirements

It is recommended that investigators receive training before carrying out an investigation. A typical training syllabus for accident investigators needs to include:

- an appreciation of the law relating to accidents and the investigation of accidents (*see* **Chapters 9** and **10**);

- the techniques involved in interviewing witnesses and others (*see* **Chapter 5, section 5:4**);

- the skills needed to put together the sequence of events in the accident (*see* **Chapter 6, section 6:2**);

- the skills needed to collect and analyse evidence and draw justifiable conclusions (*see* **Chapters 6** and **7**);

- an appreciation of the wider social, legal and management issues related to accidents and their consequences (*see* **Chapter 12**);

- the skills needed to administer accident investigations, including document control, continuity of evidence and the importance of information, including issues of confidentiality, and legal and insurance requirements;

- report writing and presenting information, including the briefing of senior managers;

- an understanding of the basic human factors in accidents (*see* **Chapter 1, section 1:6**).

3:2.6.1.1 More advanced training

More advanced training would include:

- the practice of assembling fault trees and event trees (such as HAZOP);

- the understanding of advanced human factors, including human error analysis.

3:2.6.1.2 The length of a course

It is unlikely that the basics of accident investigation can be covered in less than three days. A course of one day may provide some appreciation of the subject area and enable relatively minor incidents to be investigated and recorded. However, such a short period will not normally prepare anyone to undertake a more serious accident investigation or provide them with the range of skills and knowledge required.

3:2.7 Management support

Any safety policy should provide a documented record of the intended actions of the organisation's management, but this requires real and understood support at all levels, particularly at board and senior management level. Bringing support to the management and investigation process is a feature of both its safety culture and the personal attributes of an organisation's managers and supervisors. Securing the understanding and support of safety, union and other employee representatives is part of this process.

The extent of support given to accident investigation will reflect the extent to which internal controls are managed. It will also reflect the degree to which safety features as a key issue for the organisation, and how the culture of the organisation reflects health and safety values.

3:2.8 Resources

The organisation's safety policy needs to indicate who has been chosen to investigate and then provide them with the resources and training to do the job. Quality investigations can take time to conduct and deliver. Without high-level policy commitment the investigation process is likely to flounder. Recognition of this in the policy (and its subsequent communication to the rest of the organisation) is essential.

Safety policy considerations should take into account both the extent and allocation of resource requirements for an investigation. This includes both human and financial resources. Depending upon the extent of investigation required, it is likely that investigators will be unavailable for their routine tasks for some time. The investigators' absence from their regular jobs and the need to reassign duties should be agreed in advance and these arrangements should be made clear in the policy.

Again, balancing resources needs to take into account the benefits to be derived from any investigation against the costs of doing that investigation. Very often it is not until the investigation is over that the true benefit, or otherwise, is known.

In larger organisations the policy is likely to be more formal and require a degree of resourcing related to the risks involved in the work activities. Responsibility for the management of an accident and the subsequent investigation process is likely to be shared, with safety advisers and other competent persons taking a lead role (*see* **sections 3:2.5.5, 3:2.10.1** and **3:2.10.1.1**).

3:2.8.1 Money

An organisation should budget for the costs that may be involved in carrying out an investigation. Each organisation must determine the level of funds to include in its budget based on its turnover, the likelihood of an investigation being required and the nature of the investigation likely to be needed.

The additional costs which may be incurred include, but are not limited to:

- the costs of covering the investigators' regular jobs;

- administration costs;

- investigators' travel costs;

- investigators' accommodation costs, i.e. office space and overnight accommodation.

3:2.8.2 Equipment

In order to successfully undertake accident investigations investigators need to have had sufficient training to prepare themselves for the role and be able to deal with investigations confidently. They also need to have a certain amount of equipment to assist them.

Only a limited amount of basic equipment is required for most minor investigations. For more detailed investigations some extra equipment may be required and anyone serious about accident investigation will soon come to develop their own list of requirements.

3:2.8.2.1 Basic equipment

Basic accident investigation equipment includes:

- pens and notepaper (lined and preferably in a bound book so that pages can be used consecutively and not get lost);

- a tape measure;

- a camera (Polaroid or 35 mm);

- witness statement forms, equipment record logs and other administration files (*see* **Chapter 5, Figures 5:2–5:7** and **Figure 5:9**);

- a powerful torch;

- an address book with important contact numbers of managers, technical experts and external experts as well as the enforcement authorities and test houses (e.g. equipment or PPE testers).

The equipment should be kept in a bag or case, so that it is kept together and is ready for use immediately.

3:2.8.2.2 Additional equipment

The additional equipment shown below may be needed when carrying out more complex investigations:

- a tape recorder for dictating notes;

- a camcorder or digital camera for making direct pictures (which can be easily inserted into written reports via a computer);

- a mobile phone;

- overalls and other PPE;

- video playback facilities;

- a laptop computer.

3:2.9 Time off

The personnel chosen to carry out any accident investigation must be allowed time off from their normal activities to train for their investigation role. This includes time for both formal training courses, organised by the company, and other relevant safety-related and technical courses needed to broaden their knowledge and understanding of the organisation's operations. Such time off must be without loss of pay.

3:2.10 Practical matters

A number of ancillary and supporting matters need to be addressed to both prepare for and then manage the accident investigation process including:

- deciding on the role of competent advisers;
- dealing with communications and information flows;
- planning and organising expert assistance;
- responding to and dealing with legal advisers and insurers;
- organising administrative support;
- arranging accommodation;
- welfare arrangements;
- the involvement of employee representatives;
- dealing with external authorities.

3:2.10.1 Safety advisers

In organisations where there are dedicated safety professionals, the appointed competent person (appointed under the provisions of reg. 7 of the MHSWR) may be able to provide assistance or be tasked with the investigation role. Note, however, that whilst a dedicated and qualified safety professional may provide competent assistance, they will not necessarily have the competence, skills and experience for the full range of accident investigation tasks that may be required. Training will therefore be an important consideration.

3:2.10.1.1 A team approach

When a detailed investigation has to be undertaken the resources of a team are usually required. The variety and extent of tasks to be undertaken usually makes this a necessity. Detailed investigations frequently require a range of competencies that rarely exist in an individual investigator. Moreover, the team approach allows for some sharing of tasks and responsibilities. It is also essential for some of the more detailed methodologies that may be applied (*see* **Chapters 5** and **6**). Team members may be drawn from the workforce, management and the appointed competent person, such as the safety adviser.

The role of the safety adviser will be to provide a degree of independence and act as a facilitator to the investigation process. An experienced safety professional may well be able to lead the team in the use of particular methodologies and generally guide and direct the process. They will also provide technical guidance on the application of legislation, control measures and risk assessment.

3:2.10.2 Communication

Although an important part of the safety management process, accident investigations are likely to be (hopefully) infrequent. It is therefore important to maintain support for the accident management and investigation process. The policy should be communicated when introduced and then kept at the forefront of the safety approach through reminders, examples and case studies communicated to all levels of the organisation. This is especially important if a wider definition of accident is to be used and near misses identified and investigated (*see* **Chapter 1**).

3:2.10.2.1 Communication with and between investigators

Communication between investigators is vital during the investigation, especially where they are out and about following leads and interviewing witnesses.

During the course of the investigation, contact will also need to be made with a wide range of people and authorities. Mobile telephones should be issued, especially to investigators out in the field who need to make contact with base.

The more serious the incident, the more important it is to keep tabs on such contact. In addition, welfare support (such as counsellors) will need to be kept up to date. This is essential as they can mitigate the worries and fears of those involved. (They can also be a source of useful informal information, another reason to keep the accident investigation confidential (*see* **section 3:2.10.7**).)

A member of the administration team can often successfully run communications. A dedicated administrator can keep track of phone calls, enquires and messages and act as a focal point for communications between team members and the organisation.

3:2.10.2.2 Communication with senior management

Senior management will want to know what is happening and periodic structured debriefings should take place. However, the policy should spell out that the investigation has to be conducted without interference and that those in senior positions should support the need for this. However, it is important that managers know who has been affected and how, as experience has shown that failures in internal communications can be more traumatic than the events of the accident themselves.

3:2.10.2.3 Internal communications during an investigation

During an investigation it is important to keep people informed. This can be achieved by briefings, memos or through an intranet. Senior managers need to be kept up to date (as far as is possible), especially where immediate responsive action is required to prevent either a repetition or escalation of the event being investigated. Staff need to be reassured that everything possible is being done and trade union and other representatives need to be updated as to the investigation's progress (*see also* **section 3:2.5.5.4**). The extent and

137

nature of any communication with the investigators should be decided at senior level to avoid evidence collection being affected and problems with subsequent actions developing, such as insurance claims and litigation. Decisions on what to say and when to say it also frequently need to involve consultation with legal and insurance representatives.

3:2.10.2.4 External communications

Inevitably a major event, especially one involving a fatality, serious injury, unusual circumstances or a significant event will attract the attention of the media. Anticipating the need to talk to the press and control the flow of information (and sometimes site access) should form part of the planning process (*see* **Chapter 4, section 4:3.2**).

An important aspect of this is dealing with relatives and friends and avoiding unnecessary distress by handling the situation with due sensitivity (*see* **Chapter 2, section 2:6.3**).

3:2.10.3 Expert assistance

Additional assistance may be required for certain types of investigation. It is useful to maintain a list of experts in a range of relevant fields and appropriate sources of help that can be contacted if an incident occurs. The kinds of expertise required could be:

- structural/civil engineers for building related failures;

- test laboratories for fabric failures, product failures and sub-standard materials performance;

- metallurgists for the examination of equipment failures;

- public health laboratories for the testing of water supplies, environmental conditions, etc.;

- occupational hygienists for the examination of working conditions and levels of exposure to a variety of hazards.

Manufacturers and suppliers may also be helpful if involved in this process. However, their involvement should only be authorised after consultation with legal advisers and insurers. This will ensure that any questions of liability are properly addressed and the organisation's legal position is safeguarded.

3:2.10.4 Legal implications

Both at the start of an investigation and during its course, there will be a need to take advice from, or provide information to, the people acting in respect of insurance and legal matters. There is always a need to be concerned with the legal aspects of the investigation. This is particularly so with regard to future claims against the organisation and any possible enforcement action. The policy should address how these aspects will be dealt with (*see* **Chapter 4, sections 4:3.4.1** and **4:3.4.2**). In an ideal world the accident investigators should not be concerned with this. However, whilst the investigation should (in a purist sense) be concerned with finding causation, it is sometimes difficult to separate causes from liability issues. This is especially difficult in smaller organisations where the investigation may be more focussed on insurance and legal matters (*see* **Chapters 9** and **11**).

3:2.10.5 Administration

A lot of the organisational burden can be relieved by providing administration support. The larger the organisation, the more likely that there will be a number of personnel operating in a variety of administrative roles, such as finance, personnel, ordering and dispatch. Such staff will have a number of competencies that can be used to support the investigation team. For large investigations it is necessary to have administrative support dedicated to the investigation to undertake such tasks as:

- document collation;
- filing;

- letter preparation;

- arranging interviews;

- chasing reports;

- maintaining the continuity of evidence;

- typing up or examining witness statements;

- dealing with legal and insurance enquires;

- answering the phone;

- maintaining a log of all communications – both written and oral.

All these tasks, and several others, routinely occur during any major investigation and the support of competent administrators can greatly assist in the efficiency and effectiveness of the investigation itself.

3:2.10.6 Accommodation

Even in small organisations the investigator will need some room and privacy to assemble facts, reflect on evidence and discuss issues. Large and extensive investigations need a fair amount of space. In any event, most organisations are able to find some short-term room for unexpected eventualities. It is best to plan for this space and allocate it. In addition, provision of appropriate IT support for report writing and evidence analysis needs to be allowed for. If the enforcement authorities become involved they may need a suitable place or room to interview people, if required.

For extensive investigations a room (or preferably two) needs to made available to the investigation team. This allows for the containment of information, a place to think and a place to organise the various elements of investigation methodology presented in **Chapters 5** and **6**. Such a room may not be essential for lesser incidents, but for involved investigations it is *absolutely essential*. This room also needs to communicate with the outside world. A telephone (or two), a fax (with its own line) and tea-making facilities are the minimum requirements. File boxes, tables and chairs will tend to sort themselves out. Such items tend to respond to human need!

Ideally the room should be ready and waiting. This will often be impossible, so the next best choice is to have a dual-purpose room, such as a library, conference room or the large office of a senior manager (preferably the accident investigation director), which can be converted at a moment's notice.

3:2.10.7 Welfare provisions

No accident occurs without there being some repercussions on the people involved. Often the more serious the outcome, the more traumatic the effects on those involved, although this is not necessarily the case. The accident policy should indicate what welfare provisions have been made available, and what role counselling is going to play in the investigation, who will provide counselling or other support and how it will be provided.

Consideration must also be given to any possible trauma on the investigators themselves, especially in situations where the outcome is harrowing or distressing. Senior management should ensure that the investigators take adequate breaks for rest and food, as it is easy for investigators to become absorbed in the investigation and neglect their own welfare.

The impact on relatives, friends and colleagues should also be addressed. Provision should be made so that information can be given with due haste and respect for the feelings and concerns of those involved in the lives of any affected employee.

3:2.10.8 Communications with trade unions

Whatever the extent of involvement of employee representatives in the investigation process (*see* **Chapter 3, section 3:2.5.5.4**) it is vitally important to ensure a record is kept detailing the information passed to them and any questions they may have raised. This information will be of great benefit when the accident is discussed at any safety committee and when formal consultation with the representatives takes place.

3:2.10.9 External authorities

In some circumstances the HSE or police may be involved, and in the case of a fatality, a coroner (*see* **Chapter 9, section 9:7.2**) will need to be advised of progress. Such communications take time and can detract from the task of investigating. A central focus needs to be given to this communication, but unfortunately only the investigators are likely to be in a position to provide up-to-date information. It must be stressed that it is unwise to make early conclusions and the investigating team should be left to get on with the task as far as is humanly possible.

4 | Managing Accidents

Issues discussed in this chapter:

- What actions need to be taken immediately following an accident?
  - Making the accident site safe
  - Ensuring the welfare of any casualties
- Mobilising the emergency services
- Contacting the enforcement authorities and next of kin
- Dealing with the media
- What has to be reported under the Reporting of Incidents, Diseases and Dangerous Occurrences Regulations?
- How to report accidents
- How to record details of all accidents

4:1 Immediate post-accident action

When an accident occurs there will always be a need to manage the situation. The degree and extent of management required depends upon the nature and outcome of the accident, as well as the resources available.

There are a number of matters that need to be considered in the immediate aftermath of the accident. These include both dealing with the people affected by the accident, and with a range of issues that arise out of the accident. These need to be dealt with either immediately or as soon as possible.

Dealing with people involves dealing with anyone who has been injured and with other people who may have been affected by the accident. Firstly, there is a need to consider the impact of the accident on any of the people directly involved. This will include:

- removing people from the area if any immediate and continuing danger exists;

- ensuring that first aid is provided to anyone who has been injured;

- providing support to those traumatised or otherwise affected by witnessing the accident;

- informing the next of kin and others (such as close friends) about the circumstances of the accident and the condition of any casualties;

- dealing with any remaining dangers that pose a risk to workers, passers-by, including the public, or people who may subsequently happen upon the scene, such as cleaners, security guards or children gaining access after the close of business.

4:1.1 Immediate actions

4:1.1.1 Checking for any continuing dangers

In the immediate aftermath of an accident there is a need to ensure that no further danger to people, the environment or property exists. Some of the decisions and actions required will be for the investigators and others will not. It is most unlikely that the appointed investigators will be on the scene to deal with any of the early requirements for protection of people and rendering of first aid, but they will probably be the people best able to identify the immediate ramifications of the early findings of the investigation. These issues are discussed in **Chapter 8** as part of the actions resulting from accidents. It is therefore important that all employees have a general awareness of the need to assess accident situations and take appropriate action to prevent further danger or to be able to call others who can, including the emergency services.

4:1.1.2 The affected persons

People who are present at the scene of an accident may be affected in different ways. Primary concern must be for injured persons. Whilst this is not normally a role for the accident investigator, the provision of first aid is a part of accident management. Limiting consequences, preventing things from getting worse than they are already, mitigating damage and generally making sure that nobody else has the same accident are part of accident management – and the actions of first aiders and other people rendering treatment (who may not be 'qualified' first aiders – *see* **section 4:1.1.3**) may be essential information for the investigator. It is possible that the inappropriate application of first aid or the late application of first aid could have a significant impact on someone's injuries and in some cases even directly contribute to their death. It is for the accident investigator to consider including such matters in the investigation as lessons can clearly be learnt from things that have gone wrong.

4:1.1.3 Providing first aid

Employers are required by the Health and Safety (First Aid) Regulations 1981 to make provision for first aid protection for their employees (*see* **Chapter 2, section 2:7**). Administering first aid is a task for those immediately on the scene. The investigator is unlikely to be involved in the accident scenario itself and should concentrate on the investigation role upon arrival. If by chance the trained accident investigator is caught up in the accident scenario itself, or is directly responsible for it, then there has to be a question about whether they can suitably carry on as an investigator, as in such circumstances they become a witness and not an impartial party.

In the management of the accident it is necessary to ensure that first aid is applied competently and that first aid facilities and equipment are available (*see* **Chapter 2, section 2:7**). Suitable first aid provision should be located near to the areas of risk identified in the risk assessment required to comply with the guidance *First Aid at Work: the Health and Safety (First Aid) Regulations 1981 – Approved Code of Practice and Guidance* (code number L74, available from HSE Books, website: www.hsebooks.co.uk).

In ideal circumstances those immediately on the scene would be trained in first aid. However, this is not always possible and an early call for emergency services support should always be made where the circumstances warrant it.

There may be occasions when the administering of first aid and other on-site medical treatment may form part of the investigation itself. This will happen if there are questions about the efficiency and practice of first aid and the suitability of emergency facilities and equipment. For example, in a certain process area there may be a requirement to have an eye wash facility available. The effectiveness of these arrangements (or perhaps the absence of) may be matters for the accident investigator to consider.

4:1.1.4 Removing further risks

It is a normal and imperative requirement in any situation where an accident has occurred, including near misses and especially those dangerous occurrences reportable under the Reporting of Injuries, Diseases and Dangerous Occurrences Regulations 1995 (RIDDOR), to ensure no further and immediate danger remains. This can arise when structures become unstable, for example those damaged in an explosion, loads become unstable, substances are spilled and cave-ins or landslides occur during excavation work.

The extent and effectiveness of the control of immediate danger to victims and to others may form part of the accident investigation. This will also include the arrangements for identifying, notifying and ensuring people can be removed from immediate danger – a duty under the provisions of reg. 8 of the Management of Health and Safety at Work Regulations 1999 (MHSWR).

4:1.1.5 Rescue and recovery

It is important that those on the scene are able to distinguish between rescue and recovery.

4:1.1.5.1 Rescue

Rescue relates to the removal of injured and other live persons from an area of danger or imminent danger. The nature and extent of the rescue attempt will depend on the immediate circumstances. Rescues should only be attempted where there is a reasonable chance of success. Rescues frequently involves a rapid and often uncalculated assessment of the risks by the rescuers.

Rescues should not be attempted where it puts the rescuer(s) at risk. There are unfortunately many examples where well-meaning rescuers have met their deaths (*see* **Figure 4:1**). Where there is no effective rescue procedure in place, the emergency services should be called.

Preparation for foreseeable rescue scenarios can prepare rescuers for the dynamic risk assessment they will need to make at the scene. For example, the 'man overboard' procedure was developed for rescuing persons from water, whether or not they have actually fallen from the rescue vessel. Similarly, in confined space working, a procedure should be in place to facilitate an emergency response.

Rescue scenarios should form part of the risk assessment process for any hazardous working and any working where there is a likelihood of danger should control measures fail. Those responsible for authorising such work and accepting working procedures should also ensure that emergency plans are developed, and wherever possible, trained and practised. For work that is of a long duration, or is of a continuous nature, emergency plans should be reviewed and checked to ensure they are still appropriate for the circumstances. Regular checks should be made on equipment provided for emergency rescue to ensure that it is in good condition and available at the designated location. Checks on plans and equipment should be made at a frequency commensurate with the work, the equipment, the location and the risk.

4:1.1.5.2 Recovery

Recovery refers to the retrieval of bodies from an accident scene. The process of recovery is generally more considered than that for rescues; it does not need to be done as an emergency in the same way as rescue. Body retrieval is undertaken when there is no longer any danger to persons involved in the accident and any live casualties having already been removed. Therefore, recovery should not put at risk the people undertaking the recovery and entry into the danger area should be strictly controlled and monitored to ensure that lives are not lost during the recovery operation.

FIGURE 4:1 RESCUE OR RECOVERY?

How four men climbed to their deaths

The four men – let's call them trainee technician A, 20, labourer B, 20, engineer C, 26, and ganger D, 26 – died in a 4.25m-deep drain inspection chamber due to asphyxiation from breathing non-respirable gases.

The sequence of events:

1. Technician A was the first to climb into the manhole. He climbed back up half way coughing and spluttering. He fell back in. Student engineer E ran to get help from workmates on the site.

2. Labourer B and engineer C arrived within one minute. First B and then C went into the manhole, without safety lines, to help their colleague. B collapsed. E returned to the manhole.

3. Resident engineer F arrived. He saw C trying to prop up A. E went in search of a rope long enough to reach the bottom of the chamber. He returned with it.

4. F half entered the manhole and saw that C had now collapsed. F came out of the manhole. D arrived within a few minutes, tied a rope around his waist and started down the manhole.

5. D tried to grab one of the men but he too collapsed. Those on the surface pulled on the rope, but it slipped over D's limp arms.

Twenty minutes later the manhole was purged with oxygen and rescuers were able to enter the manhole safely.

Figure 4:1 illustrates some of the issues that should be looked at when deciding upon a rescue or recovery operation, and the need for a safe system of work when entering a confined space, and the possible consequences for not having one! The system of work must be based on a suitable and sufficient risk assessment (such as that required in the Confined Spaces Regulations 1997 (S.I. 1997 No. 1713)) which should include:

- the measurement of the atmosphere;

- having a trained and competent workforce;

- having adequate rescue procedures and equipment.

4:1.2 Remaining dangers

Immediately after an accident there may be a number of dangers still existing which need to be controlled The absence of, inappropriateness of or less-than-adequate early attempts to mitigate any remaining danger may mean the accident scenario continues. For example, a fire, a release of gases or the spread of contaminants may exacerbate the accident and increase damages and injuries beyond that reasonably expected in the circumstances. As well as being issues that require managing, accident investigators will need to decide if such events are to be included in the investigation, as lessons can be learnt from any failings to mitigate danger. The matters to be considered include:

- containing hazards arising out of the incident;

- the escalation of the incident;

- the evacuation of personnel.

4:1.2.1 Containing hazards arising out of an accident

On many occasions when an accident occurs certain hazards remain that need to be dealt with immediately to prevent further danger. For example, the collapse of a scaffold may require immediate work to prevent the remaining scaffold from falling into sensitive areas, such as on roadways or plant. The people in the vicinity need to have the authority and competence to act quickly to prevent the hazard causing further injuries or damage.

As far as possible, foreseeable scenarios should have been considered as part of the risk assessment process, as should the subsequent arrangements for removing people from imminent danger and putting contingency arrangements in place. Identifying competence and authority should be part of the organisation's policy for dealing with the management and investigation of accidents. In many cases it will be necessary for those on the spot to have the authority to act in such circumstances, and this means they should be provided with the skills and knowledge to take charge in the event of an emergency arising.

4:1.2.2 Escalation of an accident

There is sometimes a possibility of an accident escalating. An example of this would be a fire in one part of a plant that may spread to another where the effects may be even greater. The classic example of escalation is the so-called 'domino effect', where an incident at one site is so large that it impacts on neighbouring sites. This is a factor taken into account in the former CIMAH regulations for site control measures and emergency planning, and has been followed through into the latest Control of Major Accident Hazards Regulations 1999 (*see* **Chapter 10, section 10:8.2**).

Sometimes when an accident occurs there is an immediate need to ensure the events cannot escalate or continue. For example, stopping a small fire in the windings of an electric motor driving some process equipment, may prevent the spread of the fire to other parts of the plant or premises. In such cases it is obviously important to act quickly as the spread of fire is clearly a recognisable escalation. Such prevention is likely to be undertaken by the people on the spot and not the accident investigators.

However, there is another way escalation needs to be considered, as an imminent danger may not be so obvious. For example, if an item of equipment is found to be defective, that is, it fails in use or whilst being tested, then it may be necessary to stop all further work with that equipment until its safety can be assured. The failure may be a result of a particular part wearing, a design failure or a usage for which the equipment was not intended. Where the equipment is in widespread use, say across several sites or in several premises, the actions to prevent (or control) further immediate danger must include these other sites or locations and not just the site or location where the accident has occurred.

4:1.2.3 Implementation of an evacuation plan

Where appropriate, the evacuation plan will need to be implemented (*see* **Chapter 2, section 2:6.5**). The effectiveness and efficiency of the evacuation arrangements following an accident may well form part of the accident investigation process. It is always advisable to review evacuation plans in the light of actual experience as the way systems and people behave in reality is often different to that during rehearsals.

4:1.3 Providing support for those who are affected

The majority of accidents, and some near misses, will give rise to emotions and feelings of stress amongst many of those involved. This includes onlookers and helpers, as well as casualties.

Two ways of dealing with emotional reactions could be considered after an accident. The first is 'defusing' and the second 'debriefing'.

4:1.3.1 Defusing

Research has shown that the process of defusing is a natural reaction to incidents in many organisations. The term 'defusing' likens the process to dealing with a fuse in an explosive device. By removing or 'calming' the fuse, the explosion (i.e. the unwanted psychological trauma) is effectively reduced or eliminated. The defusing process involves the employees getting together to talk over the events they have been involved in and to share their own thoughts and feelings. This does not need to be a formalised process and in many situations it often occurs naturally. What is important is for management to understand that this process is necessary and should be encouraged.

The need for the defusing process will sometimes cross paths with the actions and needs of the accident investigators and the investigation. It is important for the investigation that evidence is kept as clear and 'unpolluted' as possible. Allowing those involved to talk freely about the accident can sometimes interfere with the way that witnesses report what they recall; their memories are conditioned by what others tell them. This, to some extent, can be overcome by using some of the approaches suggested for interviewing witnesses immediately after a traumatic event (*see* **Chapter 5, section 5:5.3.1**).

Management of the defusing process should:

- allow or assist people to comes to terms with what they have seen or been involved in;

- offer support by supporting the process, allowing time for it and being sympathetic;

- provide information on additional help if it is required.

4:1.3.2 Debriefing

Debriefing as a technique was developed to help emergency service personnel cope with the mental effects of attending incidents involving severe physical trauma, i.e. injuries and death. Originally the debriefing was seen as a rigorous process with a set of rules and prescribed processes and time sequences. This process had precise criteria for the debriefing, stating when it should be carried out and how it should be used. To a large extent the concept of debriefing has developed over time and now exists in a number of different forms without much of the original rigour. The central idea of debriefing is to provide a structured approach for steering individuals and groups through a 'review' of the events.

A central theme of debriefing is usually to expose those involved in a traumatic event to a re-run of the event itself. The underlying principle is that the debriefing process itself will lessen mental effects, especially post traumatic stress disorder. It is not just about going through the re-run of the events, but also taking part in the structure and format of the debriefing, sitting with others talking about the events and reliving rather than analysing what they have been through.

There is some controversy over whether the debriefing process works or not. This is partly because the evaluation of the process is itself difficult. Some studies have shown debriefing has no real benefit; some reports have even suggested that debriefing may in fact be harmful. It is important, therefore, before embarking on any debriefing process as part of a structured approach to dealing with traumatic events, that specialist advice is sought from psychiatrists practised in this field. The advice should include whether debriefing is appropriate in the circumstances, and also the timing and content of the debriefing programme.

4:2 Emergency services

Factors that need to be considered when the emergency services are involved in dealing with the consequences of an accident include:

- calling the emergency services to the site;

- providing information;

- providing access;

- providing equipment;

- offering support and assistance.

4:2.1 Mobilising the emergency services

The first management decision to be made when an accident occurs is to notify the emergency services. It is important to ensure that emergency services are mobilised as soon as possible, and an early decision must be taken on this issue.

Where a serious injury has occurred and treatment is required over and above minor first aid the local ambulance service should be requested. The on-site first aider or appointed person has the duty to ensure medical services are made available; this person could also be given the task of calling the fire brigade and/or the police. Only one emergency call is required using the 999 system; the operator will contact the other emergency services if requested to do so. In any event the organisation's policy and procedures for emergency response and contingency arrangements should have established this role and ensured those tasked with it are competent to make the necessary decisions.

Where possible the following should be noted and advised to the call handler:

- a description of the accident;

- the nature and type of injuries (if possible);

- the approximate number of casualties.

This will allow the fire and ambulance crews to prepare for what they are going to have to deal with.

Many rescue situations and incidents involving fire will need the attendance of the local fire brigade. It should be borne in mind that the fire service in the UK only has a statutory duty to attend and fight fires; however, there is a general practice for fire brigades to attend incidents for the purposes of undertaking rescue. The pre-accident arrangements should ensure that the local fire brigade is familiar with the site and any specific hazards it contains.

The police should also be called immediately if there has been a fatality or where assistance may be required for dealing with on- and off-site control. This is especially so in larger incidents where, for example, there is a need to secure a path for other emergency service vehicles, for the evacuation of large numbers of people or for general crowd control. In certain circumstances the police may also take on the rescue role, but this will depend on the nature of the incident and the resources available to the local constabulary. Examples of this would be search and rescue in water, and high line rescue capability. In cases of fatality the police may take the prime role in investigation in liaison with the Health and Safety Executive (HSE) or local authority (*see* **Chapter 5, section 5:5.7.5**).

4:2.2 Information when an accident occurs

When the emergency services arrive on site they will need the latest information about the incident and details of who and what is involved. The information provided to the 999 call handler should be repeated to the crews on their arrival and updated with any relevant information.

Any first aid given to casualties should be noted and passed on to the ambulance crew on their arrival. The crew should also (depending on circumstances) be met by someone in authority, and any technical expertise should be made available. This could include maintenance personnel to explain the workings of machinery (in the case of someone trapped), chemical or laboratory staff to explain the properties of substances and chemicals, or engineers to describe conditions in the plant or underground.

It is vitally important to advise the attending emergency services crews of any hazards in the location of the accident/casualty that may affect them, for example fire, hazardous chemicals and substances, and potential building collapse.

This information will be needed so that the emergency services do not expose their own staff to unknown or unnecessary risks.

4:2.3 Access

The emergency services must be able to access the accident site easily, even at security-controlled entrance points. In addition, on large sites it may be necessary to send somebody from the accident to direct the emergency services to the scene. In exceptional circumstances a landing site may need to be found for HEMS (helicopter emergency medical services), which operate in a number of areas. These landing sites need to be pre-arranged and should be discussed with the HEMS flight control operator if there is a possibility that the site may be used for landing.

Consideration of emergency access points should take account of 24-hour working and the likelihood of emergencies occurring after dark and in inclement weather. The nature of the terrain should be allowed for, as most first-response emergency service vehicles are not four-wheel drive.

During construction work or alterations to sites the arrangements with emergency services should be reviewed and they should be kept informed of any temporary changes to access points.

4:2.4 Equipment

The provision of specialised equipment on site may assist the emergency services. Such equipment includes hoists and cranes on building sites, earth movers and mobile lifting machinery, railways on underground tunnelling projects, high-rise access gear and high-capacity (long-duration) breathing apparatus (including oxygen sets).

Where specialised protective equipment is involved this may also need to be utilised by the emergency services, for example noise protection or high-visibility clothing. However, in many circumstances the emergency services will not be competent in the use of on-site emergency equipment, and it is important, therefore, that pre-accident planning of emergency scenarios takes account of this. For example, if a trench collapses the fire brigade may wish to utilise the skills of site personnel in using earth-moving equipment;

likewise for protracted tunnel rescues they may need to use underground railways to gain speedy access and have breathing apparatus made available (non-standard fire service issue). The use of such equipment must be identified in advance and the fire brigade satisfied that their crews could become competent in its use (through on-site training and familiarisation) or know that others will be there to use it if requested. It is unlikely that personnel from the ambulance service would have a background enabling them to make use of such training, and therefore emergency planning would have to take account of the co-ordination arrangements needed to utilise their services.

4:2.5 Support and assistance

Where process plant or complex situations exist, for example at a chemical plant, the emergency services (mainly the fire brigade) will need the assistance of a competent person from the site to provide detailed information. Such assistance may also be needed for the other emergency services, for example advice on site security for the police.

This person may be an engineer, production manager, factory chemist or a similar competent person who understands what is involved in the accident in terms of process, equipment and risks, and can provide technical information to assist the emergency services carrying out the rescue. For example, if an accident involved a worker trapped in a rolling machine (such as at a printers), the fire brigade will not know the details of how the machine can be operated or dismantled. This information will need to be provided before the rescue operation can begin. It is therefore vitally important that those on site can identify the type of information that is required and can quickly locate the person who can provide it. Other immediate information for the fire service may be provided by on-site signage – for example HAZCHEM signs and signs posted in accordance with the Dangerous Substances (Notification and Marking of Sites) Regulations 1990 (S.I. 1990, No. 304) to indicate the presence of particular hazardous substances.

Any specialist help on site should also be brought into action, for example the utilisation of spillage clean-up teams.

Technical and other manuals should be readily available and easily accessible (i.e. somebody should be on site who can understand them and relay the information to the emergency teams). In some cases information regarding specialised equipment or machinery may have to be obtained from manufacturers or suppliers and these details should also be readily available.

The full extent of what is required should be identified as part of the risk assessment process to identify emergency requirements in the event of control measures going wrong.

4:3 Notifying the authorities and others

The immediate management of an accident from an administrative point of view is simple but important and should be straightforward providing the systems and procedures described in **Chapter 2** are in place before any accident occurs. It involves:

- notifying the appropriate authorities;

- accessing personal details and notifying the next of kin;

- notifying company contacts.

4:3.1 Notifying the appropriate authorities

4:3.1.1 The Health and Safety Executive/local authority

The HSE or local authority, depending upon the nature of the business (*see* **Chapter 9, section 9:4**), must be notified immediately when an accident which involves death, serious injury or a dangerous occurrence, and which is immediately notifiable under the provisions of RIDDOR occurs (*see* **section 4:4**).

The immediate notification may be made by telephone to the 24-hour HSE reporting line number (tel: 0845 300 99 23) or alternatively notification can be given by email (riddor@natbrit.com). Details of these contact points need to be available and accessible at a convenient location within the workplace. A note should be made of who made the call on behalf of the company. If the contact was made by telephone, then records should be kept of:

• the time of the call;

• the details provided;

• the person who took the call.

Where the contact was made by email, then a copy of the message should be printed. Where the enforcement authority is the local authority, the HSE will pass on the information.

As this is an accident that will be investigated by the organisation, accident reporting forms provided by the organisation can be used for this purpose by inserting the details in appropriate spaces (a sample reporting form is provided in **Chapter 5, Figure 5:5**). These details should be passed to the officer responsible for reporting under the provisions of RIDDOR (*see* **Chapter 4, section 4:4.1.11**) and to the person who is to take charge of the situation, a role determined in the emergency arrangements (*see* **Chapter 2**).

In addition, it should be ascertained if the enforcement authorities are intending to investigate the accident. This is particularly relevant where an accident has involved plant or equipment which needs to be examined, because if either the enforcement authorities or the police indicate that they wish to investigate it will not be possible to interfere with or otherwise examine any equipment or plant involved in an accident. This does not prevent the company undertaking an accident investigation, but it does seriously limit any physical examination of items involved. (No material items involved in the accident should be examined unless the prior permission of the proper authority (i.e. the enforcement authorities or the police) has been obtained and confirmed.)

4:3.1.2 The police

Where a death has occurred, the police must also be immediately advised. Who makes contact will depend upon the nature of the company and of the accident. However, the responsibility will frequently fall to the senior manager in attendance.

Where the death has been caused by the accident, or where the circumstances appear suspicious, the scene of the accident must not be interfered with, other than to make it safe to administer first aid and remove casualties.

The police will require to know:

- the name(s) of the deceased;

- the place of the accident;

- the time of the accident.

The police may require the area to be secured to ensure that evidence is not interfered with.

The police must also be advised of the death of any injured person if the death occurs within 12 months of the injury being caused (*see* **section 4:4.1.4**). The police will normally advise the Coroner's Office.

4:3.2 Notifying next of kin

A very important initial response to any major accident, particularly those involving fatalities and serious injuries, is to make personal contact with the next of kin of injured persons, i.e. close relatives and personal friends within the workplace (*see* **Chapter 2, section 2:6.3**).

It is vitally important that news of any serious injury or death is communicated to the next of kin before the news reaches them indirectly, for example through the news media coverage or by being told by persons who do not have all the facts or are unconnected with the management of the situation. This latter group includes well-meaning colleagues and managers/supervisors who do not understand the situation and have not been involved in the organisation's response to the accident.

Suitably trained members of the senior management team should be tasked with communicating with the injured/dead person's family. In some circumstances companies may wish to have more than one member of the management team involved, for instance where a fatality is involved. A serious injury to or loss of a loved one is extremely traumatic for relatives, close friends and work colleagues. The situation should be handled properly and sympathetically. A phone call, fax or email is not a suitable way to convey such news to a deceased's nearest and dearest.

4:3.3 Notifying key personnel in the company

It is important that senior managers of the company be notified immediately that a serious accident has occurred. This will ensure that the responsible person for the company can take all relevant action in accordance with the company's policy and procedures. This will, of course, vary and depend on the circumstances. If immediate action is required to prevent escalation or to mitigate the consequences of the accident, it is vital that those with responsibility for aspects of the work affected by the immediate action are informed. For example, the production manager may have to halt supply streams to avoid a build up of materials, as well as shut down a production area.

In many cases the occurrence of an accident will generate a whole range of information needs. During the course of an investigation information will be gathered about the accident in order to establish causes. Some of this information might have immediate and short-term relevance, for example the identification that a certain procedure is ineffective and possibly hazardous. During the course of the early part of the accident management and investigation, a number of people will require information, including:

- senior managers;

- trade union safety representatives and employee safety representatives;

- workers not directly involved in the accident or its aftermath;

- insurers;

- enforcement authorities.

4:3.3.1 Senior managers

Senior managers will need to be told about the accident as soon as possible, taking into account the circumstances and the actions being taken by the person responsible for safety and the appointed accident investigators, as set out in the organisation's policy and arrangements.

Situations may arise, especially in larger organisations, where line managers may not know their staff have been involved in or affected by an accident. It is important that managers are told when their staff have been involved and that the investigators (and others concerned with the management of the incident, such as personnel officers) are aware of what is happening.

The speed at which managers are informed and the type of information they need will, in most cases, depend on the details of the event. Accidents with serious consequences such as fatalities, serious injuries and plant/equipment damage will obviously be of interest to senior managers due to the inevitable consequences on the business as a whole. Other events will need to be examined carefully to ensure that any immediate consequences for health and safety are identified and acted upon (*see also* **Chapter 8**). Senior managers have responsibilities to contribute to the consideration of any circumstances affecting an organisation. By informing them as soon as possible, any likely consequences of the accident will be identified and suitable action taken.

4:3.3.1.1 Updating managers on the progress of the investigation

Part of the immediate response to any accident should be to inform management of any immediate consequences and what actions are being undertaken (for example, the need to take certain production equipment out of operation, the closure of certain parts of the building and the sourcing of alternative suppliers). A simple issue will be to inform relevant managers of the persons involved in the accident and the person(s) assigned to do the investigation. An early notification of insurance managers and legal advisers is often of benefit (*see* **Chapter 11**).

It is also important to ensure that during the course of the management and investigation of an accident essential senior managers are kept up to speed with the situation and the progress being made. This fulfils several functions.

- It keeps people informed and they therefore feel part of the process and can be counselled on their responses.

- It ensures the integrity of the investigation (*see* **Chapter 7**).

- It enables managers to contribute information to the investigators, particularly in areas that may have been overlooked early in the investigation process.

- It ensures that relevant personnel know that people have been injured or otherwise involved in the accident, avoiding subsequent embarrassment and stress.

4:3.3.2 Trade union and employee representatives

There is a general duty for employers under the Health and Safety at Work etc. Act 1974 (HSWA) to allow trade union and employee representatives to investigate accidents. Employee representatives cannot do this if they are not aware that an accident has taken place. Best practice is to undertake a joint investigation between management and employee representatives, although it is recognised that this is not always possible or feasible.

4:3.3.3 Employees

When there has been an accident it is often necessary to ensure all employees are informed of the earliest findings and the occurrence itself. This would also include contractors and sub-contractors. This is necessary to ensure:

- that conditions similar to those involved are highlighted and brought to the forefront of people's minds;

- that everyone is aware of who has been involved and the consequences. This avoids any embarrassment and any non-deliberate insensitivity;

- that information which may aid the investigation comes to light from people not immediately involved.

4:3.4 Notifying key external contacts

It is important that a company's insurers and legal advisers are told without delay that an accident has occurred so that appropriate advice and guidance can be obtained.

4:3.4.1 Insurers

Any event that leads to a loss (or potential future loss) may have consequences for insurance liabilities. These may arise from:

- occupier's liability;

- employer's liability;

- public liability;

- product liability;

- a combination of all four.

Liability may also arise from accidents on public highways involving a vehicle (*see* **Chapter 11**).

In most situations where injury or damage has occurred, the appropriate insurer will need to be informed of the details of the accident. Normally this involves the completion of a claims form. Insurers may wish to undertake their own investigation and may require specific information to be obtained. Depending on the circumstances, the insurer may appoint a loss adjuster to estimate the extent and value of any material loss. This is likely to be the case where property, premises, plant and equipment or stock is involved.

A copy of any accident report will normally also be required by the insurer. Communication with those involved in the incident and particularly those who may have a claim against the insurer needs to be guarded to protect the insurer's rights.

At this stage a check can be made with the insurer regarding the insurer's rights, particularly with regard to the question of liability. This should not be allowed to interfere with the safety-related investigation; whatever the insurer's position, the accident investigation must not be steered off course until underlying causes are identified. There is sometimes a danger that an insurance response is to settle and not worry about the real causes, or alternatively become overly concerned about the report apparently admitting liability. This is the balance that each organisation needs to find for itself. Those more advanced in understanding health and safety issues would not regard this as of concern.

Attention to the speed of providing particulars will need to be addressed in order that the requirements of any subsequent action in the civil courts required by the Woolf Reforms can be met (*see* **Chapter 9, section 9:6** and **Chapter 1, section 11:8**).

Note: Insurers should be advised in all circumstances, even if immediate reactions suggest that no claim will be forthcoming.

4:3.4.2 Legal advisers

Where the losses resulting from an accident are liable to be substantial, it is important that the company's legal advisers are informed at an early stage, so that guidance can be obtained on how to deal with all parties concerned (*see* **Chapters 9** and **10**).

In particular, legal advice should be sought as soon as possible in the light of any of the following situations:

- a fatality;

- a major injury;

- equipment/product failure where there may be a question of supplier/manufacturer liability;

- a request by an enforcement authority to interview witnesses or managers;

- any situation where there is a likelihood that negligence or any other serious liability has arisen;

- there is a possible breach of any contractual obligation.

Due notice should be taken of who has:

- authority to speak on behalf of the organisation;

- authority to submit evidence;

- the ability and training to handle witnesses.

In most cases insurance companies will instruct their own legal advisers. It is essential to ensure that the insurer's legal advisers are aware of and liase with the company's advisers.

4:3.4.3 Issuing a press release

Shareholders, employees, suppliers, customers and the media will all want to know what has happened and what the future effects will be. A press release from the company will help to provide the necessary information and reassurance. The press release may be issued solely to the media, although in some circumstances it may be considered prudent to circulate the document directly to others, for example the London Stock Exchange, customers and suppliers.

Press releases are best framed with the assistance of legal advice, or if that is not readily available then by somebody who is used to dealing with such matters. (This could be a company press officer, an independent press agency, somebody in the organisation's marketing department, the company secretary or a person used to dealing with media relations.)

Statements should be informative and to the point, but not revealing. Promises, accusations, suggestions and conjecture should all be avoided. The statement should only deal with factual matters and as such can be quite brief, perhaps along the lines of 'an accident happened, involving ... and is being investigated'. Where appropriate, statements may also be included confirming that business will not be affected. The journalistic maxim is to keep to the facts.

4:4 Reporting and recording accidents

All accidents that occur in a workplace must be recorded, as required by the following regulations:

- accidents reportable under RIDDOR for which legal provision is made for the nature of the record;

- accidents that need to be recorded to comply with the Social Security Act 1967;

- accidents that are not reportable under RIDDOR.

4:4.1 Reporting accidents under RIDDOR

Responsibility for enforcing health and safety at workplaces is assigned to the relevant authority by the Health and Safety (Enforcing Authority) Regulations 1998 (S.I. 1998, No. 494). This divides responsibility in most cases according to the nature of the premises/business. Offices, retail and leisure facilities are in general assigned to local authorities, whilst industrial and 'higher risk' activities are assigned to the HSE.

Accidents which fall under the definitions provided in RIDDOR should be reported to the appropriate authority – either the HSE or the local authority. In general, environmental health officers undertake the local authority enforcement and an appropriate officer will be delegated to receive reports on behalf of the local authority.

The powers and duties of both the HSE and local authority inspectors are identical. HSE officers are formally authorised to undertake the duties of the HSE. In the case of local authority inspectors, they will be formally identified by way of a 'warrant' or authorisation to undertake all or partial duties with respect to the provisions of the HSWA and regulations made thereunder.

It is important for all employers and self-employed persons to know which is the relevant authority for their work or place of work. This information should be obtained early on and kept in a relevant place to avoid legal penalties for failing to report a reportable accident.

4:4.1.1 Reporting forms

The reporting form for an accident is HSE F2508. The information can also be provided electronically at www.riddor.gov.uk. From 1 April 2001 all RIDDOR reports can be made to a single HSE office. This is at:

Incident Contact Centre
Caerphilly Business Park
Caerphilly CF83 3GG

Local enforcement officers will be notified from this central unit. For disease the form is HSE F2508A, again reportable electronically at www.riddor.gov.uk.

4:4.1.2 What to report

The reporting of certain accidents is required by RIDDOR, and employers have an absolute duty, by law, to comply. In general, these regulations apply to all work sites to which the HSWA (as amended) applies; they also apply to certain work activities carried out in UK territorial waters and the UK sector of the continental shelf. Such activities are specified by the Health and Safety at Work etc. Act 1974 (Application outside Great Britain) Order (1995) (S.I. 1995, No. 263), which provides for the extension of UK health and safety law to offshore installations, wells, pipelines and underwater mines, as well as the unloading of ships at sea, maintenance and construction at sea and certain diving operations. Separate regulations apply in Northern Ireland.

Under RIDDOR, an accident is almost certainly any event and outcome that is required to be reported to the HSE or the local authority. The reporting requirements are linked to the outcome, such as injury, and not the events that give rise to the outcome.

It is to be noted that acts of violence at work are included in RIDDOR and this has the effect of extending the meaning of accident beyond that which might normally be recognised.

Some of the diseases required to be reported under RIDDOR may arise through 'accidental' exposure. It is not general practice to regard occupationally derived ill health as being accidents, although the principles of accident investigation may be applied to investigating them.

4:4.1.3 When should accidents be reported under RIDDOR?

RIDDOR requires notification of accidents and diseases within specified timescales.

4:4.1.3.1 Immediately reportable matters

Events that are immediately reportable under RIDDOR are:

- the death of a person at work arising out of or in connection with work;

- any major injury suffered by a person at work as a result of an accident;

- any injury suffered by a person at work which requires the injured person to be taken to hospital for treatment;

- any dangerous occurrence.

The matter must be reported by the quickest practicable means available and be followed by a written report on an approved form (F2508) within ten days of the accident. In reality, this means a telephone call to the HSE's Incident Contact Centre (tel: 0845 300 99 23) or the sending of a fax to 0845 300 99 24 or email to riddor@natbrit.com.

4:4.1.3.2 Matters not immediately reportable

Any injury resulting from an accident at work which incapacitates the injured person for more than three consecutive days are usually referred to as 'over-three-day injuries'. Counting of the three days off work includes any normal rest days, such as weekends, but does not include the day the accident/injury occurred. Effectively this means the reporting requirement falls on day four.

The purpose of collecting information is to inform the authorities about the nature and extent of workplace accidents. Incapacitation for three days or more gives some indication of injuries which have a significant impact but which are not major injuries. Major injuries need not be reported under these provisions as the immediate reporting and follow-up written report required by the immediate reporting provisions will cover this, regardless of the actual time taken off work.

If a person returns to work within the three-day period (effectively within four days including the day of the accident) but is placed on lighter or restricted duties as a result of the incapacity sustained, then the injury must still reported as an over-three-day injury.

4:4.1.4 Latent fatalities

Deaths arising or resulting from an accident at work, but which occur within one year of the accident giving rise to the injury, must be reported as soon as the employer becomes aware of the death. The report must be made whether or not any injury or occurrence was previously reported to the appropriate authority under the provisions of RIDDOR, reg. 3. The report must be in writing. This implies that an employer (or responsible person) will need to keep track of any employee injured in a work-related accident for at least one year. This will apply even if the employee, for any reason, ceases employment.

4:4.1.5 Major injury

The ten types of major injuries required to be reported under RIDDOR are listed in Sch. 1 as:

1. any fracture, other than to the fingers, thumbs or toes;

2. any amputation;

3. a dislocation of the shoulder, hip, knee or spine;

4. the loss of sight (whether temporary or permanent);

5. a chemical or hot metal burn to the eye or any penetrating injury to the eye;

6. an injury resulting from electric shock or electrical burn (including any electrical burn caused by arcing or arcing products) leading to unconsciousness or requiring resuscitation or admittance to hospital for more than 24 hours;

7. any other injury:

   a) leading to hypothermia, heat-induced illness or to unconsciousness;

   b) requiring resuscitation; or

   c) requiring admittance to hospital for more than 24 hours;

8. a loss of consciousness caused by asphyxia or by exposure to a harmful substance or biological agent;

9. either of the following conditions which result from absorption of any substance by inhalation, ingestion or passage through the skin:

   a) acute illness requiring medical treatment; or

   b) loss of consciousness;

10. any acute illness which requires medical treatment where there is reason to believe that it resulted from exposures to a biological agent or its toxins or infected material.

4:4.1.6 Dangerous occurrences

Under RIDDOR, dangerous occurrences are events which are of such a nature that their occurrence is significant in terms of health and safety in that they are indicative of unsafe conditions having occurred. They are required to be reported under the same provisions as injuries and the report must be immediate, i.e. by the quickest possible means, followed by a written report within ten days (*see* **section 4:4.1.3.1**).

Figure 4:2 illustrates the requirements under Sch. 2 in relation to the more predominant events to be reported. Paragraph numbers equate to those in the schedule. Abbreviated wording has been used where this does not detract from the general meaning. Reference to the actual schedule should be made where accuracy is required, for example lifting machinery.

FIGURE 4:2 SCHEDULE 2 OF RIDDOR

1	The collapse, the over turning or the failure of any load-bearing part of any:	a) lift or hoist; b) crane or derrick; c) mobile access platform; d) access cradle or window cleaning cradle; e) excavator; f) pile driving frame or rig having an overall height, when operating, of more than seven metres; g) fork-lift truck.
2	Pressure systems	The failure of any closed vessel including a boiler or boiler tube or of any associated pipework in which the internal pressure was above or below atmospheric pressure, where the failure has the potential to cause death of any person.
3	Freight containers	The failure of any freight container's load-bearing parts while it is being raised, lowered or suspended.
4	Any unintentional incident in which plant or equipment either:	a) comes into contact with an uninsulated overhead electric line in which the voltage exceeds 200 volts; or b) causes an electrical discharge from such an electric line by coming into close proximity to it.
5	Electrical short circuit or overload	Attended by fire or explosion which results in the stoppage of the plant involved for more than 24 hours or which has the potential to cause the death of any person.

| 6 | Explosives | A wide list of reportable conditions are given including: <ul><li>unintentional explosions or ignition of explosives except where the explosion was the result of an unintended discharge of a weapon where otherwise the weapon and explosion functioned as intended and where a fail-safe device or safe system of work prevented injury;</li><li>misfire, except where a fail-safe device or system of work prevented injury;</li><li>the failure of shots in any demolition operation to cause the intended extent of collapse or direction of fall of a building or structure;</li><li>the projection of any material beyond the boundary of the site (or danger zone) in circumstances where persons were or could have been injured;</li><li>any injury to a person (other than in a mine or quarry or otherwise reportable under the Regulations) involving first aid or medical treatment resulting from the explosion or discharge of any explosives or detonator.</li></ul> |
| 7 | Biological agents | Any accident or incident which resulted or could have resulted in the release or escape of a biological agent likely to cause severe human infection or illness. |

8	Malfunction of radiation generators, etc.	Any accident in which: a) the malfunction of a radiation generator or its ancillary equipment used in fixed or mobile industrial radiography, the irradiation of food or the processing of products by irradiation causes it to fail to de-energise at the end of the intended exposure period; b) the malfunction of equipment used in fixed or mobile industrial radiography or gamma irradiation causes a radioactive source to fail to return to its safe position by the normal means at the end of the intended exposure period.
9	Breathing apparatus	Any incident in which breathing apparatus malfunctions: a) while in use; b) during testing immediately prior to use in such a way that had the malfunction occurred while the apparatus was in use it would have posed a danger to the health and safety of the user. (This does not apply to breathing apparatus used in mines or when it is being maintained or tested as part of a routine maintenance procedure.)
10	Diving operations	A range of circumstances which would put a diver at risk.

11	Collapse of scaffold	The complete or partial collapse of: a) any scaffold which is either: i) more than five metres in height which results in a substantial part of the scaffold falling or overturning; or ii) erected over or adjacent to water in circumstances such that there would be a risk of drowning to a person falling from the scaffold into water; b) the suspension arrangements (including outrigger) of any slung or suspended scaffold which causes a working platform or cradle to fall.
12	Train collisions	These are collisions not covered in RIDDOR, Sch. 2, Pt. II (see the Railways (Safety Case) Regulations 1994).
13	Wells	A range of circumstances giving rise to danger, including blowouts, detection of hydrogen sulphide where its presence was not known, failure to maintain separation distances between wells where the planned minimum separation distances cannot be maintained and mechanical failure of any critical safety element.
14	Pipelines and pipeline works	A range of circumstances presenting danger or potential danger.

15	Fairground equipment	a) In use or under test, the: i) failure of a load bearing part; ii) failure of any part designed to support or restrain passengers. b) The derailment or the unintended collision of cars or trains.
16	*Carriage of dangerous substances by road	Any incident involving a tanker overturning, serious damage to the tank and the uncontrolled release of or fire involving the dangerous substance being carried. (*This refers to the paragraphs in Sch. 2 to the Regulations which include particular requirements in two paragraphs (16 and 17) but which have the same effect.)
17	Collapse of building or structure	Any unintended collapse or partial collapse of: a) any building or structure (above or below ground) under construction, reconstruction, alteration or demolition which involves a fall of more than five tonnes of materials; b) any floor or wall of any building (above or below ground) used as a place of work; c) any false work.
18	Explosion or fire	An explosion or fire in any plant or premises which results in the stoppage of that plant or, as the case may be, the suspension of normal work in those premises for more than 24 hours, where the explosion or fire was due to the ignition of any material.

19	Escape of flammable substances	The sudden, uncontrolled release: a) inside a building: i) of 100 kilograms or more of flammable liquid; ii) of 10 kilograms or more of a flammable liquid at a temperature above its normal boiling point; iii) of 10 kilograms or more of a flammable gas; b) in the open air of 500 kilograms or more of any of the substances referred to in a) above.
20	Escape of substances	The accidental release or escape of any substance in a quantity sufficient to cause death, major injury or any other damage to the health of any person.

Schedule 2 includes industry-specific provisions for mines, relevant transport systems and offshore workplaces. This has the effect of bringing within the reporting provisions places of work previously excluded. The dangerous conditions are specific to the industries and represent the particular hazards and associated dangers of those industries.

4:4.1.7 Disease

In a very general sense diseases are seen to be those harmful effects of being at work that happen either gradually or have long-term effects. For the purpose of RIDDOR, diseases are those shown in Sch. 3 of the Regulations. The onset of most diseases is gradual and this distinguishes diseases from accidents where the harm is usually caused very rapidly. For example, damage to hearing generally happens over time (although there can be instantaneous damage).

Damage to hearing by repeated exposure to high noise levels would be regarded as disease, as would the occurrence of an upper limb disorder caused by doing repetitive tasks. A broken leg on the other hand would be regarded as being caused accidentally. It is generally more difficult to investigate the causes of work–related disease because of the circumstances in which they occur and the long time periods of exposure involved. However, to some extent the division is artificial and accident investigation methods can be used successfully to examine disease causation. The listing of diseases and activities is extensive.

RIDDOR, reg. 5 requires the reporting of diseases which are specified within Sch. 3 to the Regulations (part I, column 1) and for which only the activities in column 2 are being undertaken. This has the effect of ensuring that only diseases which might reasonably be associated with specified work activities are reported. It is not necessary to report diseases (illnesses), including communicable diseases, which are normally to be found in a community and which are not work related. The reporting requirements are thus restricted to those occupations where a risk assessment should have identified a risk of the specified illness occurring. For example:

- illnesses associated with ionising radiation are reportable only where the work necessitates activities involving ionising radiation as part of the work;

- leptospirosis (Weil's disease) is only reportable where the work activities involve:

    - working in places which are or are liable to be infested by rats, field mice, voles or other small mammals;

    - working in dog kennels, or caring for or handling dogs;

    - contact with bovine animals or their meat products, or pigs or their meat products.

In addition to a range of infections and zoonoses, the disease listing includes cancers (those commonly associated with certain work activities), poisonings from common or specific workplace substances (such as acrylamide monomer, ethylene oxide, methyl bromide and more familiar agents such as lead, etc.), musculo-skeletal conditions (especially those commonly associated with work-related upper limb disorders such as carpal tunnel syndrome and inflammation of tendons of the hand and forearm), occupational dermatitis, and lung conditions, such as asthma and alveolitis (e.g. farmer's lung).

The requirements for reporting diseases are different for employed and self-employed persons.

4:4.1.7.1 Employed persons

Reporting diseases can only be done after the receipt of a written statement by a medical practitioner. The practitioner can be a GP, hospital doctor or doctor retained or employed by the person's employer. The report should be made on form F2508A which requires details of the doctor and the diagnosis made. It is up to the employer to make the link between the disease and the activities of employment as set out in RIDDOR (Sch. 3, Pt. I for all employment, and Schs 1 and 2 for employment offshore) and ensure the report is appropriate and correct.

4:4.1.7.2 Self-employed persons

In the case of the self-employed there is no requirement for a written statement by a doctor as a trigger for the reporting process. The person, or someone acting on their behalf, must report the disease if informed by a doctor of a diagnosis involving one of the diseases listed in the Schedules. Again, the onus is on the person to make the link between the disease and the activity as described in the Schedules to the Regulations.

4:4.1.8 Special situations

There are a limited number of special situations where the provisions of RIDDOR are either extended or modified. These include:

- incidents involving gas;

- accidents involving vehicles;

- offshore installations.

4:4.1.8.1 Gas incidents

Regulation 6(1) of RIDDOR requires any death or major injury involving both pipe-distributed flammable gas and refillable containers of liquefied petroleum gas (LPG) to be immediately notified to the HSE and followed within 14 days by a written report. The trigger for the notification by the responsible person can be quite diverse and includes media reports, as well as a letter or a telephone call. It is therefore particularly important that operators of gas distribution have communication in place so that they can be told when reportable incidents occur. The person responsible for reporting such incidents must do so as soon as they become aware that an incident has occurred.

Regulation 6(2) of RIDDOR (in conjunction with the Gas Safety (Installation and Use) Regulations 1998 (S.I. 1998, No. 2451)) requires someone to be approved to report gas leaks, inadequate combustion of gas or inadequate removal of the products of combustion that is or has been likely to cause death or any major injury. This means that any competent person undertaking gas installation work, examination or maintenance work has a duty to report their findings of unsafe conditions. The decision on the extent of the safety implications and the likelihood of serious harm occurring (and thus the need to report) will reflect the competence of the particular person doing the work.

4:4.1.8.2 Vehicles

Accidents involving moving vehicles on a public highway are reportable if:

- any person is killed or injured as a result of exposure to substances being carried on a vehicle;

- any injury (or fatality) was caused as a result of work involving the loading or unloading of a vehicle;

- any injury (or fatality) was a result of work on or at the side of the highway (such as the construction, maintenance and repair of the highway, services or verges);

- a train was involved. This may occur particularly at unmanned railway crossings.

Accidents involving vehicles on the public highway are not, for the most part, reportable under the provisions of RIDDOR, as the circumstances will be covered by other legislation – primarily the Highways Acts. It is a requirement to report injuries or fatalities that occur on highways which do not form part of the public highway, for example, access roads around a large factory site.

4:4.1.8.3 Offshore installations

In the case of offshore installations, there is a requirement to report additional diseases included in RIDDOR, Sch. 3, Pt. II, as well as all the diseases listed in Sch. 3, Pt. I. The listing in Pt. II includes the majority of communicable diseases which are socially derived and transmitted, including cholera, as well as more common infections, such as chicken pox and measles.

It is clear that offshore installations are isolated communities and the impact of communicable disease can have extensive repercussions both for the workforce and the safe operation of the plant itself, especially where the 24-hour continuity of work is essential. As such, offshore installations will require a higher degree of care to ensure control of any risk of communicable disease.

Other workplaces, although not required to report such disease, may also benefit from a conservative approach to infection control for communicable diseases, especially where large numbers of workers congregate and share domestic-type sleeping and cooking arrangements as part of their workplace arrangements.

4:4.1.9 Visitors and non-employees

The provisions of RIDDOR apply to all persons at work. Where a fatality, major or over-three-day injury occurs to persons not at work, such as visitors or members of the public, this should be reported to the relevant authority if the fatality or injury was a result of work being undertaken, for example:

- a member of the public being injured by an escalator as a result of a malfunction or design fault in the escalator;

- a hospital or nursing home patient or resident injured as a result of tripping over a cable;

- a member of the public visiting a factory and being overcome by fumes.

There is no requirement to report the death of a non-employed person which occurred sometime after being involved in an accident arising out of or in connection with work. An employer or responsible person does not therefore have to keep track of the condition of any person who was not being employed at the time of the accident giving rise to the injury.

4:4.1.10 Self-employed persons' reporting requirements

The key factor in deciding who has responsibility for reporting fatalities and injuries to self-employed persons is the determination of who was in control of the workplace at the time of the accident.

In general terms, if the self-employed person was working on their own premises or on premises that they were for the time being in control of, for example a builder who has been given the keys of an empty office to refurbish, then the self-employed person should do the reporting. In the case of a fatality this would, of course, be impossible, but it is likely the matter would come to the attention of the relevant authority by way of the coroner's officer.

Accidents which result in injury to self-employed persons on their own premises do not have to be notified to the relevant authority immediately, although they have to ensure the authority is notified within ten days by completing Form F2508. This may be done by somebody acting on their behalf. Where the workplace is controlled by another person such as a main contractor on a building site, a plant operator or proprietor, then that person should undertake the reporting.

4:4.1.11 Who should do the reporting?

In the case of the reporting of injuries and dangerous occurrences to the authorities it is necessary for an employer to provide a responsible person to ensure the reports required by the Regulations are made.

Under RIDDOR the responsible person is specified for some situations. These are:

- in a mine: the mine manager;

- in a quarry: the owner of the quarry;

- in a closed tip: the owner of the mine or quarry with which the tip is associated;

- in an offshore installation: the duty holder (with certain exceptions) for the purposes of the Offshore Installations and Pipeline Works (Management and Administration) Regulations 1995;

- in a dangerous occurrence at a pipeline: the owner of the pipeline;

- in a dangerous occurrence at a well: the concession owner or a person appointed to execute the organisational or supervisory functions of any operation;

- in a diving operation: the diving contractor;

- in a vehicle: the operator of the vehicle.

Where none of the above specifically apply then the duty to report reverts to the employer in the case of a death, reportable injury or reportable disease, and in any other case to the person for the time being having control of the premises in connection to the work where the accident or dangerous occurrence occurred, such as a main contractor on a building site, a plant operator or proprietor.

4:4.1.11.1 Incidents involving gas

In the case of incidents involving gas (*see* **section 4:4.1.8.1**), the responsible person is the conveyor of any pipe distributed system or the importer of LPG containers filled abroad, the filler of a container or the wholesaler or supplier of a gas-filled container.

4:4.2 Recording accidents

The information recorded on the HSE accident and disease reporting forms (*see* **section 4:4.1.1**) or in the accident book (*see* **section 4:4.2.1**) is sufficient to comply with the relevant regulations where appropriate. However, it will often not be adequate to properly inform the accident investigators or provide all the details needed to defend a future civil claim. It is therefore best practice for organisations to have their own internal incident reporting system, using forms that record a wider range of information. This should include:

- the training, qualifications and experience of injured parties;
- the actions leading to the event;
- the equipment involved in the incident;
- whether suitable PPE was being used;
- references to other documents involved (e.g. work permits);
- the direct causes of the incident;
- the underlying causes of the incident;
- the immediate action taken;
- the possible severity of the incident;

- any further management action (e.g. to prevent a recurrence).

The recording of further information is strongly recommended. Organisations with more advanced accident recording systems may collect more detailed information than that required for RIDDOR. It is also important to keep a record of all accidents that are not required to be reported under the provisions of RIDDOR. Information contained in such records provides data for analysis of safety performance, as well as assisting in risk assessments and examination of safety control systems. The information to be kept should be the same as that for RIDDOR-reportable accidents as this allows for comparison and compatibility of data.

4:4.2.1 Accident books

Accidents need to be recorded in an accident book to comply with the provisions of the Social Security (Claims and Payments) Regulations 1979 (S.I. 1979, No. 628), reg. 25 (as amended 1987), or accepted equivalent document, for the purposes of claims made in the event of industrial injury and sick leave.

The document prescribed in the Social Security (Claims and Payments) Regulations 1979 is the B1 510A. This is obtainable from HMSO Bookshops among others. The information which must be recorded is:

- name, address and occupation of injured person;

- date and time of accident;

- location of accident;

- the cause of the accident;

- nature of the injury;

- name, address and occupation of person entering the details (where this is not the injured person);

Where the accident being recorded has to reported under the RIDDOR regulations, the form must be signed by the employer.

The records must be retained for a minimum period of three years.

The use of this book for recording RIDDOR records may be a simple way for smaller organisations to reduce the administration required. However, consideration should be given to using an electronic recording system as the requirements of RIDDOR and the accident book are not exactly equivalent (*see* **Chapter 12, section 12:8**).

Figure 4:3 provides an example of a page from an accident book.

FIGURE 4:3 EXAMPLE OF A PAGE FROM AN ACCIDENT BOOK

Person affected/injured	**Person affected/injured**
Name	Name
Home address	Home address
Occupation	Occupation
Works number	Works number
Person reporting the incident if other than injured person	**Person reporting the incident** if other than injured person
Name	Name
Home address	Home address
Occupation	Occupation
Department Date	Department Date
Accident/incident	**Accident/incident**
Date Time	Date Time
Place	Place
Equipment/machinery involved	Equipment/machinery involved
Description of incident including cause and nature of injury	**Description of incident** including cause and nature of injury
Action taken/recommendations	Action taken/recommendations
Signed Date	Signed Date

4:4.2.2 Recording RIDDOR-reportable acciden[

The responsible person should keep a record of all th[
are reported to the relevant authority under the p
RIDDOR. The record should contain the following information:

- the date and time of the accident or dangerous occurrence;

- information on persons injured, including: full name, occupation and nature of injury;

- information on any non-employed injured person: full name, status (such as customer/visitor) and nature of injury;

- the place where the accident happened;

- a brief description of the circumstances;

- the date when the event was reported to the relevant authority;

- the method by which the event was reported.

4:4.2.2.1 Form of the record

A copy of the actual RIDDOR reporting document sent to the relevant authority is often the only record that needs to be kept as this contains all the information required. This record should be made available for inspection by safety representatives and enforcement officers and should be kept for a minimum period of three years.

Other information may be kept with this record, such as claims and insurance details where this is relevant.

Providing that the information can be easily accessed and the Data Protection Act 1998 requirements are met the record may be kept in an electronic format.

5 | Processes and Techniques for Investigation

Issues discussed in this chapter:

- The general principles of doing an investigation
- Collecting evidence
- Obtaining evidence from people:
  - Eyewitnesses
  - Managers, supervisors and others
  - Interviewing techniques
- Collecting evidence from records and documents
- Modelling and re-enactments

5:1 Introduction

The main aim of any accident investigation process or system should be to enable an organisation to improve its safety management systems, so that accidents with the same or similar causes are not repeated. In order to do this successfully, it is necessary to examine all incidents where there has been a deviation from what was expected or planned, even where no injury, damage or loss resulted. Using accident investigation processes and techniques to examine near-miss events can provide information on two counts. Firstly, it can show how well the safety system is working and identify lapses or inadequacies in procedures and equipment. Secondly, lessons can be learnt from situations where there has been some recovery. Such situations can provide an insight into how more serious consequences can be avoided in future (*see* **Chapter 1, section 1:1.2**).

It is important to remember that anyone involved in an accident, either directly or as a witness, cannot be involved in carrying out the investigation.

5:2 General principles

There are a number of processes that have been established for accident investigations. Whilst there is no one 'right' way to carry out an investigation, there are a number of general principles that need to be followed and factors that need to be taken into account. Some of these are detailed below. For convenience, these are divided into the following time frames:

- before the investigation;
- during the investigation;
- after the investigation.

Figure 5:1 provides an aide memoir of these principles.

FIGURE 5:1 AIDE MEMOIR FOR THE GENERAL PRINCIPLES OF ACCIDENT INVESTIGATION

Before the investigation

- Ensure that immediately after an accident has occurred, no further harm is imminent.

- First aid and other ameliorative treatment takes precedence over any investigation.

- Maintain the scene and do not disturb evidence.

- Be sensitive to those involved and any witnesses.

- Understand the work processes involved.

During the investigation

- Be sensitive to those involved and any witnesses.

- Establish the sequence of events.

- Establish what happened.

- Establish underlying causes.

- Clarify that establishing blame is not the important issue.

- Understand that accidents do not result from a single failure in equipment or systems.

- Collect all the relevant information.

- Investigate all deviations from expected happenings.

- Report and document events so that action to remedy any deficiencies can be undertaken.

- Collect evidence thoroughly.

After the investigation

- Ensure that the results of the investigation lead to preventive action.

- Involve trade union-appointed safety representatives (or representatives of employee safety in non-unionised workplaces).

5:2.1 Before the investigation

5:2.1.1 Preventing further danger

In the immediate aftermath of an accident there is a need to ensure that no further danger to people, the environment or property exists. Some of the decisions and actions required will be for investigators and others will not. The actions needed are fully discussed in **Chapter 4, section 4:1**.

5:2.1.2 First aid/emergency treatment

Although accident investigation is a priority when an accident occurs, it is always necessary to ensure the safety of those involved first. This is generally a natural reaction to any accident and requires no further elaboration. It is important, however, that employers have suitable arrangements in place so that effective and sufficient first aid is available when required. The Health and Safety (First Aid) Regulations 1981 (S.I. 1981, No. 917) require all employers to make adequate provision for first aid treatment of their employees. The arrangements made for first aid should be suitable for the workplace and the hazards and risks it contains (*see* **Chapter 2, section 2:7**).

As a general rule those tasked with investigating accidents should not become involved with the tasks of administering first aid. In some situations and in smaller workplaces this may, however, be unavoidable.

5:2.1.3 Being sensitive to those involved

Many accidents will result in serious injury or give rise to disturbing scenes. Investigators need to be sensitive to this and moderate their actions and approach throughout the investigation. An initial response may require careful consideration of the timing of interviews (*see* **section 5:3.3.2.5**). This allows possibly disturbed witnesses to collect their thoughts and not feel that the investigators are being intrusive or callous.

Politeness and sympathy for the situation should also be evident on the part of investigators. Use of language should be controlled: making inappropriate comments, even unwittingly, could seem insensitive. Comments like 'you had that coming to you!' or 'it's your fault' are unacceptable. Indicating blame or expressing emotion can appear insensitive to those involved and, in any case, the majority of accidents are the result of a number of causes working together; they are seldom the result solely of the actions of an individual or of the failure of a single item of equipment. The principle of investigation should be to avoid assigning blame and to look for the underlying factors that caused the accident.

5:2.1.4 Maintaining the scene

Wherever possible, and whilst still preventing further danger and rendering first aid, the scene of the incident should be maintained in a condition as close as possible to that when the accident occurred. This will enable evidence to be maintained and prevent the loss of essential information that may only be obtained by observation of the scene.

Typical actions required to contain the scene are:

- ensuring people at the scene do not disturb anything. This includes handling any equipment and being generally inquisitive. On occasion people, thinking they are being helpful, will remove items to enable work to continue, for example tools and materials, and clear spillages. It is, therefore, important that the whole workforce is aware of the need to maintain an accident scene, and that supervisors keep a watchful eye to ensure the investigation process is not hampered by actions taken by people at the scene before the investigators arrive;

- cordoning off the area where appropriate using coloured tape or physical barriers such as coning and plastic fencing;

- placing suitable signs identifying the accident site as a 'no go' area;

- taking photographs, videos and sketches of the area as soon as possible. This is especially important in those situations when creating a cordon around the area cannot be achieved or cannot be justified. This could happen, for example, if someone has fallen down the only flight of stairs in a building preventing use of the stairs for an extended period would clearly not be justifiable or practicable.

Where the scene has been disturbed, investigators should obtain the details of the first people on the scene and, as soon as possible, interview them to establish the relative location of all important items, people and materials (*see* **section 5:4**).

5:2.2 During the investigation

5:2.2.1 Establishing the sequence of events

A crucial principle of any accident investigation is to create a complete picture of what actually happened. The investigation needs to build a picture of the chronology or sequence of events leading up to the accident. This sequence may go back many hours, days, weeks or even months before the actual accident occurred (*see* **Chapter 6, section 6:2**).

5:2.2.2 Establishing underlying causes

It is important that any investigation establishes the root or underlying causes of any accident. These root causes are generally to be found in management systems failures, inadequacies or absences (*see* **Chapter 1, section 1:3.2** and **Appendix 1**). Unless the underlying causes are found then it will not be possible to prevent events with the same underlying causes in the future. This is an important point as incidents with the same underlying causes can be distinctly dissimilar when they happen.

5:2.2.3 Single causes

Few accidents have a single cause. The majority of accidents, even seemingly simple ones, have a number of causes acting together. It is important that the nature and style of an investigation and the methods and techniques used will identify the various factors that had a part to play in causing the accident (*see* **Chapter 1**).

5:2.2.4 Blame

The majority of accidents are the result of a number of causes working together (*see* **Chapter 1**) and seldom only the result of actions of an individual or of the failure of an item of equipment. The principle of investigation should be to avoid assigning blame and to look for the underlying systems failures which caused the accident.

5:2.2.5 Collecting all the relevant information

There are a number of sources of information that are useful to the investigator. It is a general principle of all good investigation that all relevant sources of information are identified and recorded.

The investigation should not be concluded until investigators are satisfied that a thorough and detailed examination has been undertaken and all relevant evidence has been uncovered. This includes examining all the relevant equipment, human factors and management system issues and ensuring that all the evidence has been collected thoroughly. In their guidance on safety management (*see* **Appendix 4**) the HSE has set out one approach that can help ensure all relevant information is collected.

5:2.2.6 Documenting and recording

Accident investigations should be documented and recorded for the following reasons.

- It provides material for subsequent investigators that can be referred to should a similar incident arise.

- It forms the basis for other actions that may be required, for example legal cases and insurance claims.

- It forms the basis for report writing and for informing the organisation of the investigators' findings (*see* **Chapter 7**).

5:2.2.6.1 The important matters to record

During the course of any investigation a number of witness statements, photographs and documents are likely to be collected. It is important that these are properly recorded and filed. It is also necessary at times to obtain expert assistance; this needs to be recorded and the actions taken noted. A set of recording forms are provided in **Figures 5:2–5:7**. Where a detailed investigation is to be undertaken a copy of the incident details form (*see* **Figure 5:2**) should be completed for each person injured. This will enable the investigators and the administration team to keep a track of the various persons involved.

FIGURE 5:2 EXAMPLE INCIDENT DETAILS FORM

INCIDENT DETAILS

No. of personnel injured or affected:	Employees	Visitors	Contractors

Date:

Time:

Location:

Brief description of incident:

Line manager's details:

Accident reported to: head office/regional office/name of person spoken to

INJURED/AFFECTED PERSON(S) DETAILS

Name: [　　　　　　　　] Age: [　　] Sex: [　　]

Work No: [　　　　　] Work location: [　　　　　]

Injuries: [　　　　　　　　　　　]

Hospital
(if applicable): [　　　　　　　　　　]

Home address/
home contact
(if necessary): [　　　　　　　　　　]

Date RIDDOR completed (if applicable): [　　　　]

Date HSE/EHO contacted (if applicable): [　　　　]

How contacted:　　　　　Phone　　E-mail　　Letter

Name of person
reported to: [　　　　　　　　　　]

FIGURE 5:3 EXAMPLE ADMINISTRATION RECORD SHEET

Administration record sheet				
Record all telephone conversations, contacts, meetings and other relevant information which should be recorded.				
Date (dd/mm/yy)	Time (24 hrs)	What (tel call, meeting, conver-sation)	Note of action (include details of other parties)	Sign (initials)

FIGURE 5:4 EXAMPLE DOCUMENT RECORD SHEET

DOCUMENT RECORD SHEET			
This sheet should be used to list all documents that have been received or sent out as part of any investigation			
Title	Reference page no.	Sent	Date

FIGURE 5:5 EXAMPLE PHOTOGRAPHIC RECORD SHEET

Photographic record sheet			
Record on this sheet all photographs, videos or other images taken of the scene of the accident or plant and equipment involved.			
Photo/video/image ref	Details of source and person(s) taking photo/video/image	Date taken	Description of photo/video/image

FIGURE 5:6 EXAMPLE WITNESS STATEMENTS RECORD SHEET

Witness statements record sheet
Use this sheet to list all witness statements taken.

Name of witness	Location of witness*	Date taken	Work position#	Reference number	Taken by

* location at time of incident   # position or role in the company

FIGURE 5:7 EXAMPLE EXPERT ASSISTANCE REQUEST FORM

Request for expert assistance	
Investigator (name, address & tel no):	Authorised by: Accounts reference:
Assistance required (describe): (e.g. pressure testing, gas analysis, PPE assessment, vehicle brake check.)	
Date by which report is required:	
Incident details: (give information about circumstances to assist the expert examination)	
If equipment is to leave the site/premises control of evidence requires this section to be completed, in duplicate	
Signed out by: Date: Time:	Receipt of the items listed below is confirmed:
Description of examination/test requirements:	Received by:
	Date:
	Tel No:

5:2.3 After the investigation

No matter how well or detailed the investigation, if it does not result in some action to improve or reconsider the safety management system, then the point of the investigation will be lost. In order to determine if corrective action is required following an investigation, a review of the circumstances and a risk assessment should take place. Where corrective action is required, this should be achieved through the development of an action plan. The action plan determines the tasks to be carried out, the resources to be assigned to achieve those tasks and the date by which the corrective action must be in place. It will also set out the monitoring arrangements to ensure that the corrective action is maintained.

5:3 Collecting evidence

5:3.1 The purpose of collecting evidence

The main purpose of collecting evidence is to assemble all the relevant facts to find an explanation for the cause of an accident. Collecting evidence can be a large task, especially when the investigation aims to establish root causes as well as immediate causes (*see* **Chapter 7**).

The evidence-collection process has two key objectives:

1. to establish the sequence of events in the accident (*see* **Chapter 6, section 6:2**);

2. to establish the cause of the accident.

It is essential that investigators gain a detailed understanding of:

- the nature of the work involved. Understanding the work processes involved is essential if the full nature of the risks (including those arising from human factors) are to be identified;

- the hazards and risks. Understanding the hazards and risks involves examining any relevant risk assessments, and exploring the ways in which the accident could have happened;

- normal working procedures. These give an insight into how the work is actually carried out, particularly at the time of the accident. This exploration involves interviewing (mostly informally) others in the workplace who do the same type of job as those involved in the accident. The normal way of working may be a departure from the expected way of working as described in company procedures, safe systems of work and training;

- safe systems of work. These should be described in company training manuals, written procedures and any relevant documentation;

- roles and responsibilities. Knowing who has what role and what responsibilities gives an insight into the safety management system. It also indicates the actual arrangements the company has in place for safety controls.

5:3.2 The basic question set

In order to obtain the information set out in **section 5:3.1**, a basic set of questions should be used:

- Who?
- What?
- When?
- Where?
- Why?
- How?

From the questions in **Figure 5:8** it can be seen that a range of questions can be constructed for almost any eventuality. They need to be moulded around the events being investigated and fitted to the circumstances.

FIGURE 5:8 TYPICAL QUESTIONS FOR INVESTIGATORS USING THE BASIC QUESTION SET

Who:

- was involved at the time of the accident? (Include details of their age, work experience, training, and physical and mental condition.)
- was supervising and/or managing the work?
- was responsible for undertaking the risk assessments?
- keeps the records of inspections, tests and maintenance?

What:

- work was being done at the time?
- were the actions of the people involved in the accident?
- was the safe system of work?
- were the hazards and risks?
- was the reason for the equipment failure?
- are the normal conditions of work?
- was different on this occasion?
- software, hardware, management systems and physical aspects were involved?

When:

- did the accident happen?
- was this work/activity/task usually carried out? (Find out time of day, day, week, month, etc.)
- was the system of work last reviewed?

- was a risk assessment last carried out?
- was relevant training, instruction and information last carried out?
- did the accident happen in relation to other work/events?
- did the accident happen in relation to the sequence of work/the work cycle?

Where:

- did the accident happen? (Include a description of the location.)
- were the witnesses positioned?
- was all the relevant equipment?

Why:

- did the accident happen? (The big question.)
- was the activity being carried out at this time?
- did the equipment fail in this way?
- did it happen at this time?
- were the circumstances like this?

How:

- did this situation differ from previous occasions?
- much damage was caused?
- much (contents of a vessel, product, weight (load))?
- often (daily, weekly, monthly)?
- do the events fit together?
- do the various causes link together? (Most accidents have multiple causes.)
- did the accident happen? (Can you recreate the accident from the evidence?)

5:3.3 Sources of information

The evidence collected in any accident investigation needs to be as complete and as thorough as possible. This means all the factors that could be involved in the causes of the accident have to be identified. Evidence can be gathered from a number of information sources including:

- people (the witnesses, managers, supervisors, manufacturers and suppliers);

- records (maintenance and repair records, accident records, etc.);

- other documents (systems of work, risk assessments, etc.);

- direct observation by the investigators;

- pictorial information;

- scientific and forensic analyses;

- reconstructions and modelling.

5:4 Obtaining evidence from people

People who will be able to provide evidence in the accident investigation include eyewitnesses, other witnesses and anyone else who holds relevant information. This section outlines the interview process; how to go about getting the information needed is examined in **section 5:4.3**.

5:4.1 Eyewitnesses

Eyewitnesses are the people who saw the actual accident occurring. This is an important matter to distinguish. Very often eyewitnesses only capture part of the immediate events leading up to, or involving, the accident. For example, if three people are present when someone falls from a ladder, they may actually witness different things.

- The first witness sees the ladder slip from the wall and then turns away, only to look back again when the person on the ladder hits the ground. They hear a shout as the ladder slips and a crash when the ladder hits the ground, although they do not see the ladder actually falling to the ground.

- The second witness hears a cry and then looks round to see the person and the ladder hit the ground.

- The third witness was footing the ladder, looked up, saw the person at the top reach out sideways and then felt the ladder move. He attempted to hold the ladder as it hit the ground. The person at the top was seen to 'jump' sideways to clear the ladder as it hit the ground.

All three witnesses see something different; therefore, each can contribute something to the accident investigation: some of this confirms what happened, some of it raises questions about what happened and some of it raises doubts.

For example, the sequence of the ladder falling, the shouts heard and the position of the ladder is confirmed by all three witnesses. There remain questions about what the person on the ladder was actually doing and how the ladder was actually pitched. Some doubts arise as to the role of the person footing the ladder and whether the ladder slipped at the bottom or at the top. Further questioning may improve the information provided.

Another important point is that eyewitnesses generally see the events from different angles or positions to the event. Depending on the circumstances it is possible for witnesses to have only a partial view of a scene or situation. For example, if someone is seen to slip on a floor, a witness who is standing behind a machine will be able to only see the person from above the waist. Therefore, when they fall, the witness will only see them fall backwards and hear their cry of distress. However, if a second witness is standing behind the person who falls and only sees the back view, without being able to see the ground, he only has a partial view of what happens and is unable to provide any details of the condition of the floor. A third witness, who is walking down a staircase onto the shop-floor, will be able to see the person fall from a distance. However, as the attention of this witness will be focussed on making sure that they negotiate the stairs correctly, he only sees part of the motion of the person falling, even if they were in a position to see everything. Thus, the picture to be created of how the person fell has to be deduced from the partial views of three witnesses (and of course the injured party themselves). The main point is that witnesses can be both unreliable and biased in giving their evidence.

All witnesses have a selective memory. This is usually not deliberate but results from the way humans perceive events and situations, and the way memory actually works. Nothing should be taken at face value by investigators. It is important that any evidence from an eyewitness is corroborated by some other means or by other witnesses, if at all possible. Investigators need to gain a firm understanding of the interpersonal and other social factors which exist within the workplace. This can avoid misplaced reliance being put on evidence provided by witnesses. It will also assist investigators in managing the way the investigation is conducted and avoid insensitive approaches to witnesses. There are a number of factors to consider:

- what witnesses can actually see;
- how they see it;
- prejudice;
- trauma and emotion.

5:4.1.1 How witnesses see the accident

Witnesses will have their own knowledge and perceptions of any accident situation and the persons involved. In the example used in **section 5:4.1,** if the witnesses are aware that the floor in the area where the person slipped is often affected by spillages of machine oil, they may be tempted to say (in fact, one would be surprised if they did not) that the person slipped on the oily floor. This does not, of course, indicate that the floor was necessarily slippery or that oil on the floor contributed to the accident as the witnesses could not see the floor at the time. This information can only be gathered from other evidence.

5:4.1.2 Prejudice

What also has to be borne in mind is the relationship between witnesses and the person having the accident. If, for example, witnesses are close friends of the person having the accident, they may well deliberately alter their accounts of the accident to make it appear that the person was not to blame or to attempt to moderate the way the accident happened. This type of response is more likely to be prevalent in an organisation where the safety culture is poor and where people tend to get the blame for their own actions. Members of a peer group are likely to cover up the event to protect, as they perceive it, the person involved.

By the same token, investigators must also be aware that on occasion a witness may deliberately give a bad impression of the person who had the accident by saying things like 'they had it coming', 'it was their own fault' or 'they are always doing that', because of the poor personal relationship they have with the injured party.

It should also not be overlooked that if witnesses feel, suspect or realise that they have had some part to play in causing the accident, they are likely to give their evidence in such a way as to avoid implicating themselves.

5:4.1.3 Trauma and emotion

If a witness is close in some way to the person who had the accident, they are also likely to be traumatised by what they have seen and have an emotive response. This is to be expected of course, but it may have a bearing on the way they relate the event when being questioned. For example, they may be confused, unable to give evidence or only able to provide partial information.

The same is also true where the injuries of the people involved in the accident are serious and/or fatal. The circumstances of death and injury can have a profound effect on the way that witnesses recall and relate the events they have seen.

5:4.2 Other witnesses

5:4.2.1 Managers and supervisors

These people represent a special class of witness in workplace accidents. Firstly, they represent the management that should have been ensuring that safe systems of work and management procedures were in place to prevent the accident. Their reaction when being questioned about an incident will depend on the type of safety culture in the workplace. It is also likely that this group of people will have been responsible for ensuring that an adequate risk assessment of the work activities had been undertaken.

When dealing with this group, investigators need to be very sensitive to the role of managers and supervisors. It may often be the case that they are particularly defensive in any answers they give. This is more so if the safety culture is one where blame is a key feature, but it is also a natural human response when something bad has occurred.

Managers and supervisors are an essential source of information about:

- what was supposed to have happened;

- what normal practice actually is;

- any circumstances which were different at the time of the accident.

5:4.2.2 Maintenance personnel

Maintenance personnel will be of particular importance in any investigation involving plant and equipment. They provide a number of useful sources of information. Firstly, they are able to provide information regarding the performance, type and nature of maintenance undertaken, a view on the history of the plant/equipment performance and a first-hand account of the item in question.

As with managers and supervisors, care has to be taken to ensure that these personnel do not get the impression that they are being questioned because of their specific role and duties. Again, this is more easily achieved where the safety culture is supportive.

Secondly, maintenance personnel are often technically competent and are able to assist investigators in determining modes of failure or breakdown. They should also be able to provide access to manuals and technical literature related to the plant/equipment.

Where maintenance is undertaken as a contracted-out service, investigators will need to be careful about the way the investigation is conducted to avoid any conflict of interest. The main area of conflict will be that of any breach of contract on the part of the maintenance operation which could result in legal action (*see* **section 5:4.2.4**).

5:4.2.3 Trainers

One key issue in any accident is often training. This may be the training of the employees involved in the accident, the training of managers (and supervisors) in such matters as risk assessment and safe systems of work, or the training of managers in general health and safety management. In large organisations in particular, trainers can provide an insight into what the various people in the organisation are expected to know. The trainers should be able to provide both the background to training courses and the detailed content of them, including who has had what training and when.

An understanding of the training provided in an organisation will often be a fundamental part of any accident investigation. Not only is this a clear legal duty set out in s.2 of the HSWA (the employers general duty to ensure the health and safety of his employees is extended by s.2(2)(c) 'the provision of such information, instruction, training and supervision as is necessary to ensure, so far as is reasonably practicable, the health and safety at work of his employees'), but it is also often the main control factor in non-technical systems.

5:4.2.4 Suppliers' and manufacturers' representatives

Suppliers and manufacturers will often need to be involved in accident investigations. This is usually, and certainly in the first instance, carried out through their representatives (often the sales person or technical contact).

In any investigation involving plant and machinery, equipment and/or personal protective equipment (PPE), it will be necessary to make contact with suppliers/manufacturers for the following reasons:

- to find out if there is an issue of manufacturers'/suppliers' liability;

- to maintain the supplier-customer relationship;

- it is a legal duty of manufacturers/suppliers to comply with the HSWA;

- to ensure that a serious defect is remedied.

5:4.2.4.1 Manufacturers'/suppliers' liability

In the event of an accident investigation leading to claims of liability, either by an injured party or the employer, the manufacturer or supplier (depending on the nature of responsibility) should:

- know about the incident from the time when it first arose;

- be party to any examination of the equipment/plant/ machinery/PPE by any independent competent authority designated to assist the accident investigation;

- be able to undertake any immediate corrective action which in their opinion they feel is necessary to protect both their position and their other customers.

5:4.2.4.2 Supplier-customer relationship

It is often the case that the relationship between suppliers and their customers is well established. Confidence built up over a long period of time and the understanding between an organisation and its suppliers often goes beyond the legal confines of contracts and order books. It is important, therefore, that this relationship is not (unduly) jeopardised by the accident investigation process. Unsubstantiated comments regarding the service or product should be avoided.

5:4.2.4.3 Suppliers'/manufacturers' legal duties

Suppliers and manufacturers generally have a duty to comply without question to s.6 of the HSWA and will want to notify their other customers of any defects, failures or deficiencies in their product or services found in the accident investigation. They generally prefer to do this themselves without attracting major publicity or attention for obvious reasons.

It has to be borne in mind that s.6 of the HSWA places a duty on designers, manufacturers, importers and suppliers to ensure that any equipment supplied is fit for the purpose and safe for the purpose for which it is designed. Section 6(1) makes it the duty:

...of any person who designs, manufacturers, imports or supplies any article for use at work or any article of fairground equipment:

(a) *to ensure, so far as is reasonably practicable, that the article is so designed and constructed that it will be safe and without risks to health at all times when it is being set, used, cleaned or maintained by a person at work;*

(b) *to carry out or arrange for the carrying out of such testing and examination as may be necessary for the performance of the duty imposed on his by the preceding paragraph;*

(c) *to take such steps as are necessary to secure that persons supplied by that person with the article are provided with adequate information about the use for which the article is designed or has been tested and about any conditions necessary to ensure that it will be safe and without risks to health at all such times as are mentioned in paragraph (a) above and when it is being dismantled or disposed of; and*

(d) *to take such steps as are necessary to secure, so far as is reasonably practicable, that persons so supplied are provided with all such revisions of information provided to them by virtue of the preceding paragraph as are necessary by reason of its becoming known that anything gives rise to a serious risk to health or safety.*

The HSWA, s.6(4) applies similar duties to the manufacturers, importers and suppliers of substances.

The duties in s.6 of the HSWA have been further clarified by the Supply of Machinery (Safety) Regulations 1992 (S.I. 1992, No. 3073) and the Personal Protective Equipment (EC Directive) Regulations 1992 (S.I. 1992, No. 3139), as amended by the Health and Safety (Miscellaneous Amendments) Regulations 2002 (S.I. 2002, No. 2174). Additional requirements are added by the

Noise at Work Regulations 1989 (S.I. 1989, No. 1790), to the effect that information must be provided if any article to be used at work is likely to cause exposure to above the first action level or the peak action level defined in those regulations.

Whether the equipment is fit for the purpose(s) intended will be a question during any investigation of an accident involving equipment. The investigation should be conducted accordingly so as not to prejudice any action being taken either by the enforcement authorities or the organisation itself under civil law. This can be done by allowing the manufacturer/supplier to be represented at any testing, examination or other technical investigation. Investigators will then be able to share information without prejudicing either the position of the employer or that of the supplier/manufacturer. Unless this is done the manufacturer/supplier could argue that the test/examination process was incorrect, invalid or not reasonably and competently undertaken.

5:4.2.4.4 Remedying a serious defect

A further matter to consider is that, in the case of any serious defect, it will usually be the manufacturer/supplier who provides the remedy. This may be in the way of modification, parts replacement or radical redesign. A supplier/manufacturer who feels fairly treated in any investigation will be one more likely to respond rapidly to this situation than one who feels that the investigation is onerous and only for the purposes of seeking legal redress.

5:4.3 Interviewing witnesses

Interviewing witnesses, including the persons involved (injured or not), is one of the main forms of evidence gathering. The best approach is to ensure that anybody who is likely to be an accident investigator has received some training in interviewing techniques: interviewing is not simply a matter of asking questions and writing down the answers.

It is generally better for the investigator to take notes of the witness's words and then write these up as a formal statement for the witness to sign as a true record. Some witnesses may prefer to write their own statements. This is not a problem but can lead to discrepancies or facts being left out which investigators will then have to address, usually by drafting an additional statement for the witness to sign. In simple situations a witness statement may be left for the witness to fill in and return to the investigators. This is a reasonable approach to adopt if the matters to be addressed are factual, such as the date and time the witness undertook a certain test of equipment. For most general purposes it is better to have two interviewers, wherever possible: one to ask questions and one to take notes. With practice some investigators may be able to write up the witness statement as the interview progresses, although generally interviewing witnesses can be a long and tiring process. A sample witness statement form is shown in **Figure 5:9**.

FIGURE 5:9 EXAMPLE WITNESS STATEMENT FORM

Incident details
Investigator details Name: Contact number: Location:
Details of witness Name: Age: Sex: M/F Location/home address (if not employee):

Names of other persons present at interview	Status

Leave no gaps between lines.

_____

_____

_____

_____

_____

_____

_____

_____

_____

_____

_____

_____

_____

_____

_____

_____

To the best of my knowledge I believe this is a true statement of facts.

Signature:............................. Print name: ....

Date: ....

In the presence of:

Signature:............................. Print name: ....

Date: ....

If the witness is unwilling to sign, an investigator should sign that this is a true account of the statement made by the witness in their presence.

Witnesses have to be approached carefully and with due regard to their role, position and involvement in the accident, both immediate and underlying. There are a number of factors that need to be considered when interviewing. These include:

- the attitude of the interviewer;

- the interview location and its facilities;

- the timing of the interview;

- the style of the interview;

- the interview techniques (questioning, summarising, cross checking and confirming);

- legal considerations.

5:4.3.1 The attitude of the interviewer

When interviewing, the interviewer should ideally adopt an open attitude and avoid any suggestion of blame or retribution. At the start of the interview the interviewer should make the interviewee feel comfortable. The choice of the location for the interview will often help in this respect. The nature of the interview should be clearly explained. The interviewer should take notes and explain to the interviewee what they are doing and why. The interviewer should assure the interviewee that anything said in the interview will be confidential and individuals' names will not be used in reports other than to provide descriptions of actions and findings.

The interviewer should avoid sharing any thoughts or opinions on the nature of the accident with people being interviewed. Sometimes it can be difficult for an interviewer to disregard their own thoughts and feelings. Interviewers, as well as witnesses, have prejudices that may affect the way evidence is viewed. When interviewing the investigator should remain calm and not be roused to anger or other emotions. In many cases, a company investigator will have knowledge of the attitudes and behaviours of the workforce. For example, there may be a widely held belief that a section of the workforce have a poor attitude towards safety and are known to have frequently disregarded safety procedures. This information might influence the investigator when doing interviews.

5:4.3.2 The interview location and its facilities

It is often better for someone to be interviewed at a location they are familiar with. This both adds to their comfort and does not make them feel as if they are being subjected to any special treatment. A quiet room should be found where confidentiality can be assured.

Ideally investigators should go to the witnesses rather than around the other way. In many organisations people may feel intimidated by being requested to go to a head office for an interview.

Inevitably there are situations where others will know who is being interviewed. This presents an opportunity for people to ask each other: 'So what were you asked?'. This may mean that evidence will be affected, with questions and information being circulated among the people who have been and are to be interviewed. Wherever possible this should be avoided. Often it is necessary to ask people not to discuss the interview with colleagues. However, it is also necessary to strike a balance between ensuring the information is kept free of interference and the welfare of individuals concerned.

Interviews need to be planned and arranged so that disruption of the workplace and inconvenience to those being interviewed is minimised. Interviews should be conducted somewhere private. If possible the entrance to the interviewing room should not be directly visible so that those being interviewed can have a degree of privacy. This can be an important point when dealing with sensitive investigations, especially those involving fatalities and serious injuries. The planning and arrangement of interviews should also take account of the debriefing and welfare requirements.

5:4.3.3 The importance of timing

There are two main factors that need to be considered here:

1. the timing of the interview after the event;

2. the time set aside for the interview.

5:4.3.3.1 The timing of the interview after the event

There are mixed opinions about the best timing of interviews after an accident. When interviewing witnesses of a criminal offence, the expert police view is that witnesses tend to be better (that is, give more accurate and reliable answers to questions) when several days have elapsed after the incident was witnessed.

There is also the need to consider requirements for debriefing and the avoidance of mental trauma, particularly after harrowing accidents have been witnessed. Some investigators are of the view that information from eyewitnesses is best gathered as soon as possible after the event. The choice of timing has to be decided in each particular case, taking into consideration all the various factors involved.

One possible solution to this is to provide a compromise. Immediately (or as soon as possible) after an accident, eyewitnesses can be asked to note down pertinent details, for example:

*   where they were;

*   what they were doing (their role and activities);

*   what they saw;

*   what equipment they were using,

They should provide this information to investigators before leaving the scene or the workplace. This gives investigators time to review the scene (*see* **section 5:5.3**), assess the relative importance of witnesses and to frame a list of questions they need to ask.

5:4.3.3.2 Setting aside time

The smooth running of any interview is assisted if the interviewee knows that time has been set aside for this. They may well be under pressures to 'get on with the job' and respond to what they see as conflicting management requirements. Interviewers should arrange for time to be set aside and enlist the support of managers and supervisors so that the interview can be conducted without any external pressures being placed on the interviewee. Investigators need to be careful to set aside sufficient time and to avoid over-running.

Interviews are best conducted in work time and the person being interviewed should not be penalised for giving up their time, especially if overtime rates or piece work is involved.

5:4.3.4 Interview techniques

The best practice is to adopt an open approach to the interviewee. It should be clear at the outset what the purpose of the interview is and what the consequences will be. There should be no question of apportioning blame. This is more likely to make the interviewee reveal facts and information. The approach should be friendly, but not unduly so, and professional. The interviewer should make it clear that they have no preconceptions of the accident and its causes. An open mind is therefore required at all times.

Whilst the ideal approach is to work through the sequence of events, it is best to let the interviewee explain the events in their own words. Even though this might take longer, more information is likely to be obtained.

The interviewer should remember the role and position of the person being interviewed and take into account any prejudices or bias they may bring to the interview. Concern should be shown for the events and the persons involved without being patronising.

5:4.3.4.1 Using visual aids

From the evidence collected, investigators should draw up a plan or sketch of the site of the accident and use this to guide the interviewee. A visual demonstration of the scene will help to jog memories and verify facts. Where photographic or video evidence is available this can also be used. When asking questions about items of equipment, use an item of equipment identical to that involved and, where appropriate, the actual item.

5:4.3.4.2 Framing interview questions

The interviewer should begin the interview with general questions that the interviewee will find it easy to answer, for example:

> 'Describe what happened on the morning of the accident.'

Closed questions (questions with either a 'yes' or a 'no' answer) should not be used, for example:

> 'Did you see what happened?'.

Open questions should be used instead, for example:

> 'Could you tell me in your own words what you saw.'

The answer to this is possibly a fairly long account.

Once the interviewee has started talking, they should not be interrupted, but gently guided back to the subject at an appropriate moment, for example when there is a natural pause in their flow. Leading questions such as 'the supervisors always allow the procedure to be altered in this way?' should be avoided. This question is inviting the interviewee to agree with the interviewer.

Assumptions should not be made. For example, if the interviewee says they do something once a week, it should not be assumed that they did that in the week of the accident. Instead, ask them to confirm this.

Use probing questions, such as:

'Could you describe what condition the floor was in when you last saw it?'

A number of probing questions include the words *how, what, when* and *where?* These guide the interviewee to deliver more detail and facts about the situation (*see* **Figure 5:8**). Ask about each one in turn:

'Where were you standing/What did you see/When did you become aware there was a problem/How did ... react?'

Use more probing questions to follow up on specific details, such as:

'You said there was a noise as Mr A fell. How would you describe this?'

The interviewer should keep probing gently until all the facts relevant to the specific details have been obtained.

5:4.3.4.3 Summarising the key points

When you have exhausted a line of enquiry refresh the answers given by the interviewee by summarising them and seeking their agreement to the details provided:

'So if I have understood this correctly, on the day you were stood at the door to the production floor you saw Mr A fall. As he fell, there was a noise which you describe as similar to the guard on the rolling machine closing, but you did not see this. You then became aware that the production line stopped. Is that correct?'

To examine other areas, the interviewer should begin by going back to the start and relating it to a different issue:

'If I could take you back to the beginning, how would you describe the lighting on the production room floor that day?'

Continue the questions on the new theme (in this case, lighting) until all possibilities have been exhausted.

5:4.3.4.4 Cross checking and confirming information

Sometimes during the course of an interview there may be information which seems to conflict or contradict other statements made by the interviewee. These should not be ignored but probed (gently) to elucidate the truth. For example:

> 'Earlier you said that you were at the door of the production room when you saw Mr A fall but now I am a little confused because you also said, I think, that you saw the production manager at the other end of the line hit the emergency stop, but that position cannot be seen from the door. Could you clarify this for me?'

There may be many occasions when contradictory information is given. This should be dealt with in such a way that the interviewee does not feel that they are being interrogated or their honesty and memory is being called into question. Accidents usually happen very quickly (especially from a witness' perspective) and a witness cannot be expected to have either seen everything precisely or have a complete mental record of it.

5:4.3.5 Interviewing injured persons

Special considerations are required when interviewing injured persons. These are in addition to the normal considerations for interviewing eyewitnesses. Depending on the circumstances and the nature of the injury, it is very likely that somebody injured in an accident will feel traumatised. This may mean that they are not able to cope with the interview and will reject any approaches to be interviewed. To some extent these concerns have to be dealt with. There is no legal requirement for an injured employee to answer questions in an accident investigation. Experience shows that most are ready and willing to do so. However, there are occasions, particularly those involving loss of a limb or body part, where the individual has (understandable) difficulty in coming to terms with the accident. A range of emotions and attitudes may be involved – from bitterness to self blame for their injury.

Such situations need handling with care. Often enlisting the support of friends, family, medical personnel and trade union representatives can assist investigators. Sometimes investigators may need to build the investigation without the prime knowledge of the events that is held first hand by the injured party, who may be so seriously injured as to be unable to be interviewed or recall events. In the case of a fatality it is not always possible to gain first-hand information, unless someone directly involved in the incident has survived.

5:4.3.6 Joint interviews

Where a serious accident has occurred it may be possible to undertake joint interviews. The gathering of information and the undertaking of interviews takes time and can be stressful for the people involved. To minimise both time and stress it is sometimes possible to arrange for joint interviewing. This can involve a panel of interviewers comprising the police, the Health and Safety Executive (HSE)/an environmental health officer (EHO) and trade union safety representatives (where applicable). Whilst this may appear unusual, it may be welcomed by the enforcement authority (the police or the HSE) as the questions can help them to obtain information. The company's accident investigators will normally be both familiar with the premises, plant, processes, safe systems of work and training and may have some specific technical knowledge.

If such joint interviewing can be arranged then a protocol should be designed to ensure that it goes smoothly. The protocol should make it clear that the police have priority when interviewing, and only when they are satisfied with the questions they have asked should company accident investigators start asking questions. The benefits of this are several fold.

- The people being interviewed generally only have to be interviewed once, thereby reducing stress.

- The information gained comes from questions asked from a number of perspectives and is thus likely to be much more complete.

- Time off from the job is minimised.

- Facilities are only required once.

The disadvantage of such an arrangement is that the interviewee may be overawed by the number of people on the panel. This can be overcome to some extent by explaining the process and the benefits beforehand.

Joint arrangements are not suitable where the police or HSE are interviewing an individual from the perspective of investigating a possible offence committed by that person.

5:4.3.7 The legal aspects to consider when interviewing witnesses

Although the purpose of interviewing witnesses is to establish the sequence of events and the causes of accidents in a blame-free manner, this is not always possible. There are a number of legal considerations that need to be taken into account. These include:

- representation at interviews;

- internal discipline;

- criminal law;

- interviewing non-employees;

- enforcement authority responsibilities;

- insurers' rights.

5:4.3.7.1 Representation at interviews

There may be a need to ensure that the person being interviewed is aware of any right they may have to be represented during the interview. In the majority of cases this will not be necessary as the interview should not be for the purposes of apportioning blame or implicating the interviewee. However, where apportioning blame or determining guilt is the purpose or a possibility, then the interviewee should be accompanied by their trade union safety representative or by a solicitor.

A clear direction on this area should be obtained from the employer's legal advisers and in consultation with the trade unions.

5:4.3.7.2 Internal discipline

There may be cases where investigators believe that a matter for internal company discipline from the circumstances of the accident has arisen, such as the accident arising from a clear breach of company rules and procedures. In such cases it is important that the interview process takes account of this. It is important that disciplinary issues are dealt with in the context of employment legislation. The interview should either not take place at all or be halted as soon as the interviewer has formed this opinion.

There will not be many occasions where there is a conflict between the needs of the investigation and providing evidence for discipline, but when it occurs it is important to act properly. An event that has been the result of deliberate and malicious contravention of company rules and procedures cannot be considered to be accidental. The investigation may continue depending on the circumstances but it is usually not advisable to consider the event as an accident. An example of this is 'horseplay' or an action that has been racially motivated. This will also be the case where there has been an infringement of company alcohol and drugs policy (*see* **Chapter 2, section 2:6.11.2** and **Appendix 3**) or where alcohol and/or drugs have been responsible for the incident.

5:4.3.7.3 Criminal law

If before the interview or during the interview the interviewer forms the opinion that a crime has been committed, then the

231

interview should not take place or be called to a halt. Senior management and the employer's legal advisers should be notified and, where appropriate, the police. Such an event might be somebody being injured whilst stealing company stock or equipment, or a deliberate act of personal assault or violence with the intention of harming another person.

5:4.3.7.4 Interviewing non-employees

The interviewing of persons not employed by the company, but who may have been directly involved or been eyewitnesses must be considered very carefully; ideally legal advice should be sought. In some circumstances the investigator may be in danger of being charged with interfering with witnesses. It is important, therefore, that the roles and duties of both the police and the HSE/local authority are taken into account before proceeding with any interviewing of non-company personnel.

There is no requirement for anyone not employed by a company to co-operate with it in the investigation of an accident.

The interviewing of suppliers and manufacturers is not necessarily covered by this caveat. However, the primacy of any investigation will lie with the enforcement authority and this must be considered before interviewing suppliers/manufacturers. Although it is uncommon for action to be taken under s.6 of the HSWA, this should always be regarded as a possibility.

5:4.3.7.5 Enforcement authority responsibilities

In the case of fatalities, serious injuries and dangerous occurrences it must be expected that either the police or the HSE/local authority will undertake an investigation. It is not normally a problem for a company's accident investigator to interview employees, but this should be confirmed with the enforcement authority before commencing the interviews. Investigators should be aware of the memorandum of understanding between the police and the HSE (*see* **Chapter 9, section 9:4.7.2**).

5:4.3.7.6 Insurers' rights

Where an insurance claim may result from an accident it is important that the interviewing of witnesses does not compromise the insurer's rights (*see* **Chapter 11**). Care must be taken to ensure that liability is not admitted.

5:4.3.8 Feedback from interviews

It is important to ensure that the results of the investigation are known to all. Those involved in the incident and eyewitnesses should be informed of the outcome of the investigation and the results of the investigation report by the investigators. This should be done as soon as the investigation is over. It is a good idea to do the debrief before the final report is submitted (*see* **Chapter 8, section 8:2**).

In general terms giving feedback to the interviewees serves a number of useful purposes.

- It allows investigators to assess the response to the report and amend any factual discrepancies.

- It provides an opportunity to explain any opinions formed by the investigators, especially where evidence has been contradictory.

- The workforce immediately involved in the accident and its consequences get to hear about the report first hand.

- It is a visible demonstration that the company is promoting a blame-free culture.

5:5 Obtaining evidence from other sources

As highlighted in **section 5:2.2.5**, evidence collected in any accident investigation needs to be as complete and thorough as possible. Other sources of evidence that may be of importance in an investigation can include company records and documentation, pictorial information, scientific and medical analysis, and the use of modelling and re-enactments.

5:5.1 Equipment and process documentation

Equipment and process documentation can be a valuable source of evidence and provide information on the status of equipment, plant and processes prior to the accident. They also provide an insight into safety management in the organisation and can highlight deficiencies in procedures and the suitability of plant and equipment for the job.

Such documentation includes:

- statutory test results;

- monitoring print-outs (for equipment, plant and processes);

- previous accidents records;

- maintenance reports;

- repair reports;

- certificates of compliance with standards;

- technical files (where CE-marked equipment and PPE are involved);

- material data sheets.

5:5.1.1 Statutory test results

Under law, many items of equipment, plant and PPE have to be regularly inspected and/or tested. **Figure 5:10** provides a list of the principal Regulations that have specific requirements, and the frequency of testing where appropriate. (Note that the list is not exhaustive.)

FIGURE 5:10 REGULATORY TESTING REQUIREMENTS

Regulations	Types of equipment/ plant/PPE covered	Frequency
Provision and Use of Work Equipment Regulations 1998	All work equipment	Refer to Regulations
Lifting Operations and Lifting Equipment Regulations 1998	Cranes, slings, chains and other lifting plant/devices	Annually
	Equipment designed to lift people, including passenger lifts	Six months
Electricity at Work Regulations 1989	Fixed electrical installation of a building	Every five years
	Portable electrical appliances	By assessment
Personal Protective Equipment Regulations 1992		Refer to Regulations
Pressure Systems Safety Regulations 2000	Pressure systems, including compressors, pressure vessel	Annually
Workplace (Health, Safety and Welfare) Regulations 1992		Refer to Regulations
Control of Lead at Work Regulations 2002		Refer to Regulations
Control of Asbestos at Work Regulations 2002		Refer to Regulations
Control of Substances Hazardous to Health Regulations 2002	Ventilation systems	14 months, or as specified in the schedule of the Regulations
	Respiratory personal equipment	One month, or as specified in the Regulations

The frequency of inspection/test depends upon assessment, the regularity of use and manufacturer's recommendations. Minimum intervals are set within the various regulations for specific items of plant and equipment and reference should be made to the regulations for details.

If an item of equipment is involved in an accident, the investigator will need to examine the test results (where relevant) of the equipment involved and any other identical or similar equipment. It is possible that the test results may have indicated a failure mode or the overall status of the condition of the equipment. The duties of manufacturers and suppliers to provide up-to-date information should be borne in mind when reviewing test records. The review of this information will also give an insight into the adequacy of test methods, test recording and testing procedures.

5:5.1.2 Monitoring print-outs

In many situations, but especially in process plant, process controls and instruments will have recording mechanisms which produce logs of activity. Some alarm equipment such as fire alarms have print-outs detailing times of alarm calls and other actions. Investigators will need to capture this information as soon as possible as often it is over-written or has a limited lifetime within the system. Investigators may also need to enlist the help of production personnel, control room operators or other technical specialists in interpreting the logs/recordings.

5:5.1.3 Previous accident records

Information from previously reported and investigated accidents may be helpful.

Where a similar accident has previously occurred and remedial measures put in place it may well be that the focus of the investigation should be changed. The investigation of the latest accident may need to focus on why the recurrence happened rather than the mechanism of failure itself.

5:5.1.4 Maintenance reports

Maintenance reports provide information on the reliability of plant and equipment (including PPE). The type and style of report may be a significant factor in the usefulness of the information provided. Whilst maintenance personnel may be extremely knowledgeable and helpful it is unlikely that they will remember every detail of every job they did within the last 12 months. If the reports provided by maintenance staff are not detailed it will not be possible to gain an accurate picture of the reliability of the equipment. This situation can be overcome in some respects by interviewing other personnel such as production workers. However, it is a fairly common phenomenon for people to 'over-remember' the frequency of poor situations, such as a breakdown in equipment, and to under-emphasise reliability. This is demonstrated by the extremes in statements such as 'we are always replacing washers on that hoseline' and 'that machine never needs anything changing' when in reality the washers were only replaced every two to three months and the machine actually has needed replacement parts a few times, but not when it was inconvenient. Using records of maintenance activity is a good way to cross-check the validity of such statements.

The form of maintenance reports will depend upon the company's operating procedures and the plant/equipment being maintained. There may be a specifically designed document, or the report may take the form of a worksheet.

5:5.1.5 Repair reports

Repair reports can be of significant interest to investigators. If they are sufficiently detailed and well maintained, they should be able to provide information on the nature of breakdowns and the details of any replacement parts and modifications made. There are a number of classic examples of accidents that have occurred when repairs were incorrectly undertaken, either by using the wrong parts or involving modifications, the ramifications of which went undetected until there was a catastrophic failure. One of these is the explosion at the Flixborough plant.

A simple sample repair form is shown in **Figure 5:11**.

FIGURE 5:11 EXAMPLE REPAIR REPORT FORM

Repair report form	
Company:	
Fault reported:	Date reported:
Engineer's report:	
Date of repair:	
Repair complete?	Yes/No
Engineer's signature:	

As with maintenance reports, repair reports will vary between companies, and the plant/equipment being repaired. Most will be unique to the organisation, and in many cases the maintenance report will also be used for repairs.

5:5.1.6 Certificates of compliance with standards

The equipment which is required to have undergone a 'thorough examination' and/or have a certificate for worthiness to comply with legislation and/or insurance requirements is shown in **Figure 5:12**. Note that this list is not exhaustive.

FIGURE 5:12 EXAMPLES OF EQUIPMENT REQUIRING CERTIFICATES OF WORTHINESS

Legislation	Equipment
Lifting Operations and Lifting Equipment Regulations 1998*	Lifting equipment designed for lifting materials, including chains, straps, shackles, etc.
Lifting Operations and Lifting Equipment Regulations 1998*	Lifting equipment designed for lifting people, including passenger lifts, and devices designed specifically for the lifting of people
Provision and Use of Work Equipment Regulations 1998*	Mobile plant, for instance diggers, cherrypickers
Provision and Use of Work Equipment Regulations 1998*	Fork-lift trucks
Pressure Systems Safety Regulations 2000	Pressure systems, including compressors, pressure vessels
Control of Substances Hazardous to Health Regulations 2002	Respiratory personal equipment (RPE)
Control of Substances Hazardous to Health Regulations 2002	Local exhaust ventilation systems
*As amended by the Health and Safety (Miscellaneous Amendments) Regulations 2002.	

If such equipment is involved in an accident, it will be essential to ensure that it was compliant to any certificate issued and the accompanying standards. This will provide information that may be relevant to discovering the immediate cause of any failure, for example lifting equipment tested to a maximum working load that has been exceeded during work operations resulting in failure of the equipment. The adequacy of such certificates, their documentation, storage, retrieval and utility can often provide an insight into aspects of the management system that may be relevant to the accident.

5:5.1.6.1 Technical files (where CE-marked equipment and PPE are involved)

Technical files are a requirement of European legislation and are effectively the documented technical background to any equipment or PPE which has been CE marked. The mark should be observed, and is usually found on or near the 'Type Number' plate or stamp.

The technical files of the manufacturer, designer or supplier may provide relevant information on the equipment. This may especially be the case where detail is required of the actual purpose and conditions of use for which the item has been CE marked.

5:5.1.6.2 The Machinery Directive

The Supply of Machinery (Safety) Regulations 1992 implement the requirements of the EC Council Directive 89/392/EEC, known as the Machinery Directive.

The Directive aimed to harmonise safety standards on new machinery across the European Union, setting out general safety standards and a conformity-marking system now widely known as the CE mark. The regulations apply to 'relevant machinery', defined as a mechanical structure of powered moving parts, its power supplies, controls and detachable accessories. Unpowered or hand-powered equipment is not included.

Where other EC product safety requirements apply, e.g. electrical safety requirements, there will be a need to determine whether the item is a 'relevant machine' or an 'electrical appliance', and as such to apply conformity requirements accordingly.

The regulations require 'suppliers' of 'relevant machinery' to:

- ensure that the machinery complies with the 'essential safety requirements' set down in the Machinery Directive;

- implement a 'conformity procedure';

- mark the machine with the CE mark;

- ensure that the machine 'is in fact safe'.

5:5.1.7 Material data sheets

Copies of all material specifications and manufacturers' data sheets should be obtained by accident investigators for materials and substances used in the processes affected by the accident. These may already be available within the company, but if not they will have to be obtained from the original manufacturers and suppliers. These will provide information to back up any scientific and forensic analysis which may be needed to establish the cause of an accident. Care needs to be exercised when obtaining such data to ensure that the issues surrounding trade secrets are dealt with adequately and that a full understanding of product formulation is provided. For many substances in common use no precise formulation is available as products tend to vary from one batch to another. This may therefore require a detailed analysis to establish the precise constituents involved in any accident.

5:5.1.7.1 COSHH data sheet

The Chemicals (Hazard Information and Packaging) Regulations 2002 require manufacturers and suppliers to provide safety information on their products. This information is provided in the form of a data sheet. Copies of data sheets should be supplied with each consignment and will thus be available to the investigator. These data sheets usually form the basis for substance handling and technical information as part of the COSHH risk assessment (*see* **section 5:5.2.6**).

5:5.2 Company documentation

Many organisations will have a vast collection of documents, many of which can be relevant to an accident investigation. The retention of these documents is good business practice, but the extent to which this is done will depend upon the culture and history of the company: whether documents are retained/archived, and for how long; what documents are retained after relocation or mergers. The business sector within which the company operates may also influence what documents are retained.

Documents of this type are typically:

- plans of the site;
- sketches of the site;
- maps of the site including environmental aspects;
- 'as-built' drawings/plans for the building site;
- design and specification documentation;
- risk assessments, working procedures and safe-operating instructions.

5:5.2.1 Plans

These include the architectural drawings and drawings used by the contractor or installer of any facility or plant. They also include plans drawn up for security purposes, cable runs, process lines and any other relevant aspects of the site, facility or plant which may have been involved in the accident.

The plans may have been prepared by the company in the course of its business activities, and may record the developments of a particular office building, computer suite, workshop, plant or process. In some cases, the plans will have been prepared by contractors who have undertaken work on the company's behalf. These later documents may be the property of the contractor. If the contractor's work or design is thought to have contributed to the accident, then investigators will need to be aware of the contractor's rights when inspecting or requesting these documents.

5:5.2.2 Sketches

This refers to any sketches drawn by people at the site after the accident, including the investigators, as well as any drawn before the incident. It is sometimes possible to find that fitters, maintenance people and other service personnel have created their own 'working drawings' of fixtures, fittings and plant prior to the accident, which can be useful to the investigator. Sketches can sometimes also be produced on the spot during interviews by the interviewee to help explain to the investigators the local circumstances or the witness's view of the site and/or situation.

If an accident occurs in an area outside a company's site boundary (such as a street) a sketch may be the only 'plan' of the area concerned.

5:5.2.3 Maps

Sometimes maps are useful to pinpoint the site or other environmental aspects associated with the accident. These would include, for example, the location of other buildings, geographical features such as roads, hills and water courses, and any other relevant details. They can also give a clue to local topographical influences such as wind direction, the location of possible witnesses and traffic routes. Such information might be necessary if investigating an incident involving an air-borne substance.

5:5.2.4 'As-built' drawings

'As-built' drawings represent a special category of documentation, especially in older plant and facilities. They must be treated with caution. It is frequently found that as-built drawings do not match the actual situation at the accident site. Indeed, many accidents have been caused because reliance has been placed on as-built drawings when designing the system of work which led to the accident. The discrepancies happen because no arrangements have been made for ensuring as-built drawings are accurate when the plant/installation/building has been handed over and no arrangements have been made for updating them during modifications, upgrades and maintenance. Because as-built drawings are frequently wrong, they should be a first point of reference for many accidents involving plant and process installations to ensure that they have not themselves formed part of the problem. If they are correct they are, of course, another source of information.

5:5.2.5 Design and specification documentation

Design and specification documents should tell investigators what the original intention of the installation or equipment was, how it was meant to operate and how it was supposed to be built or put together. Often modifications during the life of plant and equipment means that it no longer functions as designed and may be exceeding design parameters. This can often be a cause of failure.

5:5.2.5.1 The Construction (Design and Management) Regulations 1994

If any construction work has been carried out since the introduction of the Construction (Design and Management) Regulations 1994 (S.I. 1994, No. 3140), then a copy of the 'health and safety file', produced under the regulations, must be available. This file will contain many of the documents referred to above. Inspection of these documents will give an investigator a 'feel' for the location/site and may reveal differences between the planned and actual location.

5:5.2.6 Risk assessments, work procedures and safe-operating instructions

Documents such as risk assessments, work procedures and safe-operating instructions are central to the accident investigation process. However, they have to be viewed with some caution. Risk assessments should give rise to work procedures and safe-operating instructions which ensure the adequate control of risks and by implication the prevention of accidents. That an accident has occurred, or at least some deviation from what was expected, should lead investigators to the view that information to be gleaned from the risk assessment (and the subsequent control measure documents) may be questionable. In the majority of cases the risk assessment will probably (or should) give a good indication of what was *supposed* to have happened. This may be useful to the investigator in analysing the evidence to determine any deviation. Such information has some utility when using logic trees and change analysis. A great deal rather depends on the initial quality of the risk assessment undertaken before the accident, its validity and reliability.

Examination of and reference to the risk assessment will be necessary when deciding on action following the accident investigation report. It is also essential as part of the risk assessment review process required by the Management of Health and Safety at Work Regulations 1999 (MHSWR).

Safe-operating instructions and procedures are often not carried out as documented. They either become redundant over time as new work practices are introduced without any reassessment of the work itself or they lapse into disuse as people become familiar with the job and take short cuts.

5:5.3 Direct observation

As soon as possible investigators should visit the scene of the accident. They should be suitably equipped to enable evidence to be captured before it is lost. (A list of equipment can be found in **Chapter 3, section 3:2.8.2.**)

Ideally the scene should be left undisturbed until the investigators have finished collecting immediate evidence. This is not always possible. The scene may be disturbed by those applying first aid treatment to the injured or carrying out rescue operations, or altered in order to prevent the problem escalating.

Where the scene has been disturbed, investigators should obtain the details of the first people on the scene and as soon as possible interview them to establish the relative location of all important items, people and materials.

As a general rule the scene should not be disturbed to allow normal work to continue. Sufficient time and resources should be provided to ensure investigators have as much access to the scene as is required to conduct a successful investigation.

Wherever possible, investigators should take the opportunity to directly observe work processes, procedures, use of equipment or practices that are similar (or preferably identical) to those involved in the accident.

In most cases a sketch plan of the scene should be made and the location of all persons, equipment and materials charted on it.

Photographs or video footage should be taken and be as thorough and as detailed as possible. Once the scene is returned to normal, any essential information not collected will be lost forever. The use of digital cameras has greatly enhanced the ability of investigators to immediately capture information at the scene.

To ensure that all relevant information is gathered, photographs should be taken from all angles. The maxim is that you cannot have too many pictures. It is useful to place rulers or other measures in the scene before photographing. This will assist investigators in understanding the physical scales.

Viewing the photographs later frequently reveals an important fact that was missed or not appreciated whilst at the scene. The sketch plan and the photographs can also be used later when interviewing witnesses and other key personnel. A sample form for recording photographs and other visual material (including videos) is shown at **Figure 5:5**.

Investigators may also be assisted by observing the work practices and procedures that were operating at the time of an accident – or as near as possible to this – by visiting the work site or similar work sites where such practices are in use (see the re-enactment in **section 5:5.6.2**). This enables them to get an understanding of actual work practices, as opposed to what may be assumed from reviewing written operating procedures.

5:5.3.1 Removal of items from site

Investigators may wish to remove from the site and retain items of equipment, plant, finished or partly finished products, or any other relevant items for further examination.

For future identification each item removed should be photographed. Investigators should list and record the items removed. Sufficient information should be recorded to ensure that the items can be identified in future. Continuity of evidence should be maintained, as explained in **section 5:5.5**.

Items removed should be put in secure and controlled storage under the direct control of the investigators.

Investigators must be aware of the requirements of the relevant enforcement authority. If the police of the HSE/local authority are involved in the investigation, items must not be removed by the investigators without their knowledge and approval.

5:5.4 Pictorial information

It is often surprising the amount of pictorial information from other sources that can become available during an investigation. Some of these sources appear quite unusual and some are fairly common. Sources of such material include:

- pictures (usually photographs) of a scene before the accident. Such pictures may include publicity material taken of plant, equipment and buildings. These photographs often appear in in-house company magazines and trade journals. They can often provide an insight into the relationship between different aspects of the scene and can be helpful if the site is unusual and has been destroyed or severely damaged in the accident;

- video footage of the accident, or part of it, taken by a witness/bystander. As will have been noted from press reports, bystanders often happen to be on hand with a video camera as an accident takes place. Care has to be taken in gaining access to this material as the proper authorities may have prior need for it;

- still photographs of the accident taken by a bystander. As with video footage, still photographs are sometimes taken by bystanders, often without any real understanding of how important such material can be. Again access to it needs to be approached with caution to ensure the proper authorities' requirements are met;

- manufacturers'/suppliers' catalogue pictures of equipment/ plant. These pictures may only be of limited use. However, they can sometimes help decide which type, make and model of equipment/plant has been involved. They can also be used to prompt witnesses. They may be particularly helpful in spotting differences that may indicate deviations or modifications from the standard design or set up;

- CCTV footage, usually from security cameras. Many sites now have CCTV cameras for security purposes. These cameras often pick up much of the movement in and around a site. Recordings of this material tend to disappear fairly quickly as the recording tape is reused. Investigators need to get hold of this material very quickly to determine its relevance to any investigation;

- designers' drawings, pictures and construction photographs. Designers and builders often take photographs as a building/plant is being constructed or installed. This is especially so if the installation is unique or of a large size. Sometimes such a photograph gives an insight into the detail of structures and plant which is otherwise obscured or has been lost in the accident.

5:5.5 Scientific and forensic analysis

The use of specialist scientific or forensic analysis can be particularly helpful (and sometimes absolutely essential) when investigating accidents involving broken plant or equipment, PPE failures, chemicals and unusual materials, and where the cause is not obvious.

Where an item of equipment has broken or failed it is essential to establish the mechanism of failure. The factors involved in the failure need to be fully understood to ensure the investigation does not lead to mistaken conclusions. Very often the reason for failure is not apparent. Specialist examination and expertise may be required to determine the precise mode of failure. Where metal parts fail through overloading, wear and tear, stress or other forces a metallurgical examination will reveal the nature of the failure. It will also be of assistance in determining if the metal used in the equipment was to specification. Failures in mechanical processes, such as gear mechanisms, lifting machinery and pressure vessels, will most often be determined by the use of metallurgy. In addition, examination and inspection by engineers expert in the design and operation of such machines can also be helpful in assisting the investigation.

A variety of accident scenarios also require the use of a range of scientific tests and examinations to gather information, for example in the determination of temperature at which items of equipment or materials fail, the contamination (or formulation) of process liquids, the composition of atmospheres, and explanations for structural collapses.

The following specialists may be of assistance:

- structural engineers;

- metallurgists;

- industrial hygienists;

- engineers (mechanical, electrical and/or building);

- physicists;

- medically qualified personnel.

Computers and computer-controlled equipment can fail through a malfunction of the control software. Where this may have contributed to an accident, software specialists and programmers will need to analyse the programs for failures and give an assessment of operating characteristics.

It is unlikely that most investigators will have access to all or any of these specialists in house. External experts will need to be engaged.

A sample form for requesting expert assistance is shown at **Figure 5:7**. The use of such a form also helps to ensure that continuity of evidence is maintained. This means that it is possible to prove that the item or substance that has been examined is the one from the accident scene. Although this is strictly required for law enforcement purposes it also has great utility for in-house investigations and can assist both legal advisers and insurers.

5:5.5.1 The medical examination of injuries

Medical personnel may also be able to assist an investigation by providing a study of the relationship between injuries and the likely ways in which the injury could have been caused. This is a very specialised area of medicine and thus specialist medical forensic assistance may be required.

This, however, raises a number of ethical and legal issues.

5:5.5.1.1 The legal position

Employers cannot insist upon employees undergoing a medical examination, unless the right has been clearly established in the contract of employment (*see* **Chapter 2, section 2:6.1**). The Access to Medical Records Act 1990 ensures confidentiality of an individual's medical history. An employer cannot approach an employee's medical practitioner without written consent from the employee.

5:5.5.1.2 The objectives of medical examination

An investigator may request a medical examination to determine the nature and extent of a person's injuries. Such an examination may help the investigator to determine how the injuries occurred. The nature of an injury can sometimes give an insight into how an accident occurred, especially where there is some debate over the precise mechanisms involved.

As the main thrust of the investigation should be about determining the nature of the event rather than its outcome, much of the information related to injuries is likely to be helpful in relation to fitness for work, liability and associated issues, matters for insurers and legal advisers to deal with.

The examination may also reveal whether the condition being suffered is an existing condition that has been made worse, as well as the extent of damage that has been caused.

5:5.5.1.3 Who should conduct an examination?

A medical examination will normally be carried out by a general practitioner or a medical specialist depending on the nature of the injury or condition of the employee; the specialist will usually be appointed by the company. If an insurance company is involved in the investigation, they may wish to appoint their own medical advisers.

A company's own medical adviser can also be of assistance in obtaining relevant information from treatment hospitals, especially from accident and emergency consultants and pathologists. This can be particularly useful where the nature of an injury is unusual and/or the events leading to the injury are dependent on medical information, for example in the case of exposure to refrigerant gases which can give rise to symptoms of a heart attack following respiratory exposure.

5:5.5.2 Alcohol and drugs

If the immediate cause of an accident is considered to be a result of human error, it may be prudent to ensure that alcohol and/or drugs was not a contributory factor. Employers may only carry out a test on an employee if they have a policy on alcohol and drugs in place. This policy must include the right to carry out tests (*see* **Chapter 2, section 2:6.11.2**).

5:5.6 Reconstructions and modelling

Another and often useful tool in piecing together the evidence in an accident is to attempt to reconstruct or replay it. A reconstruction can be done in a number of ways depending on the circumstances of the situation, the competence of those involved in doing the reconstruction and the time and effort involved. Modelling is particularly useful when much of the physical evidence has been destroyed and when there are few, if any, eye witnesses.

Reconstructions can take a number of forms:

- walk-throughs;
- re-enactments;
- theoretical modelling;
- physical modelling.

5:5.6.1 Walk-throughs

These simply involve getting the various people (or substitutes) to go through the actions that were carried out at the time of the incident. It is, of course, important to ensure that safety is not compromised, so the best that can be achieved is a role play. Walk-throughs can sometimes be helpful in jogging people's memories or highlighting questions that a desk-top approach cannot.

Care has to be exercised to ensure that people involved in the accident are not coerced into 'performing' in the reconstruction. It is important that their legal rights are not compromised and that they do not get stressed by the occasion. The appropriate use of walk-throughs is often a judgement call and legal advice should be sought before doing it if there is any doubt.

5:5.6.2 Re-enactments

Re-enactments are really a half-way house between the walk-through approach and full-scale modelling. In some situations it may be possible to re-enact the accident scenario without having the same consequences. This approach is often used by traffic accident investigators to establish how a vehicle might behave in certain circumstances. They might for example, take a car through a corner at speed to establish the likely effect this might have or go through a journey sequence in real time to establish what the various drivers involved in the accident may have seen or been able to see. Similarly, it has been possible to reproduce fire events by recreating the circumstances in a controlled environment, such as a fire research laboratory.

5:5.6.3 Theoretical modelling

In many types of accident, including those involving plant and equipment failures, it may be possible to develop a model of what may have happened. This involves examining the evidence and developing an explanation of the sequence of events based on a sound knowledge of the properties of the factors involved. These may include mechanics, fluid dynamics and product reactions, chemistry or physics, and buildings and structures.

First, the circumstances and factors involved are examined. A theoretical model is then constructed and tested to see if the events of the accident can be reproduced. It is common to use computer analysis for this type of modelling, especially where complex factors may be involved. This may simply be a mathematical model showing, for example:

- the effect of different stresses and strains on equipment, structures and plant through the use of engineering principles;

- the effect of differing combinations of products, chemicals and process components, such as heat or contact time, using the general principles of chemistry or physics.

Alternatively it may be a digital model developed by feeding various data into a computer to show, for example:

- the effects of gas cloud dispersion;

- the effects of placing loads on various parts of a structure;

- the effects of fire in a building;

- the effects of water movement in a river or stream.

During the investigation of the Piper Alpha oil platform explosion such theoretical models were constructed to establish the nature and type of explosion that could have caused the accident. This type of modelling is usually complex and requires special expertise to undertake it. Some simpler theoretical modelling may be possible, for example in attempting to establish the likely sequence of events in a chemical or process reaction. This could be achieved by establishing the type of reactions that would lead to the outcome seen at the accident, including the forces involved and the amount of energy required.

5:5.6.4 Physical modelling

It may be possible, although generally costly, to create a miniature, to-scale model of the accident scenario. This uses the knowledge of the facilities, the actions of people and the properties involved in the accident to build an actual physical model of the accident site. This can give a miniaturised picture of the site and enable a possible sequence of events to be established by using the model to re-create possible accident scenarios.

A large physical model was created to explain the sequence of events and the possible causation of the Kings Cross underground fire. This modelling 'discovered' the phenomenon of trench fires in the escalators and led to a much wider understanding of the safety issues surrounding this type of installation. Another example is the use of an architectural model to explain a structural collapse. Care has to be taken when using scale models as the scaling process can radically affect the results. What happens on a small scale may not happen in precisely the same way as the full-size, real-life incident.

6 | Collating and Analysing Evidence, and Reporting Findings

Issues discussed in this chapter:

- Establishing the sequence of events in an accident
- Analysing evidence
- Developing logic trees
- Applying fault trees to accident investigations and management systems

6:1 Introduction

In any complex accident investigation it is important to have a means by which to examine the evidence and weigh up the findings. There are three basic tasks that need to be achieved, which are:

1. to establish the sequence of events;

2. to analyse the evidence to establish causation;

3. to write a report to explain the findings and describe the causation of the accident.

6:2 Establishing the sequence of events

The first essential task to be carried out in any accident investigation is to have as complete a picture as possible of the sequence of events. The cause of the accident is described not only by the nature of any identified failures but also by the order in which events took place. This is essential to the understanding of the underlying causes and the action that is required to prevent recurrence. Events that happen in one order may give rise to a different outcome if they happen in another order.

The sequence of events is assembled as the investigation progresses. It is usual for the sequence to be put together by working backwards from the final event in the accident chain. This event is usually the point at which damage or injury occurred, or, in the case of a near miss, the point at which the deviation from the planned actions took place (*see* **section 6:3.3**).

The more complex the event being investigated, the greater the need for a structure in which to assemble the evidence, so as to find the sequence of the accident events. The main technique for achieving this is the development of an event chart.

6:2.1 The event chart

One very effective but simple method to put the evidence together is to construct an event chart. The chart is made up as the evidence is collected. For simple and less complex events, the chart may be made on paper. For larger and more complex situations, the best way to develop the chart is on a section of available wall or a series of display boards.

6:2.1.1 The components of an events chart

The main components of an events chart are:

- the time line;
- event/action cards;
- the list of players.

6:2.1.1.1 The time line

From the witness statements taken and from other evidence collected a number of appropriate time 'markers' can be deduced. These are placed horizontally on the wall at a high level. At the start of the process two nominal times will be used. For convenience these are referred to as t^0 and t^{end}.

- t^0 is the time when the accident sequence began.
- t^{end} is the time when the accident sequence finished.

The line between t^0 and t^{end} is called the time line. This time line marks the upper border of the chart.

t^0 is often not known at the start of the process and will only be decided after the evidence collection is complete. In an investigation looking at underlying causes, t^0 may be days, weeks or months before the actual accident event itself. In such cases it is not normally necessary to develop the accident sequence to such an extent.

t^{end} can be taken as the point when injury, damage or loss occurred, but this is not always the case. For example, if somebody is injured by a building or wall collapsing, the investigation is not about why the person suffered broken bones, but why the building or wall collapsed (and why it collapsed when the person was standing in a place to get injured). The t^{end} for the accident sequence is most likely to be, therefore, the point at which the structure collapsed. Other times may then be found during the evidence-collection process, and these are put on the time line, for example the time when work finished for lunch or the time a witness saw something (i.e. a time that can be confirmed pretty precisely).

The development of the chart is essentially iterative. A typical time line for an event chart is illustrated in **Figure 6:1**.

FIGURE 6:1 EXAMPLE EVENT CHART TIME LINE

t^0	12.35	13.30	14.45	16.00	t^{end}
time when accident sequence started	time when first alarm went off	time when supervisor noticed pressure increase	time when fitter called in from job site	time when fitter reports valve let by	time when vessel exploded

6:2.1.1.2 Event/action cards

Witness statements form the main source of information for assembling the chart. Each person (or team) involved in the accident is treated separately. They can be thought of as players whose positions have to be plotted on to the chart. The movements, positions and actions of each player are carefully extracted from the statements. Each movement is then written down on a small piece of paper, card or whatever is convenient. The important point is to ensure that each card only holds the movement or actions of one player (person or team) and only *one* action/event. The cards are then put on to the chart.

If an area of wall is being used, the cards may be fixed to it by Blutack®. Alternatively, if 'self-stick' notes are used as the cards, these can be stuck directly onto the wall. If a cork board or large notice-board is used, then the cards can be fastened to it by drawing pins. Once the procedure is understood, the method of doing it is up to the ingenuity of the investigators.

A typical player's card is illustrated in **Figure 6:2**.

FIGURE 6:2 EXAMPLE EVENT CARD

Player: Supervisor Mr A	Source of information: statement (page 2, para. 3)	Approximate time:
action/event	Rings maintenance manager to get a fitter on site.	About five minutes after he logs pressure rise in vessel C in report log.

6:2.1.1.3 The list of players

The names of the players should be placed in the left margin of the chart. The order in which these are put will vary for each accident scenario being investigated. A good general rule is to put the key players at the top of the chart as there is likely to be more information about them.

A typical left margin list of players may look something like this:

Players
Supervisor Mr A
Maintenance manager Mr B
Fitter Mr C
Fitter Mr D
Production manager Miss F

6:2.1.1.4 Assembling the chart

The cards for each player are progressively put onto the chart as the information comes in. The cards are placed on the horizontal line for each player and in the vertical line (on the time line) for the known or suspected time that the event took place. A typical event chart is illustrated in **Figure 6:3**.

261

FIGURE 6:3 EXAMPLE EVENT CHART

Players/time	Time when sequence started		Time when first alarm went off	Time when supervisor notices pressure increase	Time when fitter called in from job site		Time when fitter reports valve let by	Time when vessel exploded
	t^0		12.35	13.30	14.45		16.00	t^{end}
	Valve let by	Pressure increase						
Supervisor Mr A			Hears alarm	Rings Mr B			Orders evacuation	
Maintenance manager Mr B				Gets C		Sends D to assist		
Fitter Mr C				C goes to plant	Calls in		Unable to fix	Hit by hot gases & thrown to floor
Fitter Mr D						Goes to plant		
Production manager Miss F					Discusses with B / Stops production run		Notices flow still metering / Reports to B	

6:2.1.2 Considerations when constructing the chart

There are a number of considerations when using this plotting technique. These include:

- sequencing;

- using 'real' time;

- event conflicts.

6:2.1.2.1 Sequencing

The time line is crucial to the understanding of the sequence of events but it is not necessary to use actual times. Events simply have to be put in chronological order. For example, event 1 occurs to player 1 after event 5 to player 3 and before event 4 to player 2.

6:2.1.2.1.1 Using 'real' time

Sometimes it will be possible to use 'real' times. These could be taken from clocks on site, data linkages from computer print-outs, or digital displays on CCTV cameras and digital cameras.

It is important to ensure these times are synchronised. Any variation between clocks, watches and data recordings can seriously mislead the plotting of the sequence of events. The evidence needs to be checked to corroborate that stated real times are accurate and can be compared. Very often this can be verified during the investigation by comparing the times of clocks, data recorders and computers with GMT time signals. If this cannot be done all real times used to plot the sequence of events must be treated with caution and only allowed to remain if there is other corroborating evidence that indicates the sequence is correct.

6:2.1.2.2 Event conflicts

The plotting of the chart during the course of the investigation enables investigators to immediately identify where conflicts in evidence arise. By looking at the vertical arrangement of the time line against the players, it is relatively easy to identify events which could not have happened together or in the order given. This enables investigators to review the evidence and question it.

Conflicts between what witnesses did at different times/the same time or what other evidence has provided should be checked. No event conflict on the chart should be taken at face value or ignored.

6:2.1.3 The benefits of sequence plotting

This plotting method has a number of benefits, namely:

- flexibility;
- the ability to corroborate evidence;
- the ability to identify missing evidence.

6:2.1.3.1 Flexibility

The plotting of the sequence is flexible. Because all the actions have been broken down into individual components they can be analysed separately. As the investigation proceeds, investigators will understand the relationship between events that have happened. By using moveable cards/pieces of paper, the events for each player can be moved along the time line until a complete picture of the sequence is obtained. The time line can also be adjusted without too much problem.

6:2.1.3.2 Evidence corroboration

The plotting of the individual actions and events related to individual players enables investigators to corroborate evidence given by one witness against that of another. This is an iterative process. For example, if witness A says that they saw a particular event (person B walking along the edge of the roof at 12.00 hours), then it is possible to ask other witnesses who may have been in a position to see the edge of the roof if they also saw person B on the roof.

6:2.1.3.3 Missing evidence

The most telling part of sequence plotting is the gaps in the time line that exist between what players did or were involved in. These gaps very often indicate that evidence is missing. If there is no information on what somebody did (for example, an injured party) then this needs to be found. At the very least the absence of evidence must be explained in the report and some degree of reservation must be noted for the explanation of the sequence of the accident and the events leading up to it.

6:2.1.4 Applying the event chart to process accidents

This event plotting technique can also be used when the accident primarily involves equipment/plant and not people. The exact same method is employed, except in this case the list of players becomes a list of plant and equipment. The event/action cards describe the individual events/actions relating to the items of plant or equipment involved. For example, the plant list might be something like:

Equipment/Plant
valve A
XS flow valve B
stop valve C
process control A
thermostat E

An action card for a valve is illustrated in **Figure 6:4.**

FIGURE 6:4 EXAMPLE ACTION/EVENT CARD FOR A PROCESS EVENT

Equipment/Plant:	Purpose:	Time of action:
XS flow valve B	Prevents XS flow of agent to reactor vessel. Controlled by volume indicator switch (information from as-built design spec).	
Event/action	Failed to respond; stuck in open position	When reactor vessel filled to design capacity

6:2.1.5 Checking the sequence

Obtaining further evidence to check or validate the sequence of events is very often necessary. Gaps in the evidence, areas of conflict or vagueness in the sequence picture will need to be followed up. There are a number of ways this can be achieved. The two main approaches to use are:

1. modelling;

2. role play and reconstruction.

These are described in **Chapter 5, section 5:5.6.**

6:2.2 Recording the chart

It is generally good practice to transcribe the chart to some form of permanent record. This can be used in the accident report as reference material to support the presentation of evidence and as a historical record. It may also form a useful training aid. The format of the permanent record is up to investigators. It may be made on a spreadsheet, as a word-processed document or as a hand-drawn document.

6:3 Analysing the evidence

A number of techniques of varying sophistication are available to assist in the analysis of evidence. Amongst these are:

- fish bone diagrams;

- change analysis;

- logic trees (FT and ET analysis).

6:3.1 Fish bone diagrams

The fish bone is another one of those uniquely Japanese ideas that has found its way into a number of analytical techniques and is now known more by its familiar name than by its inventor. The technique is simplicity itself. The problem or issue to be examined is put at the head of a fish bone diagram (*see* **Figure 6:5**). In the case of accident investigation this is normally the outcome of the accident. Categories of contributing causes are placed at the head of each of the main bones on the diagram and then the sub-causes or issues involved are spelt out on the smaller bones under the appropriate category.

FIGURE 6:5 FISH BONE DIAGRAM

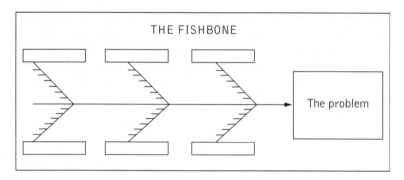

An actual example of this technique applied to a real incident is shown in **Figure 6:6** (from Hancock, B. June 1998. 'Learning from accident experience – are the old lessons really being applied?', *Loss Prevention Bulletin*, 141).

FIGURE 6:6 COMPLETED FISH BONE DIAGRAM

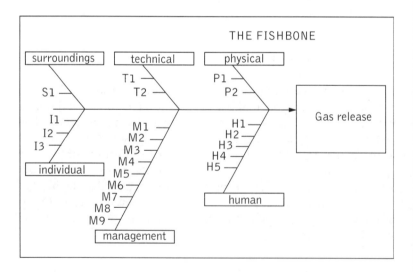

In **Figure 6:6** the accident involved a release of chlorine gas during the off-loading of a road tanker. Six categories of failure were identified, which in turn had a total of 22 contributing factors. Human factors included the failure to communicate which specific valve had to be opened. Management failures included employing an apprentice for the job when two technical staff were absent. Individual failures included lack of technical knowledge by the supervisor. The small and dirty name plates on the valves were classified as a surroundings failure. Technical failures included the design not ensuring mal-operation was prevented, and so on. Altogether some 12 people were involved in the incident that initially could have been 'closed out' by simply opening a purge valve.

The fish bone is a very useful and simple method for drawing together ideas about an accident and grouping causes in categories for attention.

6:3.2 Change analysis

Change analysis is a fairly simple technique that involves comparing the situation during the accident with what should happen in normal circumstances. Performing a change analysis requires an understanding of the normal work processes, procedures and systems in use. It is important to understand the sequence of events both in the 'normal' and in the 'abnormal' situations. The two are then compared. This is often best done using a table (*see* **Figure 6:7**). An example is shown in **Figure 6:8**.

FIGURE 6:7 CHANGE ANALYSIS COMPARISON TABLE

Issue: procedure/ equipment/ people/ technology/ operational (factors and conditions – *see* Chapter 1, section 1:3)	Expected situation/ behaviour/ operation	Actual situation at time of accident	Changes/ difference
Basic question set: (*see* Chapter 5, section 5:3.2)			
Who?			
What?			
Why?			
When?			
Where?			
How?			

FIGURE 6:8 CHANGE ANALYSIS TABLE FOR AN ACCIDENT INVOLVING THE SPLASHING OF BATTERY ACID IN SOMEONE'S EYE

Issue: procedure/ equipment/ people/ technology/ operational (factors and conditions)	Expected situation/ behaviour/ operation	Actual situation at time of accident	Changes/ difference
Who was doing the work?	Vehicle mechanic	Vehicle mechanic	No change – a competence or training issue?
What work was being done?	Replacement in service	Replacement for testing due to failure	Replaced before expected time, possible issue of shortened life?
What type of battery was it?	Gel electrolyte	Liquid electrolyte	For some reason a liquid battery had been used instead of the authorised solid gel
What PPE was being used?	Gloves and overalls	Gloves and overalls	Eye protection not identified by risk assessment – no need if battery acid is in solid gel form as specified

Issue: procedure/ equipment/ people/ technology/ operational (factors and conditions)	Expected situation/ behaviour/ operation	Actual situation at time of accident	Changes/ difference
Why was the battery carried?	Lifted from rack onto trolley	Carried in arms – no trolley available	Absence of trolley may have exacerbated movement required
Why was the battery moved?	To effect replacement	To effect replacement	Moving battery is part of normal work procedure
Why were the cell caps removed?	Not required	To check electrolyte level	Mechanic aware that battery was of liquid type but took no precautionary measures
When did the splashing occur?	No splashing expected – has not happened previously	As battery lifted from vehicle	Splashing occurred during movement of battery – not a normal occurrence
Where was the battery?	Being moved from vehicle	Being moved from vehicle	Normal action
How was it moved?	Lifted by hand	Lifted by hand	Normal action

From the example shown in **Figure 6:8**, the change in the nature of the battery acid content is quickly identified. The splashing may have been exacerbated by the extra movement required because the equipment for lifting and moving the battery (the trolley) was unavailable and because the cell caps had been removed. Removal of cell caps would not be a problem if the electrolyte was in gel form as specified. Eye protection was not identified as a necessity for this operation as the battery acid would not be able to splash.

Change analysis is useful for a quick fix, especially in situations where the evidence is unclear and time is of the essence. Changes come in a wide variety: changes in time, doing something too early or too late, changes in products, for example fuels, additives, mixtures and chemicals, changes in people (less experienced for experienced), changes in working patterns or even changes in organisational structures and arrangements, for example the person responsible for Permit to Work (PTW) authorisations reporting to a different manager who does not allow time for the PTW authorisations to be processed properly.

The main question to be asked in change analysis is: what is different? Although this is relatively simple it can also be a difficulty if the investigators do not fully appreciate the normal working pattern, equipment arrangements, etc. Therefore, it is not a substitute for thorough investigation and information collection.

6:3.3 Logic trees

There are a number of variations on the logic tree principle. The more established include fault trees and event trees (used in fault tree and event tree analysis). These have been developed largely out of the hazard and operability study (HAZOP) methodology.

The application of logic trees, especially those derived from the fault tree and event tree analysis methodologies, can be extremely helpful in an accident investigation.

6:4 Developing logic trees

There are two main modes in which the tree can be developed:

1. working backwards to causes;

2. working forwards to developments/consequences.

6:4.1 Working backwards – fault trees

These trees are often called fault trees and are used extensively in detailed analysis work. The technical fault tree must be completed with precision and probabilities can be assigned to the various levels of event. In most investigations this rigour is not necessary.

The fault tree shows all of the events that could have led to the head event (*see* **section 6:5.1**). It does not mean that all the events shown on the tree did actually happen. The tree is a tool for examining the evidence and ensuring nothing has been missed.

The fault trees represent the ways in which the causes of events combine. The points on the tree where the events combine are generally referred to as gates. There are a number of different types of gates that are utilised in the formal fault tree method. The two major ones are 'AND' and 'OR' gates:

1. AND gates indicate that the events beneath the gates all have to happen before the event above them can occur. They are shown as the symbol:

2. OR gates indicate that any one of the events beneath the gate can cause the event(s) above the gate to happen. They are shown as the symbol:

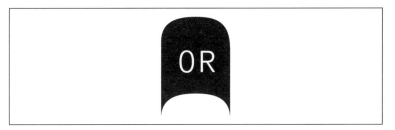

6:4.1.1 Method

The basic principles of these trees are fairly simple. The fault tree approach starts with consideration of a head or top event. Then, by using logic and working backwards, the events leading up to this top event can be deduced. A simple example is shown in **Figure 6:9**.

Starting with the head event the conditions immediately prior to this head event are described. This is the hard part of the analysis and takes some practice. It is essential to ensure the events described are the only ones that can give rise to the head event. In essence, the fault tree represents a chain of events, each happening in sequence. **Figure 6:9** shows a simple fault tree used to examine the reasons why a car fails to start.

FIGURE 6:9 SIMPLE FAULT TREE FOR A CAR NOT STARTING

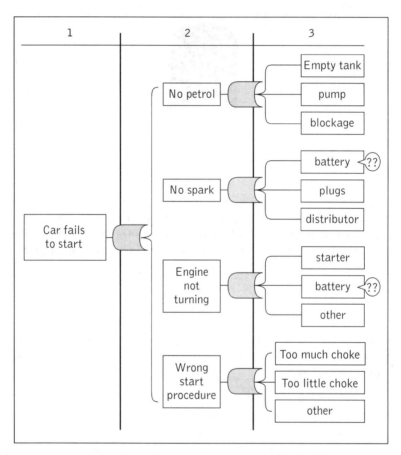

(Adapted from Kletz, T.A. 1986. Hazop and Hazan – *Notes on the Identification and Assessment of Hazards*. Institution of Chemical Engineers)

The head event in column 1 is 'car fails to start'. There could be a number of reasons for this, all of them independent. The fault tree therefore shows in column 2 four main reasons for the car not starting: no petrol, no spark, engine not turning or the wrong start procedure. As all of these are independent of each other they are shown as acting to produce the head event through OR gates. In column 2 each of these primary reasons for the car not starting are assigned their own causes. Thus there are three possible reasons why there is no petrol getting to the engine: the tank itself is empty, the fuel pump is not working or the fuel line is blocked. Each of the other primary reasons are broken down in this way (column 3). Again they all act independently: any one of them in their group could be the primary reason for the car not starting.

The tree is then developed downwards until all eventualities are uncovered or until the investigator is satisfied with the tree. Some trees can be quite complex and this can detract from the benefits that the tree offers as a means of analysing the evidence.

By examining each of the branches of the tree in turn it is possible both to identify all the possible types of causation and examine each of them to see which is the right one.

A common error when first developing fault trees is to start with events (including events in the tree) that are not immediate to the head event. For example:

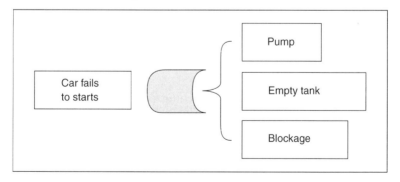

In this situation the absence of petrol in the engine has been overlooked. It is the absence of petrol that is a primary reason for the car not starting and it is this absence of petrol that needs to be explained.

6:4.1.2 Common mode failures

In technical fault trees (where calculations are undertaken to determine the probability of head events occurring), it is normal to identify common mode failures. These are failures that are identical but appear in several parts of the tree. For example, in **Figure 6:9** the flat battery appears in two parts of the tree. The failure of the battery is 'common' to two parts of the tree. If this is taken out to form a separate tree then the complexity of the tree is reduced and duplication is avoided.

6:5 Applying fault trees to accident investigations

It is possible to examine an accident in the same way that the fault tree in **Figure 6:9** was constructed to identify and then trace reasons why a car has failed to start. An accident investigator must first decide on a head event that needs to be examined. The evidence is then assembled and collated to create a fault tree to explain the head event.

6:5.1 Choosing the head event

Care has to be exercised when choosing the head event. It is important that the right event is chosen, otherwise the investigation may be misled. For example, in an accident a passenger is thrown from a vehicle. The vehicle is specialised and was designed and specified by the company. The company has very little, if any, control over the driving of others on the road and in the way the road is designed or maintained. What the company has done (or believed it had done) is to ensure the integrity of the vehicle passenger compartment. The passenger who was not wearing a restraint was thrown from the vehicle because the door failed and opened. Others in the vehicle remained safe and uninjured even though the vehicle overturned. Head event A could be the road traffic accident (RTA) and would read something like:

> The event where the vehicle went out of control and hit a road sign.

Head event B, however, would read:

> The event of the passenger being thrown from the vehicle during a RTA.

Head event A (the RTA) is usually the focus for the police and motor vehicle insurers. If the head event chosen is A, then the investigator will be trying to justify the investigation on the basis of the state of the road, the driver's actions and the circumstances of the RTA itself.

However, as the company had control (or would like to have had control) over the passenger compartment design, only head event B will lead to any meaningful explanation as to why the door failed. In order to ensure that the total event can be examined the head event description should include both the fact of the door coming open and the person being thrown out.

If the description was limited to the door coming open, then the investigators may miss the point about the wearing of restraints. Moreover, the determination of head event A focuses only on that particular RTA (a feature of most police examinations) whereas head event B will apply to all situations where the door could come open in any RTA.

Choosing the head event to be examined by the logic tree is up to the investigators. On occasions it may be necessary to examine more than one head event.

6:5.2 Describing the head event

The description of the head event should be sufficiently detailed so that the event is clear. There is a tendency when using this methodology to write down something simple like the 'the door came open'. This, however, may be misleading later on, especially when others come to examine the logic tree. A more detailed description, such as 'the door came open when the vehicle hit a road sign on the near side allowing the passenger to be thrown out', provides a much better focus for the development of the tree and makes clear what is actually being examined.

A simple work-related fault tree is shown in **Figure 6:10**. The accident involved a welder burning his hand whilst working. The head event is set out and three areas of primary reasons are identified: training, PPE and risk assessment. It is important to note that each of these reasons is set out as a failure – inadequate training, failure of PPE, inadequate risk assessment. One of the failures of PPE is that it was not worn. Although this is not strictly a failure of the PPE itself, it may well be that the need for PPE was overlooked or discounted by the welder, or perhaps it was unavailable. Both of these reasons indicate a management fault: either a lack of supervision to ensure welders wear PPE or a failure to provide suitable PPE.

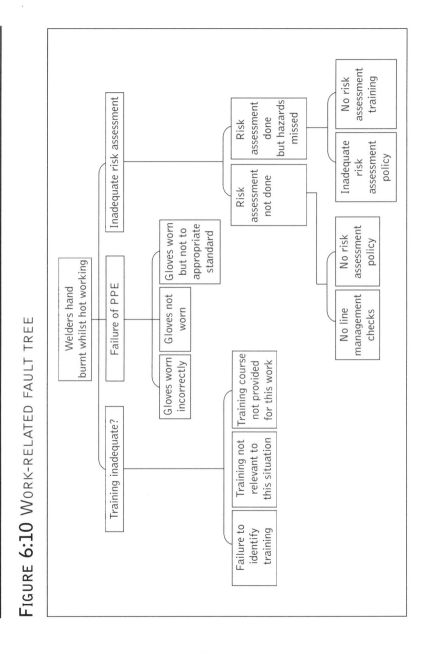

FIGURE 6:10 WORK-RELATED FAULT TREE

6:6 Using fault trees to examine systems of work and management systems

The fault tree approach can be used to simply look at the sequence of events leading to a failure/accident (the head event), even though this may be quite complex. Alternatively, the approach can be adapted to look at systems failures, especially those involving work systems and/or management systems. Commonly in accidents there are factors that are accountable in most of them. A set of events can be predicted for most accidents, for example failures in training, hazard recognition, supervision and work systems. These can be set as key events beneath the head event, for example:

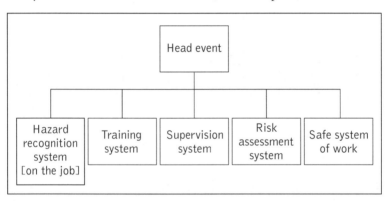

Each of the principle systems failures can then be developed to determine what evidence might be required to indicate if they failed or not in the particular accident being investigated.

In **Figure 6:11** the head event is the release of chlorine gas when a tanker was delivering to fixed plant. The danger recognition system will include such things as general warnings, alarms, gas monitors and more physical signs, such as a valve being incorrectly set, gauges reading 'strangely' and unusual operations. All of these should trigger some response from the operatives. So the questions are: did this happen? Were such signs available? Was danger recognised or not? Could it have been recognised? If it was recognised, was this too late to avoid the incident?

FIGURE 6:11 SAMPLE SYSTEMS-BASED FAULT TREE (PARTIALLY COMPLETED)

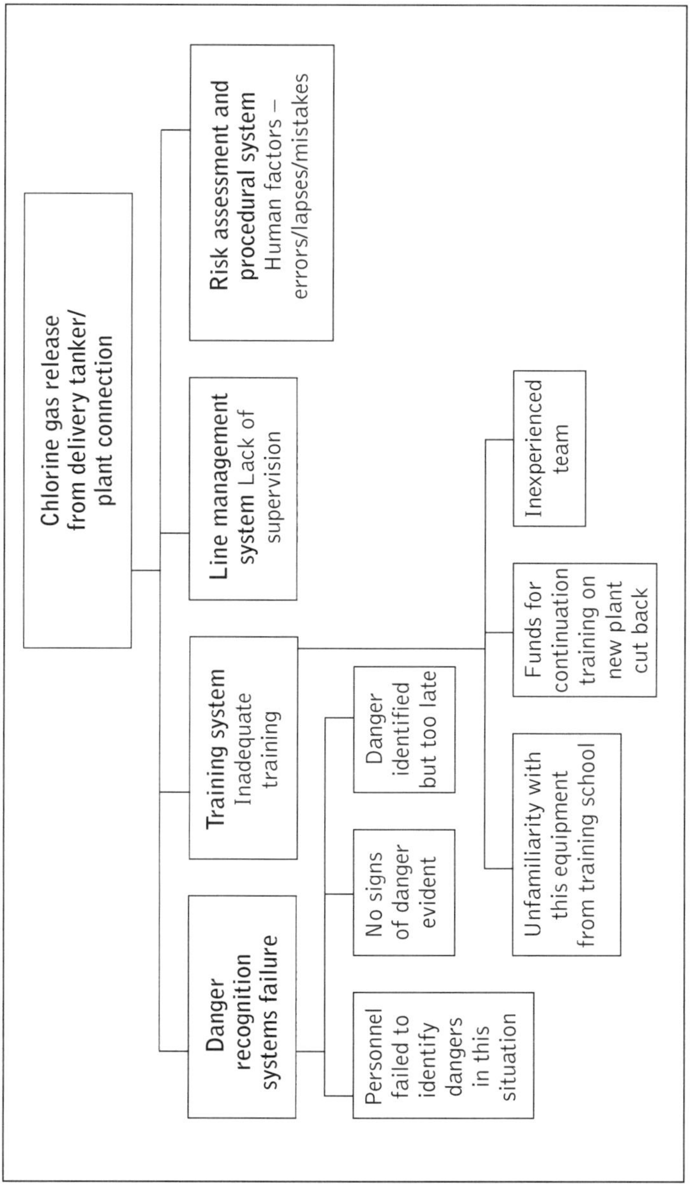

Chlorine gas release from delivery tanker/ plant connection

Risk assessment and procedural system Human factors – errors/lapses/mistakes

Line management system Lack of supervision

Training system Inadequate training

Danger recognition systems failure

Personnel failed to identify dangers in this situation

No signs of danger evident

Danger identified but too late

Unfamiliarity with this equipment from training school

Funds for continuation training on new plant cut back

Inexperienced team

The training system looks at what skills, knowledge and experience the operatives should have to do the job in question. Was this type of plant a feature of their training? Did they have the training or was there a cut back so that insufficient training had been given? Were they inexperienced in this type of work? On-the-job training is an important part of developing knowledge and skills.

6:7 The use of fault trees in accident investigations

By building up a comprehensive fault tree accident investigators should be able to probe the evidence and also the possible cause of the events being investigated. It is essential that the basic principles of logic tree development are followed and for anything but the simplest of accidents most people will require some specific training in the fault tree methodology to make full use of the approach.

Effective and meaningful fault trees are generally always better if completed by a team. This allows a number of ideas to mix and inevitably some form of brainstorming is required to get the process going. As the approach suggested here is not as rigorous as that required for engineering purposes (including risk assessments of plant and processes) some degree of latitude is allowable. The important feature is to obtain a tree that helps investigators to analyse the evidence, identify gaps in the evidence and establish some general theories about causation. It can also serve as a simple, explanatory 'picture' of the whole event, especially in complex situations.

6:8 Working forward to developments/consequences (event trees)

These logic trees work in the opposite way to the fault trees described above. When used in technical situations they are called event trees. Event trees are put together in the same way as fault trees but in this case the head event leads to further consequences. For example, **Figure 6:12** illustrates the events following a car crash.

FIGURE 6:12 EXAMPLE OF AN EVENT TREE

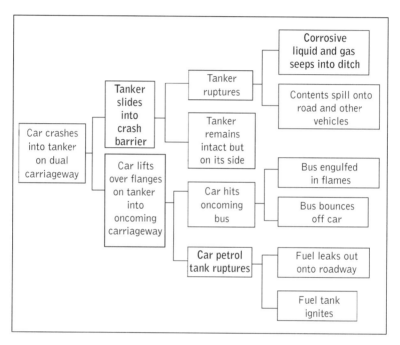

The event tree in **Figure 6:12** attempts to describe what might happen if a car was to hit a tanker on a dual carriageway. The tree is only provided as a representation of how an event tree *might* develop. Obviously in an accident scenario there are going to be some actual 'knowns' about what happened, which events occurred and which did not. However, event trees can be very useful in piecing together the underlying reasons why certain consequences happen, as in the case of the investigation following the Piper Alpha disaster in July 1988, where event trees were utilised to explain how the original fire led to such tragic loss of life and the total loss of the platform.

Event trees can be useful in accident investigations, especially when the evidence is scarce and the actual sequence of events is not understood. In the Piper Alpha inquiry an event tree was used to first postulate and then confirm the likely progression of consequences from the initial explosion.

Working forward from a head event to create an event tree is perhaps not as common in accident investigations, or as useful as using fault trees. However, the logic is the same and the development of an event tree to explain possible consequences of a postulated failure can aid the investigator in the search for evidence and the explanation of complex situations.

6:9 Bow ties

The expression bow tie is often used to describe the use of fault trees and event trees in combination. The head event is used to work backwards to describe the combination of failures that can lead to it and forwards to identify its possible consequences.

For example, **Figure 6:13** illustrates how the fault tree and event tree can be combined.

FIGURE 6:13 THE BOW TIE

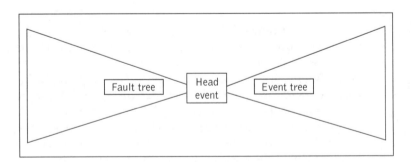

Figure 6:14 shows a simple bow tie for an accident where a cook slips over in a kitchen.

FIGURE 6:14 SIMPLE EXAMPLE OF A BOW TIE

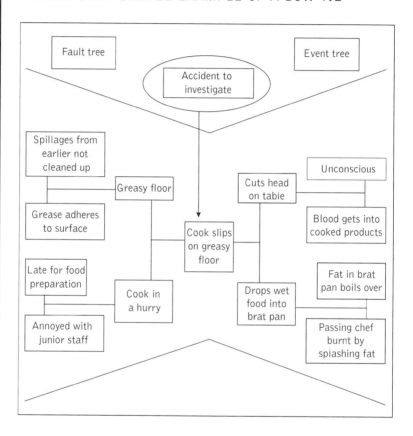

7 | The Accident Investigation Report

Issues discussed in this chapter:

- Why have an accident report?
- Who should prepare the report?
- Analysing and presenting the data
- Common errors in report writing

7:1 Introduction

The accident investigation report is the means by which all the facts and information about the accident are presented to the organisation and to those involved. In effect it is the collation of the efforts of the accident investigators and their findings. Accident reports may come in a number of guises relating to the extent of the investigation and the use to which the report is to be put.

An accident investigation report may be no more than the record made of the accident for recording purposes (a sample form is included in **Figure 7:1**), including the entry in the accident book (*see* **Chapter 4, section 4:4.2.1**). Such a report is, of course, relatively superficial and will only be adequate where the event is of minimal interest, for example where someone may have knocked their knee on an open drawer, sustaining localised bruising but with no obvious long-term effects. A quick reminder to ensure people in the immediate section where the incident took place to keep their desk drawers closed may be all that is required and an entry in the accident book may suffice. However, the accident book is not to be regarded as an accident report and is certainly not sufficient as a report of a thorough and wide-ranging accident investigation.

FIGURE 7:1 EXAMPLE ACCIDENT INVESTIGATION REPORT FORM

Company name:		
PERSONAL INFORMATION		
Name of injured person:		
Male ☐ Female ☐ Age:		
Address:		
Employee ☐	Contractor ☐ Employer:	Other ☐ Specify:
Occupation/dept:		
Nature of injury, or damage or near miss:		
First aid given? Yes ☐ No ☐		
WITNESSES		
Names of witnesses:		
Statements taken? Yes ☐ No ☐		
INCIDENT DETAILS		
Date/time of incident:		
Location of incident:		
Task being performed:		
Working conditions:		
Description of accident/incident (state possible causes):		

ASSESSMENT OF RISKS ASSOCIATED WITH ACCIDENT/INCIDENT		
What was the likely severity of injury?		
What is the likelihood of the incident recurring?		
How many people could have been affected? Risk rating =		
Risk assessment ref no (if applicable): Risk assessment amended?		
INVESTIGATOR'S CONCLUSIONS		
Causes of incident		
• Direct		
• Underlying		
Corrective action needed (including responsible person)		
Type of action	Date completed	Signature

REVIEW
Review of corrective action required?   Yes ☐   No ☐
Name of person carrying out review:
Signature/date:
Name of investigator:
Signature/date:

A separate record may be made as a 'report'. Such reports are usually for statistical interest only and may subsequently be reported to managers as part of a collated set of statistics showing relative safety performance, such as the number of minor injuries caused in offices in one year (*see* **Chapter 12, section 12:8**). They rarely provide enough information about the accident.

As soon as it becomes evident that a more detailed investigation is required, the accident record by itself will be generally insufficient to report the investigation. Whilst a Reporting of Injuries, Diseases and Dangerous Occurrences Regulations 1995 (RIDDOR) report on form F2508 contains relevant information about an accident, it does not contain all the information generated by a detailed accident investigation. A more detailed and logical report is therefore often required following an investigation. The information in the report should include:

- who was involved in the accident;

- the evidence collected (including witness statements);

- the immediate and underlying causes of the accident;

- the inadequacies in safety management, including any risk assessments undertaken (*see* **section 7:2.1**).

7:1.1 The objectives of the accident investigation report

The information contained in the report should aim to:

- present of the evidence;
- explain what has happened;
- assess/reassess the degree of risk;
- assess the control measures in place;
- prevent recurrence.

7:1.1.1 Presentation of the evidence

The report serves to pull together all the evidence collected in such a way that any reader will understand what has been considered. It is just as important for the reader to understand what evidence has not been considered and to some extent, what gaps in the evidence there may be.

7:1.1.2 An explanation of what has happened

The report should also explain and describe what actually happened. This applies not only to the immediate events preceding the accident, but also to the underlying events that contributed to the accident.

7:1.1.3 Information to assess/reassess the degree of risk

The report will also describe and illustrate how the events and control measures relate to the degree of risk. This may be the degree of risk understood prior to the event or, more likely, the degree of risk as understood after the event. In many cases the report will need to reflect the understanding of safety as is found in the expressions 'who would have thought that could happen' or 'that was never considered to be a risk'. In a sense, the accident report provides the gift of hindsight.

7:1.1.4 Information to assess control measures

Part of understanding risk will come from the assessment of the control measures that were in place prior to the accident. The report will therefore assist in assessing both the relevance and the effectiveness of these control measures. The detailing of the evidence and the explanation of the reasons for causation will be a vital part of this assessment.

7:1.1.5 Information to prevent recurrence

In a more general sense the objectives of the report combined is to provide information to prevent recurrence. The more detailed and thorough the report, the more chance there will be of obtaining information from it to prevent recurrence.

7:2 The purpose of an accident investigation report

The report serves a number of purposes. These may be regarded as internal or external: internal purposes serve the needs and requirements of the organisation directly; external purposes relate to the use the report may be put to in dealing with issues arising from outside the organisation. These purposes should generally be of secondary consideration when writing a report.

The report must be factual. It also serves to provide a history or record of what has happened in the organisation. In addition, it is documentary evidence of an accident – evidence that may be challenged.

7:2.1 Internal purposes

The main internal purpose of the accident report is to provide for the health and safety needs of the organisation. These needs will primarily reflect:

- risk assessments and control measures;
- improvements in systems and controls;
- the organisation's learning requirements.

7:2.1.1 Risk assessments and control measures

One of the main objectives of the report is to provide information so that risk and control measures can be assessed and improved. As this is one of the main purposes of the report, the style and content should be designed to ensure that the health and safety purposes can be met.

7:2.1.2 Improvements in systems and controls

A thorough and detailed report will provide information to assess the *actual* systems and control measures being used. It will generally be found that assessment of the risks and control measures after the accident will lead to a better understanding of their functionality, highlighting areas that need to be improved.

7:2.1.3 The organisation's learning requirements

The report may also be used to serve the wider purpose of organisational learning (*see* **Chapter 1, section 1:2.5**). The style and content of the report could be designed to clearly identify those areas within the business that may be improved. A report that covers all the issues in a logical way can (and should) often be shared directly with all those in the organisation so that lessons can be learned. In many situations, the material used in the investigation, for example videos made to reconstruct the accident as part of the investigation process, can be utilised with the report as training material.

7:2.2 External purposes

The external purposes for which the report may be written reflect the inevitable actions that are prompted by factors outside the control of the organisation. Principally these are matters of:

- insurance;
- litigation;
- enforcement.

7:2.2.1 Insurance

Insurance issues arise because of the nature of the various contracts of insurance that an organisation may enter into, i.e. occupier, employer and product liabilities. The in-house report provided by accident investigators may be used by the insurers to assist in their own assessment of the nature of the liabilities arising and the degree to which cover may be afforded.

7:2.2.2 Litigation

Claims against the organisation, mainly for personal injury, but also property and other liabilities, may draw upon the accident investigation report. In many cases the report may be the only detailed report that is written. However, it is normally found that an emphasis on helping the management of health and safety in an organisation may not be sufficient for the lawyers acting for the organisation in defending any claims that arise. This difficulty comes about because the emphasis of a health and safety-related accident investigation should be on discovering underlying causation, whereas litigation is generally concerned with apportioning blame.

These two purposes are often seen to conflict. The introduction of the new Civil Procedure Rules (the Woolf Reforms) should to a large extent eliminate this problem (*see* **Chapter 9, section 9:6**). A report that is open and candid about causation will greatly assist the new legal process, especially in agreeing issues of liability before proceedings. It is important to note that the wording or framing of a report can influence the impression created by it. Where a claim is likely the report can be written in a style that achieves the objectives for improving health and safety management without compromising the subsequent legal position it may have when dealing with litigation. Any internal report will (ultimately) always have to be disclosed.

7:2.2.3 Enforcement

An accident may come to the attention of the enforcement authorities (the Health and Safety Executive (HSE) or local authority environmental health officer (EHO)) by a number of routes. Most commonly the procedure for reporting under RIDDOR will highlight accidents for which enforcement action is most likely. Any internally produced report must be readily accessible to the enforcement authorities and may be used by them in deciding what action to take.

7:2.3 An historical record

In addition to highlighting the necessary steps an organisation must take to improve its health and safety standards, an accident report has an ongoing significance for an organisation as it includes the health and safety performance of the organisation over a period of time. This serves as a point of reference for future risk assessments and is a benchmark for measuring continued improvements in safety standards.

7:3 Who should prepare the accident investigation report?

The accident investigation report should be written and presented by the investigators themselves. Where a specialist has been used, for example a structural engineer brought in to examine evidence of a building collapse, the investigators will need to include this evidence in the report and include a copy of the specialist report as an appendix (*see* **section 7:4.2.3**).

7:3.1 Perspectives in an accident investigation report

The preparation, delivery and presentation of an accident investigation report has to be seen from a number of perspectives. Whilst the main aim of the investigation must be to ensure and secure improvements in health and safety, the requirements of other aspects of the organisation's business have to be borne in mind. These requirements are primarily:

- health and safety;
- insurance;
- the law;
- the organisation as a whole.

7:3.1.1 The health and safety perspective

The consideration of health and safety is the main focus for the accident investigation itself and for the report that follows from it. Whatever mistakes have been identified, duties unfulfilled or blames apportioned, the investigation and its report will have failed if lessons cannot be learnt.

This is such an important aspect that it is generally regarded that all other requirements are much less important. There are plenty of examples of how attempts to cover up findings or massage the report to provide for a better legal or insurance position are ultimately doomed to failure. If the inherent errors and underlying systems issues are not dealt with at the time, they are bound at some point in the future to reappear and cause history to repeat itself.

7:3.1.2 The insurance perspective

In many situations the consequences of an accident will involve contracts of insurance (*see* **Chapter 11, section 11:3**). It is important that the report is capable of being used by those responsible for dealing with insurance claims, but not to such an extent that only the insurance issues are covered in the report. In many cases it may be that a safety report will need to be added to to cover the insurance angles. Before writing the report the investigators should check the organisation's insurance contract to confirm whether an insurance claim is likely to be made.

This is a decision for the organisation's management to take on board and reflects the arguments:

- that accident investigation is really a part of the safety management system of the organisation;

- that organisational culture is a significant aspect of ensuring good safety performance and that a supportive culture is one in which people can learn from mistakes and failures without being blamed;

- that organisations need to learn from their accident experiences so that mistakes and failures are avoided in the future, as discussed in **Chapter 1, section 1:2.5**.

Typically reports that concentrate on who is to blame are prepared for insurance purposes. A good investigation report will concentrate on the underlying reason for the accident. Insurance considerations are normally related to the immediate causes of accidents.

7:3.1.3 The legal perspective

Legal advice should be sought when an accident occurs (*see* **Chapter 4, section 4:3.4.2**). This may not be necessary on all occasions and it is usually possible to set down some general guidelines within an organisation as to when it is required. These, for example, are occasions when legal advice should be sought:

- there is a potential personal injury claim. This can be expected with all serious injuries and fatalities;

- there is a question about supplier or manufacturer liability for failures in equipment or plant;

- enforcement action is likely, suggested or taken by any of the enforcement authorities, such as an improvement or prohibition notice or a prosecution (*see* **Chapter 9, section 9:8**).

Where a claim for damages is likely to arise, the accident investigation report, carried out for health and safety purposes, may need to be added to, providing information on any likely breaches of legislation. The organisation's legal advisers will need to see a copy of the report, but it will often be found that additional legal questions will be raised. Keeping health and safety aspects separate from any details of possible breaches of legislation which might involve a claim against the organisation will usually be found to be the best approach. Legal advisers will wish to see that the organisation is complying with the Health and Safety at Work etc. Act 1974 and regulations made thereunder.

In addition, action, ranging from prosecution through to the issuing of improvement or prohibition notices, by the enforcement authorities may result from the accident. It is frequently the case that enforcement bodies will ask for additional information about an accident and request a copy of the investigation report. The report should not be amended or written in such a way as to paint a 'rosy' picture, as this will often result in difficulties. In all cases the best approach is to be open and honest in the accident investigation report. Enforcement officers will mostly be persuaded not to take action if they can see obvious and well-intentioned actions arising from a report that is not overtly critical but is instead objective, balanced and neutral. However, it is also true that an internal accident investigation report may form the basis for an enforcement authority to take action and even institute legal proceedings as a result of its contents.

7:3.1.4 Compatibility and interactions

It can be seen from the above considerations that the health and safety, insurance and legal aspects of an accident investigation report may be incompatible. The insurance and legal perspectives will largely be about assigning liability for any accident and in some cases (if not all) be about 'protecting' the organisation, for example by seeking to minimise liability, defray costs and limit insurance premium increases. In contrast, the health and safety approach should be more about learning from the events and identifying where the management system itself has been less than adequate.

It will generally be found that the best way to deal with these apparent incompatibilities is to adhere to the adages 'putting one's head above the parapet' and 'taking a taste of one's own medicine'. In other words, in the context of any accident investigation report, being totally honest and identifying mistakes and failings in the management system is better than seeking to gloss over matters that the management board may find unpalatable. Above all, the report should be factual.

The way the report is handled and the way the consequences of the report are managed is the key to ensuring that overall damage to an organisation is minimised whilst important safety lessons are learned.

7:4 Analysing and presenting the data

In order to achieve its objectives an accident investigation report needs to have a number of properties. Factors to consider when drafting a report include:

- style;
- approach;
- expectations;
- structure;
- interpretation of the evidence;
- the use of diagrams to illustrate a point.

Before starting to write the report, investigators should consider the following list of questions:

- Have all witnesses and others with relevant information been interviewed, and have all statements been obtained?
- Have all risk assessments, work procedures and method statements been obtained?
- Have copies of all safety inspections, test certificates and reports been obtained?
- Has all the available pictorial information been collated?

7:4.1 Style

The style of the report will reflect the circumstances and to some extent the author. However, the style of the report needs to be such that it is clear, precise and relevant to the events and findings being reported.

The style of the report should match the expectations of the reader. Those reading the report will expect it to be comprehensive and fully inclusive of all the relevant issues. A well-presented and well-thought out report will create expectations in the mind of the reader. The reader will be led to the conclusions through the presentation of evidence in a way that is logical and easily understood. If the report is not presented in a clear and concise way, the reader will not be able to follow the course of events and may begin to question the validity of the report itself.

Once a style and format of report has been introduced into an organisation this creates a precedent for subsequent reports with the reader expecting to see a certain format and to see evidence laid out in a certain way. Consistency in reports is therefore an important point to consider. The investigators should check previous reports for style and format to give them a better idea of the way the content should be structured.

It is always preferable to report in the passive voice where possible. This helps maintain a high degree of independence. It also allows bias and prejudice that may arise from the investigators' own views to be avoided.

For example, avoid writing:

> '**I** then went to the end of the line and observed the machine in normal operation.'

or

> 'After questioning the occupants **we** then questioned other witnesses.'

Instead write:

> 'Observations of the machine in normal operation were made and they revealed that…'

and

> 'The occupants were questioned [give time] on the first day of the investigation [give date]; other witnesses were subsequently questioned on [date and time].'

Approach the report objectively and independently. Wherever possible, use a documentary style, reporting the events and findings dispassionately and without any colourful or emotional language. Keep sentences short and to the point. Use illustrations (photographs, plans, etc.) wherever possible to make explanations clear.

7:4.2 Structure

In order to produce clear and informative reports it is necessary to have a structure that supports the nature and style of the report. The structure should enable any reader to piece together the accident and see how the investigators have arrived at the conclusions, what evidence there is, what ideas (about causation) have been formulated and how thorough the investigation has been. It is particularly important that the report makes clear the risks that have been exposed and the controls that are involved, either because they have failed or because they did not exist.

The nature of the event being investigated and the detail of the findings will determine the length of the report. The amount of detail which should go into a report depends upon the severity of the outcome and the use the investigation and report will be put to in the future.

The structure of the report provided here holds well for most detailed accident investigations. It can be adapted to suit the needs of any organisation. The structure consists of the following sections. Although they appear in this order in the report, this is not necessarily the order they will be written in.

1. The synopsis – contains a brief outline of the accident 'setting the scene' for the report.

2. The sequence of events – is a chronological listing of the way the events unfolded.

3. The evidence – presents the collated information.

4. Hypotheses – theories of why the accident happened that are to be tested.

5. The conclusion.

6. Appendices.

7:4.2.1 The synopsis

The first part of the report should be a short explanation of what the report is about. This need be no more than a paragraph. The synopsis sets the scene for the reader and the context of the report.

This synopsis should be written after the investigation is completed. The purpose of the synopsis is to concentrate the reader's mind on the people involved, the situation and circumstances of the accident and the significant features of the consequences.

The significant parts of the synopsis are:

- date and time;
- location;
- person(s) involved, injured, etc.;
- situation/circumstances;
- the outcome;
- conclusion (why it happened).

A typical synopsis might read something like this:

On [day and date] at [time], Mr X was fatally injured whilst attempting to clean a [name of machine/equipment]. The interlock devices were not engaged at the time. His arm became trapped as his sleeve was drawn into the machine when it inadvertently started. Mr X was crushed as he was pulled between the rollers. The failure to engage the interlock devices was found to be the result of inappropriate systems of work following introduction of new equipment.

In complex accident scenarios it may be beneficial to provide a more detailed summary to assist busy managers who may need an 'executive brief' to work from.

7:4.2.2 The sequence of events

The purpose of the sequence of events section is to tell in detail what happened chronologically. It is most important that the sequence is set out clearly and precisely so that the reader can understand what happened and in what order. It is not the purpose of this section to explain why something happened.

The reader of the report will quickly understand the relevance of the actions of people, the various circumstances and the order in which events occurred. In many cases, especially for complex events, the evidence can be very detailed and complex.

By separating the description of the sequence of events from the reasons why these events happened (the evidence), the report will remain succinct and the information can be easily digested.

As with any 'story' the reader's attention will often be drawn to questions such as: why did this happen? Why did the person do such a thing? The reader is then 'primed' to understand the reasons why the events happened. These reasons will be explained in the evidence section of the report and commented upon in the hypotheses section.

For example, the sequence of events might read something like this:

> At 8.00 a.m. at the start of the morning shift Mr B the supervisor requested Mr X to clean machine 12. This machine is located at the far end of the production shed. Mr X went to the materials room and was seen there by Mrs Y and Miss W. He told them he was off to clean the machine. At about 8.25 Mr X was seen by the foreman Mr C walking in the direction of the machine pushing a maintenance trolley. At around this time Mr V saw a lock-out tag on the power supply isolator for machines 1, 2 and 3. Shortly after

this Mr X appears to have put the machine into reverse mode by manually operating the controls. At approximately 08.45 a number of witnesses heard a shout and a loud scream. Mr V ran to the area where Mr X was working and found the machine operating in normal mode and Mr X partially pulled into it between the rollers. Mr V immediately operated the emergency stop button and sounded the alarm to attract attention. Emergency services were called and the fire brigade arrived at 08.57 followed by a paramedic crew at 09.20. The fire brigade were able to free Mr X from the machine and he was released at around 10.10. During this period the paramedics provided first aid support. He was transported to hospital at 10.29 and pronounced dead on arrival.

This report of the sequence of events is brief and to the point. It draws on witness statements and describes events in the order in which they occurred. Although some explanation is given, for example 'walking in the direction of the machine pushing a maintenance trolley' and 'Mr X appears to have put the machine into reverse mode', it is only provided to assist the flow of the description. The reader does not know at this stage the relevance of the maintenance trolley or the reason or evidence for the machine being in the reverse mode. These issues are covered in the evidence and hypotheses sections. Where one has been created, the event chart (*see* **Chapter 6, section 6:2.1**) can be used to help the reader picture the sequence of events. The chart itself should be added to the report as an appendix so that it can be referred to if necessary. Alternatively, the sequence of events may be presented as in **Figure 7:2**, using the same information from the above example.

FIGURE 7:2 EXAMPLE SEQUENCE OF EVENTS

08.00	At the start of the morning shift Mr B the supervisor asked Mr X to clean machine 12. This machine is located at the far end of the production shed. Mr X went to the materials room and was seen there by Mrs Y and Miss W. He told them he was off to clean the machine.
About 08.25	Mr X was seen by the foreman Mr C walking in the direction of the machine pushing a maintenance trolley. At around this time Mr V saw a lock-out tag on the power supply isolator for machines 1, 2 and 3. Shortly after this Mr X appears to have put the machine into reverse mode by manually operating the controls.
Approximately 08.45	A number of witnesses heard a shout and a loud scream. Mr V ran to the area where Mr X was working and found the machine operating in normal mode and Mr X partially pulled into it between the rollers. Mr V immediately operated the emergency stop button and sounded the alarm to attract attention. Emergency services were called.
08.57	The fire brigade arrived.
09.20	The paramedic crew arrived.
10.10	The fire brigade were able to free Mr X from the machine and he was released at around 10.10. During this period the paramedics provided first aid support.
10.29	Mr X was transported to hospital at 10.29 and pronounced dead on arrival.

7:4.2.3 The evidence

The evidence section is designed to bring together all the evidence collected in a logical and structured way. There are a number of ways in which the presentation of evidence can be structured. The final choice depends on the circumstances and the nature of the evidence itself.

It is not necessary to put the evidence in the form of a story or even in chronological order. In fact to do so can be confusing. The important point is that the evidence is clear and can demonstrate what the investigators have taken into account and have found out about the events. The nature and type of evidence to be presented will be determined by the event and will include the range of issues detailed in **Chapter 12, section 12:8**. It is helpful if the evidence is categorised logically.

When describing the evidence it is important to ensure that the description is itself logical and coherent. The reader needs to be able to understand the evidence and its relevance at first reading. If the evidence is complicated and the description of it muddled, then the report itself will lose credibility. It needs to be borne in mind that the weight and significance of the evidence will be the major factor that managers will take into account when deciding on remedial action.

Wherever possible the evidence should be illustrated. The use of photographs and drawings can aid understanding. Using a picture can sometimes make the job of the report writer far easier. The use of video footage should also not be overlooked. Where this is to be used as evidence a brief description is required with a cross reference so that the reader can turn to the video at the right time. A video made of a reconstruction of the accident can be a powerful tool for explaining events to others, including the management (*see* **Chapter 12**).

It is important that the evidence is collated and cross referenced. In particular, items of evidence, such as witness statements, photographs, drawings and other material, should be labelled and annotated.

7:4.2.3.1 Categorising the evidence

When presenting evidence it is best to put it in categories like those shown below.

- Witnesses statements – these summarise what the witness said. The full statements should be included as an appendix to the report.

- Human factors – evidence to show that the organisation, the job or personnel influenced the accident.

- Inspection reports – recent reports of inspections carried out on the plant/equipment involved and on the location where the accident occurred. Include copies of the documents in an appendix to the report.

- Test certificates and reports – details of the dates and results of statutory inspections carried out on the plant/equipment involved in the accident, and on any others which might have had an influence on it. Include copies of the reports in an appendix to the report.

- Plans, drawings and photographs of the site/scene/equipment – include copies of these documents in the report. The originals should be kept by the investigators until the report has been issued and accepted, and then archived.

- Safety information – work procedures, method statements and risk assessments should be referred to in the report. Copies should be included in an annex to the report.

- Training records – details of the training provided to those involved (both task and safety) in the accident should be detailed. Where the quality of the training may be a factor in the accident, the training content and training methods should be included.

- Technical information – suppliers'/manufacturers' technical literature will be needed where failure of plant, equipment or of product is seen to have had an influence on the accident.

- Experts reports – reports by experts appointed to examine and carry out material analyses, structural reports, etc., should be summarised in the report. The experts' reports should be included as appendices to the main report.

In many accident scenarios it will also be useful to examine the human factors – issues relating to the organisation, working practices and individuals' characteristics (*see* **Chapter 1, section 1:6**). These should be put under the 'human factors' heading. Similarly, management system issues can be addressed as a group under a suitable heading.

Collecting the evidence will involve work over an extended time period. It is therefore essential to ensure that the evidence is kept intact and properly referenced. The forms shown in **Chapter 5, Figures 5:2–5:7** can be used to keep a record of the evidence collected. The mode of evidence collection, its continuity and the way it is referenced should be briefly referred to in the report. This can either be written as an introduction to the evidence section or addressed in each of the sections of evidence, for example:

> *the machine parts were bagged at the time and transferred to the technical department on [date and time] where they were subsequently examined by a technical expert from [name, position, etc.] on the [time and date]. This report found that the controlling interlock on the machine was designed so as to be inoperative when the machine was put into manual control mode. The experts report is provided in annex 3.*

7:4.2.4 Hypotheses

A hypothesis is described in the dictionary as:

A proposition made as a basis for reasoning without assumption of its truth – or a supposition made as a starting point for further investigation from known facts.

(*Concise Oxford Dictionary*, 9th edition)

This is a long-winded way of saying: 'we are not sure what the causes are but we have some ideas we wish to test'. An exemplum of a simple hypothesis for the example in **sections 7:4.2.1** and **7:4.2.2** would be:

Mr X was caught by the machine because he did not follow the correct procedure.

This statement can be used to test the evidence. Is there evidence that this hypothesis is true or does the evidence show otherwise?

The idea of making up hypotheses is to provide some basis for forming a judgement about what the actual causes of the accident were. At the start of any investigation the investigators will have some idea of what happened. They may be right or they may be entirely wrong. It is important that the investigators keep an open mind (*see* **Chapter 5, section 5:4.1**). However, the mind can often become clouded and the use of hypotheses can assist in showing whether the evidence supports an idea about how an accident was caused.

By constructing a hypothesis the investigators are explicitly stating the assumptions that are being made. Most hypotheses will be obvious, as they will have resulted from the information gathered during the investigation. It is, however, important to consider what might be described as 'outlandish' hypotheses in order to ensure that factors have not been overlooked.

Well-formed hypotheses can give assistance in determining if any evidence has been overlooked or if the evidence itself is insufficient. If it is not possible to say for certain that a particular event happened for a specific reason or in a specific way then it is almost certain that the evidence collected is insufficient.

Most events are the result of multiple causes (*see* **Chapter 5, section 5:2.2.3**) and thus it may be necessary to test a number of simple hypotheses in order to build a more complete picture of what the evidence is confirming.

This idea also has another utility. The reader will be examining the evidence and description of the accident and will therefore form their own ideas about what has happened. They will need to be certain that the investigators have covered every possibility. By examining the hypotheses put forward by the investigators the reader can tell if their own ideas have been addressed. It is important therefore to examine every reasonably conceivable hypothesis and not just the ones that are obvious.

For example, in the accident described in **sections 7:4.2.1** and **7:4.2.2**, one hypothesis might be:

> *Mr X was killed because another party turned on the power whilst he was working.*

or even

> *Mr X was killed because another party deliberately turned on the power whilst he was working.*

This second hypothesis is the one that any police investigation would attempt to prove (or disprove) first.

The evidence may not show that the power was turned on deliberately, but if this factor had not been considered by the investigator, then the investigation will be short on the evidence that it has considered. If, in this case, there is no evidence to show that the power was turned on by another person, then this will be stated when testing the hypotheses.

The evidence relating it to the hypotheses that have been decided upon should be discussed. Each hypothesis should be discussed in turn with the reasons for and against it being proved by using the evidence.

For example, a hypothesis for the possible reason for an accident goes something like this:

The circumstances in which Mr X was caught in the machine were a result of a failure to identify a change in the working procedures when new equipment was installed.

Drawing on evidence to prove or disprove it tests this hypothesis. For example, there may be evidence that actual procedures have changed and that this had not been taken into account. What may have formerly been a safe working procedure has been altered by common working practices. These had not made the situation unsafe until new equipment had been installed. The evidence may show that the procedures used by the workers were now no longer appropriate. The real issue is the absence or failures in the management system to both identify changes in working procedures and to re-assess their effectiveness (and the risk assessment) when a deliberate change is made, for example after the installation of new equipment.

The framing of the hypotheses and the discussion of the evidence can make reference to any fault or event trees that have been used to analyse the evidence, as well as the sequence of events (*see* **Chapters 5** and **6**).

When testing the hypotheses there are a series of basic questions that need to be addressed.

- Does the evidence support the causes identified by the hypotheses?

If the answer is 'yes', how strong is the evidence for this?

If the answer is 'no' the following questions should be answered:

- Why not?
- Which are the most likely or probable causes?
- Are the causes clear and supported by the evidence?

7:4.2.5 Conclusion

This is the easiest part of the report. It should be short, simple and to the point. The formulation and testing of the hypotheses should have covered all the ground required to analyse the evidence and come to a conclusion about the accident.

A good conclusion begins with:

The accident happened because …

Then it should describe in about one paragraph why it happened:

… Mr X slipped whilst cleaning the machine and was drawn into the rollers. This situation arose because the monitoring of safe systems of work was inadequate and the permit to work system for this procedure was not rigorously enforced. The procedure for cleaning the equipment was not in accordance with the design features and instructions provided by the machine supplier. No risk assessment had been undertaken to assess the risks and control measures required when cleaning the machine. As a result, the changes in work procedures had not been identified.

It is sometimes useful to break the reasons for the accident into the three areas identified by Bird's loss control model (*see* **Appendix 1, section A1:1.2.2**):

1. the immediate cause;
2. the basic cause;
3. the underlying cause.

The immediate cause refers to those factors that can be identified as happening immediately prior to the injury being caused, for example:

Mr X was caught by the rotating rollers as he leant into clean them and as he did so he slipped.

The basic cause refers to the factors that created the situation, in a physical sense, prior to the accident, for example:

The reason Mr X was cleaning the machine in this manner was because the permit to work system was not adhered to.

The underlying cause relates more to management system issues and can be related to the accident causation model and theories related by Reason (*see* **Appendix 1, section A1:1.3.1**). Thus, the underlying reason for the accident may be something like:

Management failed to take account of the need to ensure that changes in processes and equipment were identified and that adequate risk assessment procedures and monitoring arrangements were in place.

Or more pointedly:

There were no management systems in place to ensure risk assessments and monitoring procedures were carried out and safety-critical changes identified.

As the report will be going to the board of directors, partners or senior management, this blunt conclusion may be more palatable if expressed in the terms of:

Less than adequate management systems meant that …

It is generally the case that no individual deliberately avoids their safety duties or wishes to cause injury. This does not mean to say that violations of procedures and rules are not committed (as described in **Chapter 1, section 1:6**), only that such violations are not normally wilful or negligent in intent. In order to assist the appreciation of management system issues it is necessary to bring the relevant managers 'on board'. This will not be achieved if they are alienated by a report that explicitly states they are to blame. Whilst this approach may be suitable (and indeed expected in some cases) for external reports, such as those undertaken by enforcement agencies, it is not generally suitable for internal reports.

7:4.2.6 Appendices

The nature and extent of documents appended to the main report will depend on the incident and the evidence collected. Typically appendices will include:

- witness statements;

- records, risk assessments, working procedures, etc.);

- photographs;

- plans and drawings;

- forensic and specialist reports;

- fault and event trees, and change analysis tables;

- the event chart.

A master copy of the report should be retained together with the listing of all material collected (using the forms in **Chapter 5, Figures 5:2–5:9**) and the appendices. This material can then be passed to the legal advisers as a full and complete record of the investigation and its findings.

7:5 Challenges to the report

The information contained in the report and the way the evidence is presented in it makes it a document that can be challenged by others. As the causes of the accident are explicitly presented in the report, there may be occasions when others will seek to challenge the investigators' findings. If the report is well written and the evidence presented accurately, then the challenge can be made and proved either right or wrong quickly and accurately.

7:6 Supplementary reports

It is frequently the case that when investigating an accident, especially a complex one, a number of other safety issues may be identified that are not directly relevant to the incident under investigation. They may be of serious concern. In order not to confuse matters and to provide a manageable report, it is generally better to keep such 'supplementary' matters separate.

When critical safety issues are discovered during an investigation it is, of course, important to act, especially where there is a potentially serious risk to people. However, the issues may have nothing to do with the accident under investigation and may therefore not appear in the accident report. For example, whilst investigating why an operator was hurt working a particular item of equipment, the investigators discover that maintenance procedures are not correct. Even though these had nothing to do with the particular accident being investigated, they should, of course, be reported.

The investigators should write and submit a supplementary report to address particular safety concerns that have arisen during the investigation, but which are not directly relevant to it. Sometimes the issues raised in a supplementary report can be of greater significance than the accident investigation itself.

7:7 Common errors in report writing

Whilst the approach to report writing given here is not the only one that can be applied, there are a number of errors common to most styles of report writing that crop up. These errors are to be avoided if the report is to be clear and concise. They generally arise because the person or persons writing the report are too close to the events and have too many assumptions on board; they do not necessarily appreciate that readers of the report will be seeing this information for the first time.

7:7.1 Explaining events without evidence

In the process of formulating hypotheses it is not unusual for new evidence to be introduced. This is not only confusing but also means that the report writer has left out important descriptions of evidence in the report. It is important to ensure that all relevant evidence is explained and authenticated in the body of the report under the 'evidence' section (*see* **section 7:4.2.3**).

7:7.2 Introducing new evidence in conclusions

It is also important to avoid reaching conclusions by using evidence that has not been presented in the body of the report.

7:8 Recommendations in reports

It has been common practice for investigators to end their reports with a list of sometimes quite detailed recommendations. This practice is not generally recommended for a number of reasons.

- Investigators do not know everything.
- The report is just one of many other matters.

- Risk decisions need to be made after the investigation.

- Resource allocation – and decision making.

- The costs and benefits of actions.

- Management responsibility.

7:8.1 Investigators do not know everything

The temptation to write down explicit recommendations once an investigation has been completed is understandable. However, the range and diversity of work within any organisation and the priorities to be addressed mean that investigators cannot know everything. Furthermore, there is a danger that the recommendations will direct attention away from more significant issues, for example the next accident waiting to happen, because other aspects of the safety management system have not been addressed.

7:8.2 The report is just one of many other matters

Any accident report is just one part of a fairly large body of detailed information that any organisation should be using to monitor its safety performance. The accident report has to be seen in the light of this other safety performance information, for example audit and inspection reports. It is only when this context has been reviewed that a decision can be made on what precisely is required.

7:8.3 Risk decisions need to be made after the investigation

It also follows that the decisions about the actual risk demonstrated and presented by the accident investigation's findings can only be made in the context of overall risk. This overall risk is both that to individual employees and to the organisation as a whole. A very focussed decision needs to be made as to whether the accident investigation has highlighted:

- any new risks;

- any known risks which have not been controlled (owing to a failure in control measures);

- any known risks which have been reduced to a level that is reasonably practicable.

It is unlikely that the accident investigators will have considered all these aspects in full. This can only be achieved in the context of the safety management system as a whole and what is known about risks in the organisation.

7:8.4 Resource allocation – and decision making

If action is required following an accident, then resources will need to be allocated to deal with the work. Again, such resource allocation, usually people and money, can only be decided upon once the other factors are considered. This task is generally one for senior managers, and in many cases will be beyond the scope of the accident investigators. If investigators provide a recommendation without considering the resourcing implications, the recommendations themselves may not be put into place.

7:8.5 The costs and benefits of actions

It will be apparent that any action taken after an accident needs to be considered in terms of the costs involved and the benefits to be achieved. The case of *Edwards* v. *National Coal Board* (1949) set the legal precedent for the definition of 'reasonably practicable'. The court decided that 'reasonably practicable' was a narrower term than 'physically possible'. It seems to imply that a computation must be made (by the employer) in which the quantum of risk is placed on one scale and the sacrifice involved in the measures necessary for averting the risk (whether in money, time or trouble) is placed in the other, and that, if it be shown that there is a gross disproportion between them – the risk being insignificant in relation to the sacrifices made – the employer discharges the onus on himself.

A classic example of this is demonstrated by the Fennell Inquiry report into the events around the Kings Cross underground disaster. Although some 144 recommendations were provided in the report, only about 50% were ever carried out. This was because there came a point where the investment to achieve the suggested safety improvements was simply far in excess of the benefit to the actual improvement in safety that would be gained.

7:8.6 Management responsibility

The prime reason for not supporting the idea of adding recommendations to an accident report is simply that this is the role of management. A very simple question could be put to the senior management, who have the duty to ensure safety. This is: here is the accident report; its findings indicate what is wrong. What are you going to do about it? It should be self evident, however, that after receiving the accident investigation report and deciding what has to be done, responsible managers will have taken 'ownership' of the solution anyway without needing to be prompted.

Experience shows that it is very easy to take a list of recommendations and put them in place without any detailed thought or simply to expect them to happen anyway. There are numerous examples where recommendations made in accident investigation reports have not been followed through. This is very often for all the reasons stated in **section 7:8.5**. One effective way of making managers responsible for deciding what to do after an accident is to get them to agree to an action plan.

8 | Further Action

Issues discussed in this chapter:

- Who should be informed of the outcome of an investigation?

- Deciding what actions need to be taken:
    - immediately
    - in the longer term

- The effect of the outcome on companies listed on the London Stock Exchange

- Dealing with insurers and handling claims

- Communication with the enforcement authorities

- Reviewing risk assessments and safe systems of work

8:1 When the accident investigation is complete

There is a range of tasks to be undertaken when the accident investigation has been completed, some of which may need to be carried out before the final report is submitted. These tasks include:

- informing those involved about the accident investigation's findings;

- communicating the report;

- developing action plans;

- reviewing risk assessments;

- examining working practices and safe systems of work.

8:2 Informing those involved

It is generally good practice to share the accident investigation's findings with the people directly involved in the incident, including any casualties where possible. This is generally carried out before the report is finalised.

This achieves a number of objectives, including:

- ensuring that people are aware that the event has been taken seriously;

- by sharing the findings with those involved, allowing people to check the facts and thereby enabling any missing detail to be included;

- explaining the causes of the event, especially the underlying causes;

- supporting a 'no-blame' culture.

8:2.1 The feedback process

Feedback should be carried out by the accident investigators as part of the investigation process and generally in a face-to-face debriefing session, either with a group or as individuals. In doing so, care must be taken to liase with those managing any debriefing process that may be taking place.

The debriefing should be informal and non-threatening, by, for example, avoiding disciplinary issues and apportioning blame, as this should be part of the accident investigation philosophy anyway. The feedback meeting should ideally take place at the employees' workplace: in an area of the canteen, a rest room or a side room, if available.

The main purpose of the meeting should be one of sharing the investigators' findings and conclusions with the group immediately involved, including any injured parties. The approach should be open and if people suggest alterations that need to be made owing to misinterpretation on the part of the investigators, these should be accepted, and the points reconsidered and looked at again.

On occasion, it may be necessary to visit injured persons at home or in hospital. This should only be done with their agreement and after taking advice from any counselling staff or a personnel support manager.

As the primary purpose of the accident investigation report is to establish underlying management system failures and garner information to prevent a recurrence, it is not generally advisable to share this with people outside the organisation, such as the family of any deceased victims, at least not at this stage. They will get the opportunity at the inquest and hopefully through information from the investigating enforcement authorities. More especially, the purpose of this feedback session is to build a better safety culture within the organisation.

Issues of the organisation admitting negligence through the report or triggering any claim through this process should be disregarded. Investigators should base their report on facts alone. Where the organisation's procedures or actions appear to be at fault, this needs to stated. Given the Civil Procedure Rules (*see* **Chapter 9, section 9:6** and **Chapter 11, section 11:8**) the organisation's report will be disclosed at a very early stage and therefore the investigators should avoid any attempt to write a favourable report when there is evidence to suggest that the organisation may have been negligent.

Some solicitors in some organisations may prefer to keep a tighter reign than others on the nature of the report. This largely reflects organisational policy and where the organisation is positioned in terms of developing its safety culture, rather than an attempt to hide or suppress the facts.

8:3 Who should receive the report?

Once completed, the report should be shared as widely as possible. Recipients of the report will or may include:

- those involved in the accident. It is often useful to discuss the final draft of the report with those involved prior to issuing a final report (*see* **section 8:2**);

- line mangers;

- senior managers/the board of directors/partners;

- employee representatives;

- legal advisers;

- insurance officers/insurers;

- the appropriate enforcement authority. Enforcement authorities are likely to request a copy of the report for an accident they have been investigating or an accident reportable under RIDDOR.

8:3.1 Those involved in the accident

During the investigation process at least one feedback session should have been held with the people immediately involved in the accident, especially the co-workers of anyone seriously injured or killed. This is covered in **Chapter 5, section 5:5.8** and is part of the process of investigating to check facts and ensure consistency (of both witnesses and information). At the end of the investigation the final report should be shared with this group as part of the process of improving the safety culture. By this means the people caught up in the accident events, and probably those most personally affected by the accident, come to feel that they have been involved in the investigation and that management has taken the incident seriously. The report is best shared and discussed with them at the final draft stage so that any glaring factual errors can be corrected before it is submitted elsewhere.

8:3.2 Line managers

Line mangers may usefully be given copies of accident investigation reports as part of the organisational learning process. They can then identify any similarities with situations or risks within their own area of responsibility that they can correct without the need for overt instructions from a higher authority.

8:3.3 Senior managers/the board of directors/ partners

The discussion and acceptance of accident investigation reports by people at a senior management level is an important way of ensuring that safety performance is uppermost in the minds of those charged with direct responsibility and accountability for the overall performance of the organisation. This area is discussed in more detail in **Chapter 12**. These are also the people who will generally sanction any action plan arising from the investigators' findings and the report.

8:3.4 Employee representatives

Employee representatives can be party to an accident investigation itself as part of general good practice. Whether or not they are party to the investigation is a matter for individual organisations. However, it is certainly a function of employee representatives to be informed of the findings of any accident investigation and to be part of any safety committee whose role it is to review and comment on accident investigation reports.

8:3.5 Legal advisers

Accident investigation reports will be utilised by legal advisers as part of the evidence required in personal injury or other liability claims and also to give them an understanding of how the organisation is operating and performing. Although not all accidents that give rise to investigation reports will result in legal action, sharing the reports with legal advisers will enable them to comment and advise on safety performance in general and on any areas of non-compliance with the law. This will also include comments on possible future liability where the report indicates control systems to be less than adequate.

8:3.6 Insurance officers/insurers

Information from accident investigation reports may prove useful to insurers (agents, brokers or in-house insurance/risk mangers) both in determining liability and in indicating areas for concern. Not only will accident investigation reports identify areas where risk controls may be inadequate, but they may also indicate areas of under-insurance, for example by identifying activities or areas of involvement that have not been considered in the schedule of insurance.

8:3.7 Enforcement authorities

On occasions the enforcement authority involved may ask for further information regarding a reported accident (under the terms of RIDDOR). The accident investigation report will provide this and may be shared with the enforcement authority either as a complete document or as a summary. Legal advice would normally be sought when sharing such reports with the enforcement authority. The fact that a detailed, accurate, well-resourced accident investigation system is in place, together with a comprehensive report, may actually lessen the impact of the enforcement authority rather than exacerbate it. However, it should always be borne in mind that an internally produced report may be used or produced as evidence by the enforcement authority in any legal action against the company.

8:4 Actions to be taken

One of the first tasks after the investigation has been completed and distributed to the relevant people is to draw up an action plan. This is a responsibility of the organisation's management. It is important to note that the action plan comes after the report has been made available to senior managers. Which directors and managers are to be directly involved in drawing up the action plan will depend upon the nature and consequences of the accident and the size and culture of the organisation. The role of senior managers in deriving and resourcing the action plan and understanding the relevance of the work required should be emphasised. Supporting and directing the action plan are roles for senior managers, as is ensuring that the monitoring and evaluation of the plan are implemented and effective.

The investigators may also be included in the action plan team so that their detailed knowledge may be utilised. However, they would not normally lead the team. The purpose of the action plan is to ensure that the results of the investigation can be acted upon to prevent recurrence and improve safety. If enforcement action (such as an improvement or prohibition notice) has been taken by the relevant enforcement authority, the action plan will be a means of demonstrating the nature, type and extent of action that the organisation intends to take to remedy the defects and deficiencies identified. This will also apply if informal enforcement action has been undertaken, for example in the form of an advisory or warning letter (*see* **section 8:4.2.2**).

8:4.1 The action plan

The action plan can be dividend into two stages:

1. immediate actions;
2. longer-term actions.

8:4.1.1 Immediate actions

The immediate plan should consider the actions required to achieve an improvement in safety. The extent of the tasks to be undertaken and the resources required for them will depend on the nature of the accident and the causes identified. Likely immediate actions will include:

- reviewing the risk assessment;

- identifying resource requirements, such as time, money and people;

- supplying information to management, such as changes in priorities and realignment of projects;

- communicating findings, i.e. telling the organisation about the accident and the actions to be taken;

- agreeing on the format of the action plan for longer-term action (if required);

- dealing with the appropriate enforcement authority.

8:4.1.2 Reviewing the risk assessment – the short term

Once the accident investigation is complete a great deal of information will have been gathered about the risks involved in the accident and the degree to which, if any, the existing risk assessments (if any actually existed prior to the accident) covered the issues raised.

It is always necessary to review any risk assessments related to the tasks/activities involved in the accident. A great deal depends on the relevance of any pre-accident risk assessments to what actually happened, and whether the risk assessments were actually realistic. The fact that a serious accident has happened may indicate that the risk assessment process and its results may have been weak. This needs to be picked up as an item for the action plan, as in many cases the risk assessment issues can be quite complex (*see* **section 8:6**).

However, this early review may assist in identifying other possible immediate consequences, for example if the activity is one frequently undertaken and there is a possibility that another accident might occur. By reviewing the risk assessments a judgement can be made on what factors were taken into account in the current control measures. In turn, this will identify whether these control measures are likely to be adequate or breached (in the light of the information garnered from the investigation) in the short term.

The existing risk assessments may assist in reviewing the immediate actions to be taken. For example, an engineering failure of a metal component may have identified a weakness in the design or fabrication of the part. On the basis of the evidence from the investigation, a judgement can be made if the risk of failure of that part is likely to recur in the short term and whether a short-term solution is available, for example the use of a replacement stronger component. Alternatively, a decision may be reached that in the short term the operation of the equipment using that component should be suspended until a solution is found. The decision may largely be based on the existing risk assessment as this assessment should have included all the current knowledge about the usage and exposure of the equipment involved in the accident up until the accident occurred, for example the amount of daily usage, the likelihood of a similar set of circumstances arising, the reliability of the component, or the ability to increase the testing or inspection of the component. An early decision can then be made as to whether to continue with some temporary control measures or whether to put the work process on hold until a complete solution can be found.

8:4.1.3 Identifying resource requirements

Identifying the need for further resources as early as possible becomes crucial when there is pressure to continue working. It is helpful early on in the process of managing and investigating the accident to identify the possible resources that may be required, whilst still considering what action must be taken.

Having some idea about possible resource reallocation may be helpful, if carried out as soon a possible. This is particularly essential, for example, if there are major projects likely to be affected by the need to take remedial action, or if a particular operation, such as a production run, will be affected. It may be necessary to take people with particular skills away from their routine work in order to develop both short- and long-term solutions. Similarly there may be a need to allocate reserve financial resources or divert funds intended for other purposes.

8:4.1.4 Possible resource requirements – the short term

The extent of the commitment of resources after an accident to deal with its immediate requirements will, of course, depend on the circumstances. In the short term this will have to take account of:

- the investigators' time, including administration support and any cover required for their normal duties and roles. This may extend beyond the actual investigation period as the investigators may be required to liase with legal and insurance advisers, meet with enforcement authorities and attend court or a coroner's inquest;

- the locating and financing of replacement equipment or premises and the ensuring of short-term business continuity;

- plant and equipment. During the course of the investigation this may be taken out of use whilst the investigation is completed. Legal and insurance requirements may extend this period as the plant/equipment may need to be available for evidence or may be held whilst awaiting completion of any enforcement authority enquiries:

- the researching of the extent of the usage of any equipment or procedures either at any other sites of the organisation or in the industry sector in general. This will require one or more persons to be assigned this role and hence take them out of their normal working pattern.

Figure 8:1 provides an example of possible short-term resource requirements.

FIGURE 8:1 EXAMPLE OF SHORT-TERM RESOURCE
REQUIREMENTS

A business suffers a major accident where a fork-lift truck hits some racking, causing it to partially collapse and injure the driver. The business may experience the following:

- The fork-lift is damaged and cannot be returned to service without repair. Repairs are delayed whilst the enforcement authorities carry out their own examination of the truck. The company has other trucks but they are all fully employed and a decision needs to be made whether or not to hire a fork-lift truck for the short term.

- The racking that has collapsed cannot be used. In addition, there is every indication that the racking had not performed to industry standards and enquires need to be undertaken with suppliers, installers and other users to compare the company's installation and determine if there is any intrinsic fault (and not just the fact that it was hit by a fork-lift, an action which it should have withstood). This has wider implications for the company as it has several sites with a large area of similar racking in use already.

- Whilst awaiting the research of racking standards and suitability the company needs to make a quick decision on what it needs to do to safeguard its other areas of operation (and of course its business) and if it should suspend work in other warehouses. If so, this would represent a great loss of business for the company.

- The goods that were held at the site of the accident have had to be transferred to another part of the site but this has led to short-term 'overcrowding'. This in turn has created another hazard as working areas have become somewhat cramped and fork-lift drivers are complaining of the restriction on movement. New stock is also scheduled to arrive and the company now faces a decision on whether it needs to find some short-term temporary accommodation.

- Four members of staff have been transferred from other duties to cover the work involved in moving stock from the damaged area, researching the industry and dealing with the authorities, insurers and customers. The company is now paying overtime to ensure work can continue as normal.

- The company was proposing to open three other sites in the year. These plans now need to be reconsidered depending on the outcome of the industry-wide research they have instigated and the possibility that racking and layout will need to be redesigned and respecified. There are implications for costs as the design and specification work has already been carried out. The company's senior managers have a great deal of time tied up in the new sites project but are now having to reconsider their options as so much time is now having to be spent on the short-term consequences of the accident.

8:4.1.5 Supplying information to management

In the short term, managers need to be given by those preparing the action plan as much information as is necessary for them to be aware of the implications, or possible implications, of the accident and the impact it will have on the organisation. This can be achieved by meetings, memos or any other suitable means, and may include:

- the names and locations of staff assigned new short-term roles or duties, such as liaising with the authorities;

- the names and roles of those involved in the accident. (This may have been done on a local basis but multi-site organisations need to promulgate this information widely, not just to the site affected by the accident.) Staff do move from site to site and an open policy on such information is useful should an employee involved in an accident subsequently transfer to another site/division or function of an organisation;

- the short-term impact on the business, for example what items of equipment are suspended from use, which processes require adaptation and what short-term plan is in place to deal with these;

- what management should brief their staff on if questions are raised, especially those concerning working practices or equipment;

- requests to review risk assessments and operating practices at their sites/divisions/functions that are either directly associated with the accident or that relate to activities and conditions similar to those involved in the accident.

8:4.1.6 Communicating findings

In the short term, a message needs to go out to all employees highlighting the events that have occurred and what it means for the company and its employees. A director or senior manager would usually undertake this. If the organisation has a marketing department, they may be required to prepare the notice. For smaller incidents and minor injury accidents this may be achieved through the organisation's newsletter, intranet, email system or notice board. Larger and more significant accidents will probably require a special briefing for employees. This may take the form of a meeting or group of meetings chaired by a senior manager to inform employees of the events and what the company is proposing to do. At this stage the 'message' only needs to be informative and will be picked up again in longer-term action. Wherever possible the communication should be a joint one between the management and the employee safety representatives. If the organisation has a health and safety committee, it should be informed and used as a means of communication with the workforce.

The benefits of doing this are several fold.

- It underlines the importance the organisation is attaching to safety.

- It enables the organisation to take the information lead and prevent or discourage rumours.

- Management can be seen to be providing information and not just the safety representatives (who, because they work on the shop floor, are generally and traditionally more approachable for information than managers).

- It sets the scene for any longer-term actions the organisation intends to take.

- By informing everyone, concerns about particular risks, working practices or equipment may be more rapidly 'volunteered' by the workforce.

- It is generally supportive of a good safety culture.

The information provided should at this stage be limited to:

- the fact that an accident has occurred;

- who has been injured and what support the company has provided for them;

- what restrictions, improvements and changes to operational procedures are being introduced as an immediate precaution.

Further information and longer-term action should continue to be communicated at later stages (*see* **sections 8:5.2** and **8:5.3**).

8:4.1.7 Agreeing on the format of the action plan

Ideally this should be 'rubber stamping' as the action planning process should already be part of the organisation's general policy on health and safety. However, in many cases the action planning process will not be fully appreciated. Even where this is contained within a sound policy there is always a need to confirm the action to be taken and the method to be adopted, in particular the need to secure the agreement of senior managers to take part in the process and to flag up the possible implications for their own time and resources under their control.

8:4.1.8 Dealing with the appropriate enforcement authority

It is often essential to review the arrangements for liaison and consultation with the appropriate enforcement authority. The issues regarding authority to speak on behalf of the organisation and the likelihood and implications of enforcement action need to be addressed. The organisation needs to agree who will liaise with the enforcement authority. This will differ between organisations, but in many cases the safety adviser will be appointed to do this.

8:4.2 Longer-term action

The longer-term action plan allows the organisation to plan for the future after reflecting on the detail of the accident report. Usually those involved in the short-term plan will be involved in the longer-term proposals. They may wish to involve others, perhaps those with specialist knowledge.

Any action plan should deal with two major concerns:

1. developing an action plan to improve safety measures;

2. ancillary matters.

8:4.2.1 Developing an action plan

The action plan for longer-term safety improvement will usually be quite extensive. A logical approach to considering this plan would include:

- agreeing what needs to be done;

- agreeing the sequence of work required;

- agreeing responsibilities;

- agreeing the timetable;

- providing resources;

- establishing a monitoring/evaluation process;

- drawing up the plan and communicating it to the parties concerned.

Very often these may be considered together. However, for simplicity, each element of the planning process is considered separately. The action plan process is illustrated in **Figure 8:2**.

FIGURE 8:2 THE ACTION PLAN PROCESS

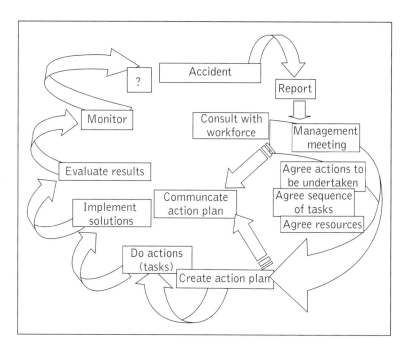

8:4.2.2 Agreeing what needs to be done

This is a task that should be undertaken by a team of representative senior managers on the basis of a detailed understanding of the risks that have been involved. Where possible, the team should include trade unions and employee representatives. The advice of the investigators may be sought if appropriate. There is no one right way to go about this. In many cases it may be that the analysis and assessment of the risks and the required control measures are so involved as to warrant being included as the first stage in the action plan itself. The risk issues are discussed in **section 8:6** as they are involved with and affect a number of other considerations.

The senior managers are likely to be drawn from all sections of the organisation: personnel, finance, law, production, risk management, safety, engineering, transport, distribution, property. The benefit of doing this is to ensure all relevant parties are involved and the support of all the top management is given to the action plan when it is completed. Even though it might be believed that some parties are not required, it very often turns out that somewhere in the delivery of the action plan their assistance *is* required.

For example, following an accident involving production plant, the action plan requires the plant to be redesigned and replaced. The original idea was to put the plant on the site of the original. However, the new design when it arrives clearly shows that using the existing site is not possible: major building modifications are required to incorporate the new plant into the production process. The company, however, already has an agreed building programme and the head of property is reluctant to get involved and commit his own budget, staff and resources. He was not party to the agreement of the action plan and is a 'latecomer' to the project. This could have been avoided if the property department had been involved at the outset, even if it was originally considered that no major building alterations were required.

It is essential that at a very early stage the required actions are understood and well thought through by all those likely to be involved. The team needs to consider:

- existing financial and contractual commitments;

- the impact of diverting funds and resources on the main business of the organisation;

- the resources, time, people and finances likely to be required;

- the competencies of those people assigned tasks within the action plan. The business record of designers and contractors should be scrutinised before any contracts are awarded;

- how the plan can be fitted into the organisation's work with the minimum of disruption

- the priority to be given to the work (based on a risk assessment).

8:4.2.2.1 Input from the enforcement authorities and lawyers

Where enforcement action or litigation is possible then the views of both the enforcement authority and legal advisers should be borne in mind. In the case of serious accidents it is likely that the enforcement authority would wish to be party to the action plan. They should therefore be kept informed of the progress of the formulation of the action plan. In such cases, the involvement of the organisation's legal advisers is essential to ensure that nothing is done or said that might prejudice the organisation's legal defence. Having had sight of the action plan and satisfied themselves that it meets certain requirements, the enforcement authority may serve an improvement notice, in effect requiring the actions in the plan to be delivered.

However, the main purpose of undertaking the investigation is to prevent recurrence and action should not be unnecessarily delayed whilst awaiting the views of the enforcement authorities.

The new process for litigation, introduced by the Woolf Reforms (the new Civil Procedure Rules) allows little if any scope for delay or positioning (*see* **Chapter 9, section 9:6**). It was once held that responding to an accident in a positive sense (by undertaking remedial measures) would be tantamount to an admission of guilt and managers were often actively discouraged from being too hasty in their response. This situation never made sense and is to be avoided.

It is sometimes the case that enforcement action can be slow and protracted. In such cases it is advisable to be guided by the officers of the enforcement authority, where possible, in ascertaining their expectations of action following an accident. A good accident investigation, which focusses on root causes, however, should provide all the evidence that is required to determine what action should be undertaken. Delays in waiting for the enforcement authority to act should not prevent the action plan being formulated.

Once the management team has reviewed the investigators' findings and considered the nature of the underlying and immediate causes (*see* **Chapter 1**), it can draw up a list of actions. In the first instance this will be in very broad terms. The list can then be considered for resource and responsibility allocation after first agreeing on the sequence of work.

8:4.2.3 Agreeing on the sequence of work

The list of actions is only the start. It is important, especially in complex situations, to agree on the sequence in which the work should be undertaken. Where different departments or functions are involved there is a potential for conflict and the wasting of time, effort and resources if work is carried out in an unsynchronised and unco-ordinated manner.

For example, an accident involving equipment on a production line may require action in a number of areas. These might involve:

- the consideration of the design/specification of the equipment;

- making alterations or improvements in the system of work;

- the training of staff;

- making alterations to production scheduling.

It is, however, pointless for each of these tasks to be carried out at the same time. Changing the system of work and training staff will be a fruitless exercise if the consideration of the equipment issues results in a completely different design and operation. The system of work and the training need to be developed to accommodate the changes in the equipment specification. By understanding the processes required to bring about improvement, a suitable sequence of work can be decided upon.

8:4.2.4 Agreeing on responsibilities

This is frequently the stage where the management process falls down. The purpose of an action plan is to have a documented and monitored means to ensure the work is actually carried out and the improvements are evaluated and maintained. This cannot be achieved if the responsibilities for carrying out the work identified in the plan are not agreed. Recommendations may have been agreed by senior managers, even in a formal process, for example at a board meeting. However, unless responsibility is actually taken for delivering these recommendations, the required work will not be done. This is not a problem if the enforcement authority is involved, but in the majority of cases action plans will be developed without any involvement on the part of the enforcement authority. It is therefore essential that a robust approach is taken and named managers are held accountable for delivering the required and agreed actions.

In organisations which have well-demarcated departments, such as production, engineering, maintenance, facilities management, production, training, personnel (to name but a few), it may be fairly obvious where responsibilities lie for the actions that are required. Nevertheless, these should be considered in detail and the precise requirements agreed and documented.

This provides for two needs. The first is the simple need to have good organisation so that somebody is actually tasked with taking responsibility for defined deliverables, for example drafting a design specification with a manufacturer. The second is the ability to monitor the action plan and ensure that there is co-ordination and co-operation and that the required work will be achieved.

Co-ordination of the action plan should be the responsibility of the director accountable for health and safety at board level in a company and in the equivalent position in other organisations.

8:4.2.5 Agreeing on timetables

Once agreement has been reached on what needs to be done and who is responsible for achieving it, it has to be decided how long each part of the plan is going to take. The aim should be to agree a realistic schedule of work that makes allowance for available time and resources and takes into account the various tasks that have to be carried out. One essential feature of the timetable process is the consideration of financial and human resources that are required. These will need to be 'released', usually from other areas of work, most of which may already be planned. The agreement of the timetable, therefore, also takes into account the commitment of others to release resources at the appropriate time to ensure the work can be achieved.

8:4.2.6 Providing resources

All action plans require a commitment to do extra work. The work is extra simply because having an accident means that the events were not foreseen and planned for. Obviously the amount of resources required, mainly in terms of human time and finances, will depend on the particular accident and the findings of the investigation. However, it is likely that if significant root causes have been established, the amount of work required will be similarly significant.

One way of dealing with the unexpected demand for resources is to create a special working team to oversee or actually carry out the action plan. The creation of such a team is, of course, a drain upon resources and will have to be met by sacrifices elsewhere. In real terms this is often a problem and the need to dedicate resources, especially human ones, can cause the whole process to flounder. Where organisations have been successful in recovering from accidents it is because they have been able to redirect resources, often at a price, to ensure the necessary action is undertaken.

Resource considerations will involve:

- people – allocating staff with the right competencies for the tasks identified (in the action plan) and either back-filling with agency or short-term staff (with probably an implied short-term training cost); arranging overtime payments; considering special responsibility allowances (for example, temporary promotion whilst on the project);

- finances – identifying where major investment is required (and therefore considering things like borrowing, raising loans, arranging repayment schedules, extending insurance, etc.);

- the impact on normal business – deferring suppliers' schedules; slowing production runs; extending delivery times to customers;

- the impact on other projects – delaying expansion; postponing site developments; re-arranging project plans.

8:4.2.7 Evaluation and monitoring

It is important to ensure that as the action plan is being put together a process is created to ensure the outcomes of the plan can be evaluated and the results monitored. The deliverable outcomes in the plan will need to be SMART:

> **S**pecific
>
> **M**easurable
>
> **A**chievable
>
> **R**ealistic
>
> **T**imely

As the purpose of the plan is to ensure accident prevention by improving safety, it is important that this is measured. For example, redesigned equipment should be tested to ensure that it meets the requirements of the job, and that new or additional hazards have not been created. This can be evaluated by trialing the equipment before using it the workplace.

A similar approach can be adopted for revised systems of work or training to ensure that the system or the training actually does improve safety.

Once the new approach is shown to be effective, then it is important to ensure that it is monitored as part of the overall management systems approach. This can be achieved with techniques such as inspection, supervision and observation.

8:4.2.8 Drawing up the action plan

The action plan can only be drawn up properly when the other matters above have been resolved. In effect the plan is the place where all the agreements, resources and objectives are set down.

The action plan should be drawn up like a project plan. This will set out the overall objectives to be achieved, the individual tasks that need to be done to deliver these objectives, the persons who are responsible for each task, the resources allocated to each task and the order in which the tasks are to be done.

Key responsibilities should be identified. The key tasks should be listed in sequential order and the time allocated to each task noted. By doing this it is possible to set a series of indicators that can be reported on as the plan progresses. The plan can be shared widely so that everybody knows what is happening.

It is also imperative that the person with overall responsibility for safety in the organisation is able to monitor the plan and ensure that the objectives are being met.

A sample action plan is provided in **Figure 8:3**.

FIGURE 8:3 EXAMPLE ACTION PLAN

Action plan requirement	Task/lead	March	April	May	June	July	Aug	Date	Resources
Research new equipment	Head of R&D								
1	Contact suppliers	1							1 admin staff £50
2	Visit suppliers	12–24							3 prod technicians £400
3	Obtain test sample		15						Driver + transport £1,300
4	Test		20						2 prod techs + 3 line workers
Review production process	H Prod Eng								
1	Establish team		15						2 engs, 2 fitters, 1 systems designer £5,000
2	Brief team		20						
3	Set pilot protocol		20–30						
4	Run pilot			5–10					
5	Report findings			20					

Action plan requirement	Task/lead	March	April	May	June	July	Aug	Date	Resources
Trial production run	Prod Mgr								
1	Start run				1				4 prod workers 1 fitter
2	Check quality				5				OT @ £15/hr
3	Rerun				6				1 quality controller p/t
4	Check quality				7				
Agree acceptance	MD/CHAIR				20				
Convert whole plant	H Eng								Est. £150,000
Separate plan Ref ai/2									

This action plan shows a set of tasks that need to be completed to replace an item of production equipment that has proved to be unacceptable as a result of an accident. The plan shows that three main objectives have to be met: researching the market-place for new equipment; reviewing the production process to enable the new equipment to work in the factory and deliver the factory's product; and doing a trial run of the new equipment and the plan (as a separate project if accepted by the board) to convert the whole of the factory.

This plan does not include any training requirements or anything about consulting the workforce or communicating the plan, etc. These issues should really be covered in the plan to enable a full picture of 'what is required' to be shown and agreed. Resources have been earmarked for the project and estimated costs have been given (shown in the right-hand column). The responsibility for each phase is assigned in the 'Task/lead' column. The expected completion times are show by the solid bars, which also indicate the phases of the plan. The figures in the columns show the estimated number of days required to complete each task with the resources provided.

There are a number of IT products which can be used to draw up simple or complex action plans, assign resources and allow effective monitoring of the plan.

8:4.2.9 Relevance to companies listed on the London Stock Exchange

For significant accidents, the action plan is likely to form part of the reporting of risk control measures to the board of the company. This is particularly relevant to companies required to report on corporate governance to the LSE, and in organisations taking a similar approach to organisational management. A significant accident would be one involving a fatality or serious injury and one likely to lead to a large fine and a high claim for compensation, or one which results in a large revenue or capital loss to the company, such as a loss of production for several weeks or months, or loss of high-cost plant and premises.

The plan will demonstrate to the board the impact of the remedial works required to rectify the failures in safety management, and also point out the extent of the work involved. It is likely that the board would also have to authorise the expenditure involved in delivering the action plan. This is likely to be a key responsibility of the director appointed to take the lead on health and safety.

8:5 Ancillary matters

Ancillary matters are important issues that need to be dealt with, but are usually outside the investigation process and fall to appropriate managers to undertake. There are two main issues that need to be addressed:

1. dealing with claims and insurance matters;

2. communicating the accident findings to the workforce and other relevant parties.

8:5.1 Dealing with claims and insurance issues

Inevitably many accidents are going to give rise to insurance claims, personal injury claims and possibly liability disputes with suppliers and manufacturers. These need to be dealt with as separate issues to the accident investigation. It is important to ensure that the issues surrounding blame and liability do not detract from the central aim of the accident investigation. This is best achieved by the investigator only reporting factually.

The insurance and litigation issues rarely deal with underlying causation.

8:5.2 Communicating with the workforce

Everybody in the organisation will probably have some knowledge of the accident, if only through rumour and general gossip. It is important that they are provided with an understanding of the causes of the accident and what management intends to do as a result. If information has been provided early (*see* **section 8:4.1.5**), then a good basis will have been developed for communicating with the workforce on the issues raised by the accident and the final action plan.

In many cases it is likely that training in revised procedures or new processes and equipment will be required following an accident. It is important that employees understand why retraining is required or why processes and procedures have been altered.

The action plan itself may take some time to deliver, especially in complex situations where the corrective measures take months or sometimes years to be fully realised. For example, consider the long time it takes to replace railway track in the UK and install train protection devices.

The benefits of communicating fully and explicitly with the workforce include:

- maintaining a focus on health and safety management;

- supporting the development and maintenance of a good safety culture;

- ensuring that the reasons for the accident and the steps being taken as a result are not forgotten or put to one side. (Old ways of working will be reverted to if the new practices are not well established and supported.);

- demonstrating management's continuing commitment to health and safety;

- providing opportunities to obtain the views of the workforce by encouraging involvement in the safety management process, such as risk assessments, accident investigations and hazard spotting;

- demonstrating to the workforce that reporting accidents and near misses can have positive benefits and lead to safer and better working.

8:5.3 Communicating with other relevant parties

These include:

- the appropriate enforcement authority;

- manufacturers/suppliers;

- industry groups;

- trade unions.

8:5.3.1 The appropriate enforcement authorities

If the appropriate enforcement authority decides to investigate the accident, it may request a copy of the report and the action plan. This request will generally come as a letter asking for more details of the accident and what the organisation intends to do about the findings. Consideration needs to be given to how the accident and the action plan are explained to ensure that no misunderstandings arise. This is just as important if the enforcement authority has been involved in the development of the action plan as when it has had no real involvement. It helps set out the record of the organisation co-operating with the enforcement authority, which is something that the courts may take into account when reaching a decision.

8:5.3.2 Manufacturers/suppliers

Where an accident has involved equipment or plant it is likely that the manufacturer/supplier has been involved at some point. However, the equipment or plant may not in fact be implicated in the accident causation. In such cases, it is likely that the supplier/manufacturer will have been left in the dark as the investigators may not have informed them in detail of the findings. It is just as important for them to know that there is no problem with plant and equipment as it is to learn of failures. Information from an accident investigation can often be helpful to manufacturers in improving the design and specification process of their products. It can also be helpful in the development of user instructions and training programmes through the elimination of any ambiguities.

8:5.3.3 Industry groups

In order to ensure that the wider lessons are learnt, it is important that information derived from accident investigation is fed into the body of knowledge within a particular industry sector. This can be achieved through user groups, collaborative panels/committees and trade associations.

8:5.3.4 Trade unions

It is important that the representatives of the workforce understand the nature and type of accidents that are occurring and (more importantly) what is being done about it. They have a vital role to play in ensuring that lessons are learnt in a wider sense, both within an industry and across industry sectors. The information derived from an accident investigation can provide good material for the training of safety representatives. It also allows a more proactive role for health and safety committees.

Trade unions and other employee representatives should be involved in the investigation process. Ideally, the representatives should form part of the investigation team and be involved in all the decisions and actions of the investigators. However, this is not always possible and, in many situations, the representatives may not want to be totally involved, but prefer to undertake their own investigation. Subject to company policy and legal advice, the investigators should keep the employee representatives fully informed of progress with the investigation, including the development of the action plan.

The single and most important feature of the relationship between the investigation, the investigators and the employee representatives should be one of trust. In most situations it is important that the investigators be allowed to have control over the release and handling of information related to the accident. Involving the employee representative in the investigation process is best practice, but it can only be successful if the roles of the investigators and the nature of the information being developed is respected by those representing employees.

8:6 Post-accident risk assessment

The advantages of having a detailed accident investigation process are that a great deal of information is uncovered and a great deal is actually learnt about the risks. In effect, a thorough accident investigation is tantamount to undertaking a risk assessment. The accident itself exposes the whole safety management system, and reveals its areas of weakness and the actual nature of the risks involved in the work processes.

Before any work commences the risk assessment is generally carried out with foresight (in many situations, there is often no certain knowledge that a risk will lead to actual harm) and as such a considerable amount of judgemental prediction is required. Once an accident has occurred, the flaws in that judgement are revealed and the predictions are held open to question.

8:6.1 The legal requirements

Under the MHSWR, there is an explicit requirement for an organisation to have:

- identified the significant risks;

- assessed them;

- eliminated further risk where possible;

- at least to have developed and maintained control measures where elimination is not possible,

in order to prevent further harm to the health and safety of employees exposed to the risks whilst at work and to others who may be exposed to the risk arising out of or in connection with the work, such as visitors, contractors and members of the public. Furthermore, subject-specific regulations, for example the Noise at Work Regulations 1989, reinforce this requirement in relation to specific hazards.

Under reg.3(3) of the MHSWR, there is a requirement to review the risk assessment if:

[a] *there is a reason to suspect that it is no longer valid;*

or

[b] *there has been a significant change in the matters to which it relates; and where, as a result of any such review, changes to an assessment are required, the employer or self employed person concerned shall make them as it is necessary to do so.*

Although there is no *specific* requirement to do this after there has been an accident, the logical inference is that an accident indicates any risk assessment (relevant to the tasks being undertaken at the time of the accident) should be reviewed and therefore it is suggested best practice to do so.

Proposals have been suggested by the HSC that a specific requirement be brought into law making it a new duty to always undertake a review of the risk assessment whenever there has been an accident related to the work covered by the risk assessment.

Where a claim is being made for damages under the new Civil Procedure Rules (the Woolf Reforms), the protocols require the risk assessment prior to the accident and the risk assessment made *after* the accident to be presented.

8:6.2 Deciding what to act on

When considering the accident report the organisation's senior management needs to know if the accident is one that indicates something is seriously wrong with the management of safety in the organisation, or whether only minor corrections are required (if indeed any). In other words:

- is there reason to suspect the original risk assessment is no longer valid?

or

- have matters changed so much that changes in the risk assessment and the control measures which follow from it are required?

There are two possibilities arising from an accident indicating that the risk assessment has either:

1. not identified adequate control measures; or

2. that the control measures have not been adequately maintained.

However, it is also necessary to consider other aspects of risk, in particular:

- the acceptability of risk;
- the 'foreseeability' of risk.

8:6.2.1 The acceptability of risk

Under the HSWA there is a legal requirement to control risk so it is 'as low as is reasonably practicable', and, in common law terms, to have demonstrated due diligence (absence of negligence) in undertaking a duty of care to another (for example, as between an employer and its employees).

It is thus possible that the evidence from an accident investigation may demonstrate that the situation is within the 'as low as is reasonably practicable' boundary. That is to say that the accident is 'acceptable'. The accident merely confirms the findings of the risk assessment and indicates that the circumstances occurred as would be expected and that control measures were working reasonably well. No review of the risk assessment is therefore required and no remedial measures need be put in place.

Whilst this possibility should be borne in mind, experience shows that this is rarely, if ever, the case. The more general finding is that accident investigations tend to identify risks that have not been foreseen and control measures that have been inadequate.

The common law findings are not so strictly bound as those of statutory law, and it may sometimes be found that a duty of care has been breached without necessarily showing that all 'reasonably practicable' steps had not been taken to control the risk.

8:6.2.2 The 'foreseeability' of risk

A central issue for risk assessment is the concept of 'foreseeability'. That is to say, it is necessary to foresee what can *possibly* go wrong in order to develop adequate control measures. If an action or consequence is not foreseen then it is unlikely that any control measure would be put in place specifically to prevent it.

Thus, one of the first questions any accident investigation must answer is: 'does this investigation provide information about risks which are either new or which have been underestimated?'

If the answer to this question is 'yes', then clearly a fairly thorough and extensive review of the situation is required. In effect a risk assessment has to be undertaken utilising the new knowledge gained from the accident investigation.

In many cases it will probably be shown that, on reflection, the warning signs were there and the risks should have been foreseen. This has been a common finding in virtually all major disaster investigations such as Kings Cross, Piper Alpha, Flixborough, Chernobyl and Bhopal.

The significant findings generally show that insufficient attention had been given to identifying or recognising risks. With the benefit of hindsight all the dangerous situations and circumstances were foreseeable before the events took place. Thus, the problem has mostly been with the state and nature of the management systems responsible for identifying risks and predicting what could go wrong.

Once an accident has occurred the events and causes now go on the list of what is foreseeable. It is therefore extremely important that findings of the accident investigation are considered in terms of:

- how they influence decisions about immediate risks and working practices;

- how they indicate risks within the management system and the extent of latent defects and failures.

8:6.3 Practical considerations

The first question is: 'was there in fact a risk assessment covering the type of work being undertaken?' If the answer to this question is 'no', then clearly a risk assessment has to be completed anyway. Assuming that some sort of risk assessment had been undertaken, the accident investigation should give an insight into several if not all of the following:

- Were the actual hazards identified and known about?

  For example, a workman loses his leg after kneeling in cement for three and a half hours whilst laying a floor for his employer. The risk assessment had indicated the general slight risk of burns from cement. However, the workman, who was only wearing torn jeans tucked into Wellington boots, did not realise the harmful effects of the cement and only discovered the burns to his legs when he took his clothing off. As a result of his injuries one leg was amputated.

- Were the working practices understood and followed correctly?

  In the above example, the working practices should have included using a kneeling board and even a 'retarder' in the cement so that the job did not have to be done at speed. One of the reasons why the workman was kneeling in the cement was to ensure he could get a flat and level finish before the cement went off.

- Were the control measures suitable for the risks?

  Control measures in this example should have included adequate PPE to protect the skin, for example thick protective overalls, cement resistant boots and gloves.

- Were all the relevant human factors considered?

  Again, in the example above, the worker felt he had to kneel in the cement as he had been instructed to complete the work quickly before the cement went off. His approach was to consider the speed aspect rather than the safety one.

- Were the instructions for the work adequately communicated?

- Was the worker sufficiently competent to undertake the required tasks?

  These two questions are clearly linked. A more competent person probably does not need detailed information if they are familiar with equipment, substances and work processes. A less competent person will require much more explicit information. Competence is a product of experience, skills, knowledge and understanding. It is achieved on the job and with training. It is therefore necessary to ask if the training was adequate for the risk and the control measures associated with the tasks.

- Did the management systems for identifying and communicating risks actually work?

  In many cases the failure to fully understand (both on the part of management and individual workers) the process of risk assessment and the development of adequate control measures lies at the heart of many accidents.

- Was everybody likely to be exposed to the risk identified?

  An adequate risk assessment must take into account the actions and likely actions of everyone around the work site and those likely to come onto it. Were the human factors associated with this work situation understood? A full understanding of human factors is required and essential to successful risk assessment.

- Was a generic risk assessment used when a job-specific assessment should have been made instead?

  A risk assessment for confined spaces will need to be reviewed for each and every individual confined space. Although generic risk assessments can be used in some circumstances, it is important to ensure they are in fact relevant to the work being done.

- Did the control measures actually match the risk and the way the work was organised?

- Were engineering failures a result of not fully understanding the purpose of the equipment/plant/machine in the work process at the design stage?

- Had the risk in fact been identified earlier but no corrective action taken?

  This would indicate a communications failure in the management system itself.

- Was the approach to risk assessment too simplistic?

  A reach-truck driver dies not only because he had not been trained, although he had several years experience, but also the company had failed to see the risk involved in not maintaining racking and in not controlling safety. As a result, when the truck driver hit racking at the company's premises it fell on him and killed him.

- Was the risk assessment or the risks themselves just ignored?

  An electrical contractor for a local authority dies after touching live wires in a concealed position that the authority knew about. However, the authority failed to either inform the electrician or provide safeguards, even though there had been a fatality in similar circumstances five years earlier.

9 | Legal Processes

Issues discussed in this chapter:

- Procedures in criminal cases
- Powers of HSE inspectors
- Police involvement
- Interviews conducted under caution by HSE inspectors or the police
  - The right to legal advice
  - The caution
- The involvement of solicitors
- Civil claims and 'duty of care'
- Procedures in civil cases – the Woolf Reforms
- Procedures involving fatalities
- Enforcement notices

9:1 Introduction

Organisations, their employees, the self-employed and others may find themselves facing litigation in the criminal courts where an accident is perceived as resulting from a breach of statutory health and safety legislation.

Actions are normally instigated by the HSE, local authorities and/or the police (the Crown Prosecution Service). Organisations convicted face substantial fines, whilst individuals face both substantial fines and imprisonment.

Action in the civil courts may be brought against organisations and individuals (the defendants) by other organisations and individuals (the plaintiffs) where the plaintiff claims that they have suffered loss or injury through the defendant's failure to exercise their 'duty of care'.

9:2 Considerations for the employer and his legal advisers facing prosecution

Employers facing a prosecution should always obtain professional advice because of the increasing gravity with which the courts are viewing breaches of health and safety. In particular, the employer will need to seek advice and, using that advice, attempt to resolve the following issues as preparation for deciding whether or not to plead guilty and in preparation for any trial or making submissions to a court to persuade it to be lenient.

Matters to be considered will include:

- obtaining full disclosure of the prosecution evidence, including witness statements, photographs of the scene, tapes or notes of interviews, other relevant materials and documents seized by the investigating officers during any search;

- consideration of the prosecution statements. Can the evidence of any of the prosecution witnesses be accepted? Are there inaccuracies? Is the evidence fair?

- gathering any further evidence. For example, do any witnesses need to be interviewed who have not been seen by the enforcement authority? Are there any other relevant documents or papers that should be examined by the legal advisers?

- finding out whether the offences alleged against the employer are to be admitted or denied. This decision will ultimately need to be made by the employer itself with some guidance from its legal advisers as to the likelihood of success if either option is taken;

- where the employer would prefer the case to be heard – a magistrates' court or the Crown Court?

- deciding if any expert evidence is required;

- what steps, if any, have to be taken to address the deficiencies exposed by the incident under review. It must be remembered that if a defence is not successful or if the employer pleads guilty, it will not bode well for the employer if he has done nothing to remedy the problem or factors giving rise to the incident. This is the case even if the offence is vigorously denied; the mere fact that the authorities are investigating may lead to a re-evaluation of risk assessments where appropriate;

- deciding if an independent audit of the company's procedures is required. It may be that the investigation establishes that the employer does not have the necessary skills and experience within its organisation to assess health and safety risks. It may therefore be advisable to instruct outside consultants to evaluate health and safety issues, and indeed insurers may be concerned to see this happen to allow them to evaluate the future risk and then require the employer to take action to reduce it;

- the state of the company's finances. Are up-to-date accounts available? This may be important when making submissions on the appropriate size of the fine;

- whether or not details of the company's general safety record are accurate and/or available. An employer who is under investigation for a particular offence should be aware that if an inspector discovers some other area where there is non-compliance he may take action in respect of this breach, irrespective of the circumstances under which he became aware of it. Therefore, the employer is wise to undertake a careful review of the documentation in his possession whether it is relevant or not to the current investigation, and ensure that it is brought up to date.

The above list is by no means exhaustive and the requirements will vary according to each individual case. Plainly there will be some prosecutions that can be contested. In others there may be scope to negotiate a reduction in the number of summonses to be admitted. In other cases the merits of entering an early and timely guilty plea will be immediately evident. Each case will depend on its own circumstances. Careful and comprehensive preparation is the key and the advantages of the early involvement of legal advisers cannot be overemphasised.

9:3 Procedures in criminal cases

9:3.1 Commencement of prosecutions

Once the enforcement authority has completed its investigation and it believes that a breach of the regulations has occurred a decision on whether or not to prosecute is taken. There are two principal considerations.

1. Does the evidence obtained provide a realistic prospect of conviction?

2. Is it in the public interest to prosecute?

A prosecution is commenced by the prosecuting authority laying an 'information' (a brief outline of the offence and provision breached) before the appropriate magistrates' court and requesting a summons. For summary-only offences there is a time limit of six months, which runs from the date of the incident to the date the information is laid at court. By virtue of s.34 of the HSWA this period can be extended if a special report or enquiry has been directed (s.14 of the HSWA) or a coroner's inquest is being held. There is no time limit for either-way or indictable-only offences.

Once a magistrates' court has issued a summons it can be served on a defendant. The summons must give the details of the date and place of the offence and the provision alleged to have been contravened. It will also be endorsed with the date, time and place of hearing. The validity of the service of legal documents is not always a straightforward issue, but in most cases the summons is likely to be served on the registered office of the company, as this is publicly available through Companies House. For other types of business, delivery to the usual place of business will be sufficient.

On receipt of the summons, the employer should seek legal advice on how to proceed if lawyers are not already involved. The arguments for instructing solicitors and general advice on whom to instruct are discussed in **section 9:4.9.1**. Provision for legal advice may be available as part of the employer's liability insurance. In any event it may be a term of the employer's liability insurance to notify the insurer. This will help a defendant to make an informed decision about plea and procedural matters. The basic procedure will vary depending on whether the plea is guilty or not guilty, and the type of offence committed (summary, either way or indictable).

9:3.2 Disclosure

The employer is entitled to certain information from the prosecution by the provisions of common law and the Criminal Procedure and Investigations Act 1996 (CPIA). The CPIA is supplemented by regulations and a code of practice that apply to all those who investigate offences and therefore the HSE and local authorities. The CPIA requires the prosecution to undertake initial disclosure of any material within its possession that may undermine the prosecution's case against the employer. If it is not possible to make copies of the material, then the prosecution must make it available for inspection by the employer. The CPIA contains provisions allowing the employer to apply for a court order to force the prosecution to disclose relevant information where the employer believes that full disclosure has not taken place. In addition to the CPIA, there are provisions in common law requiring the prosecution to make the evidence which they intend to rely on in court available to the employer, including witness statements, relevant objects, photographs and videos. There may be some reticence on the part of the prosecution in releasing this information, but if it is not forthcoming, then it should be applied for in writing from the prosecution. Opinions differ as to whether the entitlement to disclosure extends to copies of the statements or just to an outline of the allegation. Statements are normally provided and therefore it is not normally an issue.

9:3.3 The defence statement

Where a defendant is charged with an indictable offence (or offence triable either way and he is tried on indictment) he is required to provide the prosecution with a defence statement. The defence statement sets out in general terms the nature of his defence, indicates the matters where he takes issue with the prosecution and the reasons why he takes issue with the prosecution. The employer may choose whether or not to serve a defence statement on the prosecution in summary-only offences (or offences triable either way that proceed to summary trial). The purpose of the defence statement is to concentrate the mind of both the employer and the prosecution and therefore save time in court. The advantage for the employer in serving the defence statement is that the prosecution must then provide any further relevant disclosure that could undermine the prosecution's case in the light of the points at issue outlined in the defence statement.

9:3.4 The decision of the plea

The case may need to be adjourned for the provision of disclosure, experts' reports and the like to enable a decision on the plea to be reached. If the plea is guilty and the offence is either a summary offence or an either-way offence that the magistrates feel they have sufficient power to sentence, then the case is likely to be concluded on the occasion the guilty plea is entered. The magistrates would hear details of the allegation, the mitigation (i.e. the factors that should encourage the magistrates to be lenient) and then decide on a penalty.

If the magistrates decide their powers of sentence are not sufficient, they will commit the case to the Crown Court for sentence. The hearing at the Crown Court is likely to take place within three to four weeks.

If the plea is not guilty and the case is a summary-only matter, it will be adjourned for a trial. If it is an either-way offence the court has to decide whether the trial should take place in the magistrates' court or the Crown Court. Complexity, seriousness and powers of sentence are the most important considerations at this stage.

The prosecution and the employer are entitled to make representations concerning where the trial should take place. If the magistrates decide they can deal with the trial, then the defendant has a choice either to consent to summary trial or to elect trial at the Crown Court. It is generally thought the chances of an acquittal at the Crown Court are better, but penalties imposed on conviction are more significant. In any event the employer has a right of appeal to the Crown Court from the magistrates' court for a complete rehearing. However, the rehearing is not before a jury and therefore much of the advantages of the Crown Court are lost. The merits of such a decision will depend on the individual circumstances of each case. If the trial is to take place at the Crown Court, then the magistrates will send the case to the Crown Court. This will extend the length of the case by a number of months.

Where an incident occurs in the workplace it is likely that more than one breach of health and safety legislation will be alleged. This is because health and safety legislation is so widely drafted. Often the prosecution will bring summonses alleging a number of offences and this may provide scope for negotiating pleas, or 'plea bargaining'. It may well be that the prosecution will be content for guilty pleas to just some of the offences in return for not proceeding with the others. Alternatively, the prosecution, whilst not expressly accepting the pleas, may decide it is not in the public interest to have a trial if the employer does not accept an offence, when guilty pleas to other matters have already been entered.

9:3.5 Costs

The general rule is that costs follow the event. Therefore, a convicted party, whether the conviction followed a guilty plea or a trial, will have to pay the costs of the prosecution in addition to any other penalty imposed by the court. Costs are at the discretion of the court, but will normally be awarded in health and safety cases if the means of the employer permit. The prosecution's costs include the investigation costs provided they are reasonably incurred. A schedule of costs will usually be served at court. If the costs are substantial a schedule should be served in advance of the hearing to enable representations to be made in response to the schedule.

9:3.6 Will an attendance be necessary?

It is possible for some cases to be concluded without the need to attend court. Ordinarily, this would be the case only for minor offences where a guilty plea is entered. The court is also likely to excuse attendance for preliminary hearings where the case is going to be adjourned. For more serious matters and for trials, attendance will be required. However, the writer is of the view that, save for preliminary hearings, attendance is desirable. Apart from anything else it is likely to give the impression to the court that the individual or company is treating the matter with an appropriate degree of seriousness.

9:3.7 Appeals

If the decision of the court goes against the employer either as to guilt or as to the severity of the punishment imposed, then the employer may wish to consider whether or not an appeal against the decision is possible. An appeal will not be available in all cases and the recommendations of the employer's legal advisers should be sought before incurring costs on futile appeals. The procedure to be followed and the grounds upon which an appeal may be based will vary between the relevant courts. The detailed provisions and requirements are very complex and beyond the scope of this chapter. However, the most common appeals are on the grounds that the jury was misdirected by the judge as to some relevant factor (most commonly the law), but there are many other grounds that may be available in particular circumstances. An employer may appeal to the Crown Court from the magistrates' court as of right (s.108 of the Magistrates Court Act 1980) to have the entire case heard again before the Crown Court. The Divisional Court (basically a civil court) may also have a role to play in some appeals where the employer's grievance is that it believes the court to have acted beyond its powers or to have been biased. In such cases the appeal is described as a judicial review of the decision made. Due to the complexity of appeals and the multiplicity of options available to the employer, it is strongly advised to seek the advice of its lawyers before proceeding with the appeal.

9:4 Who are the enforcement authorities and what powers do they have?

9:4.1 The Health and Safety Commission

The Health and Safety Commission (HSC) has overall responsibility for the development of health and safety policy, subject to initiatives of the Secretary of State for Work and Pensions. The HSC is a tripartite body appointed by the Secretary of State. It consists of a chairman and between six to nine members (six being the minimum and nine being the maximum). The three parts (hence tripartite) that form the HSC represent employees, employers and other third parties involved in either promoting or enforcing health and safety matters. It follows that three members are appointed after consultation with employers' organisations, a further three after consultation with employees' organisations and the final three after consulting local authorities and other professional bodies and organisations.

The HSC is under a general duty to further the objectives of Pt. 1 of the HSWA. This includes the general duties owed by employers to employees. It also has further specific duties in respect of research into health and safety issues and the provision of training and information in relation to this purpose. It is required to provide an information service and must make proposals for regulations that it deems appropriate. Finally, it must produce a plan for the performance of its functions.

Pursuant to s.14 of the HSWA, the HSC has powers to order the Health and Safety Executive (HSE) to carry out an investigation into an accident. The purpose of the investigation must be the enforcement of the duties under Pt. 1 of the HSWA, which include the general duties described above or for the purposes of determining whether there is a need for further regulations. Section 14 also allows the HSC to direct the HSE to hold an inquiry where an inquiry is ordered, rather than an investigation.

9:4.2 The Health and Safety Executive

Health and safety at work legislation is enforced on a day-to-day level by two bodies: the Health and Safety Executive (HSE) and the relevant local authority. Procedures apply such that there is little scope for overlap of function, but where a particular issue or site falls under the remit of both enforcement bodies, procedures for deciding which authority shall have competence come into consideration.

The HSE was created by s.10 of the HSWA. It is a body corporate and therefore is considered in the eyes of the law to be a person. It consists of three full-time members who are appointed by the HSC with the approval of the Secretary of State. These are the equivalent of directors of a company. They have the power to appoint officers and servants. The functions of the HSE, its officers and servants are performed on behalf of the Crown.

The duties of the HSE include:

- appointing HSE inspectors and indemnifying those inspectors for honest mistakes;

- enforcing duties provided under the HSWA and other legislation;

- carrying out certain functions or duties on behalf of the HSC such as health and safety research, education and publicity concerning health and safety at work;

- publishing guidance notes and advisory literature, which are divided into different series:

  - Best Practice Means (BPM);

  - Chemical Safety (CS);

  - Environmental Hygiene (EH);

  - General Series (GS);

  - Health and Safety Regulations series (HSR);

  - Health and Safety Guidance series (HSG);

  - Industry General leaflets (INDG);

  - Medical Series (MS);

  - Methods for the Determination of Hazardous Substances (MDHS);

  - Plant and Machinery (PM);

- representing the UK in health and safety matters within the EU and other international forums, such as the World Health Organisation and the International Labour Organisation.

The HSE has seven regional offices (Cardiff, Luton, London, Birmingham, Leeds, Manchester and Edinburgh) and approximately 30 other offices (*see* **Appendix 5**).

Section 18 of the HSWA sets out which authority is responsible for enforcement of the relevant statutory provisions. The primary duty is on the HSE except to the extent that some other authority or authorities are made responsible for enforcement. Under s.18(4) every local authority must make adequate provision for the enforcement within its area of the statutory provisions for which it is the enforcement authority, and must perform the duty in accordance with guidance provided to it by the HSE.

9:4.3 HSE or local authority?

The Health and Safety (Enforcing Authority) Regulations 1998 provides for the division of responsibilities between the HSE and local authorities. The general rule is if the activity in question is specified in Schedule 1 (summarised in **section 9:4.4**) of the 1998 Regulations and the premises in question are non-domestic, then the local authority is the enforcement authority. In all other cases it is the HSE. There are also other detailed provisions that reverse the general rule in certain circumstances and state that the HSE shall be the enforcement authority. These provisions are designed to prevent conflicts of interest arising (for example, where the premises are occupied by a county council). They also recognise that the HSE is best placed to regulate certain specialist activities (for example, work with sources of ionising radiation) and therefore where such activities take place, the HSE becomes the enforcement authority instead of the local authority.

As stated above, the HSE tends to take responsibility for workplaces in which there are greater health and safety risks, or specialist knowledge about health and safety is required. For example, the HSE is responsible for mines and quarries, whereas local authorities are responsible for office buildings. It follows that HM Health and Safety Inspectors can, if they choose, specialise in certain work activities that occur on premises, such as:

- factories;

- construction sites;

- railways;

- mines and quarries;

- gas, water and electricity installations;

- national government offices;

- farms;

- offshore industries;

- major onshore hazards;

- nuclear installations;

- hospitals;

- educational establishments, e.g. schools, colleges and universities.

9:4.4 The responsibilities of local authorities

An environmental health officer (EHO) of a particular council usually performs the enforcement responsibilities for the local authority. Local authorities are generally the enforcement authority for:

- offices;

- retail and wholesale businesses;

- hotels;

- residential accommodation;

- catering facilities;

- leisure industries;

- work activities at sports and leisure events/facilities;

- work activities in places of worship.

If the offices are part of a complex on site with, for example, manufacturing activity being undertaken, then it is likely that the

HM Health and Safety Inspector from the HSE responsible for enforcement in the manufacturing plant will also take responsibility for the offices. If there is any doubt at all as to who is the enforcement authority, check with the nearest HSE office. The powers of a Health and Safety Inspector are the same for an EHO.

9:4.5 Other inspectors

Other inspections may be carried out by fire officers in connection with the precautions for protecting the workplace against fire and ensuring there are reasonable arrangements in place for raising the alarm and evacuating the building. Certain categories of building require a fire certificate before they may be occupied.

The Environment Agency (EA) has powers associated with investigating and preventing pollution to land, and controlled water and air, covering everything from emissions from boiler flues into the atmosphere to waste disposal, although in the context of office accommodation these powers are devolved to local authorities for enforcement by EHOs in a manner analogous to that for health and safety *vis-à-vis* HSE and local authority enforcement. Of course, a spill may have impacts on both employees and the environment and any response by the EA to the spill must take into account the impact on health and safety. It follows that in such situations the enforcement authorities should act in concert to protect the environment and also to safeguard employees. Equally, an employer may ultimately face liability for breaches of environmental law in addition to liability for breaches of health and safety law arising out of the same incident.

9:4.6 The powers of inspectors

Under s.19(1) of the HSWA enforcement authorities may appoint such suitably-qualified persons as they think necessary to act as inspectors. Inspectors are appointed by written instrument and this instrument specifies the powers that an inspector can exercise. He cannot act outside of these powers. When an inspector is either exercising or seeking to exercise any of the powers conferred upon him and he is asked to produce his instrument of appointment, he must either produce it or a duly authenticated copy of it. Therefore, in certain circumstances it may be necessary to examine the document appointing the inspector to confirm that he has the relevant authority to exercise the power he proposes to use. However, care should be taken in exercising this right as ultimately an inspector with the appropriate authority may be brought into the investigation, so at best the tactic will buy a little time and at worst raise suspicion and give rise to bad feeling. This is not to say that if an inspector attempts to exceed the powers set out in s.20 of the HSWA, it is not proper to question the appropriateness of his actions. Essentially, the actions of the inspector should be relevant to the investigation he is undertaking and/or part of an inspection of compliance with general health and safety laws for which the competent authority which appointed him has authority. The powers of inspectors are wide-ranging and are akin to those of the police in the investigation of a crime. They are set out in s.20 of the HSWA.

Provided the inspector is seeking to enforce any of the relevant statutory provisions within the responsibility of the authority that appointed him, and subject to his instrument of appointment, he can exercise any of the following powers under s.20 of the HSWA:

- at any reasonable time, to enter any premises which he has reason to believe it is necessary for him to enter for the purpose of carrying into effect any of the relevant statutory provisions within the field of responsibility of the enforcement authority;

- to take with him a police constable if he has reasonable cause to apprehend any serious obstruction in the execution of his duty;

- to take with him (1) any person duly authorised by his enforcement authority; and (2) equipment or materials required for any purpose for which the power of entry is being exercised;

- to make such examination and investigation as may be necessary to carry into effect any of the relevant statutory provisions within the field of responsibility of the enforcement authority;

- as regards any premises which he has power to enter, to direct that those premises or any part of them, or anything therein, shall be left undisturbed for so long as is reasonably necessary for any examination or investigation in accordance with the previous paragraph;

- to take such measurements, photographs or recordings as he considers necessary for the purposes of the investigation or examination;

- to take samples of any articles or substances found in any premises which he has power to enter, and of the atmosphere in or in the vicinity of any such premises, to dismantle any article or test any substance;

- to cause an article or substance to be dismantled or to be subjected to any process or test provided that the purpose is the carrying into effect any of the relevant statutory provisions within the field of responsibility of the enforcement authority and provided that the article or substances appear to the inspector to have caused or to be likely to cause a danger to health and safety;

- to take possession of any article or substance that appears to have caused or to be likely to cause a danger to health and safety for either further examination, for preservation in its current state (to prevent tampering) or in order to produce it as evidence in any relevant proceedings;

- to require any person whom he has reasonable cause to believe to be able to give information relevant to any examination or investigation, to answer such questions as the inspector thinks fit, to ask and to sign a declaration of the truth of his answers;

- to require the production of, inspect and take copies of, any books or documents either required to be kept under relevant health and safety regulations or any other books or documents which it is necessary for him to see for the purposes of any examination or inspection;

- to require any person to afford him such facilities and assistance within that person's control as are necessary;

- any other power for the purpose of enforcing any of the relevant statutory provisions.

9:4.6.1 The provision of evidence

The employer should note in particular the inspector's powers to compel any person who he has reasonable cause to believe to be able to give information relevant to any examination or investigation to answer such questions as the inspector thinks fit to ask and to sign a declaration of the truth of his answers. This is a rather draconian power. However, it should be noted that under s.20 of the HSWA any answer given by a person in response to a requirement being imposed by an inspector to answer the question is inadmissible as evidence against that person or the husband or wife of that person in any proceedings. Further, it should be noted that s.20 could not require an employer to disclose any documents that would be covered by legal professional privilege. This means that correspondence between the employer and his legal advisers would not have to be disclosed to the inspector nor would any documents relating to an investigation or preparation of statements, including expert witness statements created in response to a request from the employer's legal advisers. If the employer has any doubt over the right of the inspector to see these documents, then the employer should withhold them until he has spoken to his legal advisers. The employer would be advised to do this urgently.

9:4.6.2 The powers of the police on entry

It should be noted that although the inspector may authorise a police officer to accompany him if he fears that he may be obstructed by any person in the performance of his duties, this does not affect the powers of the police to enter premises in their own right under separate statutory provisions. The relevant provisions are complex and beyond the scope of this work.

9:4.7 Police involvement

9:4.7.1 General position

The police's involvement in the enforcement of health and safety legislation can occur on two levels: either as the principal investigative authority or in support of the HSE. The situation with regard to fatalities in the workplace is discussed in **section 9:7**. If general criminal offences as opposed to offences covered by health and safety legislation come to light during an investigation (for example, a fraudulent insurance claim), then the police are the relevant authority to investigate and will assist the Crown Prosecution Service if the matter develops into a prosecution. The HSE is likely to stay involved to deal with health and safety issues.

The police can support the HSE in the way outlined in **section 9:4.6** as a result of an inspector exercising his power under s.20 of the HSWA, namely to take with him a police constable if he has reasonable cause to apprehend any serious obstruction in the execution of his duty. An inspector can therefore call upon the services of a police constable if serious obstruction is anticipated or experienced. Continued obstruction either of the inspector, a police constable or both, is likely to constitute the criminal offences of obstructing an inspector or obstructing a police officer in the execution of his duties.

9:4.7.2 HSE, police and Crown Prosecution Service protocol for liaison

9:4.7.2.1 Background

A protocol has been agreed between the HSE, the Association of Chief Police Officers and the Crown Prosecution Service (CPS) in relation to work-related deaths in England and Wales where the HSE is the enforcement authority. (A protocol is planned where the local authority is the enforcement authority but currently local liaison agreements exist.) The reason behind the protocol is to ensure effective liaison between the three bodies as each have different responsibilities in relation to work-related deaths.

Moreover, the HSE is responsible for enforcement of health and safety at work (s.18 of the HSWA), but has no power to prosecute general criminal offences such as manslaughter. The police are responsible for investigating crimes in general and to recommend prosecution of offenders to the CPS. The police will also have an interest in establishing the circumstances surrounding a work-related death in order to assist the coroner for the purpose of the inquest (*see* **section 9:7.2**). It should also be noted that other authorities could also become involved, such as the Environment Agency, a fire officer (where there is suspected arson) and the coroner's officer. The CPS reviews the evidence and decides if there is a realistic prospect of a conviction and, if so, whether a prosecution is justified in the public interest.

9:4.7.2.2 The initial procedure

Where there is a work-related death, or a strong likelihood that one will result, a police detective of supervisory rank should attend the scene and:

- make an initial assessment as to whether the circumstances might justify a charge of manslaughter, or another serious general criminal offence. If this is the case, the police will commence their investigation;

- where the HSE is the enforcement authority, confirm that the death or injury has been notified to the HSE by the quickest practical means;

- liase with the HSE either to inform them that the police will be investigating or, if the initial investigations indicate that no police investigation is necessary, to discuss arrangements for preserving the scene and the nature of the assistance that the police are able to provide to the HSE investigation.

9:4.7.2.3 The investigation

As a general rule, the police will investigate the matter where there is evidence or a suspicion of a deliberate intent or gross negligence or recklessness on the part of an individual or company as opposed to human error or carelessness. Where the police investigate, the HSE is to provide technical support to the police and is to continue investigating possible health and safety offences.

The HSE should not commence any prosecution until the police and CPS have reached a decision on whether or not they will prosecute. If the decision is that a charge of manslaughter, corporate manslaughter, or any other serious offence cannot be justified, then the HSE will conclude its own investigation into potential health and safety offences.

Where the police indicate that they do not intend to investigate at an early stage the investigation will be held by the HSE. The HSE can seek the assistance of the police and can refer the matter back to them or the CPS if they find evidence indicating that an offence of manslaughter has been committed.

9:4.7.2.4 Decisions to prosecute

The protocol suggests that the police should always seek the advice of the CPS in relation to charging an individual with manslaughter and must consult them when consideration is being given to charging a company with corporate manslaughter. If it decides not to prosecute, it should quickly inform the HSE so that it may expedite proceedings of health and safety offences. There are also detailed provisions with regard to consultation and liaison between the HSE, police and CPS depending on who is the investigating and prosecuting authority, and the provisions of that deal with the retention and disclosure of material obtained during the course of an investigation.

9:4.8 Interviews

9:4.8.1 The Police and Criminal Evidence Act 1984

The Police and Criminal Evidence Act 1984 (PACE) is the major piece of legislation that deals with police powers in the investigation of offences and also contains provisions relating to the collection of evidence in criminal proceedings.

Section 66 of the PACE provides that the Secretary of State can issue and amend codes of practice setting down the detailed requirements placed on the police when investigating a criminal offence. The codes of practice cover a wide range of issues including searches, the conduct of police interviews, conditions of detention whilst under arrest and the right to have legal advice. Section 67 of PACE provides that persons other than police officers who are charged with the duty of investigating offences or charging offenders shall in the discharge of that duty have regard to any relevant provisions of the codes. Therefore, HM Health and Safety Inspectors and environmental health officers must have regard to the codes when investigating health and safety offences.

9:4.8.2 Code C

A number of codes have been issued, the most relevant of which is Code C – the code of practice for the detention, treatment and questioning of persons by police officers. Code C runs to 46 printed pages and includes five annexes, has guidance notes and is continually being updated.

As discussed in **section 9:4.8.1**, by virtue of s.67 of PACE, inspectors must comply with the Code when interviewing persons about suspected health and safety offences. The Code provides protection to those suspected of committing an offence. It applies to any questioning by inspectors in interviews whether the alleged offence or offences are committed by a corporate entity (in which case an individual will require authority to speak on behalf of the entity) or an individual. Interviews may be conducted in person or through written correspondence. In either case, the same rules apply.

9:4.8.2.1 The right to legal advice

Section 6 of the Code provides for a person at any time to consult and communicate privately with a solicitor, whether in person, in writing or by telephone.

An employer is strongly advised to take legal advice before attending an interview under caution either with the police or an inspector. Where the inspector suggests that the interview take place immediately, the employer should not be persuaded to proceed without taking legal advice. This may happen during an inspection where the inspector discovers a breach of laws and wishes to conduct a formal taped interview under caution immediately. This has the advantage for the inspector that the employer's comments, if made under caution, can be used in evidence against him in any proceedings whereas if the inspector relies on his powers under s.20 to ask questions, then any replies from the employer cannot be used in evidence against the employer.

If the interview is taking place at the police station, then an individual may be entitled to free legal advice from a solicitor paid for by the legal aid board depending on the severity of the offence. The advice is not means tested but is limited to advising whilst at the police station itself. It will not cover any subsequent consultations or advice in respect of any proceedings. The solicitor's firm will have to be registered with the legal aid board in order to claim payment and payment is limited to legal aid board rates. A corporate body will not be entitled to the advice and it is likely that in most cases the employer's usual solicitor will not be registered with the legal aid board and therefore some arrangement as to remuneration must be made.

Interviews with inspectors will normally take place at their offices and will be tape-recorded. Inspectors are usually amenable to arranging the interview at the convenience of all parties, including the solicitor.

9:4.8.2.2 The caution

The interview forms part of a criminal investigation, which may ultimately lead to proceedings being taken against the employer. The interview is a crucial evidence-gathering phase of the investigation. In order that the interviewee is completely aware how seriously the court will take their statements in the interview they must be cautioned. It follows therefore that what is, or is not, said in the interview can have a significant effect on subsequent proceedings.

Interviews under caution should not be confused with a statement taken by an inspector under s.20 of the HSWA (*see* **section 9:4.8**).

It is a matter of discretion for the inspector as to who to interview under caution. As a rule, an interview under caution is appropriate when questioning a suspect about his involvement or suspected involvement in an offence. In practice, both a statement under s.20 and an interview under caution can be obtained from the same person. However, it is arguable that there is little to be gained by the inspector in questioning the employer in detail using his powers under s.20 if there is a distinct likelihood that the enforcement authorities will charge the employer with an offence.

The interview is voluntary in the sense that the inspector does not have the power to arrest and detain for the purposes of an interview. It is rarely advisable to refuse to be interviewed, but whether or not an interviewee chooses to give responses to questions is a different matter entirely. Legal advice should always be sought in this regard.

The wording of the caution is as follows:

> *You do not have to say anything, but it may harm your defence if you do not mention when questioned something, which you later rely on in court. Anything you do say may be given in evidence.*

The caution does not have to be word perfect, but it must convey the message contained therein. If the interviewee claims that they were not cautioned correctly, then the admissibility of the evidence will be questioned. Ultimately, the court will take the decision as to whether or not the message got across. If a break is taken part way through the interview, then the caution must be repeated once the interview starts again. Each person present is also required to identify themselves on tape or their names must be recorded in the contemporaneous notes.

There are three parts to the caution:

1. 'You do not have to say anything' – a suspect has a right to silence and therefore does not commit an offence by refusing to answer questions. However, it is interesting to note that it would be an offence for the employer not to answer a question put by the inspector pursuant to his power under s.20 of the HSWA. However, it would appear that a challenge under the Human Rights Act 1998 might be possible (depending on the question asked) and for that reason it would be surprising if it were enforced in this way.

Whether it is advisable to say nothing depends on the circumstances and is one of the reasons why legal advice should be sought in all cases. In very general terms, it would be advisable to remain silent if the evidence the inspector holds does not reveal any offence to have been committed, whereas to provide responses during the interview would. The other situation where refusal to answer questions may be reasonable is where the inspector has not given the employer or its advisers access to the information leading to the interview being undertaken. Legal advice should always be sought.

2. 'But it may harm your defence if you do not mention when questioned something which you later rely on in court' – this warning means that if a suspect is questioned about something and remains silent about a fact that he later seeks to rely on in court, the court could draw a negative inference from the fact it was not mentioned in the interview under caution. It is therefore normally advisable to provide an account in interview if there is a defence to any prospective criminal charges. To do otherwise may give rise to difficulties at court.

3. 'Anything you do say may be given in evidence' – this means that the interview can be used in proceedings. An accurate record of the interview must be made whether it is by means of tape recording or contemporaneous notes (in which case the interviewee will have the opportunity to read the notes and sign them to confirm their accuracy). Equally, the interviewee is entitled to a copy of the tapes or notes made. This is particularly useful in the case of tapes, where the police or inspector will often provide a transcript for the purpose of the proceedings. It is always advisable to have the transcript provided by the police or inspector checked against the original tapes for errors in transcription.

9:4.9 Interview practicalities

Usually the request for an interview under caution will only be made after the inspector has collected evidence about the incident under review from eyewitnesses and other persons. We have already considered the extensive powers given to inspectors under s.20 of the HSWA. It is worth noting that any person required under s.20 of the HSWA to give information relevant to an examination or investigation to the enforcement authority is allowed to have present a person nominated by him whom the inspector may allow to be present. In due course – and sometimes after several weeks – the inspector may invite a representative of the employer (where it is a company or partnership) to be interviewed on the employer's behalf. The investigating authority will wish to establish that the individual nominated is authorised to speak on the company or partnership's behalf. By definition, that person is likely to be a senior employee or director of the company, and often the person primarily responsible for the management of health and safety. The selection of that representative will be critical and must be very carefully considered.

Normally the date and venue of the caution interview can be negotiated with the investigating authority and sometimes it is possible to obtain a list of the questions to be put or, failing that, some indication from the investigating officer of the topics to be covered.

It is open to the individual employer or corporate entity to decline to attend an interview under caution and the inspector has no power to compel attendance at such an interview. The only exceptions to this rule are serious criminal charges, such as manslaughter or causing grievous bodily harm, where the police may force attendance at the interview with the threat of arrest. However, occasions when refusal is an appropriate course of action may be rare, as the interview under caution provides an opportunity to put the employer's case at an early stage. Even in circumstances where the prosecution evidence is believed to be overwhelming and thus the prospect of successfully defending such a prosecution is assessed to be negligible, the interview can nonetheless be used as a vehicle to make valid points in mitigation. It may be that as a consequence of lessons learned from the accident, the employer has taken timely remedial action and the interview under caution can provide an opportunity to volunteer what response has been made to the accident. This may have the effect of encouraging the inspector not to lay charges or to lay lesser charges. The very fact that the employer has dealt with the interview under caution in a timely and candid fashion can itself be a point worth making in court should the case proceed that far.

There are occasions when the inspector will choose to put questions in correspondence to the employer rather than holding an interview in person. The employer will still be cautioned and its responses will still be admissible in evidence. This approach can have its advantages in that the employer is allowed to make a considered response to the investigating authority's enquiries. Again the role of a suitably experienced solicitor in assisting the employer to draft his responses can be very valuable.

9:4.9.1 The role of solicitors

At this stage of the enquiry, if not at an earlier stage, it may well be prudent and appropriate to appoint a solicitor to act on behalf of the individual employer or corporate entity. It is likely that the employer or employer's representative will not be experienced in dealing with such an interview, and a solicitor can assist in preparing the individual for the interview and ensuring at the interview that the questioning of the investigating authority's officers is fair and reasonable. The solicitor can assist in pre-interview discussions with the inspector, who will often be more prepared to make disclosure either formally or informally to a solicitor prior to the interview under caution. This has the advantage of allowing the interviewee some time to prepare their answers. The solicitor should also be able to advise the interviewee as to the necessary elements of the offence being investigated and therefore the appropriateness of the interviewer's questions. It should be noted that the interviewee has the right to stop the interview at any time to take further legal advice in private. This allows the interviewee to take a break in questioning and give it an opportunity to discuss the way in which any line of questioning is going and whether or not to continue to answer questions.

As is stressed throughout this chapter the appointment of competent legal advisers is essential to the successful management of legal proceedings. It is important that the employer defends proceedings to the full extent of their ability if it intends to rely on any insurance to mitigate the financial liabilities. As a matter of public policy, it is not possible to insure against fines, but should any civil liability arise, then, to the extent that the criminal conviction is relevant to any civil proceedings, the involvement of the employer's insurers may be important.

9:4.9.1.1 The selection of an appropriate solicitor

Many employers have in-house legal advisers who are able to give general advice on health and safety issues, research the particulars as necessary and advise on the use of external legal services. Even where in-house counsel can provide advice it may, in certain circumstances, be advantageous to have someone more familiar with the relevant areas of law. This is particularly the case where the interview proceeds under caution and there is insufficient time to refer to the relevant texts. There are few true health and safety lawyers; the discipline is normally combined with either environmental law or employment law. Lawyers specialising in criminal law also have relevant skills when it comes to advising on the preparation for and conduct of criminal proceedings and they may also be appropriate specialists to instruct. There are several directories of solicitors and solicitors' firms giving details on firms and their areas of expertise. These may be useful where an existing relationship with a firm of solicitors is not already established or if it is felt that the employer's current lawyers do not have the necessary expertise.

9:4.9.2 The preparation of witnesses

The employer's legal advisers, particularly solicitors, have a role in preparing witnesses for court appearances. This involves explaining the constitution of the court and therefore whom to expect to ask questions and where to address answers. The importance of this cannot be underestimated: a witness who appears confident and relaxed will be far more effective than one who appears nervous and disorientated. Knowing what to expect and how to react is likely to allow the witness the appropriate confidence. Obviously, the legal advisers do not have a role in changing the evidence to be given by the witness, although they may make suggestions as to how particular answers or statements may be interpreted. The legal advisers may wish to persuade the witness to rephrase statements to get their point across in a more helpful and appropriate way. In completing this task, the legal adviser is combining knowledge of the appropriate matters that have to be demonstrated by each side in order to be successful with a common-sense and somewhat detached approach to what is being said by the witness.

9:5 Civil claims

An employer may also face legal action by an employee in relation to an injury the employee suffers at work. The employee may make his claim under a number of headings, commonly negligence and breach of statutory duty. There may be others, but these are the most significant.

9:5.1 The common law duty of care and negligence

An employer owes a duty of care to his employee and certain other third parties at common law. This duty of care and its consequences are extended and modified by statute. An employee (or other claimant) who makes a claim against his employer (the alleged wrongdoer) for negligence must demonstrate that the employer has breached its duty of care to the claimant arising from either common law or statute. That breach of duty must then be shown to have *caused* the claimant to suffer an injury and/or loss.

The breadth of the common law and statutory requirements is such that they cannot be adequately summarised in this section alone. In general, a claimant must demonstrate the following four conditions.

1. That he is an individual to whom the alleged wrongdoer owed a duty of care. In many cases this is a straightforward issue. The duty may be set down in statute, for example an occupier owes a duty of care to visitors pursuant to the Occupiers Liability Act 1957, or it may be a well-established duty in common law, for example the driver of a motor vehicle has a duty of care to the drivers of other motor vehicles on the public highway.

   Care has to be taken to distinguish between statutory duties and statutes that impose a duty of care as they are subject to slightly different rules. The issue also becomes more complex when the claimant is not so apparent. For example, does the driver of the car causing the crash owe a duty of care to an individual who happens upon the accident and suffers a psychological reaction to viewing the grizzly scene?

2. The claimant must establish the standard of the duty owed by the alleged wrongdoer. For example, an occupier of a property is required to take reasonable steps to ensure the reasonable safety of visitors to his property. If he has done

everything that he can to ensure that safety, breach of duty is unlikely to be established. In contrast, an occupier owes a lesser standard of care to a trespasser. Here the occupier only has to do what is reasonable in all the circumstances to ensure that the trespasser is safe from the risk of injury from known dangers. For example, an occupier may only be required to inform a trespasser of the risk of falling masonry from a building, whereas he may have a duty to a visitor to not only inform them of the danger, but also provide them with personal protective equipment such as a safety hat.

3. Once a standard of duty has been established, breach of that duty must be proved by the claimant. It is a question for the judge to determine on the evidence presented whether or not the standard has been met. It will usually be apparent once the court has determined the appropriate standard, as it will then be a question of applying the facts to the legal standard established in point 2 above.

4. In some cases, a breach of duty is not necessarily determinative of the issue. Some statutes and the common law provide for a specific defence to the breach of duty. For example, under s.41 of the Highways Act 1980 the highway authority has a duty to maintain the highway at public expense. The standard of care is high because if the highway is not maintained, then the authority has breached this duty. However, a claim can be defeated by the defendant highway authority if it can use the defence afforded to it under s.58 of the Act. The highway authority has a defence against the claimant for compensation if it can show that it did all that was reasonable in the circumstances to ensure that the road was not dangerous to traffic.

9:5.2 Civil claims for a breach of statutory duty in health and safety

Certain health and safety legislation can give rise to civil liability for breach of statutory duty. The requirements placed upon a claimant making a claim for breach of statutory duty are similar to those placed upon the prosecution seeking a conviction for breach of statutory duty. However, there are a number of differences. A claimant only has to prove his case on the balance of probabilities, which makes his task somewhat easier than that of the HSE or local authority. On the other hand, the claimant has additional hurdles to overcome. Firstly, it must not be stated within the legislation that civil liability for breach of that statutory duty is excluded. For example, no civil liability arises for breach of the general duty to employees contained in the HSWA. Secondly, the breach of duty must have caused the plaintiff loss and the same analysis that applies to negligence in **section 9:5.1** applies here. Thirdly, the claimant must show that the injury he suffered was one envisaged by the statute. The courts will try to be accommodating to the claimant on this point in most circumstances. However, if the injury has occurred in an unusual way, then this may be a difficult hurdle to overcome.

9:5.3 Loss, causation and limitation of actions

9:5.3.1 Loss

In order to be able to succeed in a claim for negligence or breach of statutory duty, then a claimant must be able to show loss. Usually, the loss will be physical and the claimant will be seeking compensation for that physical loss. However, the claimant will also often be seeking compensation for financial loss, most usually stemming from loss of earnings although not exclusively so. Particular rules restrict the ability of a claimant to recover in certain circumstances and are discussed in **section 9:5.3.2**.

9:5.3.2 Causation

9:5.3.2.1 Causation in claims for personal injury

It is common sense that a claimant must show that the defendant's negligent acts caused his injuries. However, the law does not allow the claimant to recover all the losses that are said to be caused by the defendant's acts. It should also be noted that the law on recovery for breach of statutory duty is slightly different to breach of the common law duty of care, and it is the latter that is dealt with here. It is essentially a question of fact whether or not the defendant's acts caused the claimant to suffer the injury. Medical evidence is often very valuable to the court in assisting its decision making. If the issue is a complex one, then a different medical expert may be instructed by the claimant and defendant, but the court will try to encourage the parties to agree on one expert. Medical experts are now required to meet before trial to discuss their reports and to try to reach consensus on the issues. If consensus is reached, then no further debate is required in court. However, if the experts are unable to agree, then it will be for the court to decide which expert they find the more convincing. It follows that the selection of the appropriate expert is of key importance; the parties will usually rely on their legal advisers to recommend a suitable expert. This is usually someone with a recognised reputation in his or her field of expertise, but also someone used to appearing in court and facing cross-examination.

9:5.3.2.2 When can the employer be presumed to be liable?

It may be the case that the claimant can claim that the only way he could have suffered the harm is by the defendant's negligence, although he cannot point to the steps in causation leading to it. For example, an employee, who works all his life for one company and develops asbestosis, may claim that the only exposure he could have had to asbestos is at work, but he may not be able to point to any particular incident. This claim can put the burden of proof on to the defendant. In other words, it is for the defendant to show that the claimant suffered his loss due to some other factor.

9:5.3.2.3 The relevance of other factors outside the defendant's control

The issue of causation becomes more complex where the defendant's actions are not the only cause of the claimant's injury. Other factors include the claimant's own actions, his pre-existing susceptibilities to injury, and the actions of other employees and third parties. The law in this area is very complex, but a number of essential principles may be described.

Firstly, the defendant takes the claimant as he finds him. This means that even though the injuries suffered by the claimant are made worse by the claimant's particular susceptibility, the defendant is liable to the full extent of those injuries. For example, a claimant who suffered a burn to his lip at work, which due to a rare genetic susceptibility led to the claimant developing a cancer, claims compensation from his employer. Neither the employee nor employer was aware of the claimant's susceptibility. However, the defendant became liable for the full amount of the claimant's loss.

Secondly, the acts of third parties prior to the plaintiff suffering injury will not prevent the defendant from incurring liability for the claimant's injuries. If the acts of third parties are negligent, then the defendant may seek to join in those third parties as co-defendants with a view to sharing liability between them. The court will generally disregard non-negligent acts by third parties and the compensation payable by the defendant will be on the basis that they are the sole cause of the claimant's injury.

Thirdly, the acts of the claimant − if found to be contributory negligent − can be taken into account in determining the amount of compensation to be paid to the claimant.

The issue becomes more complicated where there is some other intervening act that makes the injury suffered by the claimant much worse. For example, does the act of a doctor who negligently performs surgery on the injury suffered as a consequence of the defendant's negligence break the chain of causation? The question of whether or not the defendant can incur liability in these circumstances is difficult and something that ordinarily requires expert advice. In the example of the doctor, he is additionally liable to the extent that he has made the claimant's injuries worse; the defendant would be prudent to join the other defendant in the claimant's claim so that the compensation is shared. If the claimant were unable to recover from the doctor, then the claimant would be entitled to recover the full amount from the original defendant. However, where, for example, a claimant was involved in a car crash and was hit first by one car and then subsequently by a second car also being driven negligently, then the liability of the driver of the first car would be limited to the damage caused by his impact and not the damage caused by the impact of the second driver. To a degree this is a question of foreseeability: negligent treatment is a foreseeable consequence of the claimant's injury, whereas a further impact by the second driver is not a foreseeable consequence of the first driver's negligence.

9:5.3.2.4 Foreseeability

There is one remaining concept that must be explained. The loss suffered by the defendant must be of a kind which is foreseeable. It is not necessary for the particular loss suffered by the defendant nor the way in which it is suffered to be foreseeable. However, the kind of loss must be. For example, as stated in **section 9:5.3.2.3**, personal injury is obviously a foreseeable consequence of an employer's negligence and it is established law that personal injury is a single kind of loss. Therefore, it is no defence for the defendant, where a claimant makes a claim based on skin cancer arising from a chemical burn, to claim that although a chemical burn was foreseeable the cancer was not.

Foreseeability is more of an issue in determining recoverability of financial losses. Loss of earnings or earning potential are clearly foreseeable consequences, but if an employee were to claim that his accident prevented him entering his weekly numbers for the lottery and those numbers came up, then although this loss could be said to be caused by the defendant's negligence it would not be of a foreseeable kind and therefore not recoverable.

9:5.3.3 Limitation on actions

The law does not allow a defendant to be exposed to claims following an incident for an indefinite period. The general rule is that claims for personal injury have to be made within three years of the injury. There are, of course, exceptions, including claims by children and claimants whose injuries are not apparent until some later date.

9:6 Procedures in civil cases

The vast majority of civil claims made against employers in health and safety law will be claims for personal injury from employees. This section outlines the civil procedures and some relevant considerations for employers. The procedures of civil courts are governed by a relatively new regime that came into force on 1 April 1999 called the Civil Procedure Rules (CPR). There are 54 CPR and two schedules covering, amongst many other issues, timetables for hearing cases, the format of court documents, procedures on expert witnesses, the exchange of witness statements and the disclosure of documents. A number of the most relevant rules are discussed in **sections 9:6.1–9:6.8**.

The reform of the rules governing civil procedure had two main objectives. The first was to reduce the number of claims reaching court by encouraging the early settlement of claims and the second was to streamline the court's dealing with those cases where litigation could not be avoided. Since the CPR came into force the number of claims reaching the courts has reduced significantly. The CPR contain a number of new measures to encourage early settlement, including guidance for judges on how parties should conduct litigation prior to court proceedings being issued. In particular parties are expected to follow certain procedures in the form of protocols and CPR before issuing their claims. It is essential for those investigating an accident to be very familiar with the requirements of the pre-action protocols and in particular the pre-action protocol for personal injury claims.

9:6.1 The pre-action protocol for personal injury claims

These pre-action protocols will encourage the early gathering and exchange of information by the parties, such that each party can evaluate the strength of their case and make a decision on whether or not they are willing to settle the claim without going to court. This early exchange of information has the added benefit of saving time later should the matter not be settled and proceed to court.

The benefit of the pre-action protocol for personal injury claims (the protocol) to those investigating accidents is that a three-month period is allowed by the protocol for investigation following delivery of a letter of claim. The protocol is intended to cover claims of up to £15,000, but retains the flexibility to cover larger claims where appropriate. No longer do insurers and loss adjusters have to rely upon a brief and unhelpful letter before action; the protocol requires a formal letter of claim to be delivered to the potential defendant, with a copy for passing onto the defendant's insurers. The letter should stress the importance of passing the letter on to the insurers as soon as possible and the fact that a failure to act quickly could affect the validity of the employer's insurance. The contents of the letter of claim should enable the employer or its insurers to address the allegations being made on behalf of the claimant. It is a requirement that the letter shall contain a clear summary of the facts on which the claim is based and sufficient information should be given in order to enable insurers and employers to commence investigations and at least put a broad valuation on the 'risk', and therefore conduct an investigation that is proportionate to the value of the claim. An example of a letter of claim is provided in **Figure 9:1**.

FIGURE 9:1 EXAMPLE OF A LETTER OF CLAIM

ANYWHERE & CO, SOLICITORS
Mr A N Other
Anytown

The Store
Registered Office
Little Anyhow
Knockton

Our Ref. AWS/128 1 July 2002

Dear Sir

CLAIMANT'S FULL NAME

CLAIMANT'S FULL ADDRESS

CLAIMANT'S NI NUMBER

CLAIMANT'S DATE OF BIRTH

CLAIMANT'S CLOCK OR WORKS NUMBER

CLAIMANT'S EMPLOYER'S (Name and Address)

We are instructed by the above named to claim damages in connection with an accident on 1 May 2001 at the Anytown store of The Store Limited.

Please confirm the identity of your insurers. Please note that the insurers will need to see this letter as soon as possible and it may affect your insurance cover and/or the conduct of any subsequent legal proceedings if you do not send this letter to them.

The circumstances of the accident are that our client was working at the Anytown store on 1 May 2001. She knelt down to check the price on some bleach products. Above her one of her fellow employees and your store assistant, a Mr Clumsy, were re-stocking the shelves. As Mr Clumsy did so a loose metal shelf fell onto our client's back.

The reason why we are alleging fault is that:

1. your store assistant should have cordoned off the area where he was working;

2. your store assistant should have warned our client that he working on the shelves;

3. your store assistant dropped the shelf onto our client's back;

4. you failed to review your system of work to minimise the risk to employees when re-stocking shelves; and

5. in breach of your common law duty of care to your employee you negligently failed to properly maintain the shelves and this caused our client to suffer injury.

Our client suffered a soft tissue injury to her back, which is causing continuing pain and stiffness and is expected to last for approximately three years from the accident. Our client is also suffering from disturbed sleep, interference with her normal household and social activities, and shock.

She has had to take six months off work following the accident and we understand that her approximate salary is £850 per calendar month. As you are her employer please provide details of her earnings so that we may calculate her financial loss.

She has had to have meals provided for her for ten days after the accident at an estimated cost of £200 and incurred expenses of £90 travelling to her local hospital for physiotherapy. She has also had to purchase a special orthopaedic bed.

At this stage of our enquiries we would expect the documents contained in the attached Schedule to be relevant to this action.

A copy of this letter is attached for you to send to your insurers. Finally, if you do not acknowledge receipt of this letter within 21 days then we will be entitled to issue proceedings.

Yours faithfully

ANYWHERE & CO
Enc

FIGURE 9:2 SCHEDULE TO THE LETTER OF CLAIM

List of Disclosures for Health and Safety at Work Claims

a) Accident book entry

b) First aider report

c) Surgery record

d) Foreman's/supervisor's accident report

e) Safety representative's accident report

f) RIDDOR report to the HSE

g) Other communications between the employer and the HSE

h) Minutes of health and safety committee meetings where the accident/matter is considered

i) Report to the Department of Work and Pensions

j) Documents listed above relative to any previous accident/matter identified by the claimant and relied upon as proof of negligence

k) Earnings information

l) Pre-accident risk assessment required by Regulation 3 of the Management of Health and Safety At Work Regulations 1999 (MHSWR)

m) Post-accident risk assessment required by Regulation 3 of the MHSWR

n) Accident investigation report prepared in implementing the requirements of Regulations 4, 6 and 9 of the MHSWR

o) Health surveillance records in appropriate cases required by Regulation 5 of the MHSWR

p) Information provided to employees under Regulation 8 of the MHSWR

q) Documents relating to the employer's health and safety training required by Regulation 11 of the MHSWR

The protocol goes onto list further disclosures where the following specific health and safety regulations apply:

- Workplace (Health and Safety and Welfare) Regulations 1992;

- Provision and Use of Work Equipment Regulations 1992;

- Personal Protective Equipment at Work Regulations 1992;

- Manual Handling Operations Regulations 1992;

- Health and Safety (Display Screen Equipment) Regulations 1992;

- Control of Substances Hazardous to Heath Regulations 2002;

- Construction (Design and Management) Regulations 1994;

- Pressure Systems and Transportable Gas Containers Regulations 1989;

- Lifting Plant and Equipment (Records of Test and Examination Etc.) Regulations 1992;

- Noise at Work Regulations 1989;

- Construction (Head Protection) Regulations 1989;

- Construction (General Provisions) Regulations 1961.

The employer should reply to the letter of claim within 21 days of the date of posting of the letter, identifying his insurer (if any). If there has been no reply by the employer or insurer by the expiry of 21 days, the claimant will be entitled to issue proceedings. It is likely that the employer's insurer will take on the running of the claim if they consider it likely that the claim will be covered by insurance. The employer and/or its insurer then have a maximum of three months from the date of acknowledgement of the claim to investigate. At the end of that period the employer shall reply stating whether the liability is denied and, if so, giving reasons for the denial of liability. In the event that liability is denied, the documents listed in the Schedule to the letter of claim in **Figure 9:2** should be disclosed, in addition to any other documents which are material to the issues between the parties, and which are likely to be ordered to be disclosed by the court with the letter setting out the denial.

Whilst the lists technically apply to fast-track disclosure only (*see* **section 9:6.3.2** for meaning), it is good practice to have a copy of the list to hand whilst investigating all claims. **Figure 9:3** provides a flow chart of the pre-action protocol for personal injury claims.

FIGURE 9:3 PRE-ACTION PROTOCOL FOR PERSONAL INJURY CLAIMS FLOWCHART

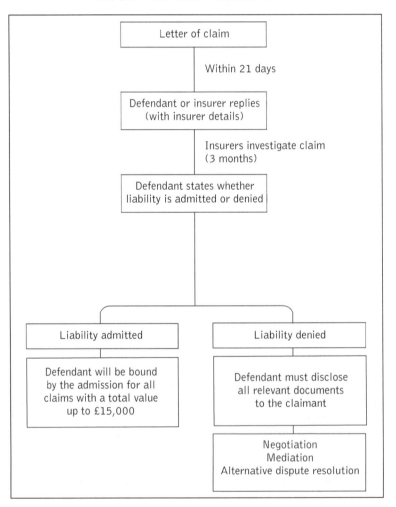

9:6.2 The instruction of experts under the protocol

Before any party instructs an expert it must give the other a list of the names of one or more experts in the relevant speciality whom they consider it suitable to instruct. Within 14 days of receiving the list the party may object to any of the named experts. If the second party objects to all the experts, then the parties may instruct their own experts and it is up to the court to decide in any subsequent proceedings whether the party objecting behaved reasonably. If the second party does not object to the witness appointed, then they cannot rely on their own expert in subsequent proceedings unless they first obtain the party's agreement or the court so directs or the first party's report is amended and the first party is not prepared to disclose the original report. The procedure is primarily aimed at medical experts, but it covers any type of expert. The parties are allowed to ask the appointed expert written questions, the replies to which must be disclosed to all sides. The protocol does not completely prohibit a party instructing its own expert, and in some cases this would still be appropriate. The failure to comply with the protocol by any party is likely to lead to the party being unable to claim back the cost of instructing the expert should that party be successful in any future court proceedings.

The three-month period following receipt of the letter of claim should not be wasted. Once proceedings are issued, judges are required to manage the case so as to bring it to trial at the earliest possible opportunity. Accordingly, the opportunity to obtain statements and evidence after proceedings have been issued will be limited. That is particularly the case with claims that have gone through the protocol as these are likely to be treated as so called fast-track claims, where no more than 30 weeks should pass between the defence being served and the trial.

9:6.3 The commencement of proceedings

Following the employer's rejection of the claimant's claim and failure to respond within the time allowed, the claimant may issue proceedings. The claimant commences proceedings by issuing a 'claim form' which is a legal document setting out the basic terms of his claim. The procedure following the issue of the claim form is set out in **Figure 9:4**.

FIGURE 9:4 COURT PROCEEDINGS

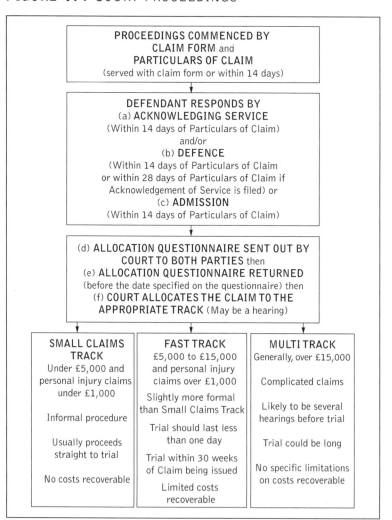

The claimant also has to serve a particulars of claim, which sets out the claimant's claim in more detail. The employer, in conjunction with his insurer where appropriate, must then decide whether or not he intends to defend the claim. If he elects to defend the claim he must serve his defence within the time limit; if he intends to accept liability he must serve an admission of liability. It is possible for the employer to accept *part* of the claimant's claim. After the employer has served his defence, the claimant is allowed to respond to the issues raised in the defence in the form of a further document called a reply. Following receipt of the defence, the court will issue an allocation questionnaire to each party, which must be filled in and returned to the court. In the questionnaire the parties will have to disclose whether or not they followed the pre-action protocol and this may be taken into account in the following directions given by the court. The court decides which 'track' will apply to the case. This is important as different rules apply for each 'track'.

9:6.3.1 Small claims tracks

For claims for less than £5,000 (less than £1,000 for personal injury (excluding special damages, i.e. out-of-pocket expenses)) the small claims track will apply. The small claims track is the least formal of the procedures and will usually be dealt with at a single hearing. The court asks the parties to follow the standard procedures for the small claims track on the disclosure of documents and witness statements. The important thing to note about the small claims track is that the successful party can recover no costs (other than court fees).

9:6.3.2 Fast track

If the claim exceeds £5,000 (£1,000 for personal injury (excluding special damages, i.e. out of pocket expenses)) but is less than £15,000, and provided that it can be dealt with by the court in less than one day, it will be allocated to the fast track. The fast-track procedure is intended to be for the more straightforward cases.

Again, the court has standard procedures for the disclosure of documents that will rarely need to be modified by the parties making an application to court. The fast-track procedure states that the trial should take place within 30 weeks of allocation to the fast track. Only very limited costs are recoverable by the successful party. In particular, the costs for the trial itself are fixed.

9:6.3.3 Multi track

Finally, for the most complicated cases and those valued over £15,000 the court may allocate them to the multi track. Claims allocated to the multi track will be actively managed by the court so as to bring it to trial as soon as possible. However, the CPR provide for no particular deadline and each case will be dealt with according to its own circumstances. There are also no specific limitations on the recovery of costs, but a party should not expect to recover its full costs even if successful and even if the case is dealt with expeditiously by its advisers.

It follows that for cases allocated to the small claims track and fast track the employer may consider it financially imprudent to appoint outside advisers. However, as the issues raised in any parallel criminal proceedings will necessitate the involvement of legal advisers, it may be that they can provide some further advice on civil proceedings at little extra cost. In the likely event that the employer is insured and the insurers wish to defend the proceedings it is likely that they have retained lawyers on special terms that make it economic for them to defend the proceedings using lawyers.

9:6.4 Directions and preliminary hearings

In the more complex cases there are a large number of preliminary issues that the parties may wish the court to make a decision on. For example, the parties may ask the court to order the other side to release documents held by them but not yet disclosed, or decide whether the employer's defence or claimant's claim is without any foundation. If the court decides that there is no basis for either the claim or the defence, then the matter may be summarily dealt with, a procedure called summary judgement. The court may also make directions for the further exchange of information and hear applications for extensions of time limits at preliminary hearings. In particular, the courts will ask the parties to exchange their witness statements. Two principal types of witness are recognised by the CPR; these are witnesses of fact and expert witnesses.

9:6.5 Evidence in civil proceedings

9:6.5.1 Gathering evidence

Once the defence has been served, the evidence-gathering process begins in earnest. A case stands or falls on the evidence. A judge can only decide on a fact based on the evidence that he has heard. It follows therefore that the evidence must be obtained in the first place, and is then presented in an admissible form.

The primary source of evidence is that of an individual who has knowledge of the facts and matters that are at issue. Other means of evidence can often be equally or more crucial. Examples of other evidence include:

- documents, for example copies of the risk assessment, accident book, correspondence between employer and employee, employment records, etc.;

- plans, for example a description of the layout of the building where relevant to the circumstances giving rise to an accident;

- photographs of the area in which the accident occurred or the equipment involved;

- video footage – the accident may have been recorded on CCTV; video footage may assist the judge in understanding the scene of a particular incident.

Different rules control the admission of evidence in criminal and civil procedures. CPR 32 deals with evidence in civil proceedings. Rule 32.1 provides the court with the power, through the judge, to control the evidence that it hears and the way in which it wishes to hear that evidence. For example, the judge may direct that the evidence is given by a statement, or by plan, photograph, video tape or video link. The judge has discretion as to the exercise of the power given to him under this rule.

9:6.5.2 The disclosure of documents

A list of the relevant documents held by each party must be assembled and disclosed. It is likely that many of these documents will already have been disclosed pursuant to the pre-action protocol. However, a formal list of documents must be served on the other side as part of the proceedings. The time period for producing this list is very short and therefore it is imperative that requests for documents by the insurers or their legal advisers are dealt with quickly.

9:6.5.3 Supervising officer

To ensure that documents are maintained both before and after an accident and are easily accessible, a supervising officer responsible for gathering documents in civil proceedings and signing disclosure statements (*see* **section 9:6.5.9**) should be appointed. Given their role, again the organisation may appoint an accident investigator to be the supervising officer. As a result, the following points on the disclosure requirements should be carefully noted.

9:6.5.4 What are documents?

'Documents' are not confined to written documents, but cover anything in which information of any description is recorded. Therefore tape recordings, videos, photographs, etc., are included.

9:6.5.5 What documents are to be disclosed?

Parties are required to give what is called 'standard disclosure' only, unless the court orders otherwise. This means that a party is required to disclose only:

- the documents on which he relies;

- the documents which either:

  - adversely affect his own case;

  - adversely affect another party's case; or

  - support another party's case.

A non-exhaustive list of the documents that are likely to be relevant is found in the Schedule to the letter of claim (*see* **Figure 9:2**).

If the employer (or insurer) has any doubt about whether a document is disclosable, it should be sent to their insurers or its nominated solicitors who can advise on this point.

9:6.5.6 Duty of search

When giving standard disclosure, the duty is to make a *reasonable* and *proportionate* search for documents which adversely affect a party's case or support another party's case. The factors relevant in deciding the reasonableness of a search include:

- the number of documents involved;

- the nature and complexity of the proceedings;

- the ease and expense of retrieval of any particular documents;

- the significance of any document likely to be located during the search.

If a category or class of document has not been searched for on the grounds that to do so would be unreasonable, that must be stated in the disclosure statement (*see* **section 9:6.5.9**) and the category or class of document identified.

9:6.5.7 Duty of disclosure limited to documents in a party's control

A party's duty to disclose documents is limited to documents that are or have been in his control. For this purpose, a party has or has had a document in his control if either:

- it is or was in his physical possession;

- he has or has had a right to possession of it; or

- he has or has had a right to inspect or take copies of it.

9:6.5.8 Duty of disclosure during proceedings

The duty of disclosure continues until the proceedings are concluded. Therefore, if standard disclosure documents come to an employer's notice at any time during the proceedings, they must be provided to the other side via its legal advisers and the employer's insurers. Furthermore, documents that may be relevant in civil proceedings must be preserved and should not be destroyed or disposed of until the proceedings are concluded.

9:6.5.9 Disclosure statement

Initially the employer or its insurers make disclosure at the end of the three-month investigation period (if they decide that a claim should be defended). At that stage disclosure is informal and a disclosure statement is not required.

Once court proceedings have started the court will make directions that disclosure of certain documents should take place by a certain date; this time period may be prescribed by the CPR for some cases. At this stage, disclosure is made by each party serving a list setting out their disclosable documents. The documents may be the same as those already disclosed before court proceedings started.

The employer's or insurer's legal advisers will draw up the list on the employer's behalf based on the information and documents provided to them. The list must also give details of any documents which *did* exist but are no longer in the organisation's control, together with an explanation of what happened to those documents. For example, the list will refer to letters sent for which there is only a file copy and the 'original' letter is no longer in the employer's possession.

The list must also include a disclosure statement signed by the proper representative (i.e. a senior employee, director or partner) of the party disclosing the documents:

- setting out the extent of the search that has been made to locate documents, which he is required to disclose;

- certifying that he understands the duty to disclose documents;

- certifying that to the best of his knowledge he has carried out that duty.

Where the party making the disclosure statement is a company, firm, association or other organisation, the statement must also:

- identify the person making the statement and the official position he holds;

- explain why he is considered an appropriate person to make the statement.

All parties in a claim have a right to inspect or obtain copies of documents which have been disclosed. However, some documents may be privileged (documents prepared for or in contemplation of litigation), and inspection may be withheld. Whether or not documents are privileged is a complex issue and one that should be determined by the employer's/insurer's legal advisers. However, insurers or solicitors will need to see any documents the organisation considers may be privileged, so that they can make a decision as to their status.

9:6.5.10 Sanctions

There are harsh sanctions for non-compliance. In view of this, it is crucial that organisations ensure that all relevant documents are gathered and sent to the insurers or nominated solicitors as soon as they are requested.

9:6.6 Statements of fact

The most frequently used form of evidence is a written and signed statement of fact. This is, in common parlance, a witness statement. The importance of carefully drafting the witness statement should not be underestimated, and although words cannot be put into the mouth of the witness, it is very important that the way in which the witness intends to put across their points is rigorously examined for weaknesses and unintentional ambiguity. The value of a properly prepared witness statement is only seen at trial during cross-examination, where the well-prepared witness will cope better with the pressure and be better prepared to answer the questions that they are asked. The main objective is to limit the number of questions that can be asked under cross-examination. Under the CPR witness statements are exchanged before trial and the parties must attempt to agree as much of the witness evidence as possible. The idea is that if as much material can be agreed the court's time is saved by being able to focus specifically on the issues that truly divide the parties. Where a witness' statement is agreed, then it is unlikely that it will be read out in court. (The judge will be expected to have read the witness statement as part of his preparation for the trial.) At the trial itself, the witness enters the witness box and the signed statement of fact stands as his evidence (called evidence-in-chief). Whilst permission may be asked of the trial judge to ask the witness supplementary questions, it is perfectly within the trial judge's power to refuse that permission and thereby restrict the witness's evidence-in-chief to those facts and matters contained in the written statement. The lawyers acting for the other side, in order to confirm the veracity of the statement and in an attempt to show weaknesses, inconsistencies and also uncertainty in the witness, will then ask him questions. This second process is called cross-examination. Finally, the lawyers acting for those that called him as a witness may ask the witness questions. This process is called re-examination.

The form of the witness statement will depend on the circumstances. It may be necessary in some hearings for a witness to swear an affidavit; in other cases it is sufficient for the witness to make a statement of truth. In the former case a solicitor must witness the swearing of an oath as to the accuracy of the statements made in the witness statement. In the latter case the witness merely signs the witness statement under a declaration that he believes the statements made by him are true.

9:6.6.1 Contents of a statement of fact

The statement will obviously concentrate on facts within the knowledge of the witness. It should not contain hearsay except in exceptional circumstances. Hearsay is where a witness reports what he has been told someone else said or saw. The fact that they can report is the telling, but not the contents of what has been told. Thus, if Bob has a fall at work, which he alleges was caused by dangerous work practices, it does not help his case for him to call as witnesses of fact his mates from the pub, whom he told of the injury and how it was caused that same evening over a quiet pint. The retelling of the facts to some third party does not in the eyes of the court make Bob's evidence any more convincing. Care also has to be taken with statements of opinion. A witness cannot report on things that are outside his or her experience. Thus, an employee cannot call his co-worker who saw him fall to give evidence on how bad a fall it was in terms of the injuries he suffered and his long-term prospects for recovery. He might be able to offer his opinion on how treacherous the floor was if he had walked on it just a few moments before the accident as it is within his ability and experience to make such a judgement. However, he is not qualified to comment on whether or not the employer had breached his duty towards his employee. These types of statement will have to be removed from the witness statements before they are exchanged with the other side. The court sets down a specific date for the exchange of witness statements. Each side is required to exchange their statements simultaneously so that neither side can gain an advantage over the other by drafting their statements in such a way as to respond to the points made in the other party's statement.

When handling a witness it is bad practice to give them the impression that he or she will never have to attend court for the purpose of delivering their evidence. Instead, the employer should explain that court proceedings and a trial are a possibility at the first opportunity, rather than surprising them at a later stage. It is also good practice to explain the form in which the witness statement will be presented for signature and the importance of ensuring that it is read thoroughly and only signed when the witness is entirely happy with its contents. If it takes three or four goes to get it right, so be it. The form of the statement itself must comply with CPR 32.8, in particular:

- the written statement should be headed with the name and number of the proceedings. (If proceedings have not begun, the statement should still be set out as if proceedings have begun, simply leaving a space for the name of the court and the claim number.);

- at the top right hand corner of the first page there should be clearly written:

  - the party on whose behalf the statement is made;

  - the initials and surname of the witness;

  - the number of the statement in relation to that witness;

  - the identifying initials and number of each exhibit referred to;

  - the date the statement was made.

It goes without saying that the statement must be in the witness' own words; those drafting statements should avoid introducing their own style, or entering vocabulary which – it will become apparent at trial – is not natural to the witness. The statement will ultimately be signed by the witness, and drafted in the first person. It should also state:

- the full name of the witness;

- his place of residence, or if he is making a statement in his professional, business or other occupational capacity, the address at which he works, the position he holds and the name of his firm or employer;

- his occupation, or if he has none, his description;

- the fact that he is a party to the proceedings or is the employee of such a party if that is the case.

The witness must indicate in his statement which parts of the statement that he makes are within his own knowledge and which are matters of information or belief and the source for any matters of information and belief. For example, the accident book may recall the precise time and date of the accident.

As a practical point, the written statement should be presented in the following format.

- It should be produced on A4 paper with 3.5cm margins and be typed on one side of the paper only.

- Pages must be numbered consecutively and the statements divided into numbered paragraphs.

- Numbers, including dates, must be expressed in figures.

- It must conclude with verification by a statement of truth; to verify a witness statement the statement of truth should read 'I believe that the facts stated in this witness statement are true'.

The witness statements will ultimately form part of the trial bundle. The trial bundle is the bundle of documents including witness statements, expert reports and relevant disclosed documents presented to the court for its use during and after the trial. This bundle of documents will have been brought together over a period of time leading up to trial in order to prepare properly for the hearing. The trial bundle will be prepared by the lawyers based on their understanding of the issues likely to be discussed at trial. The trial bundle is usually prepared by the claimant's legal advisers and is sent to the defendant's solicitors for approval. Ideally, the list of documents must be agreed so that a single bundle of files is submitted to the court. If agreement proves impossible, then a separate bundle may be prepared for each side. However, as this can cause confusion and waste time the court will expect the lawyers to have a good reason for preparing separate bundles.

9:6.7 Expert witnesses

Expert evidence in civil proceedings is governed by CPR 35. Judges have a duty under CPR 35.1 to restrict the evidence of experts to that which is reasonably required to resolve the issues in dispute. In practice, even in multi-track claims, judges are keen to limit medical experts to one per discipline. The courts will often try to avoid having experts such as employment consultants and health and safety consultants, as they are not viewed as adding enough to the issues in dispute to justify the cost of appointing them. The role of experts is to provide technical guidance to the trial judge on issues within the expert's area of expertise. It is not to provide an opinion as to where liability should fall, or to repeat evidence of fact that should properly be given by a witness of fact (*see* **section 9:6.6**). The expert has a duty to the court to help the court on the matters within his expertise and this duty overrides the duty to the person who instructed him. The expert may seek the directions of the court in the preparation of his report without consulting either of the parties. No party may call an expert without the permission of the court. The court will usually issue a direction to the parties indicating the number of expert witnesses it wishes to hear and the areas which they are to cover. If the parties wish to have further expert witnesses, then they must make an application to the court. There is no restriction on the employer appointing an expert who is already employed by him, subject to him being able to give expert evidence and him not being a witness of fact.

The court may direct under CPR 35.7 that the evidence be given by one expert only and where the parties fail to agree on a single expert, the court may appoint the expert on their behalf from a list submitted by the instructing parties. The court is more likely to take this type of action in fast-track cases, or small claims track cases. In any event, the parties should have already instructed a joint expert under the protocol (*see* **section 9:6.1**). If each party appoints its own expert, then the court may, and is likely to, instruct the experts to meet and to try to agree their evidence.

The report must state the substance of all material instructions, whether written or oral, on the basis of which the report was written. Instructions provided to the expert are likely to be considered by the trial judge as part of the overall report. It has become the practice of many experts to attach a copy of the letter of instruction to the report. The art of instructing an expert has therefore become far more important since the CPR took effect.

All expert's reports must give details of:

- the expert's qualifications;

- any literature or other material which the expert has relied upon in making the report;

- who carried out any tests or experiments which the expert has used for the report and whether or not the tests or experiments have been carried out under the expert's supervision;

- the qualifications of the person who carried out any such tests or experiments and, where there is a range of opinion on the matters summarised in the report, the range of the opinion and reasons for his own opinion.

The report should contain a summary of the conclusions reached and contain a statement of truth as follows:

I believe that the facts I have stated in the report are true and that the opinions I have expressed are correct.

The final report should be addressed to the court and should contain a statement at the end stating that the expert understands his duty to the court and confirming that he has complied with that duty.

9:6.7.1 Other types of expert report

The court has power under CPR 35.9 to direct a party with access to information, which is not reasonably available to another party, to serve on that other party a document that records the information. The document served must include sufficient details of all the facts, tests, experiments and assumptions that underlie any part of the information to enable the party on whom it is served to make or to obtain a proper interpretation of the information and an assessment of its significance. It is noted that this rule has been little used so far. However, it is conceivable that an employer could be so directed to produce such a report, particularly where the claimant has limited resources to pay for their own expert.

9:6.7.2 Expert reports and accident investigation

It is often the case that an investigation into the cause of an accident has to be undertaken to comply with health and safety laws, such as the MHSWR. For example, an investigation and a report may be necessary in order to review the risk assessment carried out under the above regulations in light of the accident. It is important to note that such an investigation is likely to be disclosable in civil proceedings. Therefore, particularly where the employer considers it likely that there will be litigation arising from the investigation, the exercise undertaken in order to comply with the requirements of health and safety legislation should be carefully scoped. In particular, experts conducting these investigations should be discouraged from commenting on the liability of the employer and should restrict themselves to the minimum necessary to properly discharge the employer's duties under health and safety law. The maker of the report can be required to attend court to give evidence on the contents of their report, although that is something that will be discussed with a judge after proceedings have been issued.

An employer faced with legal action may wish to conduct an investigation for its own purposes. The employer may take advantage of certain legal privileges that prevent some reports prepared in contemplation of legal proceedings from being disclosed. This is usually done by involving lawyers in instructing the expert, which is the easiest way of demonstrating the purpose of the report was to enable the employer to conduct his defence. In such circumstances, the employer can choose not to disclose the report if it is unfavourable. Therefore, prior to proceedings being issued, it is important that the report is obtained and understood, and, if its contents are unfavourable, consideration given to obtaining a report from an alternative expert.

9:6.8 Particular considerations in respect of medical evidence

The claimant's previous medical history may be relevant to the cause and extent of the current injuries. For example, the condition of the injured person's back may have deteriorated naturally over time, and the effect of the accident may have been to bring forward the end point by a number of years, thereby potentially limiting the claim for compensation to that period.

It follows that it is important to gather as much medical information on the claimant as possible. As medical records are confidential the employer will have to rely on the claimant to produce them as part of their list of documents (*see* **Figure 9:2**). If the claimant does not include them or it appears to the employer that there are records missing, then it will need to make a direct request to the claimant that they disclose their medical records to the employer. If the request is unsuccessful, the employer may ask the court for an order that the claimant discloses the information.

The patient has a right of access to his own medical records under the Access to Health Records Act 1990. There are limitations placed on the patient's right to see their medical records under the Act, some of which are listed below.

Disclosure may be curtailed where either:

- disclosure would cause 'serious harm to the physical or mental health of the individual or others';

- disclosure would be likely to reveal information about another person without their consent;

- disclosure would be likely to reveal the identity of another person other than a non-health professional involved in the care of the patient, who has given information to the practitioner about the individual, unless that person consents to the disclosure;

- the patient had provided the information in the expectation that it would not be disclosed; or

- the patient consented to an investigation or procedure on the basis that the results would not be disclosed.

Where the medical practitioner believes that any of the above criteria apply, he must inform the individual. Access may then be limited to whatever parts of the report that are not so affected. The employer should obtain confirmation from the claimant that there were no such restrictions placed on the disclosure of medical records by the health authorities to the claimant.

9:7 Particular considerations in respect of fatalities

9:7.1 The Fatal Accidents Act 1976

Where an accident results in a fatality, the person who suffered the injury and who would normally make the claim is obviously dead. However, their dependants will still be adversely affected financially by the loss. The Fatal Accidents Act (FAA) 1976 allows them to claim compensation.

The FAA provides the statutory right for a certain class of individuals (dependants) to claim damages for a loss of dependency against the person or persons whose wrongful acts or omissions have caused the death of the individual on whom the dependency rested. Potential claimants are limited to the class of persons who fall within the definition of dependency. Those persons are:

- a wife or husband of the deceased, or a former wife or husband;

- a person who had been living immediately before the time of the death of the deceased as his/her husband/wife in the same household, who had been so living for a continuous period of at least two years prior to that death;

- any parent (or other ascendant) of the deceased;

- any person treated by the deceased as his/her parent;

- any child or other descendants of the deceased;

- anyone who, though not actually a child of the deceased, had been treated by him/her as a child of the marriage to which the deceased was a party;

- anyone who is a brother, sister, uncle or aunt of the deceased, or any child of such person.

In order to receive compensation they must demonstrate actual dependency on the deceased.

The award itself is a single award that will be apportioned between the dependants. The amount depends on the financial circumstances of the deceased but not on the number of dependants. The usual categories for compensation are:

- general damages where the deceased has survived for a period after the accident, i.e. compensation for pain and suffering;

- the funeral expenses incurred by the dependants, to include items such as a memorial stone, but not including the cost of obtaining a grant of probate or letters of administration or the cost of administering the estate;

- the bereavement award, currently standing at £10,000 (March 2002). This is paid to a spouse for the death of a lawful husband or wife (but not a cohabitee) and to parents for the death of a child under 18 years (but not to a child for the death of a parent);

- the dependency award, including items such as loss of earnings and cost of replacing services such as childcare and do-it-yourself services.

The single biggest item in a claim within the dependency award will be the loss of earnings item. This is calculated using a multiplier and multiplicand. The multiplier is based on the number of years' loss of dependency. The multiplicand is the net annual loss of the dependants. The size of the multiplier and multiplicand must be established and in any one claim there may be more than one calculation required in order to establish the total figure. In any event the claim will be split into two. Firstly, those losses that have already been incurred, i.e. loss of earnings or services up to the date of claim, known as special damages, and secondly those losses expected to be incurred after the date of claim, known as general damages.

The multiplier will in most circumstances be based on the number of years left from the date of the accident until the anticipated retirement of the employee. The figure is reduced slightly in accordance with a set formula to take into account the value of having the money up front and therefore the possibility of investing some of it.

The multiplicand is determined by many factors and it may be that there is more than one multiplicand. For example, if it can be shown that the employee's income would have risen over his career, then a different multiplicand may be used for the first ten years from the second ten years. The multiplicand may also be affected by the other services provided to the dependants such as home improvement and childcare. The employee's income is modified to take into account the portion of it that they would have spent on themselves. This is taken to be a third where the only dependant is a spouse and one quarter where there are children. It may be that the court divides up the calculation such that it is one quarter only for the period of time, which the children remain dependants and then reverts to one third.

For example, if the deceased dies in 2000 aged 36 years the appropriate multiplier to a retirement age of 65 years is about 18. If the calculation is carried out in 2002 (two years later) the special damages will include two times the multiplicand and the general damages will be 16 times the multiplicand.

Deceased's net income:	£18,000.00
Dependants' own net income:	£7,000.00
Total income:	£25,000.00
Deduct deceased's living expenses (one third if there are no children; one quarter if there are children)	£8,300.00
Total (minus living expenses)	£16,700.00
Deduct dependant's own net income	−£7,000.00
Add any other services lost by dependants (e.g. home improvements)	£1,000.00
Total (dependency multiplicand)	£10,700.00

Therefore the total general damages for loss of income would be

$$16 \times £10,700.00 = £171,100.00.$$

It follows from the above that the preparation for claims arising out of a fatal accident must extend to identifying the existence and nature of any dependants. The absence of a dependant will render a claim of minimal value.

9:7.2 The role of the coroner's court

When an accident occurs at a workplace that leads to the death of any person, whether or not that person is an employee, a coroner's inquest is likely to be held to investigate the death. The doctor who certifies that the person is dead will normally notify the coroner of the death.

A coroner is an independent judicial officer. To be appointed the applicant must have been qualified as a solicitor, barrister or medical practitioner for a minimum of five years. The local authority makes the appointment and it is subsequently approved by the Secretary of State. The coroner will question the witnesses and, in deaths resulting from an accident at work, it is likely that a jury will be present. A coroner is appointed to a particular district and there are 148 districts in England and Wales of which only 26 are full-time posts. The death must have occurred in or near to a particular coroner's district for him to have jurisdiction.

The coroner must act in accordance with the Coroners Act 1988, the Coroners Rules 1984 and Home Office circulars. Subject to these, he has a fairly wide discretion on how to conduct proceedings. The coroner must appoint a deputy and may also appoint an assistant deputy. One or more coroner's officers will also be appointed to assist with administrative matters.

The coroner's court is unique. Its sole purpose is to make an enquiry into the death for the purpose of establishing the factual details surrounding the death, i.e. name and date of birth of the deceased; time, place and date of death; circumstances leading to the death; and the cause of death. For this reason the inquest has an important part to play in the investigation of fatal accidents. The coroner is expressly precluded from making decisions on civil or criminal liability.

The inquest will normally be opened within a few days of the death, which allows for the body to be released. It will then be adjourned pending further enquiries. The coroner is under a duty to hold an inquest as soon as practicable (subject to awaiting the outcome of criminal proceedings, for example for health and safety prosecution or a prosecution for manslaughter or corporate manslaughter). In practice there will be a considerable delay in deaths related to the workplace whilst the circumstances are properly investigated. A coroner's officer will usually be responsible for collecting witness statements and the coroner will decide which witnesses to call to give live evidence at the inquest and which statements can be read. If necessary the coroner can issue a summons requiring the attendance of a witness and enforce this summons by a financial penalty. Therefore, an employer or his employees could be called to give evidence.

Any properly interested person is entitled to examine any witness at an inquest. The questions cannot go to the issue of civil or criminal liability but are limited to the factual circumstances pertaining to the death. Whether a person is 'properly interested' is ultimately a matter for the coroner. In practice, an employer, his insurer, or in either case their legal representative would be a properly interested person in respect of a work-related death.

Legal advice should be sought on whether it is advisable to be legally represented at an inquest. It is probable that the employer's liability insurers will fund such a representation. In view of the fact that the witnesses may be examined and that this may lead to useful information becoming known it may be pertinent for the employer to be represented.

Once the coroner has heard all the evidence he will deliver his verdict. There are a number of verdicts prescribed and it must be one of these. No verdict shall be framed in such a way as to determine any question of civil or criminal liability.

9:7.2.1 Coroner's verdicts

Below are the verdicts coroners can give.

- Industrial disease.
- Want of attention at birth.
- Accident/misadventure.
- Unlawful killing.
- Open verdict.
- Suicide.
- Natural causes.

9:8 Further powers of inspectors other than prosecution

9:8.1 Enforcement notices under ss 21 and 22 of the HSWA

In addition to the general power to prosecute for breaches of legislation and the wide-ranging investigative powers outlined in **section 9:4.6**, inspectors have the power to serve notices as a means of enforcing health and safety legislation. These can be either improvement notices (*see* **section 9:8.2**) or prohibition notices (*see* **section 9:8.3**).

9:8.2 Improvement notices

Under s.21 of the HSWA, an improvement notice can be served by an inspector if he is of the opinion that one or more of the relevant statutory provisions is being contravened or has been contravened in circumstances that make it likely the contravention will be repeated. The purpose of the improvement notice is to give the employer an opportunity to get it right. It is not a criminal sanction and therefore appeals against the service of a notice are governed by civil law. An improvement notice should state:

- that the inspector is of the opinion that one or more of the relevant statutory provisions is or has been contravened;

- the legal provision or provisions concerned;

- why the inspector is of that opinion;

- that the circumstances should be remedied within a certain time. (This period must be longer than the time limit allowed to bring an appeal against the notice.);

- that the inspector may elect to specify the action or actions required to comply with the notice.

The imposition of the enforcement notice is a civil law issue. The employer has 21 days in which to appeal to the employment tribunal. However, if the employer fails to comply with the notice, the sanctions are criminal and will be dealt with by the magistrates' court or the Crown Court where the breach is serious enough. The penalty for the employer ranges from a fine up to £20,000 or a six-month prison sentence on conviction in the magistrates' court and an unlimited fine on indictment. If the employer continues to fail to rectify the situation, then a further fine of up to £100 a day may be incurred. The service of a notice does not prevent the enforcement authority from pursuing criminal proceedings. However, this would only be likely in the event that the provision breached led to an accident. A sample improvement notice is provided in **Figure 9:5**.

FIGURE 9:5 SAMPLE IMPROVEMENT NOTICE

Health and Safety Executive

HSE
Health & Safety Executive

Improvement Notice for Crown Employers

To

1 This is a formal notice to you that in the opinion of the Health and Safety Executive you are contravening or have contravened the legal provisions stated at (g) below, and that you should remedy the situation by the date specified at (h) below. The Crown cannot be prosecuted for the contravention of any of the provisions of the Health and Safety at Work etc Act 1974, or any other of the relevant statutory provisions within the meaning of that Act, nor for the failure to comply with this notice. Nevertheless, failure to comply is a serious matter and will result in a formal approach from the Health and Safety Executive to an appropriate person with higher authority in your organisation or, if necessary, from the chairman of the Health and Safety Commission to the responsible Minister.

2 An inspector may withdraw a notice or extend the period specified in the notice before the end of that period. You should discuss the matter with the inspector who has issued the notice if you wish him to consider this, and should do so before the end of the period given in it. If the inspector does not agree to withdraw the notice or extend the period, it is open to you as well as to him, to take up the matter at a higher level.

3 The inspector issuing the notice will, at the same time, give a copy to your employees or their representatives in accordance with section 28(8) of the Health and Safety at Work Act 1974.

4 The Code of Practice on Access to Government Information, makes information about this notice available to a member of the public. In general, HSE will disclose the front page of this notice upon request. If you think that disclosure would harm national security or defence or that the information is commercially confidential, you should give written notification to HSE within 14 days. HSE will consider whether release of the information falls within an exemption to the code, and if so, refuse to release such information.

(a) Inspector's full name	I (a)
(b) Inspector's official designation	one of (b)
(c) Official address	of (c)
	tel. no.
(d) Location of premises or place and activity	hereby give you notice that I am of the opinion that at (d)
(e) Delete as necessary	you are as (e) an employer / a person wholly or partly in control of the premises
(f) Other specified capacity	(f)
	(e) are contravening / have contravened in the circumstances that make it likely that the contravention will continue or be repeated
(g) Provisions contravened	(g)
	The reasons for my opinion are:
(h) Date	You should remedy the said contraventions or, as the case may be, the matters occasioning them by: (h)
	(e) in the manner stated in the attached schedule which forms part of this Notice.
	Signature Date
	Being an inspector appointed by an instrument in writing made pursuant to Section 19 of the Health and Safety at Work etc Act 1974 and authorised by the Health and Safety Executive to issue this notice.
	(e) An improvement notice is also being served on:
LP52 (rev 04.97)	of related to the matters contained in this notice.

9:8.3 Prohibition notices

Under s.22 of the HSWA, an inspector can serve a prohibition notice in respect of activities which are governed by the relevant statutory provisions if he is of the opinion that the activities involve, or will involve, a risk of serious personal injury. ('Personal injury' includes any disease and any impairment of a person's physical or mental condition.) The purpose of a prohibition notice is to suspend dangerous activities while a system of work, particular procedure or process is modified, or personal protective equipment is either repaired or provided, such that the risk is reduced to a level satisfactory to the inspector. The inspector has sufficient flexibility to defer the prohibition notice so that it comes into force, for example after a particular work pattern comes to an end and will prohibit its repetition until certain matters are eliminated or controlled. A prohibition notice must:

- state the inspector is of the opinion that the activities involve or will involve a risk of serious personal injury;

- specify the matters which gives rise to this risk;

- if any of those matters involve contravention of any of the statutory provisions of Pt. I of the HSWA, state this is the inspector's opinion, specify the provision or provisions and give reasons why he is of that opinion;

- direct that the activities are not to be continued unless the matter is specified and any contraventions of the provisions have been remedied.

A prohibition notice takes effect either at the end of the period specified in the notice or immediately. Again, failure to comply with a prohibition notice constitutes an offence that is punishable by a fine no greater than £20,000 on summary conviction and/or a six-month prison sentence or an unlimited fine on indictment and a further fine not exceeding £100 per day if the offence is continued. A sample prohibition notice is provided in **Figure 9:6**.

FIGURE 9:6 SAMPLE PROHIBITION NOTICE

Health and Safety Executive

Notice that work should be stopped
(risk of serious injury) for Crown Employers

To:

1 This is a formal notice to you that in the opinion of the Health and Safety Executive the activities named below involve or will involve a risk of seri-ous personal injury and should be stopped. The Crown cannot be prosecuted for the contravention of any of the provisions of the Health and Safety at Work etc Act 1974, or any other of the relevant statutory provisions within the meaning of that Act, nor for the failure to comply with this notice. Nevertheless, failure to comply is a serious matter and will result in a formal approach from the Health and Safety Executive to an appropriate person with higher authority in your organisation or, if necessary, from the chairman of the Health and Safety Commission to the responsible Minister.

2 Where this notice is not to take immediate effect, an inspector may withdraw the notice or extend the period specified in the notice before the end of that period. You should discuss the matter with the inspector who issued the notice if you wish him to consider this, and should do so before the end of the period given in it. If the inspector does not agree to withdraw the notice or extend the period, it is open to you as well as to him, to take up the matter at a higher level.

3 The inspector issuing the notice will, at the same time, give a copy to your employees or their representatives in accordance with section 28(8) of the Health and Safety at Work etc Act 1974.

4 The Code of Practice on Access to Government Information, makes information about this notice available to a member of the public. In general, HSE will disclose the front page of this notice upon request. If you think that disclosure would harm national security or defence or that the information is commercially confidential, you should give written notification to HSE within 14 days. HSE will consider whether release of the information falls with-in an exemption to the code, and if so, refuse to release such information.

(a) Inspector's full name   I (a)

(b) Inspector's official designation   one of (b)

(c) Official address   of (c)

                                                tel. no.

hereby give you notice that I am of the opinion that the following activities, namely:

(d) Location of activity   which are being carried on by you / likely to be carried out by you / under your control*
                                 at (d)

                                 involve, or will involve* a risk of serious personal injury.

                                 I am further of the opinion that the said matters involve contraventions of the following statutory provisions:

                                 because

                                 I am further of the opinion that the said activities should not be carried on by you or under your control
(e) Date   immediately / after* (e)

                                 unless the said contraventions and matters included in the schedule, which forms part of this Notice, have been remedied.

                                 Signature   Date

                                 Being an inspector appointed by an instrument in writing made pursuant to Section 19 of the Health and Safety at Work etc Act 1974 and authorised by the Health and Safety Executive to issue this notice.

LP51 (rev 10.98)

9:8.4 Appeals against improvement and prohibition notices

Under s.24 of the HSWA a person on whom either an improvement notice or a prohibition notice is served can appeal to an employment tribunal (*see* **section 9:8.5**) within 21 days from the date of the service of the notice. The tribunal can extend this time either before or after the 21-day period where it is satisfied it was not reasonably practicable for the appeal to be brought within the period. On appeal the tribunal may either affirm or cancel the notice. If it affirms it, the tribunal has the power to do so with additions, omissions or amendments.

An appeal automatically suspends the operation of an improvement notice but a prohibition notice continues to apply unless an application is made for a suspension to the tribunal and such application is granted.

Notices tend to be affirmed with modifications in the majority of cases. The initial burden rests on the inspector to show the various criteria outlined in **sections 9:8.2** and **9:8.3** are satisfied. If he does this on the balance of probabilities, then the burden shifts to the appellant to show, again on the balance of probabilities, that the notice should be cancelled or modified.

9:8.5 Employment tribunals

The employment tribunal is wholly concerned with civil rather than criminal matters; in particular it is concerned with employment matters. Under s.24 of the HSWA an appeal against an improvement or prohibition notice is made to an employment tribunal. The procedure for such an appeal is set out in Sch.4 of the Employment Tribunals' Constitution and Rules of Procedure Regulations 1993.

10 | The Law and Other Requirements

Issues discussed in this chapter:

- What is the law on health and safety?

- What are the procedures in criminal and civil courts?

- The principal statutory health and safety duties

- An explanation of 'at work' and 'an employee'

- Guidance on using 'reasonably practicable' as a defence

- What are the statutory requirements for accident prevention, reporting and investigation?

- The particular responsibilities for the manufacture and supply of products

- What are the criminal penalties?

- The liability of directors and managers

- What are liabilities for corporate killing and manslaughter?

10:1 Introduction

This chapter presents the lawyer's perspective on health and safety as it relates to the management and investigation of accidents.

10:2 What is the law on health and safety?

An employer's moral health and safety obligations towards his employees are, as one might expect, backed up by legal obligations. An employer who fails to meet these legal obligations may face legal action by his employee, the Health and Safety Executive (HSE), the local authority and in the most serious cases the Crown Prosecution Service (CPS) (amongst others). These legal obligations fall broadly into the spheres of criminal and civil law. The consequences for an employer who is found culpable in criminal law include fines and in extreme cases imprisonment. For the employer who is found liable in civil proceedings the penalties are predominantly financial. It follows that it is very important for the employer to be aware of his health and safety duties if it wishes to be sure that it is complying with relevant health and safety laws and to minimise the risk of legal action being taken against him.

10:3 The basics of criminal and civil law

10:3.1 Criminal law

The history of health and safety legislation stretches back to the mid-19th century when the first statutes dealing with conditions in the workplace, particularly those faced by children, were enacted. The purpose of health and safety legislation has changed little since the passing of the Factories Act in 1847, in that the objective of the legislation is to reduce the frequency and severity of accidents in the workplace. However, what has developed is an increasing recognition that in order for employers to appreciate the importance of their health and safety duties to their employees, it is necessary to back up their legal health and safety obligations with criminal penalties for non-compliance. Some legislation is exclusively criminal and specifically states that it does not to give rise to civil liability (*see* **section 10:3.2**) except in certain specified circumstances (e.g. the Health and Safety at Work Act 1974

(HSWA) and the Management of Health and Safety at Work Regulations 1999 (MHSWR)). This means that an individual cannot claim compensation from the employer purely because the employer has breached his statutory obligations. In order for the employee to succeed in claiming compensation they must make a claim based on some other legal principle, such as common law negligence (*see* **section 10:4.2**).

10:3.1.1 Procedures used in criminal courts

In order to prove that a criminal offence has been committed, the prosecution (either the HSE, the local authority or the CPS) must show that the evidence proving the crime is beyond reasonable doubt. More simply the court has to be 99.9% certain that the defendant has committed the offence.

Prosecutions for criminal offences start in the magistrates' court (England and Wales) or the District or Sheriff Court (Scotland). The case may, where it is serious enough, be sent to and heard by the Crown Court (England and Wales) or High Court of Justiciary (Scotland), but the magistrates' court has jurisdiction to hear most cases.

10:3.1.1.1 Magistrates' courts

Although magistrates' courts have civil jurisdiction in family and licensing matters, they are principally criminal courts. All criminal prosecutions commence in the magistrates' court irrespective of where they end up being dealt with. Prosecutions are heard in the magistrates' court for the geographical area where the alleged offence occurred. Generally magistrates are volunteers, sit in threes, are lay persons and are advised on the law by a legally qualified and impartial clerk. Subject to this, they are the arbiters of fact and law and require only a majority to reach a decision. At larger courts, or for cases of unusual complexity or importance a stipendiary magistrate will sit. A stipendiary magistrate is legally qualified and remunerated.

Whether offences relating to breaches of health and safety legislation will be concluded in the magistrates' court depends on a number of factors including the complexity of the case, the seriousness of the alleged offence and the sentencing power of the court for that particular offence. The complicated and serious cases are more likely to go to the Crown Court.

If the magistrates' court convicts an employer he has an automatic right to appeal to the Crown Court. The appeal must be brought within 21 days of the date of conviction or sentence, whichever is the later event. This time limit can be extended but leave is required of the Crown Court who will require to be satisfied there are good reasons why the appeal was not made in time. An appeal against conviction is a complete re-hearing. An appeal against a sentence raises the possibility of the original sentence being increased, although the Crown Court is restricted to the maximum powers of sentence that were available to the magistrates.

10:3.1.1.2 Crown Courts

Crown Courts are principally concerned with criminal matters. They hear the cases that are either considered too serious to be dealt with in the magistrates' court or where the defendant has elected to be tried by the Crown Court. Whether or not a case is too serious for the magistrates will depend on a number of factors including the complexity of the issues, particularly legal issues, and whether or not the magistrates consider that they have sufficient powers to adequately sentence the employer if he is found guilty. The Crown Court also hears appeals against sentences or convictions from the magistrates' court. Generally, a judge and jury will preside over a trial (where the jury are arbiters of fact and the judge the arbiter of law); a judge alone for sentencing; and a judge and two magistrates for appeals from the magistrates' court.

The Crown Courts' sentencing powers are much wider than the magistrates' courts (*see* **section 10:10.5**). The Court of Appeal has given consistent guidance in recent years concerning employers breaching health and safety legislation and the appropriate penalties.

The clear message is that the courts should be imposing more substantial punishments and, where appropriate, not be afraid of putting employers out of business. It is likely that the proportion of health and safety cases being dealt with in the Crown Court will therefore increase.

It is also possible to appeal against conviction or sentence from the Crown Court but the leave of the Court of Appeal is required. Appeal is to the criminal division of the Court of Appeal and to complete the hierarchy of criminal courts the next level is the House of Lords.

A company can be prosecuted and convicted of a criminal offence and more importantly its directors may be punished personally by imprisonment for certain offences (*see* **section 10:10.2**).

10:3.2 Sources of criminal law

Criminal law is predominantly in the form of legislation, although there are a few areas which are still based on common law principles. However, the importance of these few should not be underestimated as they include murder, breach of the peace and manslaughter. The law on murder is now partially statute based. The common law doctrine of murder has been modified most notably by the Homicide Act 1957, which introduced defences to a charge of murder of diminished responsibility and provocation. (These partial defences had already existed for some time in common law, but they were clarified by being put on a statutory footing.) The principle source of criminal law in health and safety is the HSWA. This is essentially a criminal statute and its implications are discussed further below. The fact that it is a purely criminal statute is important because it means that it does not give rise to a right of action in civil law if its requirements are broken.

10:4 Civil law

The right for an employee or any other claimant to claim compensation from an employer is found in civil law. The claimant's claim may be based on more than one legal argument. For example, he may make a claim for compensation based on the employer's negligence, breach of statutory duty and even breach of contract, all of which are civil law concepts. However, although he may show all his arguments are correct he can only recover one lot of compensation. The service of improvement and enforcement notices by either the HSE or local authority is also an important civil law matter. Although failure to comply with the notice is a criminal offence, the service of the notice and surrounding issues are all civil law issues.

The claimant is a person, partnership or company that commences legal action in the civil courts against another person, partnership or company.

10:4.1 Procedures used in civil courts

In order to prove that a person is liable under civil law, the claimant must show that the defendant is, on the balance of probabilities, liable. The balance-of-probabilities test may also be described as a requirement to show something is more likely than not. Claims by employees may be commenced in a number of courts including an employment tribunal, the County Court and the High Court. The appropriate court for commencing proceedings is decided by the value and subject matter of the claim. Appeals may be made from the employment tribunal to the High Court, from the High Court to the Court of Appeal and ultimately to the House of Lords. Legally qualified judges make the decisions of all civil courts in health and safety claims. The employment tribunal is the only exception to this rule as it sits with three lay people familiar with industrial disputes. The civil law is further complicated by the impact of European legislation on domestic English law. Moreover, in areas pertaining to the interpretation and implementation of

European law, appeals may be made to the European Court of Justice in Strasbourg. This is the highest court of the European Union and its decisions are binding on all UK domestic courts including the House of Lords.

10:4.2 Sources of civil law

There are two important sources of civil law. These are:

1. the common law;

2. legislation.

The common law is the most difficult to conceptually understand. It is established by decisions of the courts. These decisions are in turn based upon the court's reading of what society believes should be a rule, which if broken gives rise to a legal right to claim a remedy enforceable in a court of law. In order that there is certainty in the common law, courts have observed a doctrine of legal precedent. This doctrine requires courts to follow the decisions of higher courts and therefore only the House of Lords (as the highest court) and parliament (see below) can truly change the common law. The law of negligence is a particular area of common law that is pertinent to civil claims in health and safety. For example, the common law says that an employer owes a duty of care to his employees not to act negligently with respect to their health and safety. It follows that if an employee is injured at work and the employer has acted negligently and that negligence has caused the injury, then the employee has a right to claim compensation from the employer.

Statutes (Acts of Parliament), statutory instruments (Regulations and Orders) and European laws (EC/EU Regulations, Directives, Decisions, etc.) are all forms of legislation and share the common theme of being made by the exercise of government or parliamentary power. The common law position may be changed by new legislation and common law principles may be put on a legislative footing without, in reality, any material change in their

441

meaning. Legislation is the most rapidly developing area of law and has great relevance to health and safety. The courts still have a role in developing legislation by making decisions about its interpretation, and again courts must follow the decisions of higher courts in interpreting the law. However, the role of the courts here is more ancillary to the main driving force in the development of this area, which is the Government. It should be noted that there is overlap here with the criminal law in that a piece of legislation may give rise to both criminal and civil liability for the employer.

10:5 What are the principal statutory duties?

10:5.1 The Health and Safety at Work etc. Act 1974

The principal piece of legislation that governs health and safety at work is the Health and Safety at Work etc. Act 1974 (HSWA). The HSWA is primarily a criminal statute in that it creates statutory duties that are enforced by the state, usually in the form of the HSE (*see* **Chapter 9, section 9:4.2**) or local authority. The most important and overarching duties are contained in the Act, such as the duty on an employer to ensure, so far as reasonably practicable, the health and safety of his employees. The HSWA is supplemented by regulations (statutory instruments) made by the Secretary of State under s.15 of the Act. Although obligations pursuant to the regulations made under the HSWA are often also backed with criminal sanctions, they are not covered automatically by the exclusion of civil claims that apply to the duties in the HSWA. The scheme of health and safety law does involve other legislation, such as that relating to product liability and legislation that was enacted before the HSWA, but has not yet been replaced by regulations made under the HSWA, either because the opportunity has not yet arisen or there has been no practical need. However, the vast majority is now contained either in the HSWA or regulations made thereunder. The remainder of this section goes on to discuss the principal pieces of health and safety legislation that underpin any discussion of health and safety law. It is not within the scope of this work to go through every piece of legislation that might give rise to liability in particular circumstances. Rather, it is intended to concentrate on the key pieces of legislation and those others that are most likely to be relevant to either the effective management of an accident or that most frequently give rise to legal action as a consequence of an accident.

10:5.1.1 Duties under the Health and Safety at Work etc. Act

As stated in **section 10:5.1**, the HSWA contains the overarching legal health and safety obligations. The principal ones are dealt with here, as is an explanation of the relevant terms. A breach of these duties can give rise to criminal prosecution, but a claimant who suffers loss does not become entitled to compensation simply because of a breach of these duties under the HSWA by their employer. The claimant may still be entitled to compensation, but their claim must be based on some other legal footing, i.e. under the civil law. The general duties of employers to employees are contained in s.2 of the HSWA:

Section 2(1). It shall be the duty of every employer to ensure, so far as is reasonably practicable, the health, safety and welfare at work of all of his employees.

Section 2(2). Without prejudice to the generality of an employer's duty under the preceding subsection, the matters to which that duty extends include in particular:

a) the provision and maintenance of plant and systems of work that are, so far as is reasonably practicable, safe and without risks to health;

b) arrangements for ensuring, so far as is reasonably practicable, safety and absence of risks to health in connection with the use, handling, storage and transport of articles and substances;

c)   *the provision of such information, instruction, training and supervision as is necessary to ensure, so far as is reasonably practicable, the health and safety at work of his employees;*

d)   *so far as is reasonably practicable as regards any place of work under the employer's control, the maintenance of it in a condition that is safe and without risks to health and the provision and maintenance of means of access to and egress from it that are safe and without such risks; and*

e)   *the provision and maintenance of a working environment for his employees that is, so far as is reasonably practicable, safe, without risk to health, and adequate as regards facilities and arrangements for their welfare at work.*

Section 2(3). Except in such cases as may be prescribed, it shall be the duty of every employer to prepare and as often as may be appropriate revise a written statement of his general policy with respect to the health and safety at work of his employees and the organisation and arrangements for the time being in force for carrying out that policy, and to bring the statement and any revision of it to the notice of all his employees.

Subject to the defence of 'reasonable practicability', ss 2 and 3 of the HSWA create offences of absolute criminal liability. This means that the prosecution does not need to show the employer was at fault. The employer's duties towards people who are not his employees are contained in ss 3 and 4 of the HSWA.

Pursuant to s.3(1), the employer is under a duty to conduct his undertaking in such a way so as to ensure so far as is reasonably practicable that persons not in his employment who may be affected by it are not exposed to threats to their health and safety. This duty will apply to a contractor or visitor to the employer's place of business.

Section 3(2) of the HSWA goes on to impose an identical obligation on self-employed persons. However, the duty extends not only to others but also to the self-employed person himself. This extension of the duty is justified by the central purpose of the HSWA, which is to reduce the number of accidents in the workplace. Therefore, Parliament has elected as a matter of policy not to allow the self-employed person to avoid liability by claiming that the only person they put at risk was themselves, as this would still be a breach of their statutory duty.

10:5.2 Explanation of terms

10:5.2.1 'At work'

'At work' is defined for the purposes of health and safety legislation as the time when the employee is in the course of his employment, but not otherwise. This definition applies to the HSWA, but care should be taken in other circumstances as the HSWA allows the Secretary of State to make regulations extending or otherwise modifying the meaning of 'at work' in particular circumstances.

10:5.2.2 'Employee'

An 'employee' (and employment is construed accordingly) is a person who is under a contract of employment. The contract of employment can be express or implied, made in writing or made orally. The only employees exempted from health and safety legislation are domestic servants employed in a private household.

Thus, the definitions of 'employment' and 'at work' are very wide and could cover the movement of an employee from one place of work to another, travelling on business trips, working at home or being away from the office. Remember, the duty of the employer is to do all that is reasonably practicable to protect the health and safety of the employee. Therefore, it would not necessarily be reasonably practicable to protect an employee who works from home from the risk of trip injuries within their own home. However, it would be reasonable for an employer to check any equipment that is provided to the employee for the purpose of working at home. The regulations pertaining to manual handling/display screens, for example, would still apply in full.

10:5.2.3 The defence of doing all that is 'reasonably practicable'

The prosecution (i.e. the HSE, the CPS or the local authority) must show that the defendant is culpable beyond reasonable doubt. Even if the prosecution can show this, the defendant may not be guilty if he can successfully argue that he has a defence to the prosecution's claim. The defence that is most commonly available in health and safety law is that the defendant did all that was reasonably practicable to comply with its statutory duty. It is for the defendant to show that this defence applies using the balance-of-probabilities test. Thus, the burden of proof has moved from the prosecution to the defence. In order to benefit from this defence the employer must show that he has done all that would be reasonable taking into account the cost and inconvenience of doing so to protect the health and safety of his employees. However, although the employer is not expected to disregard cost as a factor, it is only a small factor and the benefits of expenditure must be looked at very carefully. It is only if the expenditure in time, effort and money would be wholly disproportionate to the risk averted that the employer can claim to have done all that is reasonably practicable. The employer is expected to keep abreast of technological developments and, therefore, the assessment of risk versus cost needs to be constantly under review. The relevant point in time when the employer's assessment of the risks should be judged by the court is the period immediately before the accident. It follows that it will not assist the defendant to argue that at the time he made the decision as to which working practices to use, the costs of a safer alternative were prohibitive, if that was no longer the case when the accident happened. In deciding what is reasonably practicable, guidance and Approved Codes of Practice available from the HSE are of particular importance. An employer who is able to demonstrate that it has done all that is required by the guidance transfers the burden of proof back to the prosecution. The prosecution must then show that even that was not enough. Otherwise the defendant will have successfully raised the defence.

10:6 The statutory requirements for accident prevention

The central tenet of accident prevention within health and safety legislation is risk assessment. The principal regulations dealing with this issue are the MHSWR. These regulations are accompanied by an Approved Code of Practice (ACOP) (Ref. L21, HSE Books), which assists in understanding the requirements of the regulations. Section 3 of the ACOP gives an outline of the main statutory requirements that relate to accident prevention (*see* **section 10:6.1**). A failure to comply with these requirements could give rise to a criminal liability, depending on the circumstances and consequences of that failure. It should be noted that with the exception of duties in respect of new and expectant mothers and young persons, a breach of the MHSWR does not give rise to civil liability. It should also be noted that the failure of an employee or a competent person appointed under the MHSWR to act appropriately is not a defence to any criminal prosecution brought against the employer for breach of the employer's obligations.

10:6.1 The Management of Health and Safety at Work Regulations 1999

Under Reg. 3 of the MHSWR employers must undertake a suitable and sufficient risk assessment of:

- the risk to the health and safety of his employees to which they are exposed whilst they are at work;

- the risk to the health and safety of persons not in his employment arising out of or in connection with conduct by him of his undertakings,

for the purpose of identifying the measures he needs to take to comply with the requirements and prohibitions imposed upon him by or under the relevant statutory provisions.

The risk assessment must be suitable and sufficient, which means the scope of the risk assessment must be appropriate for the work being assessed and it must identify the risks arising from that work. It must also enable the employer to identify what action needs to be taken to meet his statutory obligations and also to prioritise those actions. The assessment must be such that it will remain valid for a reasonable period of time and it must be reviewed on a regular basis, particularly where there has been a significant change in the nature of the work or where the employer has reason to suspect that it is no longer valid. Where the employer has five or more employees the results of the risk assessment must be recorded. It follows that the suitability and sufficiency of a risk assessment is likely to be examined by an enforcement authority as part of its accident investigation. It is submitted that an accident at work should lead an employer to suspect that the risk assessment is no longer valid and therefore to lead to it being reviewed. In any event it would be good practice to do so and would demonstrate to any enforcement authority the seriousness with which the employer viewed the accident. The employer should also note that risk assessments done before and after an accident are likely to be disclosable in civil proceedings.

The regulations also require employers to have and to implement, where appropriate, procedures in the event of a serious and imminent danger to persons in his employment. The employer is required to appoint sufficient competent persons to effect an evacuation plan, if required, and also to restrict the access of employees to areas where such a serious and imminent danger is present. Only those employees whom have received appropriate training should be allowed access. The employer is also under an obligation to ensure that contacts with the emergency services are maintained.

10:7 The statutory requirements for accident reporting

The regulations in **section 10:7.1** deal with the statutory requirement for reporting accidents to the authorities and other interested parties such as safety representatives – *see also* **Chapter 4**.

10:7.1 The Reporting of Injuries, Diseases and Dangerous Occurrences Regulations 1995

The purpose of the Reporting of Injuries, Diseases and Dangerous Occurrences Regulations 1995 (RIDDOR) is to allow the enforcement authorities to gather information on the success of health and safety measures generally, and to discover where a tightening of regulations is needed. It assists in monitoring the success of individual sites at accident prevention. It also allows the enforcement authorities to investigate serious accidents. In short, RIDDOR requires the responsible person, the identity of whom will depend on the particular circumstances (*see* **Chapter 4, section 4:4.1.11**), to notify the appropriate authority and subsequently send a report in the approved form and keep a written record of the event for at least three years. The event that triggers the obligations under RIDDOR will be either death, major injury (as defined in Sch.1 of RIDDOR) or a dangerous occurrence (as defined in Sch.2 of RIDDOR). Additional provisions also apply for the reporting of cases of diseases and gas incidents (*see* **Chapter 4, section 4:4**).

Notifying by the quickest practicable means will normally mean a telephone call to the local office of the enforcement authority. Alternatively, the call may be made to the incident centre in Caerphilly. The HSE hopes that this will remove the concern experienced by some of those responsible for reporting injuries that they have reported to the wrong enforcement authority. Telephone, fax or the internet can be used to make the report. The caller should take the name of the person to whom the incident was reported, and

449

a note of the information provided to them. Ideally, any telephone reporting should be confirmed in writing either by fax or by email. The two prescribed forms for reporting the event, either F2508 or F2508A depending on the type of event, can also be submitted electronically at www.riddor.gov.uk/reportanincident.html. If you report by telephone the HSE will send you a copy of the form and you will have an opportunity to correct it. Failure to report under RIDDOR is an offence under the HSWA and is punishable by a fine.

10:8 The statutory requirements for accident investigations

Certain specific regulations impose requirements on employers to carry out an accident investigation following an incident. The various regulations in **sections 10:8.1–10:8.4** are examples of these types of requirement.

10:8.1 The Transport of Dangerous Goods (Safety Advisers) Regulations 1999

The Transport of Dangerous Goods (Safety Advisors) Regulations 1999 apply to the transport of dangerous goods (generally hazardous goods such as those listed in the approved carriage list, explosives or radioactive material) by road, railway and inland waterway. Safety advisers must be appointed by the body undertaking the transportation of the goods. The safety adviser must advise his employer as to health, safety and environmental matters in connection with the transport. If an accident occurs during the transportation of dangerous goods that affects the health or safety of any person or causes damage to the environment or property then the safety adviser must ensure a report is prepared following such an accident. Annual reports must be prepared on activities concerning the transportation of dangerous goods. These reports must be kept for a minimum of five years. Furthermore, when required by the Secretary of State, either accident reports or annual reports must be provided.

10:8.2 The Control of Major Accident Hazards Regulations 1999

The Control of Major Accident Hazards Regulations 1999 (COMAH) apply to operators of establishments where dangerous substances (as defined in the regulations) are present at an installation in quantities that could cause a major incident or accident. There is a general duty to take all measures necessary to prevent major accidents and to limit the consequences to persons and the environment. Operators must have a documented policy with respect to the prevention of major accidents and must notify the relevant authority of various matters, send them safety reports, provide information when required to do so, make certain information public and establish emergency plans. The regulations also provide for inspections and investigations by the relevant authority.

10:8.3 The Ionising Radiation Regulations 1999

The Ionising Radiation Regulations 1999 impose requirements on employers that work with radioactive substances. These regulations require certain work with sources of ionising radiation to be notified to the HSE in advance of the work being undertaken. The regulations also require an employer to take action following incidents that may have caused a person to be overexposed to radiation. The employer will first have to investigate the incident to determine whether it can be shown beyond reasonable doubt that the overexposure has not occurred. If the investigation fails to demonstrate that no overexposure could have occurred, then the employer will be required to notify the HSE, the person affected and where that person is not their employee then that person's

451

employer. A similar investigation must be carried out in the event that the employer suspects that either a release of a specified amount of radioactive material has either been made to the atmosphere or to the ground or radioactive material has been lost or stolen. Again, unless the investigation shows beyond reasonable doubt that the above could not have happened, then the employer must notify the HSE.

10:8.4 The Railways (Safety Case) Regulations 2000

Under the Railways (Safety Case) Regulations 2000 controllers of railway infrastructures (as defined in the regulations) must prepare and submit a 'safety case' containing the information specified in Sch.1 to the regulations. This safety case must be approved by the HSE and must be reviewed at such intervals as the HSE may direct, failing which every three years. If an operator becomes aware of non-compliance with the safety case the operator must notify the HSE within seven days of the date of knowledge and state what course he has taken or proposes to take to achieve compliance. The effect of these provisions is to allow pre-emptive action by the HSE rather than action occurring only in the light of a serious accident.

10:9 Product liability

Product liability and health and safety are linked in so far as products supplied for use at work have the potential to injure employees. The obligations of the employer whose business is to supply articles for use at work are wide ranging and generally beyond the scope of this work. However, worthy of note is s.6 of the HSWA.

10:9.1 Section 6 of the Health and Safety at Work etc. Act 1974

Under s.6 of the HSWA a designer, manufacturer, importer or supplier must ensure so far as reasonably practicable that articles for use at work and substances used at work are safe and without risks to health at all times. Although the obligation falls on the designer, manufacturer, importer and supplier it is sufficient for only one of them to do the necessary work and testing and for the others to rely on that work.

10:10 What are the consequences of a breach of health and safety law?

If an accident occurs in the workplace and is related to part of an employer's undertaking it may give rise to the prospect of proceedings by the HSE or other enforcement authority under the HSWA and its related regulations or by an employee in civil law. The accident itself may trigger an investigation by the authorities or the employer (*see* **section 10:7.1**) even if there is no proof that actual harm to an individual occurred.

Accident investigators, whether from the HSE or the local authority, are likely to focus on the company's safety systems and procedures and their investigation will not necessarily be restricted to the specific details of the actual accident.

10:10.1 Criminal penalties

As a result of these proceedings, criminal proceedings under the HSWA may be brought against the employer under s.33(1) which provides an exhaustive list of offences. The offences include the failure to discharge a duty, including the general duty to employees to which an employer is subject under ss 2–7 of the HSWA (s.33(1)(a)). It is also an offence to contravene any health and safety regulations or any requirement or prohibition imposed under such regulations (s.33(1)(c)). It is also an offence to fail to comply with a prohibition or improvement notice (s.33(1)(g)).

Under s.33(1) of the HSWA:

1. *It is an offence for a person:*

    a) *to fail to discharge a duty to which he is subject by virtue of sections 2 to 7;*

    b) *to contravene section 8 or 9;*

    c) *to contravene any health and safety regulations or any requirement or prohibition imposed under any such regulations (including any requirement or prohibition to which he is subject by virtue of the terms of or any condition or restriction attached to any licence, approval, exemption or other authority issued, given or granted under the regulations);*

    d) *to contravene any requirement imposed by or under regulations under section 14 or intentionally to obstruct any person in the exercise of his powers under that section;*

    e) *to contravene any requirement imposed by an inspector under section 20 or 25;*

    f) *to prevent or attempt to prevent any other person from appearing before an inspector or from answering any question to which an inspector may by virtue of section 20(2) require an answer;*

    g) *to contravene any requirement or prohibition imposed by an improvement notice or a prohibition notice (including any such notice as modified on appeal);*

    h) *intentionally to obstruct an inspector in the exercise or performance of his powers or duties or to obstruct a customs officer in the exercise of his powers under section 25A;*

i) *to contravene any requirement imposed by a notice under section 27(1);*

j) *to use or disclose any information in contravention of section 27(4) or 28;*

k) *to make a statement which he knows to be false or recklessly to make a statement which is false where the statement is made:*

  i) *in purported compliance with a requirement to furnish any information imposed by or under any of the relevant statutory provisions; or*

  ii) *for the purpose of obtaining the issue of a document under any of the relevant statutory provisions to himself or another person;*

l) *intentionally to make a false entry in any register, book, notice or other document required by or under any of the relevant statutory provisions to be kept, served or given or, with intent to deceive, to make use of any such entry which he knows to be false;*

m) *with intent to deceive, to forge or use a document issued or authorised to be issued under any of the relevant statutory provisions or required for any purpose thereunder or to make or have in his possession a document so closely resembling any such document as to be calculated to deceive;*

n) *falsely to pretend to be an inspector;*

o) *to fail to comply with an order made by a court under section 42.*

10:10.2 Corporate killing and manslaughter

The offences that may be committed by an employee are not restricted exclusively to s.33(1) of the HSWA. Companies may also be charged with the offence of manslaughter, also referred to as corporate killing. The difficulty for the prosecuting authorities (in such cases usually the CPS) is to show the 'guilty mind' which is a necessary ingredient of this crime. For example, in *R v. Great Western Trains Co*, Great Western Trains was charged with manslaughter as a result of the fatalities caused by the Southall train crash. The prosecution was ultimately unsuccessful because the prosecution failed to identify any directing mind within the company that possessed the appropriate guilty mind. The attorney general (a government lawyer) sought the opinion of the Court of Appeal on this point and the court stated that it was necessary for an individual within the company with the power to control the company in some significant way to have the guilty mind. It is unlikely that such an individual will exist in a large company where many people collectively operate the business. Therefore, the majority of successful convictions are likely to be of small companies where the controlling mind of the company is more easily identifiable. This is ably demonstrated by the Lyme Regis bay case where an activity centre was successfully prosecuted for the manslaughter of four teenagers who drowned whilst canoeing across Lyme Regis bay in March 1993. The managing director of the centre was imprisoned for a period of three years. The Government has responded to a feeling of injustice that was held by the general public by issuing a consultation paper in May 2000. It put forward proposals to introduce a new offence of corporate killing that will not require the prosecution to demonstrate the controlling mind. If such an offence is introduced and is widely enforced, then health and safety will be propelled up the boardroom agenda.

10:10.3 The liability of directors and managers

Occasionally, although this occurs less often, proceedings may be brought against a director or manager of a corporate body in a personal capacity under s.37 of the HSWA. However, the enforcement authorities very rarely pursue this type of prosecution, as it is fraught with difficulties. The enforcement authority is only likely to pursue such a prosecution where it is confident that it can show that the offence was due to some serious dereliction of duty on the part of the director. In legal terms the section goes wider than directors and can enable prosecutions of managers and those persons purporting to act in such a capacity and also the owners where they have a controlling influence. It is important to note that this discussion on liability applies to the breach of the company's obligations under the HSWA to its employees and to the breach of the employee's duty to his fellow employees under s.7 of the HSWA.

Section 37 of the HSWA – offences by bodies corporate – states that:

(1) Where an offence under any of the relevant statutory provisions committed by a body corporate is proved to have been committed with the consent or connivance of, or to have been attributable to any neglect on the part of, any director, manager, secretary or other similar officer of the body corporate or a person who was purporting to act in any such capacity, he as well as the body corporate shall be guilty of that offence and shall be liable to be proceeded against and punished accordingly.

(2) Where the affairs of a body corporate are managed by its members, the preceding subsection shall apply in relation to the acts and defaults of a member in connection with his functions of management as if he were a director of the body corporate.

10:10.4 Types of criminal offence

All criminal offences (which includes health and safety offences) are classified into one of three types, which correspond with the seriousness of the offence and therefore the court in which the case will be tried.

10:10.4.1 Summary-only offences

These are dealt with by the magistrates' court. It is not possible for offences of this type to be tried or sentenced at the Crown Court. The only way the Crown Court deals with these matters is on appeal. An example would be contravening any requirement imposed by an inspector under s.20 of the HSWA.

10:10.4.2 Either-way offences

These are offences that can be dealt with either in the magistrates' court or the Crown Court and at such stage a decision has to be made as to the appropriate forum. The majority of health and safety offences are either-way offences, for example breaches of any of the principal duties (*see* **section 10:5.1.1**) imposed on an employer by ss 2–7 of the HSWA, the vast majority of health and safety regulations, and the contravention of any requirement of an improvement or prohibition notice.

10:10.4.3 Indictable-only offences

These are the most serious offences and therefore can only be dealt with at the Crown Court. As already stated, they would still be commenced in the magistrates' court, but the initial hearings before the magistrates would be concerned with directing the case to the Crown Court. Corporate manslaughter or manslaughter are indictable offences.

10:10.5 Penalties

The extent of any penalty will obviously depend on the circumstances. The more serious the breach, the more serious the punishment will be. The court is, to some extent, expected to disregard the consequences of the breach (except where it forms part of the offence such as manslaughter) in determining the likely sentence. Thus, if the actions of the employer were only slightly below what was required of him but the consequences were unexpectedly severe, then strictly speaking the consequences of the breach should not be taken into account except insofar as they are a measure of how poorly the employer has behaved (*see R v. F Howe and Son (Engineers) Ltd*). In practice this is very difficult for the court to do and in many cases the court's sentence does not take into account the consequences. In general terms the punishments that may be imposed range from hundreds of pounds to millions. The highest fine ever imposed is £1.5 million. However, the average fine imposed under the HSWA is a mere £6,223. It should be noted that the level of fines is on the increase as courts take non-compliance more and more seriously. This trend was highlighted by the case of *R v. F Howe and Son (Engineers) Ltd* (*The Times*, 27 November 1998) which recognised the need for fines to be large enough to make employers sit up and take notice of health and safety issues. The Court of Appeal who decided this case stated:

> ... *that fines need to be large enough to bring home the message to employers that they must take their duty of care for those who work with them and the public who may be influenced by their business seriously.*

Whilst a fine should not generally be so large as to imperil the earnings of employees or create a risk of bankruptcy, there may be cases where an offence is so serious that the defendant ought not to be in business. The relevant factors for consideration identified by the Court of Appeal in the above case were as follows.

- To assess the gravity of the breach – how far short of the appropriate standard did the employer fall in failing to meet the reasonably practicable test?

- Death or serious injury as a consequence of the breach is to be regarded as an aggravating feature.

- Were costs cut to improve profit at the expense of protecting employees? Any deliberate breach of health and safety legislation with a view to profit seriously aggravates the offence.

- The standard of care imposed by the legislation is the same regardless of the size of the company.

- What were the degree of risk and the extent of dangers created by the offence?

- What was the extent of the breach or breaches?

- Was there a failure to heed warnings?

- Was there a failure to take the necessary steps to protect health and safety or was a specific risk run to save money?

The Court of Appeal also identified the following mitigating features:

- prompt admission of responsibility and timely plea of guilty;

- steps taken to remedy deficiencies once they had been drawn to the defendant's attention;

- a generally good safety record.

The law on penalties for health and safety offences is currently under review by the Government. There is recognition that the current level of fines does not act as an effective deterrent or punishment for companies to make health and safety a sufficiently high priority. In its strategy statement dated June 2000, the Government stated that it would legislate to provide the lower courts with greater sentencing powers, both in terms of giving the court wider powers to impose fines of up to £20,000 and to imprison employers for health and safety offences. To date no specific action has been taken by the Government in terms of new legislation. The increase in the level of fines is to be accompanied by a policy of naming and shaming on an annual basis by the HSE, much in the same way as the Environment Agency names and shames 'the worst polluters'. The strategy document also suggests that individuals should be given greater rights to pursue private prosecutions by removing in many cases the current requirement for the individual to have the consent of the Director of Public Prosecutions (the head of the CPS) to commence the prosecution. The removal of this limitation is likely to increase the number of individuals that pursue vexatious prosecutions against employers and may therefore be strongly resisted by industry.

The penalties that can be imposed by either the magistrates' court or the Crown Court are governed by ss 33 and 42 of the HSWA and depend on the type of offence that has been committed. Section 42 of the HSWA allows the Court to order someone convicted of an offence to remedy the breach of health and safety law instead of or in addition to another punishment. There are three general categories:

1. Breaches of ss 2–6 of the HSWA (including the principal health and safety duties placed upon employers):

   a) magistrates' court – £20,000 fine;

   b) Crown Court – unlimited fine.

2. Breaches of a HSWA s.42 order (i.e. an order by the court following a conviction to remedy an offence) or breaches of an improvement or prohibition notice:

   a) magistrates' court – £20,000 fine and/or six months' imprisonment;

   b) Crown Court – unlimited fine and/or two years' imprisonment.

3. Others, principally breach of health and safety regulations by making a false entry in any register, book or notice required under the regulations:

   a) magistrates' court − £5,000 fine;

   b) Crown Court − unlimited fine (and in some limited circumstances the power to imprison for two years).

4. Contravening a requirement or preventing a third party complying with a requirement imposed by an inspector under s.20 (inspectors' powers) or s.25 (powers to deal with a cause of imminent danger) of the HSWA:

   a) magistrate's court only − £5,000 fine.

11 | Insurance

Issues discussed in this chapter:

- Why do we need to insure?
- Statutory requirements for insurance
- 'Utmost good faith'
- The duty to disclose material facts
- The payment of claims
- Insurable and non-insurable risks
- What insurance cover is available?
- Buying direct and through a broker
- Claim procedures
- The effects of the Woolf Reforms

11:1 What is insurance?

Insurance is the transfer of risk from the purchaser to the insurer (the company or companies covering the risk). For the sake of good order we will assume those purchasing the insurance cover are private or limited companies or partnerships but will refer to them as the proposers or the company.

Insurance contracts are agreements that insurers will pay any loss covered by the insurance policy. For accident managers and investigators the problem is that these losses will occur and will be investigated in the future. Effectively this means that insurance coverage purchased today may not be tested until a claim occurs, and with some classes of liability business these claims could occur in 20 or 30 years time! If there is a defect in the insurance placing, such as wrong information being given or the wrong type of cover being purchased, a claim may not be paid. Insurance cannot be arranged or negotiated retrospectively, so when cover is purchased insurers must be given full information and the insured purchase the right amount of cover. It is essential that a company's insurance programme is exactly placed without any errors and it is strongly recommended that, as part of their risk management programme, accident managers and investigators examine their insurance cover and satisfy themselves that their insurance programme has been correctly placed and covers all exposures that need to be protected and any additional cover purchased.

This chapter deals both with the action that should be taken to arrange cover and that to be taken should a loss occur. Close attention should be paid to the exclusion clause in a policy. Whilst today's insurance cover is very broad it is not possible to cover every risk. Insurance will pay for a building to be replaced, a liability award made by courts and the costs of defending any action. There are items that insurance cannot and does not cover, for example fines imposed for breaking health and safety regulations. Such payments could be considered as encouraging negligent practices and are seen to be against public policy. Equally, insurance policies do not help the adverse publicity that can follow a substantial accident.

11:1.1 Loss following an accident

An accident could result in death or bodily injury to employees and third parties, and damage to both property from the organisation's operations and third parties. Additionally an accident could lead to legal action, loss of earnings and pecuniary losses (i.e. currency fluctuation/fall in investments). These exposures need to be analysed and the decision made whether to insure or self-insure against potential financial loss. Some exposure must be insured by law (*see* **section 11:2.3**). The cost of the insurance cover and the protection it gives should be considered against the likelihood of a loss as a result of an accident, the financial loss it will produce and the ability of the company to meet this loss out of existing assets.

The loss following an accident should be categorised into:

- losses that could prejudice the survival of the business;

- losses that could impair profitability;

- losses that could result in action being taken for third-party liability, employers' liability, products liability or third-party damage;

- losses that would have a negligible effect on the business.

By categorising exposure in this way it is possible to organise insurance in the most advantageous way.

11:1.2 Asset protection

A company's assets are the means by which it generates turnover. Most are property exposures such as buildings, machinery and plant, computers and office equipment, stock and motor vehicles. These assets are used to produce income and the loss of these assets would result in financial loss. These assets should therefore be protected by conventional property insurance.

Use of these assets may result in accidents. Therefore, it is essential that any exposure to loss or damage by means of an accident is quantified and the appropriate insurance cover sought. Accidental discharge of gas or fuel, for example, could totally destroy a major industrial site.

11:2 Statutory requirements to insure

There are statutory duties to insure **certain risks**:

- employer's liability risks are insured under the Employers' Liability Act 1969;

- motor third party risks are required to be insured under the Road Traffic Act 1988.

The cover provided by an insurer is against the financial consequences of civil action; there is no cover for any penalties or fines.

Compulsory insurance is also required for riding establishments. There is a statutory obligation to buy public liability insurance under the Riding Establishment Act 1930. The Act gives no indication of what limit of liability is required.

Accountants, solicitors and insurance brokers must buy professional indemnity insurance as conditions of membership of their own professional body or trade association. The Law Society lays down minimum requirements as does the British Insurance Brokers Association and the General Insurance Services Council.

These issues are not covered in this chapter but anyone who feels they have an exposure in these areas should consult an insurance company or an insurance intermediary.

11:2.1 The Employers' Liability Act 1969

There is an obligation for employers to insure against their legal liabilities for illness or injury to employees arising out of and in the course of their employment under the Employers' Liability Act 1969. The intention of the Act is to protect employees and to ensure that all injured employees can be compensated. It is not enough for the employee to show they were injured at work; they must show that their employer was liable for the injury. Usually the employee will allege the employer was negligent in not providing a safe method of working or safe working conditions. Under the Employers Liability (Compulsory Insurance) Regulations 1998 the minimum legal limit of cover that should be purchased for each employee is £5 million. In practice most insurance policies have an indemnity of at least £10 million per employee. Employers' liability policies provide wide cover and protect employees such as apprentices, persons under a contract of service, non-executive directors, persons supplied, hired or borrowed in the course of business, subcontractors, drivers or operators of hired plant and persons working under a community service order. Cover is given for anyone who has a contract of employment. Since 1999, such policies have had to be retained for 40 years.

Anyone visiting a place of employment would be covered by public liability insurance.

The Act does not apply to local authorities, statutory corporations and nationalised industries such as the Civil Aviation Authority.

There are special rules that relate to a small family business. For example, it is not compulsory to insure certain close relatives. For example, a husband-and-wife team running a corner shop do not need to buy cover. Equally if a son, daughter, stepson, father, mother or brother is employed there is no need to buy employers' liability cover. However, a prudent employer would surely buy such cover.

Only insurers authorised by the UK's Department of Trade and Industry can write employers' liability business. Only authorised insurance companies will offer employers' liability cover and brokers are aware which companies are authorised. The insurance company will give the employer a certificate stating they have employer's liability insurance with them. This must be displayed in a prominent position in the employer's premises. Any company that does not purchase employer's liability cover or fails to display the certificate can be fined. This fine can be levied against both individuals (such as managers and company secretaries) as well as the company itself.

11:2.1.1 The Employers' Liability (Defective Equipment) Act 1969

The Employers' Liability (Defective Equipment) Act 1969 makes an employer liable for any injuries to employees caused by defective equipment supplied by the employer. It is no defence that the defect is due to the fault of a third party.

A separate employers' liability policy must be purchased for each company. Where there are associated companies a separate policy has to be purchased for each company. This rule does not apply to subsidiaries of holding companies.

11:2.2 The Road Traffic Act 1988

The Road Traffic Act 1988 states that there is a requirement to arrange motor insurance against any legal liability (other than contractual liability) to any third party (including passengers) for death, injury or third-party property damage. Only if there is a contractual agreement between the parties that excused liability is the duty negated. This would also cover passengers being driven or being carried in the course of their employment. Employees who are injured arising out of and in the course of their employment whilst passengers in a motor vehicle which the employer is legally responsible for insuring are by law covered under the employer's motor insurance policy and not under their employer's liability policy. The Act does not apply to county council authorities, police authorities and vehicles used by the armed forces.

11:2.3 Statutory responsibilities

Under the following legislation a duty of reasonable care is required and therefore there is a need to insure.

- Health and Safety at Work etc. Act 1974;

- Factories Act 1961;

- Offices, Shops and Railway Premises Act 1961;

- The Occupiers' Liability Acts 1957 and 1984;

- Defective Premises Act 1972;

- Environmental Protection Act 1990;

- Construction (Design and Management) Regulations 1995;

- Consumer Protection Act 1987;

- Food Safety Act 1990;

- Supply of Machinery (Safety) Regulations 1992.

The first three Acts place a duty of reasonable care on employers to provide a safe and healthy environment for employees and members of the public with whom they may come into contact. Whilst the employees' insurance needs are met by the employer's liability insurance policy, a separate public liability policy will also be needed to cover anyone who is affected by the organisation's operations and who are not employees.

11:2.3.1 The Occupiers' Liability Acts 1957 and 1994

The Occupiers' Liability Acts 1957 and 1994 place an occupier under a duty to provide safe premises (this includes land, buildings and any fixed or moveable structure, including any vessel, vehicle or aircraft).

The occupier may be the landlord, although not necessarily so. The decisive factor is whether a person has some degree of control over the use of or activity in the premises. Exclusive occupation is not required, and there may be two or more occupiers in the premises at any one time. For example, a landlord who lets the premises to a tenant is treated as parting with all control, except that he is still regarded as the occupier of any parts of the premises retained by him and excluded from the tenant's holding, such as common staircases, lift shafts and entrance halls.

The Occupiers' Liability Acts cover damage to property as well as death and/or personal injury arising from acts or omission that relate to things to be done on the premises. The occupier owes all lawful visitors a 'common law duty of care'. The 1994 Act extends the duty owed to non-visitors (e.g. trespassers), persons acting in the exercise of some right, or persons lawfully exercising a private right of way. Under the Occupiers' Liability Act 1957, s.2 an occupier owes a duty to all visitors to take reasonable care of their safety.

Under s.2(4) where damage is caused to a visitor by a faulty construction, maintenance or repair by an independent contractor employed by the occupier, then the occupier is not liable if he has acted reasonably in entrusting the work to the independent contractor and had taken reasonable steps to satisfy himself that the contractor was competent and the work had been done properly.

11:2.3.2 The Defective Premises Act 1972

The Defective Premises Act 1972 imposes a non-excludable duty on builders who build new dwellings. They must be built in a workmanlike and professional manner and must be fit for human habitation on completion. The Act does not apply to buildings covered by a National House Building Registration Council certificate. The duty does not cease if the building is sold. There is a common law duty on builders for liability in negligence for any injury or damage caused by defective work. The Act provides for a statutory form of negligence which makes 'repairing landlords' liable for defects in the premises, provided they knew or ought to know about the defect.

Under the Act where a landlord has an express obligation to his tenant to maintain and repair the premises, the landlord owes a duty of care to anyone who might reasonably be expected to be affected by defects in the state of the premises. Under s.4(1) of the Act the landlord must ensure the premises are reasonably safe. If the lease gives the landlord the right to enter a premises to carry out maintenance work, then under s.4(1) the landlord is treated as if he were under an obligation to the tenant to repair and maintain. The landlord does not owe any duty in relation to a defect in the premises if this defect arises from the tenant's failure to carry out an obligation imposed expressly upon him.

11:2.3.3 The Environmental Protection Act 1990

The Environmental Protection Act 1990 controls pollution from certain industrial processes and regulates waste on land. It places a duty on local authorities to detect a statutory nuisance and to investigate complaints.

11:2.3.4 The Construction (Design and Management) Regulations 1994

The Construction (Design and Management) Regulations 1994 not only ensure safe working practices operate on a building site but also take into account the health and safety of the general public, occupiers and those who will work in the building in the future.

11:2.3.5 The Consumer Protection Act 1987

The Consumer Protection Act 1987 (CPA) imposes strict liability on the producers of goods for death, personal injury or damage to private property.

The CPA ensures that a victim has an easily identifiable target by rendering potentially liable both the actual producer and certain other persons (which includes companies) who are not involved in production. Liability extends to:

- a 'producer';

- an 'own-brander' (i.e. a product produced by a manufacturer as another's own brand, e.g. Tesco baked beans made by another company);

- an importer of a product from outside the EU;

- a supplier who cannot trace the product back to the actual producer.

The Act runs alongside existing civil laws (such as the Sale of Goods Act 1893) but applies only to goods supplied after 1 March 1998. Any injured person must prove the product caused the injury but there is no duty to prove negligence or presence of a contract. There are six limited defences available including the following:

- there is no need for a contractual relationship, i.e. any victim can sue;

- there is no need to establish fault, i.e. no matter how hard the producer tries to avoid supplying a defective product, he is legally responsible for the insuring against injuries and losses a defective product may cause. This is known as 'strict liability';

- producers are more vulnerable to legal action;

- producers should check they have adequate insurance to cover their potential liability exposure.

While there have so far been few cases brought under the CPA, it is noticeable that producers have been taking far greater preventative measures since its implementation, e.g. widespread adoption of applicable British Safety Standards.

11:2.3.6 The Food Safety Act 1990

The Food Safety Act 1990 imposes the registration and licensing of food premises and hygiene training. It is an offence to sell food which fails to conform with safety regulations or renders food injurious to health.

11:2.3.7 The Supply of Machinery (Safety) Regulations 1992

The Supply of Machinery (Safety) Regulations impose a duty on designers and manufactures to produce safe machinery. The regulations apply to machines which are powered and have moving parts, and require producers to produce machinery to the health and safety standards of BS 5304:1988 (Safety of Machinery). These regulations implement the requirements of the EC Council Directive 89/392/EEC, known as the Machinery Directive, which set out to harmonise safety standards on new machinery across the

European Union, setting out the general safety standards and a conformity marking system now widely known as the CE mark.

11:3 Insurance contracts

Insurance contracts are subject to contract law. There are a number of principles that must be observed which can invalidate a contract.

11:3.1 The principles of insurance

When claims are made following an accident, the employer will find that insurers will pay any claim that is covered by a policy that is in force, subject to the conditions of the policy.

Insurers will investigate the circumstances of the claim and are entitled to refuse to pay the claim if there has been a breach of one of the principles of insurance or the conditions of the insurance policy. It is therefore essential that the following points are considered and that checks are made to make sure the information supplied to insurers meet these principles.

11:3.1.1 Utmost good faith

The term 'utmost good faith' concerns the information disclosed by the purchaser of an insurance policy as they prepare to buy insurance. At this stage, before the policy incepts, the purchaser is known as the proposer.

As insurance policies are only truly tested when a loss occurs, buying insurance is very different from buying other items such as property or a car. For example, when buying a car the subject matter of the contract, i.e. the car, can be examined and tested and expert advice can be sought if necessary. With insurance the position is very different. Whilst the proposer can be given a specimen copy of the policy, the insurer would have difficulty examining all aspects of the proposer's business and their activities. For this reason contract law imposes a greater duty of disclosure on parties to insurance contracts than to parties for commercial contracts.

The definition of 'utmost good faith' is provided in *Rozanes* v. *Bowen* [1928]:

> *As the underwriter knows nothing and the man who comes to him to ask him to insure knows everything, it is the duty of the assured, to make a full disclosure to the underwriter without being asked of all the material circumstances. This is expressed by saying it is a contract of utmost good faith.*

11:3.1.2 Duty of disclosure

Over the years insurers have had many problems with non-disclosure of information and many legal cases have been fought over this issue.

The duty of utmost good faith has gradually evolved and it is the duty of the proposer to voluntarily disclose, accurately and fully, all the facts material to the insurance risk being proposed, whether requested or not.

The duty of disclosure applies to both proposer and insurer. The insurer must disclose all information regarding the cover given by the policy to be purchased and its conditions. The duty to disclose begins when negotiations about the policy begin and lasts until the policy incepts. It is revived at each renewal of the policy. Again the duty lasts while renewal negotiations are conducted and ends when the policy is renewed. Some policies extend this duty of disclosure so that it continues throughout the policy period and any new material information must be disclosed. Equally, if during the period of the policy there is a need to amend the cover by, for example, adding new premises or amending the policy limit, the duty of disclosure is revived because effectively a new policy is being formed.

11:3.1.3 Material facts

Insurers are most concerned about non-disclosure of material facts. These are facts that are so important to the insurer that had they been made aware of them they would either not have insured the risk or would have done so on different policy terms and premium. Material facts were defined in the Marine Insurance Act 1906 as follows:

> *Every circumstance is material that would influence the judgement of a prudent insurer in fixing the premium or determining whether he will take the risk.*

If there is a failure to disclose a material fact or circumstance insurers can avoid the claim. The problem here is that the disclosure of the circumstance of an accident could lead to insurers deciding they represent a material fact and that the claim will not be paid.

11:3.1.3.1 Association of British Insurers: Statement of General Practice

The Association of British Insurers (ABI) has clarified the position in the UK by issuing a Statement of General Insurance Practice. This statement only applies to private and personal insurance but commercial insurers also tend to use the ABI Statement as a standard procedure for disclosure. The statement says that matters which insurers have found generally to be material will be the subject of questions in proposal forms. This means that insurers will put any question that they regard as material into the proposal form and will not rely on the defence of non-disclosure of a material fact should a dispute occur. For example, insurers might investigate a motor claim and find that the driver had a number of speeding convictions. If insurers have asked on a proposal form for details of previous driving history and these speeding convictions had not been revealed they may reject the claim on the basis of non-disclosure. If, however, insurers did not ask this question, they have no right to repudiate the claim.

This puts the onus on the insurer to ask the relevant questions about the risk but also means the policyholder must disclose full information. It also says that unless the proposal form contains details of the cover being offered there must be a statement that a copy of the policy form is available on request. It is up to insurers to make sure that the proposer knows what is covered under the policy.

11:3.1.3.2 Physical and moral hazard

In practice most problems relate to information about the policyholder or their insurance history. Material facts can relate to both physical hazards and moral hazards. Usually the questions on a proposal form or the questions asked during negotiations establish what the physical hazards of the risk are. It is more difficult to ask specific questions on moral hazard, but information on whether insurance has ever been refused and the claims experience of the proposer is of vital importance and will be asked. Not everyone keeps a detailed record of what losses they have claimed from insurers over the years. The problem for a proposer in this situation is that they could provide loss information that is incorrect in that one or more losses are missing. This information would suggest to insurers that the risk is better than it actually is and they may charge too little premium or give too wide cover. In these circumstances there has been a breach in the duty of utmost good faith (*see* **section 11:3.1.1**).

11:3.1.4 Supplying information

If when completing a proposal form or supplying information the proposer does not supply what the insurer considers to be full information about the risk to be insured, the insurer will ask the proposer for more information about the risk or ask for a fuller disclosure of information.

11:3.1.4.1 Test of materiality

The test of whether or not a fact is material will be decided by the courts. If there is a dispute, the insurers would be able to refuse to pay claims on the grounds that the policy was invalid due to non-disclosure of a material fact. The court would hear evidence as to whether such a fact was material and would look at what position a prudent insurer would take in the same circumstances.

11:3.1.5 Effect of breach of duty

When there has been a breach of the duty of disclosure both the insurer and the proposer can set the policy aside *ab initio*. This means that they have the right to treat the policy as if it had never existed. If the breach was made by an insurer, the proposer would receive back any premium they have paid but the policy would no longer exist. If the breach was made by a proposer, the premium would be returned but no claims would be paid under the policy.

Where there is non-disclosure of information by the proposer the policy is voidable. This means the insurer has the right to refuse to pay claims. Much depends on the extent of the non-disclosure. If an insurer has been misled over the proposer's claims experience they would not be sympathetic. On the other hand, after a minor breach of non-disclosure insurers may pay the claim but only continue cover if the proposer pays some additional premium.

It should be noted that the Rehabilitation of Offenders Act 1974 could overrule the duty of disclosure. This Act allows a convicted person to act as if he or she has never offended provided there has been a period of 30 months since the completion of a custodial sentence. Thus a driver convicted of causing death by dangerous driving would not have to disclose this crime under this Act. Equally an employee would not have to tell an employer of a custodial sentence and thus this information could not be passed on to insurers.

For the employer the prime concern is ensuring the duty of utmost good faith is observed. The temptation to keep quiet about facts that may increase premium must be avoided. When examining a claim that is to be presented to insurers, if the accident investigator becomes aware of a breach of the duty of utmost good faith they should inform insurers immediately.

11:3.2 Insurable interest

Only risks where a company has a legal and financial interest, whereby they benefit from its safekeeping or are prejudiced by its loss, can be insured. This is called insurable interest and it includes the right of a company to insure any exposure that could give rise to financial loss. Thus a company has the right to insure against financial loss that could be caused by an employer's liability claim.

The term is used because it is the proposer's interest in the subject matter (the risk being covered) that is the prime consideration of insurers. There must be a legal relationship between the proposer and the risk. For accident insurance policies, insurable interest must exist both at the time the policy is issued and the time of the loss. For example, if a company owned a subsidiary and later sold it, insurable interest would exist at the time the policy was issued but would not exist at the time of loss.

11:3.2.1 When insurance interest must exist

For accident insurance, insurable interest exists as a company would be liable to pay damages and pay legal fees should an accident occur. Where there can be a problem with insurable interest is under contract. It may be that a company can be exposed to an unknown risk because of an agreement in a contract. It is essential that all risk that the company has insurable interest in is evaluated and insurance purchased if necessary.

11:3.3 Indemnity

When an accident occurs damage and/or harm is almost inevitably caused. Insurers will indemnify the insured for this damage/harm. This may relate to the company's own property and equipment but can equally involve death or injury to employees and third parties and damage to their property.

Indemnity effectively means putting the insured in the same financial position they would have been in had the loss not occurred. Whilst the company should not benefit by their loss equally it should not suffer any financial disadvantage from the loss.

Thus part of the principle of indemnity is that the insured must not profit from a loss. For physical damage this will mean either paying for the rebuilding of property and equipment destroyed or damaged as a result of an accident, or repairing or replacing the property/equipment.

For commercial policies an amount is deducted for wear and tear of the items (i.e. depreciation) but it is often possible to buy cover that will pay losses in full. These are known as reinstatement policies. Some special types of property policies just cover part of the exposure. For example, if the exposure is a store of a raw material it may be impossible for the full amount at risk to be damaged or destroyed as a result of an accident. In these circumstances the insured can buy a first-loss policy, which represents the maximum amount they consider to be at risk.

The traditional way of indemnifying for property losses caused by accidents was by payment of cash sums. Insurers are now changing their practice and are using nominated suppliers such as retail chain stores. Thus instead of paying the company the full value of their damaged property, insurers buy direct from a chain store or supplier and replace the lost or damaged item. As insurers buy many items during the course of a year their buying power enables them to obtain a large discount which reduces the costs of the claim. If the insured does not want the property replaced and instead wants the full cash price of the lost or damaged goods they will receive the amount the insurers would actually have paid the retailer.

With liability insurance, indemnity is deemed to be the payment of any loss awarded by a court and the costs of defending the action up to the agreed indemnity limit in the policy. Insurers will pay either the award made by the court or the cost of any out-of-court settlement made. They would in addition pay both the claimants' and company's costs. The only limiting factor is the limit of indemnity that applies to the policy.

11:3.4 Payment of insurance

11:3.4.1 Average

Insurers will pay claims in full provided the insured has purchased sufficient cover. For property insurance the sum insured is based on the total value of the insured risk. Insurers base their premiums on the policy sum insured so it is only fair that claims should also be based on the sum insured, i.e. if the policy were not insured for its full value insurers would not receive the full premium. To protect their financial position, insurers use an average clause that reduces the payment of any claim if the property has not been insured for its full value to the difference between the sum insured and the full value. Any balance is deemed to be covered by the insured. Under the average clause insurers take the sum insured under the policy, divide it by the value of the property and then multiply by the amount of the loss.

For example, if the insured believed a factory was worth £8 million and insures it for that amount, when a loss occurs and is investigated and the true value of the factory is found to be £10 million, then the insurers would use the average clause to reduce the claim. They would take the £8 million sum insured, divide by the actual value of £10 million and multiply the resulting sum by the £5 million loss. The company would receive just £4 million for a loss of £5 million.

$$\frac{\text{Sum insured } £8\text{m}}{\text{Value of factory } £10\text{m}} \text{ x Loss } £5\text{m} = £4\text{m}$$

11:3.4.2 Subrogation and contribution

One reason why insurers want to work closely with accident investigators is to preserve the insurers' right of subrogation. This is the right of insurers, following the payment of a claim, to recover all or part of a claim where a third party has been responsible for the loss. For example, a contractor is working on a factory and negligently causes damage. The company could try and recover its loss from both their insurers and the third party. This would be unfair and against the principle of indemnity. Insurers therefore use subrogation clauses that state that insurers have the right to stand in the place of the company and 'to avail themselves of all rights and remedies'. Effectively the company can either make a claim under the policy or a claim against the third party. As the claim against the insurer is more certain, the company will inevitably take this option and let the insurers take action against the third party.

The principle of subrogation is defined in *Castellain* v. *Preston* [1883] as:

> *The right of one person, having indemnified another under a legal obligation to do so, to stand in the place of that other, and avail himself of all the rights remedies of that other, whether already enforced or not.*

Without this principle the insured would be able to claim both from his insurer and from the third party who caused the accident.

The common law requirement that subrogation only exists after a claim has been paid often causes problems. Under English law an action becomes time barred after three years for property damage and six years for death or bodily injury. Time bars also exist in other countries and if insurers delayed taking action until actual payment of the claim they could find their right to take legal action barred. For this reason insurers include a condition in the policy giving them subrogation rights before the claim is paid. The only limitation is that the insurer cannot recover from a third party until they have paid their own insured's claim and that they can only recover what they have paid out. In *Yorkshire Insurance Co* v. *Nisbet Shipping Co Ltd* [1961] the insurance company paid a claim of £72,000. Due to the length of time the action took and change in rates of exchange, the insurers recovered £127,000. They were allowed to keep £72,000 but had to pass the balance of £55,000 to the insured.

Usually there is only one insurance policy covering property or liability risks. However, it is possible by error or confusion for two policies to be in effect on one risk. For example, when new equipment is purchased the supplier automatically includes insurance against damage during delivery. Unknowingly the purchaser buys the same cover. This is known as contribution and occurs when two or more policies of indemnity cover a common interest and common peril and each policy must be liable for the loss. When this happens the loss is divided between the two policies. The insured has the choice of claiming from either policy. The first insurer will then claim back part of the claim from the second insurer.

11:3.4.3 Proximate cause

An insurance contract is a promise to pay claims and insurers will be expected to pay all losses that are covered by the policy. The problem for insurers is where does a claim start and where does it finish? For example, a fire policy would cover loss caused by fire but should this include smoke damage or water damage caused when putting the fire out? The obvious answer here is yes, but there may be other circumstances where it is difficult to decide exactly what is covered. To protect both insured and insurer the doctrine of proximate cause has been adopted. The accident investigator can be confident that if the loss is caused by a peril mentioned in the policy all losses will be paid.

11:3.4.3.1 The effect of doctrine

Proximate cause means that when a loss occurs insurers will identify what peril has caused the loss. They will then pay all losses that are caused by the action of the peril that are covered by the policy. The definition of proximate cause comes from *Pawsey* v. *Scottish Union and National* [1907]:

> *Proximate cause means the active, efficient cause that sets in motion a train of events that brings about a result without the intervention of any force started and working actively from a new and independent source.*

An example will help illustrate the principle. A commercial motor vehicle develops an electrical fault and catches fire. Prompt action ensures that the vehicle is not badly damaged but cannot be moved under its own power. Whilst this is being arranged, the vehicle is maliciously damaged by vandals. The proximate cause of the first loss is fire and this peril is covered under the owner's motor policy. The cause of the second loss is malicious damage that could be excluded by the policy.

11:4 Insurable and non-insurable risks

Not all risks are insurable. A risk can only be insured if:

- it is insured against a fortuitous event. Risks can only be insured against if the cover is for accidental and not inevitable loss. For example, a private medical health policy will cover illness. It would not pay for treatment such as plastic surgery designed to hide the ageing process;

- there is insurable interest. Insurable interest is the legal relationship between the insured and the financial loss they will suffer if an event that they were insured against occurs;

- there is homogeneous exposure. There must be a sufficient number of similar risks so that the insurer can calculate an expected loss frequency. For example, it would be impossible to insure the US space shuttle. There are only four of these vehicles so it is impossible to spread the risk over a number of insurance policies. Equally, it is hard to fix an adequate premium as it is difficult to build up adequate experience with just four actual losses;

- insuring the risk is not against public policy. The contract must not be against public policy. An example is insuring a shipment of illegal drugs against loss in transit.

Risks that cannot be insured include:

- risks that cannot be measured in financial terms. Some risks cannot be quantified in financial terms, for example the choice of a new untried risk management system;

- speculative risks. These are business risks or risks of trade, for example the designing of a new type of safety equipment;

- fundamental risks. These are risks which are beyond the control of one individual. Fundamental risks are often catastrophic and arise out of social, political or natural causes. Examples are economic recession, war and famine. A company could not insure against losses suffered due to a downturn in economic activity or buyers going bankrupt. Whilst the fundamental risk itself is not insurable the effect of individuals can be insured. So although a company cannot insure against loss of profits following an economic recession, an employee of that company can cover the risks of him or her becoming unemployed, a particular risk during a recession.

11:5 The types of insurance cover available

This section provides an overview of the main types of insurance cover available. Further information on the cover and the exclusions of individual policies must be discussed with the insurer or insurance intermediary.

Property insurance covers:

- loss or damage to buildings (including plant and machinery, fixtures and fittings);

- stock (raw material to finished goods);

- the contents of the building, which can include computer records, patterns, models, moulds and designs.

In addition, cover can be purchased for business interruption insurance. This will compensate the insured for loss of any profits that follow a claim recoverable under a property insurance policy.

Whilst at first sight it would seem that property insurance should form no part of a book on accident management there is in fact a strong connection between the two. The plant and equipment contained in buildings are a frequent source of accidents and it is necessary to be aware of what is covered by these classes of business. Equally it may be that following an accident a company's business interruption policy may pay claims.

11:5.1 Property insurance

Traditionally property insurance has covered a number of named perils in the policy, such as 'fire and explosion'. Today companies and their intermediaries demand wider cover and pressure has been put on insurers to extend cover from named perils to all risks.

11:5.1.1 Named-perils cover

The perils named in a standard fire policy are fire, lightning and explosion. The risk of explosion is limited to domestic boilers situated in a building used for domestic purposes only, although fire following an explosion is covered. Excluded from the policy are:

- property which spontaneously combusts, such as coal or fishmeal;
- property which is undergoing the application of heat;
- earthquakes;
- subterranean fire;
- riots, civil unrest and war.

This basic cover is usually extended by purchasing a special perils extension, which covers:

- damage by aircraft;
- explosion;
- riots and civil unrest;
- malicious damage;
- earthquakes, storms and tempests;
- floods, burst pipes and sprinkler leakages;
- impact subsidence;
- subterranean fire and spontaneous combustion.

A large number of extensions to this cover are available which range from cover for architects' fees to temporary removal of property.

11:5.1.2 All-risks cover

All-risks insurance on commercial or industrial property is available from some insurers. As with any all-risks policies the name is misleading in that the policy will have many exclusions which will take-away much of the cover. This term can cause confusion and misunderstanding between the company and its insurers.

Typical all-risks policies for buinesses cover accidental loss, and destruction or damage to the property insured. As insurers do not intend to cover all risks of physical damage there will be an extensive list of exclusions. The following are examples of typical exclusions, although this list is not exhaustive:

- losses caused by faulty or defective design;
- the explosion of a boiler or pressure vessels (other than domestic boilers);
- damage caused by sonic boom;
- the collapse or cracking of buildings;
- theft;
- mechanical or electrical breakdown;
- burst pipes when the building is unoccupied;
- subsidence;
- settlement;
- property in transit or undergoing any process;
- excluded property (usually property held in trust or valuables);
- damage to computer equipment, glass or china;
- property in the course of construction or erection;
- livestock;
- war risks;
- pollution.

Payment of an extra premium can add cover for engineering risks, theft, subsidence, transit and computers.

Anyone needing full details of cover should discuss the excluded risks with their insurer or broker.

11:5.1.3 Limits of indemnity

First-loss policies are offered where it is virtually impossible to lose all the property insured from one loss. A typical example is if there are a number of large stocks of raw materials insured against the risk of fire where it would be impossible for all the raw materials to be destroyed at any one time. Insurers will limit their liability to an agreed amount, which represents the maximum that could be lost at any one time. Premiums are reduced to allow for the reduction in cover.

11:5.2 Business interruption insurance

Loss or damage to property will inevitably affect production and it would be prudent to purchase cover that would reduce the financial impact of such losses. A separate policy must be purchased and this cover is called business interruption insurance, also known as loss-of-profits or consequential loss insurance.

When an accident occurs it may cause the shutdown of a production unit. Whilst insurance will pay for the replacement or rebuilding of the unit it will not pay the financial losses that will be suffered by the company. The company will have to pay its workforce whilst the unit is idle or lay them off, taking the risk that skilled workers will not return. Profits will be lost which could lead to a loss of confidence among shareholders. This could result in a drop in the company's share price and make the company vulnerable to a hostile take-over. Equally, although the unit is not producing, certain standing charges, such as rates, will still be payable. All these financial exposures can be covered by a business interruption policy.

The insured can recover the loss of profits caused by any reduced turnover and any reasonable additional expenditure. There must be a separate property insurance in force covering the same loss and usually these are placed with the same insurers. Business interruption insurance is seen by insurers as being the highest risk facing UK business and greater than pure physical risk exposure. Pre-risk surveys are usual required. Business interruption insurance can be extended to cover other areas such as brand and shareholder values.

There are a number of different forms of business interruption cover but the most common is gross profit. Insurers pay the gross profit that would have been made had the loss not occurred. In effect the insurer pays the amount of the net profit made by the insured plus the expenses (i.e. the various standing charges) that have to be paid by the company even though it may not be trading. Insurers compare the actual turnover (following the loss) to the expected turnover for the year. They will pay the amount produced by applying the rate of gross profit to the reduction in turnover.

If it is possible to make up any shortfall by paying overtime or incurring costs by switching production to another unit, insurers will pay any additional costs of working as this is cost effective and can reduce the cost of the claim.

The insured has to select an indemnity period that represents the maximum period it would take to get back into full production and to recover market share. This could vary from as little as 12 months for a simple organisation to as long as four years where a complex manufacturing process is involved.

Cover can be extended to cover items lost whilst they are at a supplier's, customers' or adjacent premises and to cover damage to supply lines of utilities (e.g. gas and electricity supplies). These exposures are not included under a standard policy and must be requested. It may mean that the perils under the policy will have to be extended. If a supplier (or a customer) were based in Japan, for example, it would be prudent to have cover for earthquake risks.

11:5.2.1 Limits of indemnity

The policy should cover the anticipated gross profit for the forthcoming fiscal period. This is then increased to take into account the indemnity period of the policy (for a three-year indemnity period the figure would be trebled) and then an allowance added for any expected increase in business activity. Often insurers will add on up to a further 33.33% to cover inflation and/or growth. There is no average clause (*see* **section 11:3.4.1**) and therefore no penalties for underinsurance. Every year the premium is adjusted to take into account the actual achieved gross profit by the insured.

11:5.3 Pecuniary cover

Pecuniary cover is designed to protect the rights and interest of insurers. It covers exposures of credit and fidelity. Of particular interest to accident managers is legal expenses insurance. This covers the company against the cost of fighting or defending a legal action. Cover can vary from insurer to insurer but typically covers:

- the cost of defending an action under the HSWA;

- disputes regarding contracts of employment;

- defending actions for purchase or supply of goods;

- defending criminal proceedings and the costs of compensation in unfair dismissal cases.

The insurer must approve all cases before action is taken.

11:5.4 Liability insurance

Liability insurance covers the insured's legal liability to pay losses. Insurers will pay any awards paid by the courts plus the cost of defending any action. They will not in any circumstances pay any fines imposed by the courts. Such action would be against the public interest. Damage or injury alone will not trigger a claim under the policy; the insured must be found to be legally liable for any injury or damage.

11:5.4.1 Employers' liability

There is an obligation for employers to insure their legal liabilities for illness or injury to employees arising out of and in the course of their employment under the Employers' Liability Act 1969. The Act is intended to protect employees and to insure that injured employees can be compensated. Employers' liability insurance will enable the employer to meet the cost of compensating an employee's injury or illness caused in the course of their employment. This injury/illness can happen on or off site provided it occurs as part of the employee's working activity. An employee commuting to or from work in their own or their employer's vehicle is NOT covered by employers' liability insurance. However, an employee travelling as part of their employment is covered whether as a passenger or driver regardless of whether they are in their own vehicle or in their employer's vehicle.

The wording of most employers' liability policies is very wide and covers injury or illness caused at work due to an unsafe working practice, using unsafe machinery or the place of work being unsafe. It must be shown that the employer was negligent in not providing these safe working conditions. In the event of death, any action will be taken by the employee's estate and any award will go to his or her next of kin.

11:5.4.1.1 Limits of indemnity

The Employers Liability (Compulsory Insurance) Regulations 1998 came into force on 1 January 1999. This increased the minimum legal limit of cover for each employee from £2 million to £5 million. In practice most insurance policies have an indemnity of at least £10 million per employee and major companies have much higher limits of indemnity. Insurers pay any damages awarded against the insured plus the claimant's costs and the insured's legal costs for any loss caused during the period of the insurance. When purchasing cover the employer must consider what limit of indemnity they need and what deductibles they will accept. The employer needs to take into account the potential for multiple injuries, that the limit of indemnity in the policy applies to both liability claims and the cost of the defence of these claims, and that disease claims will be regarded as a single occurrence per employee. This last point is important as each claim will have the full limit of indemnity available BUT each claim will bear its own deductibles.

The Act says an employer must display a certificate in a place conspicuous to employees stating that insurance exists.

Employers' liability policies that began or were renewed in 1999 must be retained for 40 years. Employees in businesses subject to long-tail exposure, such as those who may contract asbestosis, often make claims years after their employment ceased. Policies can cover subsidiaries of holding companies but associated companies have to provide their own policies.

11:5.4.1.2 Definition of employee

The term 'employee' means anyone employed under a contract of employment or apprenticeship. The term also includes:

- apprentices and/or students undergoing work experience who do not have a contract of employment;

- persons under a contract of service such as IT consultants;

- non-executive directors;

- persons supplied, hired or borrowed in the course of business, for example temporary staff;

- subcontractors, drivers or operators of hired plant;

- persons working under a community service order.

Cover usually includes contractual liability and will indemnify the employer where contractually required (subject to control of the claim by the insurer) and the contractor acting as if he were the insured. If there is any doubt concerning contractual responsibilities, the contract should be sent to the insurers, either directly or via the employers' insurance broker.

11:5.4.1.3 Definition of employment

The policy covers employees during their 'normal course of employment'. This can cause problems in interpretation in the area of travel to and from work. The general rule is that work starts on arrival at the workplace. There have, however, been exceptions found in the courts. Employees working away from their normal place of employment, travelling in their employer's time and with their authority are covered. Since the Motor Vehicles (Compulsory Insurance) Regulations 1992 came into effect on 1 July 1994, the exclusion of employees being carried in the normal course of employment has been removed and thus a motor policy would respond to any claim and not the employers' liability policy. The Road Traffic Act 1988 states that there is a requirement to arrange motor insurance against any legal liability (other than contractual liability) to any third party (including passengers) for death, injury or third-party property damage. This would also cover passengers being carried in the course of their employment. Employees who are injured arising out of and in the course of their employment whilst passengers in a motor vehicle, which the employer is legally responsible for insuring, are by law covered under the employer's motor insurance policy and not under their employer's liability policy.

The Act does not apply to county council authorities, police authorities and vehicles used by the armed forces.

11:5.4.1.4 Territorial scope

Not all employees spend all their time in the UK. Employers' liability policies have territorial limits that give cover for Great Britain, Northern Ireland, the Channel Islands and the Isle of Man. Employees who are *temporarily* employed abroad are covered. Employees who are resident abroad or have employment contracts for areas outside these territorial limits will need special attention. You would need to consider local employment laws and buy appropriate cover. Most policies have a jurisdiction clause that says litigation can be brought in any territory other than North America.

11:5.4.1.5 Restriction of cover

Accident investigators need to bear in mind that insurers can restrict cover for some occupations. For example, where a company is involved in building work, height restrictions for using portable scaffolding towers could be applied. The insurer's aim is to keep their exposure within reasonable grounds. Breaching these restrictions would result in any claim being refused. Care *must* be taken to ensure any restrictions are strictly adhered to.

11:5.4.2 Products liability

Products liability insurance covers the legal liability for injury or damage to purchasers or users of the insured's products. The loss could be due to a defective manufacture, incorrect use, inadequate warning or misleading labelling, which are all covered by a product's liability policy. There is no statutory obligation to insure but there may be contractual liability under contracts of sale that implies the goods are fit for the purpose intended.

The exposure can be catastrophic and it is essential that any manufacturer insures against their products' liability to purchasers. There can be particular problems with exports to the US and companies with this exposure should seek expert professional advice.

11:5.4.2.1 Limit of indemnity

Cover is arranged for a specific limit both per claim and for all losses that are payable in the 12 months the policy will run. Some products (for example chemicals) can take many years to produce claims and here cover may be changed to claims-made basis cover.

11:5.4.3 Product-recall insurance

Product-recall insurance covers the cost of recalling and replacing products. When a defective product is discovered, insurers will pay for this product to be recalled from wholesalers and retailers premises and will also pay the cost of replacing the defective product.

11:5.4.4 Engineering insurance

Engineering insurance covers the plant which is used in buildings. This covers such items as boilers, electrical plant, lifts and computers. The main exposure is against explosion, breakdown and accidental damage.

11:5.4.5 Motor insurance

Third-party insurance for motor vehicles being used on the public highway is compulsory (*see* **section 11:2.2**). Cover for private motor cars can be purchased in two ways: comprehensive and third-party insurance. Comprehensive motor policies cover both damage to the vehicle insured and third-party liability up to an unlimited amount. Third-party policies cover third-party liability only, although cover may be extended for losses caused by fire and theft.

11:5.4.5.1 Limit of indemnity

Third party covers against death and/or bodily injury and is usually issued for an unlimited amount. Commercial vehicles have a limit for third-party property damage of between £1 million and £5 million.

11:5.4.5.2 Territorial scope

Under the Third EC Motor Directive (implemented by the Motor Vehicles (Compulsory Insurance) Regulations 1992) policies give cover for other EU states. This is either for the minimum amount required in the country being visited or the minimum requirement that would apply in the country where the vehicle is registered and normally kept, whichever is the greater.

11:5.4.6 Public-liability insurance

Public-liability insurance covers the insured against any legal liability to third parties for death, injury or third-party damage. The main risk is members of the public and third parties visiting the insured's premises, although cover is included for nuisance trespass. Insurance of these risks is not compulsory although in practice all prudent companies buy cover.

11:5.4.6.1 Limits of indemnity

Public liability cover is provided up to an agreed limit of indemnity to pay compensation for accidental death, injury or disease to any person and accidental loss or damage to property. In addition to any court awards, insurers will also pay the insured's costs incurred with insurer's written consent and legal costs in defending the action and representing the insured at any inquest or fatal enquiry or court of summary jurisdiction. Cover is included for nuisance, trespass or interference with any right of way, light, air or water.

11:5.4.6.2 Territorial scope

The policy will usually have territorial limits of Great Britain, Northern Ireland, the Channel Islands, the Isle of Man and offshore installations in territorial waters around Great Britain and its continental shelf. Policies can be extended to give worldwide cover.

11:5.4.7 Home workers

It is now quite common for staff to work wholly or partly at home. This could cause a problem both for the insurer and the accident investigator. From the insurance perspective, the exact nature of the work needs to be considered. If the employer is installing computer equipment, fax machines, etc., this needs to be covered. It may be possible for the home worker's own home insurance policy to be extended to cover these but not all home workers are happy with this. The area of public liability needs special consideration. If the home worker meets other members of staff and/or clients of their employer at his home there could be a real exposure and insurers would want to be aware of this. Employers' liability insurance for the home worker is not a problem as it will automatically cover them.

11:6 Buying insurance

Insurance can be purchased in many ways: direct from an insurer by letter, by phone or over the internet, through an intermediary or by setting up a self-insurance organisation. The general rule is that the more sophisticated the need the more advice should be sought. Thus buying cover for a simple risk could be done directly from an insurance company, for example motor insurance, but buying product liability for a major multinational would need an intermediary or a self-insurance manager.

11:6.1 Buying direct

The UK insurance industry has undergone major changes in the last few years. Until recently every major insurance company had a large number of offices across the UK. Today they are concentrating their resources in a much smaller number of branches with call centres being used for the most popular classes of business. For this reason it may not be possible to find a local representative of an insurance company. This will not pose a problem for simple risks, but may mean delays when dealing with more complex risks. Therefore, the more complicated the risk, the greater the requirement for an intermediary.

Individual insurers will only provided details of their own company policies and prices and the insured may lose out, as there will be no competitive element. It is likely that the premium will be the same whether or not a broker is used. In the event of a dispute the insured can usually ask the Association of British Insurers to intervene on the insurer's behalf. Insurers can offer package policies that meet the total needs of a company.

11:6.2 Using an intermediary

The intermediary is the agent of the insured. They are subject to the normal rules of agency. Intermediaries are usually appointed in writing but can be appointed verbally. The intermediary must carry out all legal instructions and must excise an appropriate level of skill. This would be higher for an insurance broker than for an accountant acting as an insurance agent. The intermediary must act in good faith and not conceal any information from their principal. If they are negligent they are liable for any damages caused by this negligence. It is possible to place part of a company's needs directly with insurers and still use an intermediary for other parts.

11:6.2.1 Choosing an insurance broker

Insurance brokers are experts in insurance and insurance law whose full-time occupation is the placing of insurance. They provide independent advice on a wide range of insurance matters and can find the best cover for the client from the most suitable insurer. Brokers can recommend the appropriate type of cover and can recognise subtle differences between cover offered by different insurers; thus they can help the insured buy the right level of cover. They can also offer expert services in reducing or eliminating risks. In the case of dispute they will be able to help the insured pursue their claim.

When choosing a broker, the size of the broker and their ability to handle technical services should be considered. Some brokers have specialists who can analyse a client's exposure to potential losses and suggest ways to limit or eliminate exposures. They have surveyors who will carry out pre-insurance surveys to suggest housekeeping improvements. The larger brokers will often have specialist policy drafters who can prepare individual policies for clients.

If the insured is an international organisation, the need for the broker to service overseas risks also needs to be considered. The broker should be willing to give an indication of what service they offer. Some brokers specialise in certain areas. This may be important if they match the need of the insured.

Regardless of their size the aim of every broker is to find the best cover at the most economical rate for their principal. They are the agent for the insured and could be held liable for any errors in arranging cover. Today brokers are evolving into 'risk solution providers'. They will provide a risk management service that will analyse the insured's exposure and suggest ways to control or limit these risks, whether to insure or self-insure the risk and the best way to provide an insurance programme. Obviously the larger the broker, the more resources they have to carry out these services. Access to the Lloyd's insurance market is usually via a broker.

11:6.2.1.1 Regulation of insurance brokers

Until mid-2004 regulation on insurance brokers will be on a voluntary basis. The industry has set up the General Insurance Services Council (GISC). The Board of the GISC is made up of representatives from both brokers and insurance companies. It has strict rules on protecting the interests of the insured and lays down minimum standards on how brokers should operate. These standards include the broker purchasing professional indemnity insurance. The Council's rules apply both to insurance brokers and insurance companies. The largest association of insurance brokers in the UK, the British Insurance Brokers' Association (BIBA), is a supporter of the GISC. Members of the GISC carry the body's logo on their letterheads.

BIBA membership is only open to insurance brokers. It is the major trade association for British brokers and has around 3,000 members. Members have to comply with a code of professional conduct that stresses the need for utmost good faith and that client needs come first. It seeks to maintain and improve the highest standards of business behaviour.

Some insurance brokers feel that the GISC will not serve their best interests and are supporting the rival Institute of Insurance Brokers (IIB). Like BIBA, the IIB sets down rules for solvency, professional indemnity cover and standards of practice.

11:6.2.1.2 Non-registered intermediates

These are individuals or companies who operate using the title of 'consultant' or 'adviser'. They comply with ABI standards.

11:6.2.2 Finding and briefing an intermediary

A list of brokers is available from BIBA, the IIB and Lloyd's of London.

11:6.2.2.1 Trade organisations

Cover may be arranged for a specific industry and such schemes may involve insurance brokers setting up a special scheme for those involved in the specific trade. These policies are generally well designed and may contain cover that is not available under standard market policies. The premiums charged should be competitive, although a narrow industry sector may suffer an adverse claims experience. Here the low-risk insured could find themselves subsidising their less careful colleagues.

11:6.3 Self insurance

Unless insurance is compulsory (*see* **section 11:2**) a company does not have to insure. If fact many major multinationals decide rather than pay premiums to insurers they would rather self-insure part of their insurance exposure. This can be a decision not to insure certain risks or the setting up of an in-house captive insurance company. These usually take the first part of any major loss with the reinsurance industry paying any losses above that amount.

11:7 Making a claim

Most insurance policies contain instructions regarding claims. The common feature is that insurers must be informed of a loss and that insurers have the right to control the claim. As it is their money that is being paid out they want to make sure it is being used properly. With employers' liability insurance it may be possible to agree specific figures for notification of claims. Insurers do not need to know every slip or cut and may agree that losses under a certain figure do not need to be advised.

Where insurers feel the claim may be contentious (or for large or detailed claims) insurers will often appoint loss adjusters. These are independent experts who will process, investigate and recommend the settlement of claims. They are paid by the insurer but represent the interests of the insured. The adjuster will check that the policy covers the loss and that the sum insured/limit of indemnity was adequate. They will attempt to minimise the loss and aim to help the claim get settled as quickly as possible.

The main consideration here is information. Provided the insured tells the insurers exactly what is going on immediately and co-operates with the insurers there should be little or no problems.

11:7.1 How to make a claim

There will be major differences to making a claim if an intermediary has been used to place the business. If a broker has not been used the claim will normally be made as follows:

Step 1

Notify insurers of any serious loss/fatality immediately (by telephone, fax or email).

Step 2

Notify insurers of all claims in writing within three or four days, keeping a copy of all correspondence and policy records.

Step 3

Admit nothing! Do not enter into any correspondence with any third party or their solicitors.

Step 4

Maintain records of the steps taken to correct defects and improve safety.

Step 5

Establish a procedure for notifying the insurer of any employee injury/illness and check these are covered in the policy conditions. If they are not, examine the correspondence between the parties when cover was being purchased and check that the right cover was purchased.

Step 6

Consider the appointment of a joint loss adjuster for tenanted property. The loss adjuster is appointed by the insurers to settle claims but acts independently of insurers. It will be simpler to have one loss adjuster rather than two and the loss should be settled quicker.

Step 7

Consider whether interim payments in respect of property or interruption claims are appropriate.

Step 8

Check the position on public and product liability insurance indemnity limits and excesses with insurers.

Step 9

Where machinery or plant has been damaged insurers may appoint an engineer to represent their interests. Agree a limit with the insurer for repairs that can proceed without waiting for the engineer. This may speed up the repairs of damaged equipment.

And where a broker has been appointed:

Step 10

Discuss with the insurance broker the most practical reporting procedures, and any specific requirements relating to claims handling and accident prevention.

11:7.2 Claims handling

11:7.2.1 Claims notification

Insurers are most concerned with claims notification. They feel that prompt advice of a loss will allow them to respond as soon as possible and will reduce their exposure. Insurers should be informed of any loss, however small, even if it seems unlikely that they will get involved. For any serious loss you should phone, fax or email the insurers immediately. They will probably give instructions to a loss adjuster who will protect the insurer's interests but in any event follow the initial advice with written confirmation within two/three days. Most policies have a 'reporting conditions' clause that lays down how and when losses must be reported. These clauses vary between different insurers and should be observed to the letter. For certain policies the reporting conditions require that every accident must be notified whereas other policies ask for information that only leads to a claim. It is not uncommon for the reporting conditions to state that insurers must be informed of losses within 21 days or even 'as soon as reasonably possible'.

Often insurers will supply a claim form to be completed. This will give insurers information required for a claim, such as the time of the accident, the place it occurred, the type of loss incurred, the anticipated financial losses, etc. Often insurers will telephone asking for more details. Any supporting documents, such as estimates, invoices, third-party correspondence, etc., should be sent within the terms of the policy. It is important to keep copies of these documents and a note of any telephone conversations with insurers (i.e. who was spoken to and what instructions were given).

As well as enabling insurers to appoint any experts (such as lawyers or loss adjusters) to help with the claim, an early notification will allow them to investigate the opportunity of recovering any of the loss from any third party. The tight deadlines imposed by the new Civil Procedure Rules make prompt action necessary (*see* **section 11:8**).

11:7.2.2 Third-party correspondence

Any third-party correspondence should not be replied to. Similarly if any telephone calls are received from a third party or their representatives they should be dealt with by politely refusing to discuss any aspect of the claim. A note should be made of the conversation and passed on to insurers. Similarly any correspondence should be forwarded to insurers immediately. In both circumstances under no account should any admission of guilt be made.

11:7.2.3 Claims review

For a major claim, immediate action will be taken to control or minimise loss. When things are more settled the insurer's claims expert will review the claim and examine certain features. These include (but are not limited to):

- **the amount claimed**;
  - How does it relate to the reported damage or injury?
  - Is it reasonable?
  - Is the insured claiming more than they are entitled to?
  - Are they looking for more than indemnity?

- **the proposal form;**

  - How does the information on the form relate to the claim?

  - Do the circumstances of the claim contradict earlier statements?

- **the policy.**

  - Is the loss covered by the policy and was the policy in force at the time of the claim?

  - Were there any policy conditions that have been broken, making the policy void?

  - Was the claim advised in time and correctly?

  - Do any exclusions apply that restrict the claim?

11:7.2.4 Claims investigation

Depending on the seriousness of the claim the insurer may wish to investigate the circumstances of the loss. With liability claims involving bodily injury, the insurers will want as much information as possible, for example what work was being undertaken and whether it was included within the description of the business made when the policy was taken out. Insurers may instruct their own claims inspectors to report to them on the circumstances of the claim or may appoint an independent loss adjuster to investigate the claim on their behalf. The insurer needs to determine which claims can be settled at an early stage and those that they will want to fight all the way. Where it is apparent that the insurers are liable for the loss they find it more cost effective to agree to pay the loss and to just argue over quantum. In the past few years insurance fraud has become a major problem in the industry and insurers have agreed to fight all losses that do not appear to be justified.

11:7.2.4.1 Economic considerations

With a small claim a decision needs to be made by the insurer to determine whether the expense of obtaining extra documentation or an expert's advice/report is commercially worthwhile. It may be financially better to pay a claim than become involved in a dispute which will involve heavy investigation and legal costs. An insurer's claims official will make this decision.

11:7.2.5 Settling a claim

Does the insurance company follow policy conditions to the letter, or does it prefer to be more generous with its claims payment in the belief that it is better to pay the odd claim that may not strictly be recoverable rather than face court action?

Usually the above consideration produces one of three responses: to pay the claim, to negotiate a smaller amount or to reject the claim altogether. Full reasons for the last two options should be given to enable the insured to decide whether to accept or to fight the decision.

Another alternative may be the *ex gratia* settlement – literally a payment 'out of grace'. *Ex gratia* payments are made where:

- the circumstances of a loss are unclear;

- there was a genuine mistake by the insured;

- to refuse the claim would cause great hardship to the insured;

- to refuse the claim would result in lengthy and expensive court action;

- the insurer would be exposed to bad publicity;

- the insurer has a good relationship with the insured and does not want to jeopardise this.

11:7.3 Claims handling – the intermediary

When risks have been placed using a broker, the broker will become involved in the claims process by advising the insured on what action to take and by collecting the amount of the claim from the insurers. The intermediary not only eases the flow of information to the insurers but can also reassure the insured and the insurers that the correct action is being taken.

When a loss occurs on a policy placed by an intermediary they will usually advise the insurer of the loss. Intermediaries are aware of the need for prompt action and will make sure the insured meets the policy conditions on claims notification and discloses all material facts about the loss. They will often complete any claims forms on the insured's behalf and will provide other documents (for example copies of the policy and/or cover notes) that may be required.

The main benefit of using an intermediary is that they have great experience in dealing with these situations. They will 'broke' or present the claim to insurers. They will discuss the claim and answer any technical questions the insurer has. If any questions cannot be resolved the intermediary will investigate the situation and report back to the insurer. The intermediary can use their understanding of insurance and the technical issues involved to negotiate on the insured's behalf. They will be aware of arguments or points of persuasion that have been successful with insurers in the past. If the insurers are unhappy with the claim they can understand these problems and find ways to resolve them. There are therefore considerable advantages for the insured of having a broker rather than having a direct relationship with his insurers.

11:7.4 Disputes

The vast majority of insurance claims are settled satisfactorily but if a dispute does occur the intermediary can be of assistance to the insured. They can help by drafting a reply to the insurer's declinature of the claim and can meet the insurer's representatives to explain the insured's position. The intermediary will try and negotiate a compromise or *ex gratia* settlement and if all other actions fail will help the insured take legal action against insurers. With intermediaries there is another reason to make these payments: an intermediary will produce a book of business to the insurers. They may be unwilling to risk losing this portfolio of risks by not paying a claim.

Businesses with a turnover of more than £100,000 can appeal any decision to the Financial Ombudsman.

11:8 Reform of the civil justice system

11:8.1 Legal aspects of civil justice reform

Since 1999 insurers have been faced with reforms to the English legal system proposed by Lord Woolf. The reforms made major demands on insurers and in return they expect more responsive action from policyholders. The main change is that insurers expect policyholders to report claims and incidents that could lead to claims as quickly as possible.

The Woolf reforms are intended to ensure that legal action is a last resort and is not part of the normal process of negotiating a settlement. The aim of the reforms is to give claimants, defendants and the respective insurance companies information on losses so that the facts of the claim can be established and a compromise negotiated before legal proceedings become necessary. In theory, in future the parties will meet to discuss the key points of the case rather than become involved in long and expensive litigation.

The reforms have developed a three-tier court system:

1. small claims – where the anticipated recovery is less than £5,000 or £1,000 for personal injury;

2. fast track – where the anticipated recovery is up to £15,000;

3. multi track – for losses over £15,000.

11:8.2 Small claims procedure

The small claims procedure will be almost identical to the existing system. Small claims relate to losses of not more than £5,000 for property or £1,000 for personal injury. The court may give directions for the exchange of information and fix a date for a hearing. The key features of the small claims procedures are:

- no oral or written expert evidence without the court's permission;

- the hearing is informal;

- only fixed costs are allowed unless a party has behaved unreasonably;

- there is a limited right of appeal.

11:8.3 Fast-track trials

Fast-track trials must be listed within 30 weeks of the filing of the defence, with the exchange of witness statements, expert advice and disclosure documents during this period. Any trial should last no longer than one day with limited oral evidence and fixed trial costs. The fast-track system is expected to be the most commonly used and the limits of the scheme are expected to rise shortly.

Under the personal injury protocol the claimant's solicitor sends a letter of claim to the defendant and/or his insurer setting out the details of the claim. Insurers have only 21 days to acknowledge this letter and failure to respond will allow the claimant to issue proceedings without cost penalty. Even if the insurers acknowledge within 21 days, they have only three months to investigate the claim and either admit or deny liability. The protocol also calls for documents to be disclosed even if these are against insurers' interests. Any breach of the protocol could be considered 'unreasonable conduct' and the court could apply sanctions such as fines.

The changes mean insurers will have to make early decisions on liability and the amount being claimed. Although insurers have reorganised their systems and procedures, they have yet to impose any new restrictions or duties for policyholders, instead relying on existing policy conditions. These conditions will be reiterated so that policyholders advise insurers of any claim or potential claim as soon as an accident and/or loss occurs.

It is expected, however, that insurers will introduce new and more stringent claims notification clauses when policies are renewed. Policyholders will find that loss adjusters are now appointed by their broker from a panel approved by their insurance company to save time.

Insurers are not expecting problems with personal lines business (i.e. business purchased by individuals such as motor or buildings and contents insurance). However, other classes of business are causing concern. The exposure in commercial insurance is immense and there is a tendency to delay advice of losses.

The insurers' trade association, the Association of British Insurers, has given no lead to the Woolf reforms. Rather than the industry having a united front, insurers are all responding in their own way in terms of handling and reporting claims.

11:8.4 Multi-track claims

Multi-track claims are claims that are worth over £15,000 or for claims that are not suited to the small-claims or fast-track procedures, perhaps due to their complexity. The court will consider which system is suitable and if it feels that neither the small-claims nor the fast-track systems can be used it will give directions for the multi-track system to be used. The court will give directions for an exchange of information and will set a date for a management conference where the parties will address the court on how they believe the case should be handled. This will include estimates of costs. If either side's costs significantly exceed their estimates they may be prevented from recovering any additional costs.

11:9 Troubleshooting

11:9.1 The Policyholders Protection Acts 1975 and 1997

The Insurance Companies Act 1982 controls UK insurance companies and legislates that the insurers must be solvent. Insurers must apply for permission to trade and to show that their managers are of sufficient quality and probity.

In theory a UK insurer cannot go bankrupt but to protect individuals, sole traders and partnerships the Policyholders Protection Acts provide compensation to policyholders if an insurance company becomes insolvent and cannot meet its claims. These Acts, however, do not apply to claims from corporate bodies (i.e. companies). For example, if an employee is injured at work he would be able to recover any loss from say a personal accident policy as an individual. Whilst the insurance company is insolvent the Policyholders Protection Acts allow for a levy to be made and the funds raised will be used to reimburse the employee. If the employee was employed by a sole trader or a partnership the funds raised by the Policyholders Protection Acts would be used to pay their claims. A corporation though cannot recover under the Act.

The Acts provide that 100% of all claims for compulsory insurance will be paid. This would cover motor insurance and employers' liability insurance. For all other classes of business 90% of all claims would be paid. For example, only 90% of all business interruption insurance losses would be paid.

The claims are met by a levy on insurance companies. Only risks inside the European Economic Area (EEA) are covered. Losses outside the EEA cannot be covered.

11:9.2 Handling claims disputes

There are three ways to settle a disputed claim:

1. negotiation of a settlement;
2. litigation;
3. alternative dispute resolution.

The traditional form of settling a dispute is litigation. It is expensive and will result in a decision based on the facts and the law surrounding the dispute. Legislation is formal, often lengthy and very public. The judge hearing the case may be learned in the terms of law but may not have the expertise for an insurance dispute, although it does have the advantage of being binding on both parties. However, because of the many disadvantages of litigation for both insured and insurers, alternative resolutions to disputes are sought.

11:9.2.1 Alternative dispute resolution

Alternative dispute resolution (ADR) is relatively new. The term ADR means any form of dispute resolution that is not litigation. In some ways ADR is a structured version of a negotiated settlement. It may take the form of mediation, arbitration, structured settlement or judicial appraisal (*see* **section 11:9.2.2**).

11:9.2.1.1 The advantages of ADR
The advantages of ADR are that:

- it offers greater flexibility over litigation. There are a number of types of ADR and they do not comply with statutes or rules of court. Once litigation has started neither party can withdraw without the consent of the other. If the parties cannot negotiate a solution, the courts will impose one;

- it is much quicker. The ADR system is simpler than the UK court system, and so time is saved. Fewer documents need to be prepared or exchanged;

- it offers considerable cost savings. The simpler system means less time is spent on hiring expensive specialist third parties;

- it offers greater confidentiality as hearings are behind closed doors.

As ADR procedures are less formal both sides retain more control of the dispute. Whereas litigation tends to produce a legal resolution to the dispute, ADR ensures a more commercial decision is achieved.

11:9.2.1.2 The disadvantages of ADR

The disadvantages of ADR are that neither the decision nor any award are binding nor can either party insist that an ADR process is used. In addition, either side can withdraw from an ADR at any stage. Furthermore there are no rules on disclosure for ADR and the full facts may not be known as there is no equivalent of discovery (the right to be given information from the other party in the dispute). Lastly, ADR needs both sides to want to resolve the dispute. If either side is reluctant then the process will fail.

11:9.2.2 Types of ADR

11:9.2.2.1 Mediation

In mediation both parties present the facts of the case as they see them to a mediator who is selected by a third party. In most insurance contracts there is an arbitration agreement that permits mediation. This lays down how a mediator will be appointed. It also lays down procedure for the appointment of a mediator by a third party who is usually a market figure (e.g. the chairman of Lloyd's or the chairman of the Association of British Insurers) who will be asked to appoint a suitable mediator.

The mediator discusses the case with both sides and will help them see each other's point of view and suggest areas where they agree and alternatives which they should consider. The mediator will identify the main points at issue, advise both parties on their options and suggest constructive solutions. Usually the mediation takes place in one building. Each party is allocated an office and the mediator moves from one party to another. The problem with mediation is that neither side has to be bound by the mediator's decision, although this is not usually a problem. Costs of this method of ADR are lower than for arbitration.

11:9.2.2.2 Arbitration

Arbitration is more formal than mediation and is subject to the Arbitration Act 1996. The arbitrator is appointed in a manner laid down in the policy. The arbitration clause lays down that arbitration should be sought first rather than a legal settlement and that arbitration does not take away the right of either party to start legal proceedings. Both sides can provide names for arbitrators but if they do not agree then a market figure (e.g. the chairman of Lloyd's) would be asked to provide an arbitrator who will hear the arguments of both sides in private. They will then give a decision. Arbitration is binding but there are often limited grounds for a review of a decision. Costs are lower than for litigation and any award is enforceable.

12 | Reporting to Senior Management

Issues discussed in this chapter:

- The need for the involvement of directors and senior managers in safety management
- Influences on safety management improvement
- The importance of board-level decision making
- The Government's strategy – *Revitalising Health and Safety*
- The costs of safety
- The cost of accidents
- Techniques for reporting accident information

12:1 Introduction

Ultimately the responsibility for acting upon an accident investigation report lies with those charged with managing the organisation at the highest level. The decisions made by the managers in an organisation will be influenced by several factors, including:

- reports they receive about health and safety and other risk performance in general, including accident investigation reports;
- influences on safety management improvement and understanding, such as legal requirements, changes in best practice and evidence-based approaches;

- the importance of board-level decision making and the effects this has on the organisation as a whole;

- the allocation of resources;

- the threat of enforcement action;

- the way safety performance information is presented to them.

12:2 Reporting to managers and the board

In order for the management team to have some idea of how well the organisation is doing in terms of safety management and overall loss control, it is important that they consider reports of accidents together with the failures and inadequacies in the management systems that caused them. Accident reports may only contain minimal information (*see* **Chapter 7**), for example the summaries of F2508 forms completed under the provisions of RIDDOR, whereas more detailed accident investigation reports will identify system failures and inadequacies.

Accident reports are part of the reactive monitoring aspects of the safety management system (*see* **Chapter 1**).

The consideration of accidents at senior management level should ensure that:

- safety performance is understood;

- the extent of losses is realised;

- impetus is given to both the investigation process and the remedial actions required.

The nature and type of events that should be reported to senior management will depend on several factors:

- the nature and size of the organisation;

- the types of risks and activities involved;

- the extent and understanding of safety management systems in the organisation;

- the nature and extent of accident reporting and recording systems.

12:2.1 The nature and size of the organisation

Companies listed on the London Stock Exchange (LSE) are required to maintain an understanding of the control measures they have in place for risks. These risks include health and safety risks as well as financial ones. This requirement forms part of the corporate governance codes (*see* **Chapter 1, section 1:2.2**) to ensure diligent management. It is thus to be expected that the boards of LSE-listed companies will receive reports of losses caused by accidents.

Similarly in the public sector and for local authorities there is a requirement to have a risk management approach in place that will parallel certain aspects of the corporate governance control of risk in the private sector. (For more information, see *Statement of responsibilities of local authorities and their auditors*, The Audit Commission, May 2002, available on www.audit-commission. gov.uk/publications/sor2002_5.shtml or from Audit Commission Publications, PO Box 99, Wetherby, West Yorkshire LS23 71A, tel: 0800 502030). As part of this approach it is to be expected that a local authority management board and the authority itself will require reports of accident losses.

12:2.2 The types of risks and activities

It is to be expected that industries in high-hazard environments will have a greater focus on risk and potential losses, if only because the consequences of exposure to risk will be more severe. However, the reporting of accidents will often be determined by an organisation's expectations of what should be happening. In an organisation used to dealing with risks, there may be an expectation that certain types of events will happen anyway. The result of this attitude is that reports of accidents may simply be taken 'as read' and not sufficiently acted upon. In a similar manner familiar events may not even be considered as 'accidents' and hence not reported, or if reported, not acted upon.

The classic example of this is the background to the fire at Kings Cross underground station in 1987. Part of the cause of this major disaster was the acceptance of small fires on the escalators almost as routine events to be treated as nothing particularly serious. The neglect of this situation revealed itself with the last fire to be ignored. It resulted in the deaths of 31 people. This example illustrates that minor as well as major accidents are worthy of reporting. Organisations should not be lulled into a false sense of security by only allowing themselves to be concerned with 'major' events.

High-frequency, low-consequence events such as minor injury accidents each with only one or two days 'lost time' can be just as damaging to an organisation as a major one-off accident involving large numbers of people. When added together the costs of lots of small incidents may be equal to, or even greater than, the costs of a large one-off incident. Major events tend to attract attention and management will expect to receive a report on them. The board may consider that having to examine lots of smaller accident reports at more frequent intervals is both trivial and time wasting. The consideration of apparently trivial incidents can, however, provide useful information about the nature and level of safety performance in any organisation (*see* **Chapter 1, section 1:1.3.1**).

12:2.3 The extent and understanding of safety management systems

Organisations that have a firm understanding of the requirements of a safety management system and are working to develop and maintain one will have effective accident reporting systems in place. In such situations accident reports will be accorded a high degree of importance. A well-honed system will seek to provide information regarding safety performance from all events. Reference to the management models described in **Chapter 2** can be used to demonstrate this.

12:2.4 The nature and extent of accident reporting and recording systems

It is only possible to analyse and report on those events that are reported and recorded. The degree of sophistication in the accident reporting procedure will thus be reflected in the type and extent of reports that can be provided to top management.

The important aspect of any reporting system is that all staff need to be able to identify the events that need reporting. Unless one can be sure that reports are complete and accurate it will be difficult to be fully certain that the reports being provided to top management actually give a true picture.

For example, if the reporting system only picks up on a reportable event under RIDDOR 1995 (*see* **Chapter 4, section 4:4**), then it will not be possible to make any assumptions about the extent of minor accidents or near misses. Even where there is complete compliance with the duty to log all injury accidents in the accident book (*see* **Chapter 4, section 4:4.1.2**) these will not of themselves provide sufficient information to enable useful reports to be put together.

As a minimum requirement, all accidents including very minor incidents and near miss incidents should be reported and recorded in a consistent format.

A number of fairly simple yet useful computerised information collection and analysis systems exist in the market-place. These can be used to prepare reports for management on the trends and patterns which are evident from the data collected.

The recording and reporting of accidents is discussed more fully in **section 12:7**.

12:3 Influences on safety management improvement

A number of factors influence safety management in an organisation. Significantly, these include:

- the responsibilities of directors;
- the likely financial effect of failure;
- the financial commitment required.

12:3.1 The responsibilities of directors

In the consultative document, *Directors' Responsibilities for Health and Safety* (HSC CD 167), the HSC proposed that six areas require management by directors to demonstrate a commitment to health and safety. These are given below.

1. The board needs to accept formally and publicly its collective role in providing health and safety leadership in their organisation.

2. Each board member needs to accept their individual role in providing health and safety leadership for their organisation.

   It can be argued that unless there is a strong commitment to the thorough and detailed investigation of accidents insufficient information will come to the board's attention to enable them to exercise these responsibilities. Furthermore, the board also needs to be committed to responding to accident reports in a firm and positive manner.

3. The board needs to ensure that all board decisions reflect their health and safety intentions, as articulated in the health and safety policy statement.

This responsibility is clearly one that is moderated by whatever it is that the board has in fact signed up to as their expectations of health and safety for the organisation. One clear objective should be the investigation and management of accidents, with a clear directive to learn the lessons. It is frequently established that the underlying causation of accidents is to be found in decisions made where the safety implications have not been considered (*see* **Appendix 1, section A1:1.3**).

4. The board needs to recognise its role in engaging the active participation of staff in improving health and safety.

This is a key point. It reflects the need to ensure that staff are actively involved both in any accident investigation and the provision of solutions when problems are discovered. More particularly it may be argued that the involvement of safety representatives and other employee representatives in the investigation process is to be encouraged and actively sought.

5. The board needs to ensure that it is kept informed of, and alerted to, relevant health and safety risk management issues. The HSC recommends that boards appoint one of their number to be the health and safety director.

Clearly the reporting of accident investigations to the board fulfils part of these responsibilities.

6. The HSC recommends that boards appoint one of their number to be the health and safety director.

Following consultation with unions, employers and other organisations, guidance incorporating these proposals was published on 25 July 2001 as *Directors' Responsibilities for Health and Safety*, ISBN 0717620808. This is available in packs of ten or individually free of charge from the HSE. They can be ordered online at www.hsebooks.co.uk or from HSE Books, PO Box 1999, Sudbury, Suffolk CO10 2WA, tel: 01787 881165, fax: 01787 313995. The document can be accessed online at www.hse.gov.uk/pubns/indg343.pdf.

Whilst these are only suggestions from the HSC they clearly reflect the desirability for directors to take on explicit responsibilities for health and safety. It also reflects the requirements for corporate governance for LSE-listed companies (*see* **Chapter 1, section 1:2.2**) and the proposed requirements for public bodies.

12:3.2 The financial effects of failure

In addition to the remedial and investment costs (discussed in **section 12:5.1**) there are three significant financial consequences of failure to secure and maintain safety in any organisation. These relate to:

1. the level of criminal fine imposed;

2. the level of damages paid out through civil law actions;

3. the impact upon business reputation and market share.

12:3.2.1 The level of criminal fine imposed

Figure 12:1 shows the level of fines imposed for a number of major health and safety-related cases since 1998. Most of the companies mentioned are well known and the cases were all reported in the press at the time. The table only shows the level of fines imposed by the courts and does not include the actual legal costs of the cases.

The level of fines imposed by the courts is increasing significantly. In a recent case Mr Justice Higginbotham stated:

> *any fine needs to be large enough to bring home the message about health and safety to both management and shareholders.*

FIGURE 12:1 FINES IMPOSED ON VARIOUS COMPANIES FOR BREACHES OF HEALTH AND SAFETY LAW

Company	Sector	Date	Fine in £000s
Doncaster Metropolitan Borough Council	Public – local authority	August 1997	400
Sainsburys	Food retail	November 1998	425
Balfour Beatty	Construction	February 1999	1,200
Geoconsult	Specialist construction consultant	February 1999	500
London Underground	Transport	July 1999	300
Great Western Trains	Transport	July 1999	1,500
Keltbray Ltd	Construction – demolition	September 1999	200
Costain	Construction	October 1999	200
BG exploration	Extraction	February 2000	300
Friskies Petcare (UK) Ltd	Manufacturing	March 2000	600 (reduced to 250 on appeal)
Railtrack	Transport	July 2000	200
Corus UK	Steel	September 2000	300
Mayer Parry Recycling Ltd	Reclamation and recycling	September 2001	200

As part of the Government's attempts to highlight the importance of health and safety, the names of organisations convicted of health and safety offences are posted on a database accessible on the internet (*see* **section 12:4.3.3**).

12:3.2.2 Civil law damages actions

The financial cost to businesses and organisations of civil actions probably exceeds criminal law fines by a significant percentage. The increasingly litigious nature of society and the development of 'no-win, no-fee' legal practices is likely to see an increase in the number of civil law cases taken, no doubt made more speedy by the new Civil Procedures Rules (*see* **Chapter 9, section 9:6**). Almost any injury which arises in the workplace (or as a result of work activity) is possibly going to give rise to a civil claim for damages. In many cases these claims are dealt with before reaching court or as part of an insurance claims payment. Reports in the health and safety literature indicate that the payments made as a result of civil actions are extensive with increases in the size of the awards being made. These costs are discussed in **section 12:6.2.1.6**.

12:3.2.3 Business reputation and market share

It is difficult to quantify the impact on business reputation and market share and the financial losses which result. In a number of high profile incidents various enterprises have clearly suffered on both counts. Market share loss can result after an accident from a difficulty in maintaining demand, say for a product or service, as other companies fill the gap. The market share seldom appears to recover to its previous level. It is difficult to determine how much the law of supply and demand affects the ethical operation of organisations. The failure to operate an enterprise safely may cause clients and customers to search elsewhere for goods and services. The losses due to reputation are thereby subsumed into the market share losses. Some studies have shown that share price is affected by reputation and that shareholders are willing to pay a premium for shares in organisations which are well managed in terms of environmental and health and safety matters. The impact on business reputation is no doubt mitigated by the way a major accident is handled, especially in terms of media coverage. These issues are discussed further in **section 12:4.8**.

12:3.3 Financial commitment

Organisations need to demonstrate that they have allocated sufficient funds to meet their health and safety responsibilities. This demonstration needs to be based on sound evidence, much of which will be derived from an understanding of the risks involved and the level of controls required. A system needs to be in place so that senior managers in any organisation can be made aware of the actual safety requirements of the organisation and the level of funding required to control them. For example, financial allocation may be necessary for training, safety inspections, procedural development and the provision of equipment.

12:3.3.1 Cost-benefit considerations

Boards and senior managers will need to consider the cost-benefits of the proposals they may wish to introduce to manage health and safety. Some people would regard this as a wider part of the risk assessment process itself. This may well be true. It is important, however, to realise that part of the decision-making process is to ensure money is well spent. A risk to the organisation which may result in a loss of £10 should not cost £2 million to fix; on the other hand if you can demonstrate that the investment of £2,000 in a health and safety initiative can produce savings in excess of that figure, then clearly the money is well spent. Managers, especially fund-holders, need this type of information. Deciding on the best course of action after an accident requires a careful consideration of risk and the costs and the associated benefits involved. This is another good reason for dissuading accident investigators from providing recommendations. Real solutions can only ever be arrived at by a full consideration of everything involved and by ensuring that effort and resources are not wasted on issues of minor importance whilst more important (and hence riskier) situations are not being dealt with. The tragedy is that health and safety effort may often be directed at the areas of least return or of least importance.

12:4 The importance of board-level decision making

It is important that the board actively and explicitly make decisions about matters reported to them, including accident reports and accident investigation reports. They also need to actively seek the required information to enable them to make relevant health and safety-related decisions, for example, about whether to invest in new plant or equipment when the main reasons for doing so are on the grounds of safety (with the implication that there are no apparent profit benefits). Similarly when making decisions to cut costs by cutting back on staff or reducing the time available to undertake certain production processes health and safety considerations must be addressed.

The visible or transparent nature of board-level considerations and decisions is an important factor, both in showing how well the board has managed the company in terms of accident avoidance and how well it has responded to accidents.

There are three significant issues that need to be considered by any board when making its decisions, especially in the light of any serious failure in the safety management system reported to them. These are:

1. factors that a court may take into account when deciding on sentence;

2. the actual extent of any consequences resulting from failure;

3. the Government's strategy for improving health and safety.

In addition, the board will need to consider:

- the redirecting of resources;

- the involvement of employee representatives;

- internal disciplinary proceedings;

- the impact of media coverage;

- involvement in public inquiries;

- attending coroner's inquests.

12:4.1 Factors that a court may take into account

In the court case of *R. v. F. Howe and Sons (Engineering) Ltd* [1998] TLR (CA), the judge set out guidelines that should be used to determine the level of fine to be imposed on a company that has been found guilty of health and safety offences. These guidelines are likely to be in use for some time and reflect the concern that was previously being expressed about the apparent low level of fines and other sentences being imposed by the courts. The factors that a court will take into account include:

- the extent of the shortfall in the level of care (*see* **Chapter 9, section 9:5**) which the case against the company shows that there has been;

- evidence which reveals that the company has been skimping on health and safety precautions to save money;

- evidence that shows that the company has been tolerating low levels of compliance with health and safety law in order to create or maintain a competitive advantage;

- a failure by the company to heed warnings that have previously been given to it about the circumstances which have led to its appearance in court;

- failure to co-operate with enforcement authorities;

- a history of repetitive failings and evidence of widespread systemic or cultural failings.

These are the negative 'attributes' that a court may consider when considering the fine that should be imposed. In addition, the court should also take into account the company's ability to pay and the effect of the fine on the viability of the company.

It should be noted that if the company does not submit any evidence regarding their ability to pay the court is entitled to conclude that a defendant is able to afford any penalty the court may impose. Evidence on ability to pay comes from annual accounts and any other information the defendant wishes to rely upon. Importantly the details must be submitted to the prosecution in good time for them to be considered by the court.

Thus, any board would be well advised to ensure they have positive evidence to counter the factors established in the *Howe* case. In particular they need to be aware of the need to co-operate with enforcement authorities and ensure that sufficient funds are being made available to secure an adequate level (as a minimum) of safety performance. One of the most important monitoring tools available to the board to avoid getting into a situation where the *Howe* guidelines will be applied is to frequently and thoroughly examine accident reports and take appropriate corrective action.

12:4.1.1 Mitigation

Positive matters the court may consider in mitigation include:

- a prompt admission of guilt;

- pleading guilty in a timely fashion (i.e. not hindering the court by arguing over the finer points of the case);

- swift steps being taken to remedy any deficiencies found. These will mostly be identified by an adequate and detailed accident investigation;

- a demonstration of a good safety record prior to the offence.

Clearly when an accident report is received by the board it needs to be aware of these aspects and ensure that the system in place for dealing with any offences is suitably compliant (i.e. guilt is recognised and admitted) and, perhaps most importantly, quick action is taken to remedy the defects identified.

12:4.1.1.1 What this means for directors and senior managers

Senior managers and directors ought to be aware that a 'measure' now exists which sets a standard against which their performance will be assessed. Internal reports therefore need to point out the extent to which required duties of care are being maintained, for example ensuring risk assessments are adequate and complying with the appropriate regulations such as COSHH and PUWER.

Senior managers and directors also need to be responsive to any warnings they receive about concerns in safety performance. Such warnings may come from the workforce, trade union representatives, junior managers, supervisors and enforcement officers. Any warning has to be taken seriously and followed up.

Board members and individual directors must be conscious of the financial implications for safety in their decision making. If they knowingly 'cut corners' without considering the safety impact, they will be in a very poor position should an accident or incident happen. If they deliberately attempt to save money by not implementing safety requirements, they will be in serious trouble should the company ever be taken to court for health and safety offences.

It is important that all those managers and directors who are likely to come into contact with, or whose duties mean they are responsible for communicating with enforcement authorities should be aware of the need to co-operate.

Board members and directors should receive sufficient reports to enable them to determine the extent of health and safety controls operating in the organisation. This will enable them to take appropriate action if there is evidence that there are repetitive failings in the management of safety or that the culture of the organisation does not support safety.

12:4.2 The consequences of failure

12:4.2.1 Corporate liability

The board and individual directors may become liable in the event of failures to ensure health and safety duties are complied with. This needs to be considered both at the time an accident occurs and, more especially, when the board is receiving accident investigation reports. The fact that they become liable means that the board should take a very close interest in accident investigation processes and the reports that are produced as a consequence of these processes. There are two factors to consider here:

1. directors' responsibilities;

2. criminal sanction.

12:4.2.1.1 Directors' responsibilities

In addition to those specific recommendations made by the HSE regarding directors' responsibilities for health and safety, the requirements for corporate governance for companies listed on the LSE means that the board of directors should ensure the company is complying with the requirements set out in the Turnbull Report (*Internal Control: Guidance for Directors on the Combined Code* – available from the Institute of Chartered Accountants in England and Wales: www.icaew.co.uk/internalcontrol). The principles laid out in this guidance are applicable to all companies in terms of the generalities of what is required to ensure a company is effectively managing all its risks, including health and safety risks. The broad principles of this guidance are set out in **Chapter 1, section 1:2.2**.

12:4.2.1.2 Criminal sanction

Two aspects need to be considered here:

1. offences by corporate bodies. Section 37 of the HSWA makes it an offence for an individual acting on behalf of a company, such as any director, manager, secretary or other similar officer, to have connived or consented to the neglect of a company in discharging its health and safety duties under the Act. This is of particular interest where a death has resulted.

2. involuntary manslaughter. Individual directors may be personally liable for breaches in the company's health and safety duty of care if they are found guilty of gross negligence. Although this charge has often been difficult to prove there have been occasions when individual company directors have been successfully charged with this offence. The form of the indictment is '[name of person − {company director}] on the day of [date when death occurred], unlawfully killed [name of victim]…'.

This is a very blunt and strong reminder for directors that failure to comply with health and safety duties may result in their name being put at the head of this indictment. It is clearly an issue for boards to consider when presented with accident investigation reports. In addition, it can be incorporated as an explicit point by anyone preparing or presenting reports for the board's consideration, especially in cases of near miss reports or when a reappraisal of risk decisions is required, for example when evidence from an accident investigation report suggests that there are possibly serious deficiencies in safety management which require resources to be allocated. The board may be reluctant to expend resources when there is no direct evidence of actual loss but only the possibility of loss.

12:4.2.1.3 Disqualification of directors

Proposals put forward by the Home Office in May 2000 address some of the difficulties being encountered in making individual directors liable for deaths caused whilst at or arising out of work. These proposals suggest that:

- directors and officers of companies may be disqualified after the company has been convicted;

- they may be barred from holding management roles;

- a separate prosecution may be undertaken for an offence of contributing to management failure.

According to the proposals:

> *There is management failure if the way in which activities are managed or organised fails to ensure the health and safety of persons employed or affected by those activities.*

The extent to which these proposals will be put in place is not as yet known as it represents a fundamental change in the law and may be difficult to implement. The proposals support the intention of the Department of the Environment, Transport and the Regions/HSC strategy outlined in *Revitalising Health and Safety* (*see* **section 12:4.3**).

12:4.2.2 Public bodies

The law applies equally well to public bodies. Although there is, as yet, no direct equivalent of the Turnbull Code for the management boards of public bodies, each of the members may be liable to a charge of 'misfeasance in office' (i.e. wrongful exercise of lawful authority) (*see* **section 12:2.1**).

12:4.3 *Revitalising Health and Safety*

Boards will also need to consider the way health and safety is likely to change in the future, and how the performance of any industry sector or company is likely to be measured. In particular they will need to consider how enforcement authorities are likely to view accidents and accident prevention strategies in the longer term.

A good guide to this has been provided as part of a strategy for dealing with health and safety entitled *Revitalising Health and Safety*, published by the now-defunct Department of the Environment, Transport and the Regions and the HSC in June 2000. The aim of the document is to inject impetus and to re-launch the health and safety agenda 25 years on from the enactment of the HSWA.

The impetus is underpinned by a strategy, which, summarised, is to:

- promote better working environments;

- promote the contribution of a workforce that is 'happy, healthy and here' to productivity and competitiveness;

- maintain occupational health as a top priority;

- recognise a need for the positive engagement of small firms;

- motivate employees to improve their health and safety performance;

- cultivate a culture of self regulation, especially amongst small firms;

- have the Government encourage a 'partnership on health and safety issues';

- have the Government lead by example.

These set the future direction for workplace health and safety. They highlight the importance of promoting better working environments to deliver a more competitive economy, motivating employees to improve health and safety performance and simplifying overcomplicated regulations.

535

Copies of this document are available from:

ODPM Free Literature
PO Box 236
Wetherby LS23 7NB
Email: dft@twoten.press.net
Tel: 0870 1226236
Fax: 0870 1226237
Textphone: 0870 1207405
Product code: OSCSG0390

The strategy statement can also be downloaded from www.hse.gov.uk/revitalising/strategy.pdf.

12:4.3.1 The reasons for the strategy

The strategy has been developed for four main reasons.

1. The rate of reduction in the number of workplace accidents is slowing down.

2. The nature of work is changing, creating new hazards and risks.

3. There is a need to explore new ways to bring about change.

4. There needs to be a clear target for improvement.

12:4.3.2 Targets to be achieved

The strategy sets a number of targets, including:

- reducing by 30% the number of days lost due to work-related injuries;

- reducing by 20% the incidence of work-related ill health;

- reducing the fatal and major accident incidence rates by 10%.

These are to be achieved by 2010 and to be half fulfilled by 2004.

12:4.3.3 Penalties for offenders

The strategy includes the introduction of innovative penalties for health and safety offences and the 'naming and shaming' of companies that have been prosecuted and convicted for health and safety offences.

The first 'name and shame' report was issued in the year 2000 and reported on all offenders for the period 1 April 1999 to 31 March 2000 (*Health and safety offences and penalties, a report by the HSE*, available at www.hse.gov.uk/policy/enforce.pdf; details of the cases are available at www.hse-databases.co.uk/prosecutions). The explicit aim of the 'name and shame' approach is to encourage all those people involved with a business to put pressure on it to achieve high standards in health and safety. These people would include shareholders and investors, suppliers, main contractors, insurers and those seeking work.

The strategy also makes a business case for focussing on health and safety losses, in terms of:

* the cost of failures;

* the impact of losses in the supply chain;

* insurance.

12:4.3.4 Other proposals

The range of proposals suggested in the revitalising document include issues raised elsewhere, for example corporate manslaughter and directors' responsibilities. These are likely to be incorporated into a new Safety Bill sometime towards the end of 2002. They include:

* **increasing the fines under the HSWA.** The Government will seek to provide the courts with greater sentencing powers for health and safety crimes. The key measures envisaged are to extend the £20,000 maximum

fine in the lower courts to a much wider range of offences which currently attract a maximum penalty of £5,000.

- **providing the courts with the power to imprison for most health and safety offences.** In May 2000, the Home Office published a consultation document on reforming the law on involuntary manslaughter with a view to introducing a new offence on 'corporate killing' (*see* www.homeoffice.gov.uk/consult/invmans.htm). This law is highly contentious and there is doubt whether it would be passed. Nevertheless the Government intends to put health and safety on the boardroom agenda and therefore facilitate prosecutions of individual senior managers;

- **enabling private prosecutions.** The Government will consider amending the HSWA to enable private prosecutions in England and Wales to proceed without the consent of the Director of Public Prosecutions.

12:4.4 Future developments

In addition to the firm proposals already put forward, the HSC has highlighted the following to be considered in the future:

- fines linked to the turnover or profit of a company (there has been a request for employers to provide the past five years of turnover and profits of the company to the courts for their information);

- the prohibition of directors for a fixed period;

- the suspension of managers without pay;

- suspended sentences pending remedial action;

- compulsory health and safety training;

- a penalty-point system along the driving licence model;

- fixed-penalty notices for specific offences;

- deferred prohibition notices on welfare issues.

12:4.5 Redirecting resources and effort

It is vitally important that the board and senior managers ensure their response to any accident is well considered and appropriate for the circumstances.

There is a tendency for many managers to oversimplify the accident situation and their response to it. This type of approach can lead to an overzealous response which is full of short-term remedies but will be ineffective in the longer term. One of the great 'dangers' is to ensure that the response to an accident is not merely to ensure prevention of the *last* accident that has occurred; the real aim of accident prevention and the systematic management of safety is to ensure the potential for accidents is removed (or at the very least tightly controlled).

The response may fail anyway if the general workforce or lower management perceives the response to be overzealous and ineffectual. There is some evidence to suggest that the effectiveness of any response to an accident is limited by the perception of risk within an organisation.

The traditional approach has been to either devise a rule or to invent a technical solution that will control the circumstances that gave rise to the accident. Unfortunately this approach only really deals with the immediate causes of accidents (*see* **Chapter 1**). What the board of directors needs to understand is the underlying causes and failures in the safety management system and the degree to which they represent an overall risk to the organisation and the people working in it.

In making their decisions about the actions after an accident the directors and senior managers need to take account of the overall picture and to seek evidence from other sources, such as proactive monitoring, inspections, audits and compliance with standards. This should all be part of the action planning process (*see* **Chapter 8**). At the same time warnings about risk and evidence of failings in the risk control system should not be ignored.

12:4.6 Reporting to and involving employees

The Health and Safety Commission's commitment to the involvement of employees, mainly through their appointed safety representatives, is very clear. The modern setting for workplace safety is in the spirit of partnerships between workers and managers.

In an ideal world employee representatives and managers would work together closely to investigate and report on accidents. Although this may not be achieved in the real world and may for many organisations represent an ideal and for others a difficulty, it should nevertheless be the approach to be aspired to.

Boards should be encouraged to receive reports from their employee safety representatives and safety committees should be empowered to work on behalf of the board to secure health and safety in the workplace through combined reporting and investigation of accidents.

12:4.7 Internal disciplinary proceedings

Where appropriate, the board will need to consider the need for and extent of any disciplinary actions. The need to apportion blame to individuals must be considered very carefully, especially where the failures are a result of inadequate safety management systems. The action taken will, to a large extent, reflect the culture of the organisation (*see* **Chapter 1, section 1:5.1.2**).

12:4.8 The impact of media coverage

Media coverage can lead to loss of confidence in the company by both suppliers and customers and may also result in a fall in the share price (*see* **section 12:3.2.3**). This also brings with it the whole spectre of 'trial by media'. The board will need to assess the consequences of its approach to dealing with the media.

12:4.9 Involvement in public inquires

Where the incident has been a significant one there may be a call for a public inquiry. This in itself will create a large volume of work for any organisation caught up in the issues to be addressed by such an inquiry. This in turn may lead to government involvement and changes in legislation.

12:4.10 Attending coroners' inquests

In the case of fatalities during or arising out of work activities (*see* **Chapter 11**), the board will need to consider the level of attendance and representation at the coroner's court as well as the provision of information to the coroner.

12:5 The costs of safety

Reporting accidents to senior management and board directors should influence the way the business is managed. The report should make clear the extent of any losses that may have occurred as well as the extent of investment required.

There comes a point when investment in safety is optimised. That is to say the costs incurred by investing in health and safety bring the maximum amount of benefit. After this point the return in terms of value for money diminishes. Company managers and board directors should be able to ascertain that they are getting value for money by investing in safety. Unless this is achieved it is very likely that they may seek to achieve only minimum legal compliance without fully understanding the actual (or potential) loss to their organisation. *All* the costs to the organisation, discussed in **section 12:6.2**, need to be considered when making such judgements.

Health and safety arrangements are a financial consideration for any organisation, and a cost to every line manager in their own particular part of the operation. This cost is often considered as an 'on cost' which is not really necessary. The link between safety and profitability is not generally appreciated or accepted. Safety is seen as additional expenditure rather than as a cost which is intrinsic or implicit to the business. Information obtained from an accident investigation can assist in reconciling investment costs with assurance of safety.

12:5.1 Investment costs

Investment costs include:

- **capital costs** for safeguarding machinery and ensuring a safe workplace. Capital costs are the opposite of consumable costs, i.e. they are fixed and usually require a loan of some sort to finance them; machinery is a capital cost item, as are plant, equipment, vehicles and buildings;

- **maintenance costs**, which are costs incurred from maintaining plant, equipment and structures in good and safe working order;

- **personnel costs**, which are costs incurred from the recruitment, selection and training of staff to work safely and the staff which supervises, manages and directs them. In addition, there are costs in training accident investigators, which in an ideal world would be unnecessary if there were no accidents to investigate.

- **administration costs**, which arise from the company being involved in consultation with employees, reporting on safety reviews and inspections, undertaking audits and responding to the needs of managers for information.

- **information costs**, which are incurred in communicating safety policies to the workforce and managers, tracking safety-critical plant and equipment (e.g. for specialist testing and insurance certification) and reporting safety information (including collection, collation and analysis of safety data).

12:6 The financial costs of accidents

One of the significant impacts of accident on a business is financial. In *The Costs of Accidents at Work*, HSG96, the HSE sets out a number of case studies highlighting the costs of accidents to business.

In this report the HSE concluded that whilst many organisations may consider that financial losses due to accidents are covered by insurance (*see* **Chapter 11**), this is not necessarily correct. The HSE study found that comparisons made across several industries revealed that for every £1 of costs that were covered by insurance, between £8 and £36 were taken up in uninsured costs. The costs of accidents to the companies were found to range between around 1% and 5% of operating costs.

Smaller-scale accidents should be regarded as just as important as the very obvious impact of large-scale events. The drain on resources is just as serious with a multitude of smaller incidents as it is for one very large incident; it is just that they go unnoticed and unremarked.

12:6.1 Revenue costs

In the HSE publication *The Cost of Accidents at Work* it was found that the overall direct burden on business of accidents is around £700 million per year (with the cost of ill health being between £4,000 million and £9,000 million per year). This is equivalent to a cost of around 5–10% of gross trading profits. However, total costs to the country as a whole are way in excess of this. If the effect of accidents and ill health on the provision of services, such as the National Health Service, is taken into account, then the total cost to the nation is estimated at between £10 billion and £15 billion per year, or between 1–3% of the gross domestic product.

12:6.2 Actual costs

The actual costs of accidents and other safety-related events can be viewed in terms of direct costs and indirect costs. These cannot be quantified here as they will depend upon the seriousness and extent of the accident. They will also depend upon the structure and cost base of the organisation.

12:6.2.1 Direct costs

These are the costs that can be directly measured and reflect the sums that the company has to pay out. They are seen as a true cost in terms of accounting principles.

These costs include:

- treatment costs;

- lost output;

- business interruption;

- lost business reputation;

- loss of investment opportunities – opportunity costs;

- sick pay;

- employers' and occupiers' liability payments;

- the cost of remedial work;

- fines and litigation costs.

12:6.2.1.1 Treatment costs

These include, but are not limited to the:

- cost of first aid supplies and their disposal, for example the disposal of clinical waste;

- cost of first aiders' time and their time away from normal duties;

- transportation of injured person(s) to first aid areas or to hospital. The NHS can charge for a range of services, including being picked up at a road traffic accident by an ambulance (for which the vehicle insurer normally pays);

- downtime costs of staff who accompany the injured to treatment centres.

12:6.2.1.2 Lost output

These costs include, but are not limited to:

- **replacement costs:**

  - of machinery and equipment that was broken in the accident;

  - of property that has been damaged in the accident;

  - of raw materials which may have been destroyed, damaged or contaminated in the accident;

  - for the selection, recruitment and training of temporary and/or full-time staff who are required to replace injured persons unable to work for some time or have retired. In addition, there is the cost of providing supervision for and training of the new starters whilst they acquire the necessary skills and experience to take over the injured persons' workloads;

- paid to staff to fill the gap left by absent skilled staff where it is not possible or feasible to train up new staff to fill the vacancy created by the accident, for example train and bus drivers working overtime to cover absences. The cost of absence is a significant burden and also gives rise to a number of indirect costs (*see* **section 12:6.2.2**).

Some of these costs may be met by insurance, for example insurance to replace machinery or key workers such as senior directors (*see* **Chapter 9, section 9:3**), but there may be a significant gap between making and settling the claim.

- **business interruption.** The inability to temporarily provide normal services or continue with normal production will involve the company in additional costs or losses. The extent of these will depend upon the length of the period during which disruption continues.

Typical costs or losses incurred might include but are not limited to:

- wage and salary costs of staff laid off because service/production has to be suspended until the accident site has been cleared, repairs have been completed or replacement equipment found. Dependant upon the nature of the damage sustained and the number of staff involved, these costs may be significant;

- failings in the supply chain and therefore the inability to meet a customer's deadline. This may result in the customer requesting a discount on their invoice, refusing to pay the invoice or taking their business elsewhere;

- being unable to meet invoice payments by expected or agreed deadlines, and having penalties imposed for late payment or loan arrangements having to be renegotiated (at unfavourable terms);

- the loss of cash-flow, resulting in failure to meet loan repayments and the need to extend credit;

- the loss of market share as competitors move in to take up the shortfall created by the company's loss of production;

- the cost of marketing strategies aimed at regaining market share and customers' confidence;

- having to find alternative storage facilities where suppliers are contracted to deliver raw materials, etc., and where space is no longer available as either a direct result of the accident or because production has slowed down resulting in a build-up of materials on site;

- having to source products or materials from competitors in order to maintain customer services, often at a premium rate;

- additional security for any areas that need to be guarded or which have become more vulnerable to theft, arson or vandalism;

- the cost of using alternative facilities whilst remediation and reinstatement (or re-build) of the company's own premises is effected.

Many of these costs may be covered by insurance, especially where a good business continuity plan has been devised to meet such circumstances.

To mitigate the possible costs/losses, organisations should maintain a 'business interruption' plan, which should be regularly practised and reviewed (*see* **Chapter 2, section 2:8**).

- **business reputation.** Failure to meet customer demand can have a serious impact on business reputation. The impact of media coverage should not be underestimated as the market position of a company may be adversely affected. This may also be reflected in share price. Reputation costs are difficult to quantify but they can be illustrated by what happened to Perrier when their product became accidentally contaminated. This sparkling water company lost all of its market share for a brief period of time whilst it sorted out the problem. Competitors quickly came into the market and some estimates are that Perrier only regained something of the order of 35% of its original market share. This had an impact on share price as well as the short- to medium-term effect on the desirability of the company's product as perceived by consumers.

  Similarly the number and extent of train crashes in the UK between 1998 and 2001 has had a significant effect on the numbers of people travelling by train, an impact on train operators' profits and the development of a very bad press for the industry as a whole.

  Costs may also be incurred to present a better public image by hiring in public relations consultants to deal with statements to the media and respond to outside enquires made to the company.

- **loss of investment opportunity – opportunity costs.** Opportunity costs reflect the situation where a company would have been in a position to make planned improvements, increase its product range or offer expanded services, only to have this curtailed by an accident. The accident absorbs the finances that would have otherwise been used to improve the business. The opportunity to improve is therefore lost.

Such costs might include:

- the inability to upgrade equipment or production processes as investment monies are re-directed towards dealing with the accident situation. Railtrack and the position of the rail industry is an example of this. After the Hatfield crash in October 2000 monies had to be allocated to track replacement rather than to improvement in existing services;

- losing the opportunity to expand into new markets as time and resources are taken up dealing with the accident situation, undertaking remedial works and being generally unable to focus attention on the new business areas;

- the loss of advertising fees by having to abandon new market areas or put back a new product launch for which an advertising campaign had been contracted.

12:6.2.1.3 Sick pay

Any 'lost time' injury will require some form of sick pay to be paid out. This will either be statutory sick pay (SSP) or SSP plus contractual (or occupational) sick pay. Under the Statutory Sickness Pay (General) Regulations 1992, employers have a duty to pay employees who are absent from work due to personal sickness (including both ill health or injury) a minimum level of pay for a defined period. The rate of SSP is fixed and reviewed by the Government regularly. The figure currently stands (as of 6 April 2002) at £63.25 per week.

Employers are responsible for the administration of SSP, and it is not permissible for them to require employees to contribute, either directly or indirectly, towards the cost of providing SSP. An administration cost is therefore incurred for every work-related injury or ill health absence that occurs.

Employers can recover the amount by which their statutory sick payments for a particular month exceed 13% of their total Class 1 National Insurance contributions (employer's and employee's combined) for that month. This scheme applies to all employers. The scheme effectively allows employers to recover SSP when payments have exceeded a certain level for a particular month.

There is no legal obligation on employers to pay an employee any salary or wages during periods of sickness. It is a question for each employer to decide as a matter of company policy, so long as employees' entitlements are clearly defined and communicated. Many employers operate a scheme whereby payment of sick pay is made according to a formula that defines specific entitlements according to an employee's length of service. Other employers operate a discretionary policy. This contractual sick pay is thus a cost to the organisation where an occupational or contractual sick pay scheme exists.

Many of these costs may be covered by insurance.

12:6.2.1.4 Employers' and occupiers' liability claims

These claims will be met in terms of the contract of insurance (*see* **Chapter 11, section 11:3**) but there may be some residual costs to be met by the company and usually a deductible will be incurred. This means that the insurers only meet part of the claim, with the company having to pay a percentage of the claim, usually quoted as a fixed amount such as the first £50,000. Payments under such a claim may give rise to an indirect cost.

Likely direct costs to be incurred are therefore:

- the deductible;

- administration costs for the scheme. This can be costed as 'so much per claim handled or received over the course of a year'. For example, if a quarter of one person's time is spent dealing with employee liability insurance matters and 100 claims are handled each year then the cost per accident injury is worked out as the cost of the person's time divided by 100. A similar cost can be worked out for property damage and for other insured areas;

- time (the number of person-hours) spent dealing with insurers in negotiating settlements and agreeing damages and areas of cover, especially for major accident events.

12:6.2.1.5 The cost of remedial work

These include the repair and replacement of damaged plant, equipment and structures. Included in this will be the downtime resulting from any area or plant being out of commission. This will also include the period during which the investigation is taking place (and therefore when the site or plant cannot be used (*see* **Chapters 3** and **5**)).

Remedial costs include:

- obtaining estimates, preparing specifications and researching or investigating possible solutions to the situation;

- visiting and interviewing suppliers and manufacturers to ensure specifications can be met and negotiate delivery times and finances;

- installing new plant and equipment, which involves the time and expertise of company staff to assist or direct suppliers and installers;

- financing the cost of replacing and meeting any short fall in insurance cover;

- reworking or reviewing working procedures for new plant/equipment or premises.

12:6.2.1.6 Fines and litigation costs

If the company is taken to court, either by the enforcement authority or by an injured party, there will be costs to be met. These costs will include:

- legal adviser fees;

- court attendance administration costs;

- expert witnesses' costs (e.g. time, travel and subsistence costs);

- damages awarded by the court;

- fines imposed by a court.

Although it is not possible to insure for the monetary costs of actual fines, it is possible to obtain insurance cover for the costs of legal work and legal representation and the overall costs of any legal action. The fine will always come out of the company's finances.

12:6.2.2 Indirect costs

A number of indirect costs also arise with any accident; sometimes these are extensive and generally are greater than those of direct costs. These costs tend to be subsumed within the overall accounting of the organisation and as a result go unnoticed. In the report, *The Cost of Accidents at Work* (HSG96) the HSE shows these costs to be in the order of eight to 36 times greater than the known direct costs. They include:

- investigation costs;

- administration costs, compensation claims, insurance, HR costs, etc.;

- action plan costs, including costs of managerial debate;

- the costs of maintaining morale and reducing stress;

- reinstatement costs – clean up and repair;

- welfare costs;

- insurance premiums;

- training;

- reputation.

552

12:6.2.2.1 Investigation costs

The time and effort spent on accident investigation is generally not accounted for. The time costs can be measured in terms of pro rata salaries for the investigation team and overhead contributions. The money an investigator is being paid would normally result in some productive outcome, but is being diverted to carrying out the investigation instead.

The taking of witness statements will also remove witnesses from the workplace for a period and this cost can be accounted for in terms of pro rata salaries and overhead contributions.

Other costs include the administration of the accident investigation process, paperwork, telephone calls and similar tasks, such as:

- recording, writing up and verifying witness statements;

- generating accident investigation reports;

- completing and filing RIDDOR reports, if required;

- making telephone calls to external and internal experts, enforcement authorities, manufacturers/suppliers, customers, employee representatives, employees, etc.;

- doing general administration such as filing, collating information and documenting evidence.

These all depend, of course, on the circumstances and consequences of the accident.

12:6.2.2.2 Administration costs

Apart from the administration of the investigation itself there will be a range of administrative tasks to be undertaken. These include all the human resource management tasks, such as:

- handling sick pay, checking sickness absence, filling in forms, monitoring payments of both statutory and contractual sick pay, notifying payroll, and obtaining and filing medical certificates;

- dealing with industrial injury compensation benefit claims, filling in forms, checking medical referrals and obtaining relevant information;

- selecting and recruiting replacement staff for any shortfall as a result of absence;

- training new staff (*see* **section 12:6.2.2.8**);

- conducting return-to-work assessments;

- dealing with the next of kin and relatives (where relevant/appropriate);

- liaising with counsellors or welfare support.

Other administrative tasks include:

- dealing with insurance reports and the submission of insurance claims and details;

- contacting insurers and filling in and vetting claim forms;

- providing information for public relations purposes and informing employees;

- dealing with employee representatives;

- booking rooms or venues for meetings;

- organising diaries and scheduling meetings;

- dealing with the post.

This is only a short list as the range of actual administrative tasks can be quite extensive. Most if not all of them will be undertaken as part of somebody's everyday work and thus the actual cost of doing them is not accounted for.

12:6.2.2.3 Action plan costs

The process of putting an action plan in place following an accident can be quite extensive (*see* **Chapter 8**). A significant proportion of senior management time may be taken up debating the work to be done and estimating the costs and resource allocation for the work required. These costs generally go unnoticed as they are taken up as part of normal managerial work. The costs exist because without the accident the managers would normally be spending their time on more productive areas of work.

The actual process of implementing action plans will also require the addition of resources and time. Employees who are tasked with implementing control are normally pulled away from other work and are thus subsumed in the overall costs of the company. They do, however, reflect an opportunity cost, for without them the company would be devoting its attention to its main business.

Many of the action plan costs are the result of staff time spent on the various activities involved and can be allocated as pro rata hours worked plus overhead contributions. These may involve:

- attendance at meetings;
- developing, agreeing and monitoring the action plan;
- assigning and managing resources;
- maintaining the action plan documentation (both a management cost and an administrative cost).

12:6.2.2.4 The costs of maintaining morale and reducing stress

All accidents have an impact upon company morale and increase stress among staff. It is difficult to predict the size or nature of the stress response but it can be certain that accidents cause stress amongst both workers and managers. The usual response to stress will be a diminished level of productivity, an increase in minor accidents and a higher sickness absence. This is an area which is difficult to quantify and often will go unmeasured, but nevertheless has to be seen as an indirect cost to the company.

Examples of such indirect costs might be:

- time spent by staff talking about the incident;

- the effect on managers' productivity worrying about the situation and their personal position;

- increased sickness absence among workers as a result of stress.

12:6.2.2.5 Reinstatement costs

After an accident there is generally a period of cleaning up and undertaking immediate repairs. The clean-up costs are often not explicit and are seen as part of the company's normal business. In more extensive accidents the clean-up costs can become a significant direct cost. For example, the clean up of a major industrial site following a fire can be expensive, although insurers will meet most of the direct costs. The costs will need to be clearly identified.

Typical reinstatement costs might include:

- the hiring of specialist cleaning contractors;

- waste removal and disposal charges;

- overtime for in-house cleaners;

- the cost of extra cleaning materials;

- the redecoration of affected areas;

- the use of alternative accommodation, for example portable cabins;

- the refurbishment of the site, including landscaping and rebuilding of roads, footpaths, walkways, etc.;

- the repair/replacement of broken glazing;

- the cleaning and flushing of drainage systems.

12:6.2.2.6 Welfare costs

Supporting people who have been involved in an accident will give rise to welfare costs. These will involve the costs of:

- visits to people at home or in hospital;
- support for immediate financial loss and assistance with debt, all of which may have resulted from the workplace accident;
- professional counselling or psychiatric treatment;
- debriefing and talking with employee groups and relatives and friends.

Some welfare costs may be direct costs funded by the company through its occupational health programme.

12:6.2.2.7 Insurance premiums

Insurance companies tend to examine a company's past claims history when setting its overall premiums (*see* **Chapter 11**). They obviously take into account the range, size and extent of any accidents that have already occurred. A company's accident history will thus figure as an element in the setting of premiums. In most cases, companies may not realise this as the insurers may not be explicit or make it obvious to the company that they are basing their assessment of insurance risk on past performance either of that company or of the industry sector as a whole.

Indirect insurance costs may include:

- increased premiums following a single claim for a serious accident exposure;
- increased premiums as a result of an increase in the number or size of claims;
- increases in the deductible set;

- the inability to place certain types of risk in the insurance market, therefore resulting in the company having to self-insure.

12:6.2.2.8 Training

Nearly all accidents have some element of lack of training in their causation. The individuals involved somewhere within the chain of events will have failed to demonstrate the competencies that would normally be expected, for example in designing a safe system of work, in estimating human fallibility or in selecting and/or using the right equipment. The cost of retraining or introducing new training may often be a direct cost as it is measurable as a training course or training development project. However, it is not often seen to be the case. Training is often seen as a normal part of a company's operations and the additional training costs go unremarked and become subsumed in general accounting.

Typical training costs may include:

- training-needs analysis following an accident;
- the development of new training objectives;
- sourcing training providers;
- developing training materials.

12:6.2.2.9 Reputation

In addition to the direct reputation cost mentioned in **section 12:6.2.1.2**, indirect costs may also be incurred.

Many companies now contract out work of one sort or another. This creates supply chains and reliance on contracted services. A client company would normally be expected to examine the prospective contractor's loss and risk performance record as part of its selection processes. A company which is interested in maintaining market position or the quality of its services (especially in the public sector) will be reluctant to take on a contractor who has a lot of down time and expense as a result of accidents. The supply chain issue is seen as a driver for improved health and safety performance in the Government's *Revitalising Health and Safety* strategy (*see* **section 12:4.3**).

Such costs will result from:

- an inability to persuade customers/contractors that the business is successful;

- poor financial or other references (from customers, suppliers, etc.);

- being listed in the HSE's 'name and shame' list (*see* **section 12:4.3.3**), resulting in the company not being short-listed for contracts, work, supply, etc.;

- a perception by the public and in people in the business world that the company is a poor performer, having been associated with a serious accident which received extensive media coverage, again resulting in failure to make the selection break when bidding for work.

12:6.3 Estimating costs

Given the number of variables which might need to be considered in reaching a true cost of an accident or a series of accidents to an organisation (*see* **sections 12:6.1** and **12:6.2**) it is necessary to construct some ready reckoners.

One way of doing this is to set a series of price limits for different categories of accident. The price list can be constructed by roughly assigning monetary values to each of the factors listed in **section 12:6.2**.

As serious accidents are infrequent, it is sometimes not possible to come up with a ready price for such accidents. To overcome this problem a factoring process can be used.

Figure 12:2 shows how the factoring process works. As a rule of thumb, a change in the accident category results in a ten-fold increase in costs. In this case, the cost of a fatality has been taken as the figure used in risk calculation (i.e. the value of life saved). If a fatality is calculated to cost £2 million, by this basis a major injury accident is costed at £2 million ÷ 10 = £200,000, and so on.

FIGURE 12:2 THE ACCIDENT FACTORING PROCESS

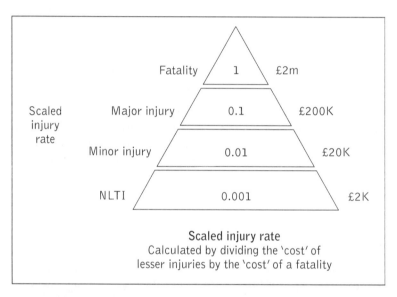

Notes: NTLI = no-lost-time injury; scaled injury rate is discussed in **section 12:7.2.7.**

In **Figure 12:3** a more accurate assessment has been made by working out a price for a larger range of accident categories and then using the same idea to work out the individual cost of each type of accident. In this case the prices reflect those as at 1995 but are based on an 'accurate' calculation of actual costs in a real organisation.

FIGURE 12:3 A MORE DETAILED ACCIDENT FACTORING PROCESS

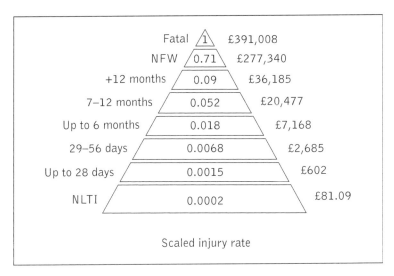

Scaled injury rate

NFW indicates an injury sufficient to make the person not fit for work. This equates to the higher level of reported injuries under RIDDOR. These figures are conservative: for example, an actual period of lost time of 28 days is likely to cost much more than £602. It should be noted that costs increase significantly, as to be expected, when the chance of returning to work is reduced. Generally it is found that after six months it can be very difficult to get people back to work.

That these figures are realistic can be judged by comparing them with figures quoted elsewhere, for example £33 for a first-aid-only injury, £141 where there is damage to plant and equipment but no injury results and an average of £2,097 where there has been an absence from work though injury; the HSE estimates a cost of between £17,000 and £19,000 for a major or serious injury (both quoted from *Health and Safety Competent Person's Newsletter*, GEE Publishing Ltd, May 2002). The high cost of NFW and fatal injuries reflects the level of compensation paid out as well as legal fees.

By presenting actual or estimated costs of an accident (or sometimes 'guesstimated' costs, bearing in mind that actual costs may not be exactly as predicted by the factoring process and actual costs may not always be available), board members gain a better picture of actual costs to their organisation. Of course, the better the accounting used, the more accurate the figures become.

The HSE has introduced a ready reckoner available on the internet at www.hse.gov.uk/costs, which may be particularly useful for small- to medium-sized organisations. Although not all the costs listed in **section 12:6.2** are included, the major costs are and there is a facility for adding a number of costs specific to the organisation. The website is accompanied by a free leaflet entitled *Reduce risks – Cut costs: the real costs of accidents and ill-health at work*, available at www.hse.gov.uk/pubns/idg355.pdf or through HSE Books.

12:6.4 Predicting enforcement action

Boards will also need to be made aware of the likelihood of enforcement action following on from an accident. This is not to ensure defence mechanisms can be instituted, but rather because it heightens the awareness of what the accident actually means for the organisation. It also serves as a reminder of the seriousness of any accident reported within an organisation, however minor it may first appear.

Factors to consider are:

- the breach of any obvious duty of care, especially under specific legislation;

- the extent of any injury or damage that has resulted;

- the opinions of competent safety advisers and the legal advisers;

- any previous history of similar events;

- any failures to initiate or follow through on action plans already agreed upon;

- the existence of risk assessments which have not been actioned.

12:6.4.1 Breaches of any obvious duty of care

It should be immediately obvious if a specific duty set out in legislation has not been met (*see* **Chapter 1**). For example, if a pressure system fails, then there may well have been a breach of the pressure system regulations. Likewise an exposure to noise resulting in hearing loss would likely be a breach of the noise-at-work regulations. Most obvious will be the absence of any risk assessments for the work involved in the accident.

In very general terms the enforcement authorities tend to react to the extent of the injury or damage that has resulted. A fatality will always give rise to an investigation by the enforcement authorities (*see* **Chapter 4**) and each case will be taken on its findings. However, a death generally indicates that some form of enforcement action should be expected. Likewise with serious injuries. The difficult area is perhaps predicting action when the event has had the potential to cause serious injury (or even a fatality) but this has not actually occurred. The general rule of thumb is probably the greater the injury, the greater the likelihood of prosecution when taking into account the extent of the breach of any statutory duty.

12:6.4.2 The opinions of competent safety advisers and legal advisers

Depending on their experience and knowledge of the relevant facts, both legal advisers and the competent safety advisers (ideally working together) should be able to give some insight into the possibility of enforcement action. Safety advisers are in all likelihood the people who have been liasing with the enforcement authority, reporting RIDDOR incidents and seeking advice on particular issues and may therefore have a good insight into the way the enforcement authority may be thinking. The legal and safety advisers will be reviewing and monitoring published reports and should have a fair understanding of what action has been taken in similar cases elsewhere.

12:6.4.3 The history of similar events

If the organisation has had experience of the same or similar types of accidents and if these have been reported to or commented on by the enforcement authority, then there is naturally going to come a point when someone in authority is going to ask *why* this has happened again. This in itself may be sufficient to prompt a more thorough look at the organisation by the enforcement authority and hence predicate grounds for some form of enforcement action. Likewise similar events occurring in other parts of the same industry sector can be a good indictor that enforcement action may follow.

12:6.4.4 Failures to initiate or follow through on action plans

Where an organisation has already been subject to enforcement authority inspections and agreed action plans or programmes of improvement, and these have not been followed through and an accident has resulted, it is highly likely that enforcement action will be taken.

12:6.4.5 The existence of risk assessments

Where an organisation has undertaken risk assessments and has identified significant risks but has not taken the action required to control those risks and an accident results, then again enforcement action is highly likely.

12:7 Techniques for reporting accident and incident information

12:7.1 Introduction

A major problem for anyone responsible for providing information on health and safety performance is determining and identifying what information is required.

Many of the health and safety information approaches adopted within organisations (what information they collect, how they collect it and the reasons for collecting it) rely upon the collection of certain injury (and fatality) data. Often these approaches collect information on fairly specific areas of interest. Such data may not reflect the real situation, especially if it is limited to certain categories of injury and events, such as RIDDOR. Data collected in most organisations and by national bodies reflects the history of injury causation; it provides very little knowledge of the potential for loss and the effectiveness of the management in ensuring the potential for loss is minimised.

One approach that is often adopted is to collect information and then for someone to decide what to do with it. For example, every aspect of every accident is recorded and then the data collated and the 'results' subjected to some form of analysis. This generally ends up with descriptive reports which detail how many injuries occurred involving specified activities or situations. Information collected on a construction site might include accident reports recording 'body part injured' and equipment and activities involved. An analysis of reported accidents on building sites might show a number of head injuries related to objects dropping from a height onto people working below, whilst in an office there might be a number of back injuries resulting from muscle strains during filing work in unsuitable storage areas. The report for these accidents would only *describe* the nature of the injuries and the activities involved (for example, over-head working involving hand tools) but would not *explain* why the injuries or the incidents occurred. There could be a variety of reasons why objects were being dropped and a number of reasons why injuries were occurring, for example the use of inappropriate hand tools, failure to secure the work area and provide protection to people working below, poor job planning causing people to work in danger areas unnecessarily, poor site supervision and horse play. Injuries to the head might be a result of failure to wear the head protection provided, inappropriate head protection or lack of provision of head protection. Falls, slips and trips might be the result of poor housekeeping, or leaving cables across the floor or rubbish lying around. By having only a description of the accidents a more detailed examination is required in order to assess the precise causes so that preventive action can be taken.

Simply reporting head injuries or incidents of workers not wearing head protection to the senior managers or the board of directors could possibly lead to the response that 'head protection is provided and they ought to wear it', with the resulting action that 'this is a supervisory problem'. This response would overlook underlying reasons why workers were not wearing helmets. One reason why workers may not be wearing head protection could be that the provided head protection does not fit and is uncomfortable. As a result, it is not worn. Another reason might be that the provided head protection gets in the way of doing the job.

A more rational approach to deciding what information to collect and report is to determine what *answers* are required and then seek the information that can produce those answers. The type of answers required will be identified by asking questions about risks and monitoring arrangements. For example, if a company wishes to know whether head protection is being properly worn on a construction site it may not be sufficient simply to record all injuries. The circumstances in which these injuries arise are equally important (in this case the monitoring process for the provision and wearing of head protection). The company may need to know why the helmets are not being worn, why they are being removed or if indeed they are performing to specification. It will also be important to establish why the work has been arranged so that people are working in dangerous areas, i.e. where they may be subjected to objects falling on to them. Whilst it is a legal requirement (Construction (Head Protection) Regulations 1989 (S.I. 1989, No. 2209)) and general good practice for head protection to be worn on building sites it is important to ensure that the helmets are the last line of defence in ensuring safety and not the first. There is a requirement to ensure safe working conditions (s.2 of the HSWA) and this will include the plan of the work, arrangements for working (for example, ensuring that overhead jobs are not done when people are working beneath them) and the general protection of the workplace (for example, providing netting or boarded flying scaffolding to catch anything that does fall).

It is important, therefore, to ensure that accident reporting reflects the information requirements of the organisation, especially at board level. Generally it is not sufficient to report simple numbers of accidents occurring, such as so many head injuries, slips and falls. What is required is to provide information that allows for the overall monitoring of safety performance and the establishing of effective corrective action. The information collected and reported on should reflect the risks in the organisation and the preventive measures that are put in place.

Thus, in reporting accidents to senior managers and the board of directors it is important to do so in the right context and with clarity. Context requires matching the information presented to the risks and control measures. For example, when reporting accidents resulting in back injury, the type of activities and tasks being undertaken needs to be included and any deficiencies in manual handling risk assessments should be pointed out. Not all back injuries result from manual handling operations. For example, someone tripping over a wire in the office may well wrench muscles in their back, giving rise to the same sort of pain as results from lifting a load badly. Reporting on such incidents needs to be clear so that those responsible for instigating corrective action (as well as monitoring safety performance) can readily determine the relationships between cause and effect. Clarity involves ensuring that the information is precise and accurate and reflects what is actually happening.

12:7.2 Analysing and presenting data

12:7.2.1 Collecting information

Deciding on what information to collect and how to handle it is a science in its own right. In order to use accident data for monitoring and corrective purposes it is necessary to look beyond the simple recording and reporting of accidents.

It is necessary to go beyond the outcomes of the events (i.e. the injuries) and look more at the events themselves. It is very likely that the events leading to loss are themselves predictable from inherent failures or weaknesses in safety management systems. Part of the purpose of reporting accidents is, therefore, to enable managers to understand what is happening in the systems they are responsible for and what inherent weaknesses may exist.

12:7.2.2 Collection of data/information

The information that can be used to report to senior management is available from a number of sources. These generally include:

- accident records, including accident book entries;

- reports made to the enforcement authorities on form F2508;

- accident investigation reports;

- insurance claims, including both public and employee liability as well as property insurance;

- results of legal action, including out-of-court settlements and litigation judgments in cases of compensation.

Depending on the amount of information available from these sources and how easily it can be collected and collated (which depends on the sophistication of the collection and analysis system in place), a number of different approaches can be adopted to analyse and present the information.

12:7.2.3 Reliability and validity of information

It is necessary to ensure that reports made to directors are accurate; this requires a consideration of the reliability and validity of the information used to present the analysis.

12:7.2.3.1 Reliability

There are several factors to be considered here. These involve:

- the means of collecting data;

- the interpretation of data when it is being collected;

- the extent of reporting and recording the data.

12:7.2.3.2 The means of collecting data

Care has to be taken to ensure that the way information is collected on accidents and incidents does not affect the way the information will eventually be used and interpreted. For example, if the accident book is used as the only means of collecting information, then there will only be a limited amount of information available. This will make it almost impossible to undertake a detailed analysis. Recording in accident books tends only to involve one line about the nature of the injury and to whom it happened. If information from accident book entries is used together with separate information from an accident reporting system, then the information will be 'mixed' and it will be necessary to check details from the accident book against those entered on the accident record. If minor injuries are recorded in the accident book but the accident recording system only records more serious events, assumptions will have to be made about the reliability of the data. For example, should events that result in a very minor injury, such as a paper cut, be included when presenting information on accidents to senior management? These are decisions that the organisation will need to make and then stick to! In an office environment details of paper cuts are not important, but they would be in an environment where contamination of the cut from biological agents was possible.

12:7.2.3.3 The interpretation of data

When an accident recording form is being used to collect data there may be occasions when some form of interpretation has to be made, either by those completing the form initially or by those collating the information for a report on accident performance. An example of this would be a question that asks 'was the appropriate procedure being followed or correct PPE being worn?' Whoever fills in the form needs to know both the risks involved in the activities being undertaken (when the accident occurred) and the procedure that should be followed or the PPE that should be used. If the person completing the form does not know, misunderstands or simply guesses the answer to such a question, the data immediately becomes unreliable.

Another form of this problem would be accident records that are incomplete. Someone collating a series of records to form a report on accident performance would have to make some assumptions about the missing information. For example, if the time of day is left off the accident report, then it will not be possible to reliably analyse the data to establish if this is an important factor in accident causation, as would be the case if a type of accident was particularly associated with shift-work patterns, i.e. people rushing at the end of the shift to get work completed.

12:7.2.3.4 The extent of reporting and recording

This is a very simple issue to address. It is only possible to analyse what is collected. If the accident recording/reporting system is rudimentary then only a very simplistic analysis will be possible. Any analysis or presentation of information is based on the principle 'what you get out is only as good as what you put in'. The extent of the information reporting/recording system will, to a large extent, determine the degree of reliability in the results that are reported from an analysis of the available information.

12:7.2.3.5 Validity

The issue of validity is very important when dealing with any data analysis to provide information on performance, such as safety performance assessed by the number and types of accidents occurring. The histogram provided at **Figure 12:7** appears at first sight to show that the biggest area of concern over safety performance is in the production area. To some extent this is true, as the number of accidents are very high and clearly something has to be done about them. It is not possible, however, to make any real conclusions about safety performance overall in this organisation as the histogram is itself very misleading. No account has been taken of the relative risks in the areas involved and, perhaps more importantly, of the numbers of people involved. The validity of presentations using actual numbers of accidents/injuries, described in **Figures 12:4–12:7**, has to be questioned. This is because they are presenting 'raw' data, which creates problems that may mask variations in both the activities and numbers of people employed in each of the divisions.

For example, if the data presented in **Figure 12:7** is re-examined to take account of the number of people involved in each unit (production, cleaning, maintenance, etc.) a different result emerges. The way this is achieved is by using indices (*see* **section 12:7.2.5** and **Figure 12:13**).

12:7.2.4 Analysis of information

There are a number of simple ways to analyse and present data. These include:

- pie charts;
- histograms;
- graphs.

12:7.2.4.1 Pie charts

Pie charts, as the name suggests, represent figures (data) in the form of a pie that has been cut into sections, each section representing some value or property that is of interest. This enables some easy analysis to be done.

A simple pie chart indicating the three main groups of accidents in a company over one year is shown **Figure 12:4**. The pie chart easily enables the relative contribution of each of the type of accident to be displayed.

FIGURE 12:4 PIE CHART SHOWING THE THREE MAIN
GROUPS OF ACCIDENT IN AN
ORGANISATION

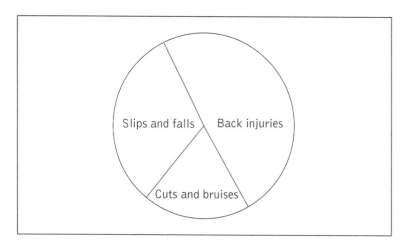

The pie chart in **Figure 12:5** shows the distribution of accidents by cause. The chart shows the relatively high contribution made by slips, trips and falls on a level, and back injuries due to manual handling operations, to the overall numbers of accidents.

FIGURE 12:5 PIE CHART SHOWING THE DISTRIBUTION OF ACCIDENTS BY CAUSE/ACTIVITY INVOLVED

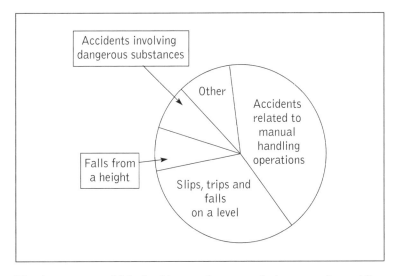

Pie charts are useful in looking at the general picture and providing some, if limited, analysis indicative of where problems may be occurring. They can therefore be useful in prompting further analysis by other means. They have the advantage of being relatively easy and simple to put together and can have an immediate impact on the way the information is presented. The main disadvantage of the use of pie charts is that they do not account for the underlying differences in the groups, activities or risks that are responsible for the distribution of the reported accidents. What the charts in **Figures 12:4** and **12:5** do not show are the relative consequences of these accidents. For example, falls from a height result in a high proportion of fatalities, whereas falls on a level may result in no more that minor contusions and bruising.

12:7.2.4.2 Histograms

Another way to analyse and present information is to display it graphically as a histogram or bar chart. The histogram in **Figure 12:6** displays accident data collected from three sites of one organisation over a year and is broken down into the total number of accidents for each quarter.

FIGURE 12:6 HISTOGRAM SHOWING THE DISTRIBUTION OF ACCIDENTS ACROSS THREE SITES OF A COMPANY DURING ONE YEAR

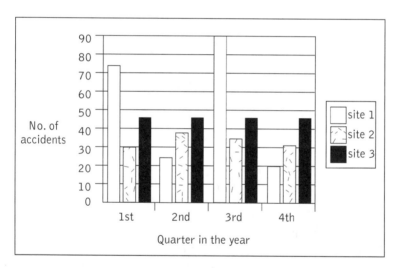

Another way of analysing accident data using histograms is to look at the contributions made by various groups in the workforce to the overall totals. **Figure 12:7** shows the relative contribution made to the accidents in an organisation by the type of worker employed.

FIGURE 12:7 HISTOGRAM SHOWING THE DISTRIBUTION OF ACCIDENTS BY WORKER GROUP

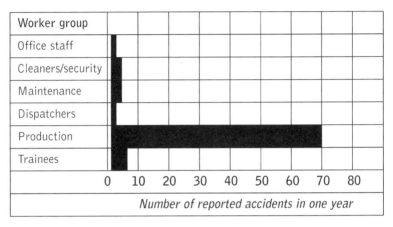

Worker group									
Office staff									
Cleaners/security									
Maintenance									
Dispatchers									
Production									
Trainees									
	0	10	20	30	40	50	60	70	80
	Number of reported accidents in one year								

This type of presentation reveals the relative contribution made by various worker groups and thus indicates to some extent what sort of activities might be involved. The production area clearly experiences more accidents than any other group in this case. Care, however, has to be exercised when making conclusions from this sort of representation as the data is relatively raw and may not be fully representative (*see* **section 12:7.2.5**).

12:7.2.4.3 Patterns and trends

One of the ways to consider what is happening in systems is to look at the patterns and trends that collated data reveal. Patterns indicate groupings or clusters of events or a certain distribution of events that may raise interesting questions about performance in specific areas. Trends are predictive, indicating that a situation is likely to continue, get worse or improve.

12:7.2.4.3.1 Patterns

The graph in **Figure 12:8** presents a pattern of safety events showing a seasonal variation. The number of reported accidents are presented (y axis) for each of the four quarters of a year (x axis) for three sites of a company. The events depicted on this graph possibly reveal a seasonal variation with peaks in the second and third quarters. The graph also shows that the sites have very similar accident experiences.

FIGURE 12.8 GRAPH SHOWING SEASONAL VARIATIONS IN THE NUMBER OF ACCIDENTS ACROSS THREE SITES OF A COMPANY

Number of accidents	1st	2nd	3rd	4th
10				
9		① ③	③	
8		②	①	
7				
6			②	
5				
4	② ③			②
3	①			① ③
2				
1				
0				
Quarter	1st	2nd	3rd	4th

Legend: ① Figures for site 1
         ② Figures for site 2
         ③ Figures for site 3

This information may indicate that there is some factor at work which is resulting in a higher number of accidents in the second and third quarters of the year. This may be for a variety of reasons, such as increased production, faster working areas or different methods of working. Only a more detailed analysis of the underlying causes of the accidents and the associated activities will determine why this variation is occurring and more importantly what corrective measures need to be applied. Again, overall the graph indicates consistency across the sites, *possibly* indicating that what is happening at one site is the same as at the others and that the same corrective action is required. Presenting information in this way can be useful to give some indication of what else needs to be examined and what needs to be explained.

Figure 12:9 shows a similar situation, but in this case the figures collected for each quarter show that there are apparent dissimilarities between the sites. Although some seasonal variation is revealed, at least one of the sites is not following the pattern of the others. Different causes and underlying reasons may be at work and different corrective actions may be required. This may reflect different management approaches at the sites or the fact that there are some fundamental differences in the way work is being carried out.

FIGURE 12:9 GRAPH SHOWING SEASONAL VARIATIONS AND DIFFERENCES IN THE NUMBER OF ACCIDENTS ACROSS THREE SITES OF A COMPANY

Number of accidents				
10				
9				
8	③	①	①	
7		②		
6		③	②	
5				
4				②
3			③	① ③
2	① ②			
1				
0				
Quarter	1st	2nd	3rd	4th

Legend: ① Figures for site 1
         ② Figures for site 2
         ③ Figures for site 3

12:7.2.4.3.2 Trends

The graph shown in **Figure 12:10** depicts the total number of accidents (y axis) that a company has had at three sites over the course of four years (x axis). This graph shows that there is a downward trend in the numbers of accidents reported year on year. If this trend were to continue, the company would be on target for zero accidents in year 5. However, what normally happens is that the graph levels out and the downward trend, despite all accident prevention efforts, does not continue. This is shown in the second graph (**Figure 12:11**).

FIGURE 12:10 GRAPH SHOWING YEARLY ACCIDENT FIGURES FOR A COMPANY WITH THREE SITES

Number of accidents				
10	③			
9	②			
8	①			
7		②		
6		①		
5		③	③	
4			①	
3			②	②
2				①
1				③
0				
Year	1	2	3	4

Legend:　① Figures for site 1
　　　　　② Figures for site 2
　　　　　③ Figures for site 3

FIGURE 12:11 GRAPH SHOWING RECORDED ACCIDENTS FOR SITE 1 OVER A 12-YEAR PERIOD

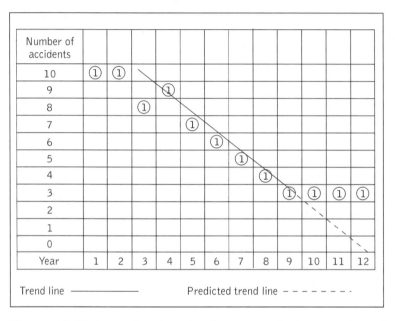

Figure 12:11 shows that there has been a steady downward trend in accidents until year 9. The prediction from this trend would be for zero accidents in year 12. However, the number of accidents levels out in year 9.

Depicting accidents in this way and analysing the trends is useful in monitoring improvement over time. Some of the more sophisticated health and safety information packages available will automatically identify both patterns and display trends, providing the correct information is fed into them. Trend analyses can be particularly useful as accident numbers do not normally follow a steady pattern but fluctuate over time. Increases in accidents in one year may mask a general downturn in the actual number of accidents. This is illustrated in **Figure 12:12**. The same is also true of decreasing numbers which may mask an actual increase in accidents overall.

FIGURE 12:12 GRAPH SHOWING A GENERAL DOWNWARD TREND IN THE NUMBER OF ACCIDENTS AT SITE 2

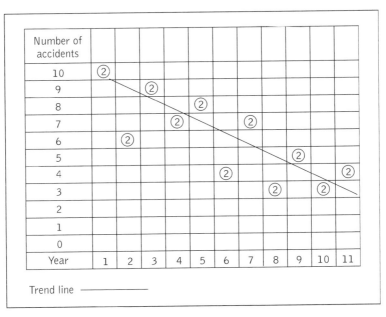

Trends analysis is particularly useful for monitoring a safety intervention over time. For example, it is possible to compare the accident 'picture' before the introduction of new procedures with the safety 'picture' after the procedure has been introduced and follow this through, over time, to establish if any permanent improvement has actually been achieved.

12:7.2.5 Indices for presenting accident data

Indices or rates are used to ensure variations between different sets of data do not obscure the true picture of what is happening. This is especially useful when comparisons are being made.

They take the form of X/Y where X is the item of information being considered and Y is the population (group or sample) containing the events causing X. Sometimes this is referred to as a rate or so many X per Y.

A multiplier is often used to ensure that the index is a simple and easily understandable figure. The multiplier has nothing to do with the answer and is usually a very high number such as 100,000 or a million. It is usual to define the index by a time period such as in one year (per annum) or location (such as per country).

For example, a typical index is an injury rate. This represents the number of injuries (X) per number of person employed (Y). A multiplier will be used if the number of injuries (X) is very low as the answer would be a very small figure.

For example, if company A has six injuries in one year and company B also has six injuries, do they both have a similar safety performance?

If company A employs 100 workers and company B employs 1,000 workers, it is obvious that they do not have the same safety performance. The rate of injury shows this very easily. The rate is X/Y where X is 6 and Y is 100 for company A and X is 6 and Y is 1,000 for company B.

The results are:

Company A injury rate = 6/100 = 0.06 per employee

and

Company B injury rate = 6/1,000 = 0.006 per employee

If we use a multiplier of 1,000, then these figures become easier to handle. The injury rate (per 100,000 employees) for company A is then 60 and for company B is 6. This quickly shows a tenfold difference.

Presenting accident information by using indices can make all the difference to understanding what is happening and, perhaps more importantly, what needs to be done. Using the information presented in **Figure 12:7** a second histogram can be drawn, but this time the data is presented as the number of reported accidents per 100,000 employees in each work group.

The original bar chart (**Figure 12:7**) looked like this:

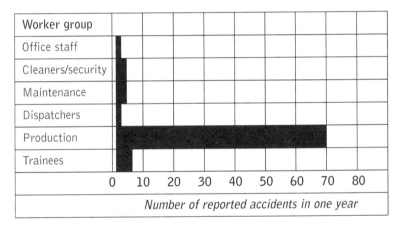

By applying the injury rate concept to this, it is possible to calculate the number of accidents per 100,000 employees in each work group. The result is **Figure 12:13**.

FIGURE 12:13 HISTOGRAM SHOWING REPORTED ACCIDENTS PER 100,000 EMPLOYEES

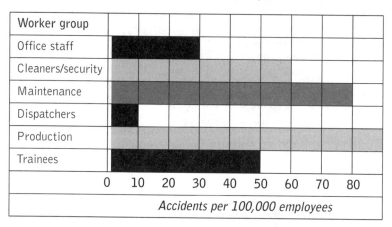

Worker group								
Office staff								
Cleaners/security								
Maintenance								
Dispatchers								
Production								
Trainees								

0 10 20 30 40 50 60 70 80

Accidents per 100,000 employees

Figure 12:13 clearly shows a marked difference in the interpretation of the accident data. This happens because the relatively low numbers of employees in the non-production areas obscures the actual safety performance in these groups. By using the index approach it is possible to identify some extremely important features of the accident performance in this particular organisation. The results clearly show that maintenance workers have nearly the same exposure to accidents as production workers; cleaners and security staff (put together because they are a very small group) also have a higher exposure than previously thought. The trainee group appears to be much more significant in the chart than when it appeared in the original presentation.

The use of such indices is therefore vital if valid conclusions are to be drawn from the reporting and presentation of accident information. In the example given (**Figures 12.12** and **12.13**) it is important to present the total number of accidents happening in the production area as being of some concern. Further analysis would be required to establish what particular causes and activities were involved. However, the managers responsible for cleaning, security and maintenance staff and the trainees also need to be concerned as clearly their safety management performance could also be called into question.

12:7.2.6 Other useful indices

These include the:

- fatal accident rate (FAR);
- accident frequency rate;
- accident incident rate;
- severity rate;
- injury incidence rate;
- injury frequency rate;
- property damage rate.

12:7.2.6.1 Fatal accident rate

$$FAR = \frac{\text{Number of fatalities per year}}{100,000,000 \text{ person hours worked}}$$

For example, an organisation employs 6,000 employees who work a total of 10,000,000 hours per annum. During the year there were two deaths.

The FAR can be worked out by using the following calculation:

$$\text{The total number of hours worked} = \frac{10,000,000}{100,000,000} = \frac{1}{10}$$

$$FAR = 2 \div 1/10 = 20$$

12:7.2.6.2 Accident frequency rate

$$\text{Accident frequency rate} = \frac{\text{Number of LTAs}}{\text{Total number of hours worked}} \times 100,000$$

where LTAs = lost time accidents*

*The LTAs do not take account of minor injuries so only injuries resulting in time away from work are counted.

As an example, for a company with 50 LTAs in one year and a total available work time for the whole workforce of 94,000 hours (50 people working a 40 hour week for 47 weeks of the year, on average) the AFR works out as:

$$\frac{50}{94,000} \times 100,000 = 53$$

12:7.2.6.3 Accident incident rate

$$\text{Accident incident rate} = \frac{\text{Number of notifiable accidents}}{\text{Number of employees}} \times 100,000$$

This rate is calculated from the actual number of RIDDOR-reported accidents each year divided by the number of employees employed through the year. It is general practice to take the actual employment figures at mid-June (i.e. the half-year employment figure) as the figure to be used for number of employees. The actual number of employees will vary throughout the year, retirement, recruitment and long-term sickness being the chief reasons for this. Taking the mid-June figure for the number of persons on the payroll is an arbitrary but valid way of getting around the variation. Care has to be taken, however, if there has been significant downsizing over the year or significant recruitment of new staff.

12:7.2.6.4 Severity rate

$$\text{Severity rate} = \frac{\text{Total number days lost}}{\text{Total number of hours worked}} \times 1{,}000$$

The total number of days lost in this equation refers to the actual number of working days lost through accidents; the total number of hours worked is taken from adding up all the hours worked by every employee for the year. Some assumptions may have to be made and unless there are significant variations in numbers employed – through downsizing or recruitment over the course of the year – an approximate calculation (providing it is made consistently) can be used by simply multiplying the normal hours worked in a day by the number of days worked by each employee in the year (allowing for holidays and sick leave).

12:7.2.6.5 Injury incidence rate

$$\text{Injury incidence rate} = \frac{\text{Total number of injuries}}{\text{Total number of employees}} \times 100{,}000$$

This rate takes the number of all recorded injuries. It is thus important to ensure all injuries are recorded. There is often a balance to be struck between recording insignificant injuries and the utility of this index, which is designed to show the overall performance of an organisation. It measures injuries and not accidents. **Figure 12:13** illustrates how this rate can be presented.

12:7.2.6.6 Injury frequency rate

$$\text{Injury frequency rate} = \frac{\text{Total number of injuries}}{\text{Average total hours worked}} \times 1,000,000$$

This is similar to the injury incidence rate, but reports injuries against hours worked, rather than numbers of employees. If used with the severity rate, it gives a good indication of the impact of accidents on the business of the organisation as together these rates show the effect on time taken away from work.

12:7.2.6.7 Property damage rate

This is a rate that is not commonly used, but can be calculated using the principles defined as for the other rates described. The purpose of this rate is to give some idea of the effect of property-only accidents on an organisation (although some may of course involve injuries as well). It can be derived from counting the total number of incidents involving property damage (such as damage to buildings and equipment) and dividing it by the number of persons employed for the year. Sources of information can include insurance claims as well as property defect reports.

$$\text{Property damage rate} = \frac{\text{Number of property damage incidents}}{\text{Number of persons employed}}$$

As well as describing the effect on property, it also gives some indication of how careless people have been, notwithstanding that the carelessness may be a result of management deficiencies, such as the failure to protect the corners of walls on routes used by a high volume of pallet movers.

12:7.2.7 Scaled injury rates

Most accident and health and safety performance criteria are related to fatalities. For example, overall risks are generally given as a risk of fatality. This is because death is the most obvious and serious consequence of a safety management failure.

The outcomes from safety management failures include a range of injuries and not just death. In order to provide some measure to compare cost and performance it is necessary to develop a means of comparing a given outcome with that of a fatality. This is usually achieved by means of scaled rates. If the value of death is taken as 1, then it could be said that the impact of a disabling accident (i.e. an accident which causes a serious injury involving disablement but not death) is 10% of that or 0.1. In any assessment of the impact of this type of injury the scaling factor (0.1) is used to account for the relative effect of the injury compared to a fatality. Thus, if assessing risk and the chance of death is 1 in 100 the multiplier can be used to give a chance of serious injury as 1 in 1,000 (i.e. 10% of the risk of death). This is calculated as follows:

If the chance of being killed is	1 in 100 = 1/100 = 0.01
Then the chance of being seriously injured	1/100 x 0.1 (i.e. 10% the risk of death)
=	0.01 x 0.1
=	0.001
=	1/1,000

If working out the costs and the cost of a death is known to be £1 million, it is possible to give the cost of serious injury as 10% of this – that is, multiply £1 million by 0.1, a cost of £100,000.

It is also possible to say that the multiplier for a non-serious injury is 10% of serious injury or 1% of a fatality or 0.01, and so on. The cost of a non-serious injury would then be:

£1 million (cost of death) x 0.01 = £10,000

These rates become useful for indicating to senior managers and the board the relative seriousness and degree of risk involved in any one accident or series of accidents. This is particularly important when considering the cost-benefit of any remedial actions proposed or intended to be taken after an accident has occurred.

Appendix 1
Using Models

Whilst they are largely theoretical and conceptual, models can be useful in accident investigations as they provide a framework to explain how accidents happen. Models can therefore be used to show where and how accident investigations should be carried out. No one model will provide all of the framework, as accidents involve a range of factors and conditions. Nevertheless it is important to have some idea of how accidents occur so that the methods used for an investigation uncover the causes of an accident successfully.

A1:1 Simple models used to explain the theory of accidents

Figures A1:1–A1:4 provide a conceptual view of the possible ways an accident may arise. These concepts were developed to examine the effectiveness of accident prevention strategies. They are provided here to challenge the traditional thinking of investigators and to set the scene for the more detailed models that follow.

Key to figures:

- **Precursors** refer to conditions that exist before the accident sequence takes place, for example a crane driver hurrying to get a job done before the wind gets too strong.

- **Chance** assumes that events and occurrences are random in nature and that there is no way of predicting what precisely will happen. It is possible that the range of likely events is not infinite, but it may be very difficult to predict how

591

many possibilities there are. It is similar to the throw of a dice, but without knowing how many faces there are and what the numbers on each face are.

- **Cue** is similar to the cues that actors use, for example responding to a word or action by another actor before coming on stage. Traffic lights present cues: when the lights change to green it means go. However, responding automatically to this cue may mean that a driver collides with an emergency vehicle coming through a red light from another direction. The cue causes the driver to act, but the action may not always be the right one. A typical cue might be a signal from a banksman to a crane driver who, responding to the signal, inadvertently drops a load in the wrong place.

- **A question mark (?)** indicates there may be a choice but it is not possible to say with any certainty whether a particular event will happen, either by chance or in response to a cue.

A1:1.1 Concept 1

FIGURE A1:1 A SEQUENCE OF EVENTS

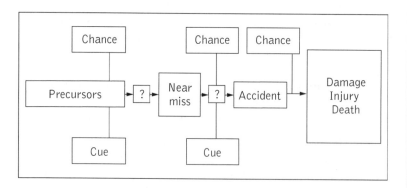

Figure A1:1 shows that accidents may be caused by a sequence of events that is controlled by chance or by cues. Not all of these will lead to the damage or loss that is called an accident. A cue might be a traffic light turning green and chance might be oil on the road. A car goes through the green light (on cue) and hits the oil on the road. By chance there are no other vehicles on the road. The car slides but the driver is able to continue without hitting anything – a near miss. The driver has received skid pan training (a precursor) and is skilled enough to avoid an accident.

Other precursors will include the driver's ability and driving style, and the cause of the oil being on the road (for example, a spillage from a tanker).

If the driver is unable to avoid other traffic there will be a collision (normally called an accident) and damage, injury and/or death will result. This is a simple model that shows a linear relationship (i.e. one event leading to another) between the factors and conditions.

A1:1.2 Concept 2

FIGURE A1:2 LINKING PRECURSORS TO OUTCOMES

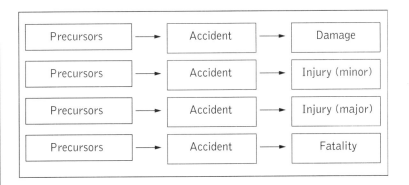

Figure A1:2 shows that the outcome (i.e. the consequences – the loss or damage that results from an accident) may have entirely different causes, meaning that the investigation will need to look for *different* precursors for the different types of outcome.

For example, the degree of skill of an operator (precursor) may be reflected in the type of accident that occurs and the damage (outcome) that results. A skilled driver driving at speed, such as an emergency service vehicle driver, may be able to control a vehicle so that if anything goes wrong only minimal damage will occur, whereas an unskilled driver involved in a similar set of circumstances is more likely to have an accident resulting in a fatality. The precursors for the unskilled driver may include age and sex (for example, younger male drivers being generally more 'reckless') or peer-group pressures (young males together late at night in a vehicle egging the driver on). This contrasts with the precursors for an emergency service vehicle driver, such as the type of call being attended, the level of responsibility they hold (towards others) and maturity. Therefore, any investigation is likely to follow different routes of inquiry for different situations.

A1:1.3 Concept 3

FIGURE A1:3 OUTCOMES DETERMINED BY CHANCE OR CUE

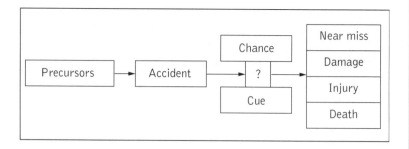

Figure A1:3 is similar to **Figure A1:1** except here the outcome is the result of some chance or cue and is not dependant on the causative factors. This means that the outcome of accidents have the same or similar set of precursors, but these are relatively unimportant. The accident itself is bound to happen when the precursors are in place as it assumes that the precursors are always present, but they only become operative when the right cues are provided or chances exist.

For example, a reckless young driver will always be reckless; an accident only happens when he drives through a red light and by chance a car is coming from another direction, or, taking his cue from another driver, overtakes when he is overtaken, but the gap is not big enough and he crashes into an oncoming car.

The type of outcome is determined by chance or by cues.

A1:1.4 Concept 4

FIGURE A1:4 LIMITED OUTCOMES

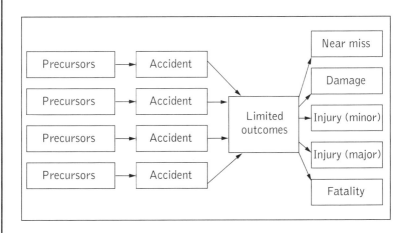

In **Figure A1:4** accidents have different causes but the outcomes are limited to what is possible. For example, if somebody has itchy eyes and a runny nose, they may be unable to identify whether this is caused by hay fever (an allergy), a cold (a virus) or a chemical. The human body only has a limited number of ways of showing ill health, but the number of causes is much greater. If the precursors are in place, the accident is bound to happen. (Chance and cues are not included.) This approach also makes it possible to envisage that a number of precursors have to be in place before an accident situation can develop. For example, genetic disposition, the presence of a respiratory irritant and a weakened immune system all act together to give rise to an asthma attack.

A1:2 Linear models

A number of linear models of accident causation have been developed to deal with some of the complexities illustrated in the simple models provided in **section A1:1.1**. The earliest generally recognised model is that produced by Heinrich in the 1930s and is discussed in **section A1:1.2.1**. Another linear model was provided by Frank Bird in the 1960s and is discussed in **section A1:1.2.2**. The Heinrich and Bird models were developed from a knowledge and analysis of accident reports collected for mainly insurance purposes. These linear models are relatively straight forward and do not provide the depth of understanding that is offered by the multi-factorial models discussed in **section A1:1.3**.

A1:2.1 Heinrich's sequence (the domino model)

Heinrich developed a linear model to explain how accidents are caused. This has come to be referred to as the 'domino model' and is shown in **Figure A1:5**. It is an early example of an attempt to provide a structured approach to describe accidents. It is often used in reference texts to explain how accidents are caused.

FIGURE A1:5 HEINRICH'S SEQUENCE
(THE DOMINO MODEL)

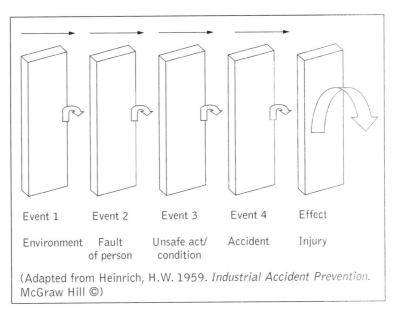

Event 1	Event 2	Event 3	Event 4	Effect
Environment	Fault of person	Unsafe act/ condition	Accident	Injury

(Adapted from Heinrich, H.W. 1959. *Industrial Accident Prevention*. McGraw Hill ©)

Figure A1:5 attempts to show that accidents are the result of a chain of events which need to occur together. The events involve, in turn:

- **the working environment**, i.e. the working conditions such as temperature, lighting, working space, etc. The model assumes that if these are not adequate then the next step or event in the accident sequence may happen;

- **the fault of a person**, i.e. human error. A worker may make a mistake that leads to the next step or event in the accident sequence, for example positioning a ladder in the wrong place for the work required;

- **an unsafe act or condition**, i.e. an unsafe act is undertaken, for example leaning out whilst working off a ladder, or an unsafe condition arises, for example the foot of the ladder becoming unstable;

- **an accident**. Following the example above, the ladder moves and the worker falls off. This is the event which results in:

- **injury** – the worker hits the ground and suffers concussion and a broken arm.

Heinrich postulated that accident prevention could be brought about by controlling any one of these factors. The sequence of events is linear, like a row of dominoes with each falling domino knocking the next one down. Experience, however, has shown that this is a very simplistic way of looking at accidents as it overlooks a number of factors involved in accident causation. As such it does not offer any help to accident investigators. Accidents are seldom the result of such a neat and structured set of circumstances.

A1:2.2 Frank Bird's model

Figure A1:6 is a model produced by Frank Bird to explain the causes of accidents. It is another example of a chain-of-events model.

FIGURE A1:6 BIRD'S ACCIDENT MODEL

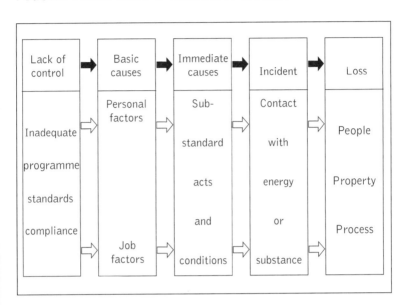

In this model there is a pre-existing set of factors which involves an absence or deficiency in the control measures. These appear in the first column headed 'Lack of control'. The lack of control may, for example, be the absence of a health and safety plan, deficiencies in standards or failures to comply with laws and Approved Codes of Practice.

The Health and Safety Executive would expect to see a health and safety plan in larger organisations and would certainly expect all relevant legislation and codes of practice for a particular industry (or work activity) to be known about and complied with. If this lack of control exists, then there is a high likelihood that the organisation will be unsafe.

Basic causes (the second column) are defined in terms of personal and job factors. Personal factors relate to the skills, knowledge, attitude, age and other characteristics of the individuals involved. Job factors relate to the work activities being undertaken, for example having to complete tasks in a certain time or operating under stress.

Immediate causes (in the third column) are related to acts and conditions that exist or happen just prior to the accident. For example, the immediate cause of someone falling over may be a cable stretched across a floor, i.e. the cable is the immediate cause! A person trips over this cable (the incident − column 4) and breaks an arm (the loss − column 5).

The lack of control, basic causes and immediate causes result in an incident. An incident is described in terms of contact with a substance or energy. This concept of contact with energy is the basis of a very useful tool in accident investigations: energy barrier analysis. The idea is that for damage or injury to occur there must be some exposure to some form of energy. This energy may result from a collision with a moving object, contact with the ground following a fall from height or a chemical reaction as is caused by acid attacking human skin, or exposure to electric current.

As a result of exposure to the energy some loss occurs (the last column). The loss can be very general or very specific and is closely associated with the idea of loss control.

Like Heinrich's model, this model is often seen as too simplistic. It is useful in identifying the underlying or root cause, but it does not explicitly address the possible multiplicity of causes that often result in accidents. By focussing on a sequence or chain of events, an investigator is likely to miss or overlook causes that are acting together. Having identified a possible causative chain the investigator stops investigating and fails to examine the other factors that combined to actually cause the accident.

A1:3 Multi-factor models

Accidents tend to have many, sometimes called multi-factorial, causes. Several ideas have been put together to explain this.

A1:3.1 Reason's model

James Reason's model is a multi-causal or multi-factorial model that has been developed to explain the causes of accidents in complex organisations. It works on the principle that an accident is caused by a combination of management and personal failures. The underlying management of an organisation has within it latent failures. These failures are like pathogens in a human body just waiting for the circumstances to be right to cause illness. Defence against these 'pathogens' is provided but can be undermined by personal failures, for example erroneous decisions made by managers and workers within the organisation (i.e. psychological aspects of human factors).

The model is based on the identified basic elements of production. Production includes all the forms of organisational deliverables (i.e. the outcomes or outputs that the organisation is set up to achieve), from manufactured products to services and energy production.

These factors are based on common elements in any organisation.

- Decision-makers – decision-makers set goals for the organisation and direct the strategies that are designed to meet these goals. These goals are based upon outside requirements, such as the need to supply products or services, for example a better road transport system in the case of a public body, or increased production and profitability for a manufacturing company. Decision-makers are concerned with the deployment of resources to maximise the desired outcomes (which include productivity and safety). Resources are finite and their allocation subject to restrictions. Resources include money, time, equipment and people.

- Line management – line managers are specialists who implement the strategies of decision-makers within their sphere of responsibility and competence, such as operations, training, maintenance, finance, personnel, etc.

- Preconditions – preconditions represent qualities required by machinery or equipment and people. Technical qualities include reliability, work schedules, equipment suitability, etc.; human qualities include skills, knowledge, motivation, attitudes and behaviour.

- Productive activities – these are simply the activities that the organisation carries out as part of its business. These include the actions undertaken by both humans and machines.

- Defences/safeguards – these refer to the ways in which hazards and risk are controlled so as to prevent loss. They include everything from the guarding of machinery to the supply of PPE and the development and operation of safe systems of work.

Reason couples these factors with the contribution made by humans to develop a model to explain the complexity of accident prevention and causation.

An accident results when inadequate performance by the factors combine to create an unsafe situation. This unsafe situation is largely a result of human fallibility. The model recognises the significant contribution of human factors in accidents. Reason uses the metaphor of 'pathogens' to explain how an accident is caused.

A1:3.2 The idea of latent pathogens

The pathogen metaphor that Reason uses explains accident causation as analogous to certain disease states, such as coronary heart disease. Such diseases result from a variety of interacting factors. For example, on the basis of current knowledge a number of factors have been identified as having some part to play in the causation of coronary heart disease, including lifestyle, exercise, blood cholesterol levels, diet, smoking habits and body fat. Some of these factors are largely pre-determined. For example, a person's blood cholesterol level is thought to be mainly a result of his or her genetic make-up, but it is controllable in some respect by diet. The amount of exercise somebody takes is mostly a result of self-made decisions: some people choose to exercise; others do not.

These factors and the way they work together are complex. What is known is that the more factors you have the more chance there is of getting heart disease. For example, high blood cholesterol levels increase the chance of heart disease. With the other contributing factors there is an inevitably that heart disease will occur. If the body's defences are weakened due to stress for example, then a heart attack becomes even more likely.

In his model, Reason refers to organisations as having 'resident pathogens' with latent failures at various points in the management system. These resident pathogens are analogous to the high cholesterol levels in the human body; they exist in the system waiting for the right circumstances or opportunities to become effective. The latent failures are like the other factors involved in heart disease, for example an under-exercised body which is not able to take any sudden strain placed upon it; it is time and chance that dictate when the disease will eventually occur. The latent failures become evident when an active failure or error occurs. An active failure would be synonymous with a person under stress running for a bus and then finding that their coronary system was not up to the strain, resulting in a heart attack. For example, Reason describes the active failures in the Kings Cross fire in 1987 as starting with a 'failure' when a discarded cigarette set light to the grease and debris on an escalator. The latent failures he describes include the presence of wooden escalators which were recognised as being prone to fire, organisational changes which had blurred maintenance and cleaning responsibilities, a focus on operational safety (i.e. running trains safely) and smoke detectors not being installed because they were regarded as too expensive, as well as a whole range of other similar issues.

If a bad design decision has been made which is not detected or acted upon, then the engineering defect that results from that decision will act like a pathogen. The effects of the decision will be waiting for the right circumstances for them to cause a problem, such as the decision not to install smoke detectors on underground escalators at Kings Cross Underground station.

A design failure can also be seen to be acting as a pathogen in the following example. A walkway collapses as people embark on a ferry. The design was basically poor but this had not been detected. The design failure only had an effect when the walkway was put into use, resulting in its collapse, loss of life and injuries. The *actual* failure was an engineering one, the component parts not being strong enough. However, a combination of *latent* failures in both management and engineering design and build probably contributed to the accident.

Examples of such failures would be:

- the failure to recheck calculations;
- incompetent engineering design;
- the failure to monitor the use of untried techniques.

Reason's model superimposes the human contributions onto the organisational factors. Most failures are controlled by various organisational processes. These processes include sound engineering, good management, doing audits and making inspections, validating and checking processes and systems of work, and employing competent personnel. An accident may occur when these control processes fail. They can combine to cause an accident at times when the defences of the organisation are weakened, as shown in **Figure A1:7**, in a similar way that humans are vulnerable to heart disease when under stress.

FIGURE A1:7 REASON'S MODEL

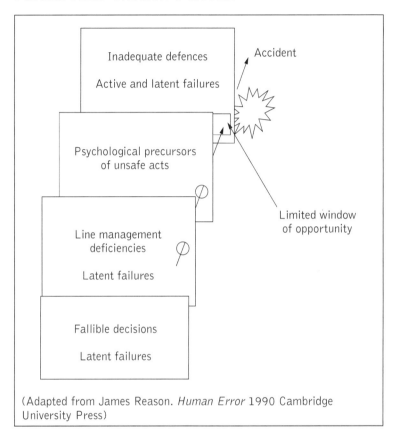

Inadequate defences

Active and latent failures

Accident

Psychological precursors
of unsafe acts

Limited window
of opportunity

Line management
deficiencies

Latent failures

Fallible decisions

Latent failures

(Adapted from James Reason. *Human Error* 1990 Cambridge
University Press)

The following is a key to Reason's model:

- **Fallible decisions** – the human contribution is most significant at the top management level where decisions are made and resources allocated. Fallible decisions made at this level have far-reaching effects on the organisation as a whole. For example, these decisions can be about the balance between safety goals and production goals. Putting resources into production at the expense of safety may

605

create a latent failure. For example, on London Underground before Kings Cross, the effort was put into operating the railways and so not enough attention was given to passenger safety in the station areas.

- **Line management** – line managers have a more limited role but they can also make bad decisions by, for example, disproportionately favouring production over safety, suffering from the stress of overwork, being ignorant of hazards and risks or not being fully competent. These types of deficiencies weaken the safety of the organisation. The model recognises that the interaction between the upper decision-making level and the lower level where unsafe acts occur is very complex.

- **Psychological precursors of unsafe acts** – the model recognises two aspects. Firstly, there are the precursors or preconditions for unsafe acts. These are also very complex. For example, the psychological precursors include the degree of motivation or stress that individuals are under, the ability of individuals to be aware of hazards, the nature of an individual's home life (i.e. whether the individual is in debt, suffering bereavement, a marriage breakdown, etc.). Secondly, there are the unsafe acts themselves that have preconditions, for example taking short cuts when starting a maintenance process or ignoring specific safety requirements because of production pressures. Again these acts are also quite complex and form part of the understanding of human factors in accident causation.

In this model an accident does not happen simply because an individual has done a single unsafe act which then forms part of a single chain of events, as is the view of the sequence models of Heinrich and Bird. Instead it describes a coming together of a complex trail of interactions. Each one by itself would be insufficient to cause the accident. Some of the events on this trail are latent errors waiting for the right conditions to come along. When they do, they cause the control system to fail and an active error occurs.

This is a very useful model as it provides an insight into the requirements of adequate investigation. To be successful the accident investigation needs to establish the nature and type of latent failures that exist within an organisation; it is not sufficient to simply look at the breakdown in defences. It is also important to look beyond the human factors associated with how people make decisions and behave; there is a need to examine organisational issues when investigating accidents as well.

A1:4 The 'behaviour in the face of danger' model

The 'behaviour in the face of danger' model was created by Hale and Glendon (*see* Glendon, Dr A. I. March 1991. Influencing behaviour: a framework for action, *Journal of Health and Safety* **6**, 23–28) to bring together a number of ideas involving human factors.

The model assumes that there is a series of decision points which account for the way humans behave when faced with danger. It assumes (and the assumption is supported by research) that generally humans do not consciously consider hazards as they go about their tasks. It also assumes that the danger is not already producing harm and that unless there is human intervention, the danger will be static, increasing or decreasing. This is termed 'objective' danger (see the bottom of the model in **Figure A1:8**). Responding to danger (i.e. learning about it at a conscious level) requires a number of sequential inputs (see the left-hand side of the model), then some processing, followed by a number of outputs (see the right-hand side of the model). The requirement is for the human to undertake the tasks in the model and achieve a positive answer to all the questions being posed. Negative answers result in the danger being left unaffected and continuing to increase.

The model uses three levels of human functioning: skills, rules and knowledge, shown in the left margin. These represent the main categories of functions where human error can occur. The model was designed to show how an individual would process information and utilise various decision-making skills. It works equally well for an individual exposed to hazards, a manager making decisions about the exposure of subordinates and a designer designing a workplace or machinery.

The following is an example of the 'behaviour in the face of danger' model:

A train driver is informed of on-track working which has altered the nature of signalling on a known route. The level of functioning is that of a train driver in what could be described as a fairly routine mode and with it go the skills and knowledge of the train driver plus the rules that are to be adhered to (the left-hand side of the model).

In these given conditions it is possible to use the danger model (*see* **Figure A1:8**) to examine what the driver might do and what the responses might be in certain situations.

Starting at the bottom left-hand side of the figure in the box 'Programmed or insistent danger signals?' the following situations can occur.

Situation 1

On approaching a clearly signalled danger area, the driver sees the warning signal, responds in the right way and the danger stays under control. Following the model through:

- obvious warning detected – Yes;

- procedure known and chosen – Yes;

- response carried out – Yes;

- danger brought under control.

Situation 2

Driver misses the obvious warning and the model moves to the 'Hazard seeking initiated?'. If the driver has missed a signal this will not happen and so through the 'No' option the model takes us to 'Danger unaffected'. In other words, the danger is there and the likelihood will be a crash.

Situation 3

If the hazard seeking is initiated, the driver does 'tests for danger known': for example, he may radio the signal box that he thinks he has missed a signal. He accepts the 'need for action' and, following the model round to the right, accepts responsibility and plans and carries out the correct approach in the circumstances. (This will now include the signaller also recognising the danger and taking avoiding action with other trains on the line.) Eventually the danger is brought under control.

Situation 4

The driver fails to realise he has missed a signal and gets around the model to the box: 'Need for action recognised?' He does not recognise that action is required and immediately the model takes us straight to 'Danger unaffected'. Again a crash is likely.

All these situations exist within a system boundary which in this case is the signalling and control system that operates the railway, including the communications between signallers, controllers and train drivers.

FIGURE A1:8 THE 'BEHAVIOUR IN THE FACE OF DANGER' MODEL

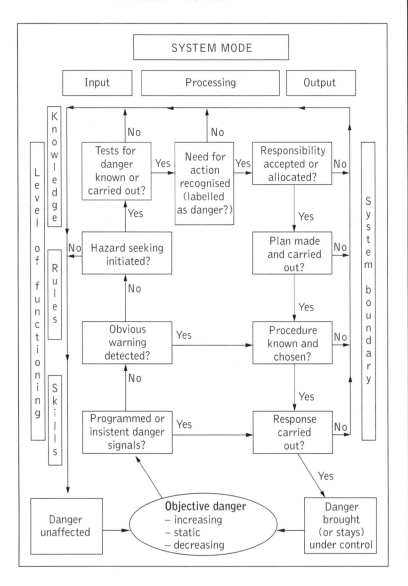

Appendix 2
Model Visitors Policy

Safety policy for visitors

1. This policy applies to all staff who are responsible for inviting visitors onto the premises, escorting them at different times or for maintaining parts of the premises such that visitors may safely visit.

2. The organisation shall undertake to protect the health and safety of visitors.

3. On arrival, visitors shall be required to record their details by signing in as visitors in the visitors' book. No person shall be permitted into the premises without complying with this requirement, however brief the proposed stay.

4. On signing in, each visitor shall be advised as to the policy on smoking (that is, the permission to smoke only in designated areas) and their attention drawn to the fire evacuation procedure.

5. During the visitor's stay on the premises he/she will be allocated to a member of staff, and required to comply with any health and safety arrangements that this member of staff advises.

6. In the event of an emergency or test evacuation of the building, all visitors shall be required to participate, and be guided from the premises by the member of staff to whom they have been allocated, or by another member of staff who takes on this responsibility.

7. Visitors will be required by their allocated staff member to comply with any other health and safety requirement, such as the wearing of hearing defenders in plant rooms, compliance with 'No Unauthorised Persons' notices at entrances to roof voids, etc.

8. On leaving the premises the visitor will be required to sign out in the visitors' book.

Appendix 3
Model Alcohol and Drugs Policy

Policy on alcohol and drugs

It is the policy of XYZ Ltd to offer help and support to any employee who suffers from a problem associated with the abuse of alcohol or drugs. This will include providing employees with information and encouragement to obtain specialist help. This policy applies to all staff.

The objectives of this policy are:

- to provide a framework for the prevention and management of alcohol and drug-related problems;

- to assist in the early identification of employees whose conduct and/or job performance is affected by the misuse of alcohol or drugs;

- to encourage staff with alcohol or drug-related problems to seek and accept help to overcome the problem;

- to maintain a safe working environment;

- to create an awareness of the lifestyle factors which may contribute to the misuse of alcohol and drugs.

The problems associated with alcohol or drug abuse can result in a number of problems for the company and for the individual as follows:

- damage to the individual's health;

- poor time-keeping;
- frequent absences from work;
- loss of efficiency;
- reduction in work output;
- unacceptable behaviour;
- risks to safety.

Although every individual is responsible for their own conduct and job performance, managers are often best placed to identify problems and offer appropriate help to their staff.

The benefits of this policy are:

- employees who are suffering from alcohol or drug-related problems are encouraged to take steps to solve the problem rather than lose their jobs;
- the company gains in efficiency and productivity;
- absenteeism and lateness are reduced;
- staff morale is improved;
- risks to safety are reduced.

Employees who believe or suspect that they may have an alcohol or drug-related problem are encouraged to come forward to their manager/the company doctor for a confidential discussion about the problem. Employees should note that it is not the company's policy to inform the police where an individual volunteers information about his/her use of illegal drugs. The employee will subsequently be afforded every help and support in obtaining the appropriate medical treatment, counselling and/or rehabilitation.

Managers who believe or suspect that an employee may have an alcohol or drug-related problem should take appropriate action to discuss the matter with the employee. Managers may draw conclusions about an employee's alcohol or drug problem as a result of observations of deteriorating work performance, erratic timekeeping and/or behavioural problems. Such observations provide a manager with legitimate grounds to enter into private discussions with the employee about the problem.

If a colleague notices obvious signs of alcohol or drug abuse in another employee, this should be reported to the immediate line manager who will similarly arrange to interview the employee concerned without revealing the identity of the person who provided the information.

The company's policy of support includes:

- referral to the company doctor in the first instance;
- referral to appropriate treatment agencies with the individual's consent and in conjunction with the individual's own GP's advice;
- allowing appropriate time off work for such treatment;
- appropriate modification to duties or hours during any period of treatment (with the employee's consent);
- recognition of any periods of treatment as periods of sickness absence under the company's sickness absence procedure;
- payment of normal salary under the rules of the company's sickness absence policy;
- suspension of disciplinary procedures during periods of treatment and rehabilitation.

Where the individual seeks, or is willing to accept, help to overcome a problem associated with alcohol or drug abuse, the company will suspend disciplinary proceedings. However, in the following circumstances, the individual will be subject to discipline, including dismissal:

- where the individual refuses to accept there is an alcohol or drugs-related problem but job performance, attendance or behavioural problems indicate that such a problem exists;

- where the individual accepts that there is an alcohol or drugs-related problem but refuses to accept or seek help;

- where the individual embarks on a programme of medical treatment and rehabilitation, but fails to complete it;

- where an individual who has undertaken a course of treatment shows evidence of recurrence of the problem. In this situation the company may, at its discretion, provide further support and treatment.

The company will provide appropriate education and information to all employees about alcohol and drug abuse including:

- recommended safe limits for alcohol consumption for men and women;

- the effects of an over-indulgence of alcohol on health;

- the effects of drug taking on health;

- the prevention and recognition of drug-related problems;

- sources of support in relation to alcohol and drug-related problems.

Appendix 4
The HSE Framework
for Accident
Investigation

The following sequence is one approach, recommended in *Successful Health and Safety Management* (HSE Books, HSG65), that may be used as a guide to analysing the immediate and underlying causes of events. It can be used as the basis for designing an approach that suits the individual needs of an organisation.

Although this example is very manufacturing- and heavy industry-based, HSG65 is applicable to all workplaces.

A4:1 Immediate causes

A4:1.1 Premises

Consider the premises and place of work first and ask 'Was there anything about the place, the access or egress which contributed to the event?', for example holes in floors causing tripping, inadequate ventilation and inadequate weather protection. The most likely conclusions may be:

- premises are not a significant factor – go to **section A4:1.2**;

- adequate premises/access and egress provided but not used: consider working procedures – go to **section A4:1.3**;

- adequate place of work initially provided but not maintained: consider planning – go to **section A4:2.1**;

- adequate place of work was never provided: consider planning – go to **section A4:2.1**.

A4:1.2 Plant and substances

Consider the precautions for plant, equipment and substances and ask 'Was there anything about the adequacy of the controls which contributed to the event?', for example inadequate guarding and poor local exhaust ventilation. (Remember plant and substances may be products supplied by the company.)

The most likely conclusions may be:

- plant and substances are not a significant factor – go to **section A4:1.3**;

- adequate controls provided but not used: consider working procedures – go to **section A4:1.3**;

- adequate controls once provided but not maintained: consider planning – go to **section A4:2.1**;

- adequate controls never provided: consider planning – go to **section A4:2.1**.

A4:1.3 Procedures

Consider the systems, instructions and methods of work and ask if they contributed to the event, for example failure to use equipment properly. (Consider both normal operations and emergency procedures.)

The most likely conclusions may be:

- correct system/method in use – go to **section A4:1.4**;

- correct system/method devised but not used – consider:

- the clarity and adequacy of instructions – go to **section A4:2.3.3**;

- the adequacy of supervision – go to **section A4:2.3.1**;

- the behaviour of employees – go to **section A4:1.4**;

• correct system/method once devised and used but now lapsed: consider the adequacy of monitoring – go to **section A4:2.4**;

• correct system/method never devised: consider planning – go to **section A4:2.1**.

A4:1.4 Human behaviour

Consider the behaviour of the people involved and ask: 'Did they do or fail to do anything which contributed to the event?' The most likely conclusions may be:

• human behaviour was not a significant factor;

• the people were unsuitable for the job (e.g. they had a physical disability or a sensitivity to certain chemicals). Consider whether these individuals were:

- never suitable: look at recruitment/selection/placement – go to **section A4:2.3.4**,

- once suitable: consider the adequacy of health surveillance – go to **section A4:2.2**;

• the people were suitable but not competent: consider whether individuals were:

- never competent: look at training – go to **section A4:2.3.4**,

- once competent but performance not sustained: look at supervision (go to **section A4:2.3.1**) and monitoring (go to **section A4:2.4**);

- the people were suitable and competent but did the wrong thing. Possibilities include:
  - unintended actions:
    - ‰ slips (doing the right thing in the wrong way);
    - ‰ lapses (forgetting to do the right thing);
  - intended actions;
    - mistakes (choosing the wrong action in error);
    - violations (purposely doing the wrong thing – routine/non-routine).

Consider therefore:

- training – go to **section A4:2.3.4**;
- controls/supervision – go to **section A4:2.3.1**;
- monitoring – go to **section A4:2.4**;
- communication – go to **section A4:2.3.3**;
- planning – go to **section A4:2.1**;
- co-operation – go to **section A4:2.3.2**.

A4:2 Underlying causes

Underlying causes can include failures in risk control systems (RCSs) and management arrangements.

A4:2.1 Planning

RCSs are necessary for the supply, use, maintenance, demolition and disposal of premises and the supply, storage, handling, use, transport and disposal of plant (including all types of equipment) and substances.

Where inadequate premises, plant and substances or procedures have been provided, consider the adequacy of the RCSs for the:

- premises, including factors such as:
  - the design of structures/buildings;
  - the control of structural design changes;
  - the selection of buildings/workplaces;
  - the purchase of buildings/workplaces;
  - the maintainance of buildings/workplaces;
  - security;
  - demolition;
- procedures, including factors such as:
  - preparation, circulation and revision;
  - practicalities;
  - technical adequacies;
- plant and substances, including factors such as:
  - the design of plant/equipment;
  - the control of design changes;
  - the selection of plant/equipment;
  - the supply of plant;
  - the selection or purchase of substances;
  - the supply of substances;
  - the construction and installation of plant;
  - the transport of plant and substances;
  - maintenance;
  - commissioning;

- the selection of equipment on hire;
- the control of equipment in use by contractors;
- changes to process/plant/equipment/substances;
- emergency arrangements;
- decommissioning/dismantling;
- the disposal of plant and substances;

When RCSs are absent or inadequate, consider risk assessment arrangements – go to **section A4:2.2**.

Where RCSs are not used, consider:

- risk assessments – go to **section A4:2.2**;
- communications – go to **section A4:2.3.3**;
- organisational controls – go to **section A4:2.3.1**;
- people – go to **section A4:1.4**;
- monitoring – go to **section A4:2.4**.

Where procedures involve contractors, consider competence – go to **section A4:2.3.4**.

A4:2.2 Assessing risks

Consider the adequacy of risk assessment arrangements. If methods of hazard identification and risk assessment are:

- absent, consider organisation control – go to **section A4:2.3.1**;
- inadequate, consider the competence of those choosing them – go to **section A4:2.3.4**;
- adequate but not used, consider:
  - organisational controls – go to **section A4:2.3.1**;

- – monitoring – go to **section A4:2.4**;
- satisfactory but the results are inadequate, consider:
  - – the competency of those using them – go to **section A4:2.3.4**;
  - – the adequacy of technical standards used – go to **section A4:2.3.3**;
  - – the clarity of results – go to **section A4:2.3.3**;
  - – the involvement of employees – go to **section A4:2.3.2**.

A4:2.3 Organisation

A4:2.3.1 Control

Where arrangements/procedures/systems are absent or not used, or supervision is inadequate, consider the responsibilities of those devising, operating and maintaining the procedures/systems. Ask:

- are responsibilities clearly set out?
- are responsibilities clearly understood?
- do those with responsibilities have the time and resources to discharge their responsibilities?
- are people held accountable for discharging health and safety responsibilities?
- are people rewarded for good performance?
- are people penalised for poor performance?

If not, consider:

- competence – go to **section A4:2.3.4**;
- the senior management's commitment and the resources devoted to health and safety.

A4:2.3.2 Co-operation

Consider how those working with risks are involved in risk assessments and devising procedures (including the operation of any health and safety committee). If inadequate, consider:

- competence – go to **section A4:2.3.4**;

- the senior management's commitment to co-operation.

A4:2.3.3 Communication

Consider whether or not:

- there is sufficient up-to-date information on the law and technical standards to make good decisions about how to control risks;

- written instructions for internal use are clear and sufficiently detailed;

- versions of available instructions are up to date;

- there is sufficient information supplied to the users of products;

- there is sufficient senior management commitment to health and safety.

A4:2.3.4 Competence

Consider the adequacy of arrangements for:

- the recruitment, selection and placement of employees to ensure that they have the right physical and mental abilities for their jobs including, where necessary, medical examinations, and tests of physical fitness, aptitudes or abilities;

- assessing the health and safety competence of contractors as part of contractor selection;

- identifying health and safety training needs at the recruitment stage when there are changes in plant and substances, technology, processes or working practices. There may be a need to maintain or enhance competence by refresher training, and organise training for contactors' employees, the self-employed or temporary workers (and even assessments of their competence);

- competence cover for staff absences, particularly for those people responsible for critical health and safety and emergency procedures;

- health checks and health surveillance based on risk assessments (including assessments of fitness for work following injury or ill health);

- provision of health and safety assistance.

A4:2.4 Monitoring

Consider the adequacy of the checks and inspections of workplace precautions and risk control systems before an accident (i.e. were they frequent enough, and did they look at the right things in sufficient detail to ensure the safe use of premises, plant and substances and the implementation of procedures?). If checks were:

- absent, consider organisation control – go to **section A4:2.3.1**;

- not adequate, review risk assessment arrangements – go to **section A4:2.2**;

- not completed, consider organisational controls (go to **section A4:2.3.1**) and reviews (go to **section A4:2.5**).

Consider any previous accident events similar to this one and examine if the investigation or lessons are helpful. The company should have recorded any incidents in an accident book. If previous events have not been thoroughly investigated, consider:

- organisational controls – go to **section A4:2.3.1**;
- competence of those responsible for investigating these incidents – go to **section A4:2.3.4**.

If the lessons have not been put into effect, consider:

- organisational controls – go to **section A4:2.3.1**;
- the review system – go to **section A4:2.5**.

A4:2.5 Review

Consider the arrangements for taking action to remedy health and safety problems.

If work is outstanding beyond the deadline, consider:

- organisational controls – go to **section A4:2.3.1**;
- the adequacy of resources and commitment to health and safety.

If a second incident occurs before corrections were made, consider:

- the mechanisms for prioritising remedial actions in the investigation process;
- the competence of those prioritising remedial action – go to **section A4:2.3.4**.

Appendix 5
Useful Addresses

Association of British Insurers
51 Gresham Street
London EC2V 7HQ
Tel: 020 7600 3333
Fax: 020 7696 8999
Email: info@abit.org.uk
Website: www.abi.org.uk

Association of Insurance and Risk Managers
6 Lloyd's Avenue
London EC3N 3AX
Tel: 020 7480 7610
Fax: 020 7702 3752
Email: enquiries@airmic.co.uk
Website: www.airmic.com

Association of Insurance Intermediaries and Brokers
Stuart Fyfe Suite
854 Brighton Road
Purley CR8 2BH
Tel: 0807 87 80 60
Fax: 020 7216 8811
Email: aiibi@lineone.net
Website: www.aiib.org

British Insurance Brokers' Association
BIBA House
14 Bevis Marks
London EC3A 7NT
Tel: 020 7623 9043
Fax: 020 7626 9676
Email: enquiries@biba.org.uk
Website: www.biba.org.uk

British Safety Council
70 Chancellors Road
London W6 9RS
Tel: 020 8600 5567
Fax: 020 8741 4555
Website: www.britishsafetycouncil.co.uk

Chartered Institute of Environmental Health
Chadwick Court
15 Hatfields
London SE1 8DJ
Tel: 020 7928 6006
Fax: 020 7827 5866
Website: www.cieh.org

Chartered Institute of Loss Adjusters
Peninsular House
36 Monument Street
London EC3R 8LJ
Tel: 020 7337 9960
Fax: 020 7929 3082
Email: info@cila.co.uk
Website: www.cila.co.uk

Chartered Insurance Institute
20 Aldermanbury
London EC2V 7HY
Tel: 020 8989 8464
Fax: 020 7726 0131
Email: customer.serv@cii.co.uk
Website: www.cii.co.uk

Confederation of Registered Gas Installers
1 Elmwood
Chineham Business Park
Crockford Lane
Basingstoke RG24 8WG
Tel: 01256 372200
Fax: 01256 708144
Website: www.corgi-gas.co.uk

Environment Agency
Rio House
Waterside Drive
Aztec West
Almondsbury
Bristol BS12 4UD
Tel: 01454 624400
Fax: 01454 624409
Website: www.environment-agency.gov.uk

Health and Safety Executive/Commission
Rose Court
2 Southwark Road Bridge
London SE1 9HS
Tel: 020 7556 2100
Fax: 020 7556 2200
Website: www.hse.gov.uk

HSE Incident Contact Centre
Caerphilly Business Park
Caerphilly
Cardiff CF83 3GG
Tel: 0845 3009923
Fax: 0845 3009924
Website: www.riddor.gov.uk

HSE Information Centre (for enquiries)
Public Information Network
Health and Safety Laboratories
Broad Lane
Sheffield S3 7HQ
Tel: 0541 545500 (Information line)

Revitalising Health and Safety Team
Health and Safety Executive
Strategy & Analytical Support Directorate
8/SW, Rose Court
Southwark Bridge
London SE1 9HS
Tel: 020 7717 6000

OR

Department for Work and Pensions
Health & Safety Sponsorship Division
4/13 Great Minster House
76 Marsham Street
London SW1P 4DR
Tel: 020 7944 4877

HSE Area Offices

East Anglia
(Essex, Norfolk, Suffolk)
39 Baddow Road
Chelmsford CM2 0HL
Tel: 01245 706200

East Grinstead
(Kent, Surrey, East Sussex, West Sussex)
3 East Grinstead House
London Road
East Grinstead RH19 1RR

East Midlands
(Leicestershire, Northamptonshire, Oxfordshire, Warwickshire)
5th floor
Belgrave House
1 Greyfriars
Northampton NN1 2BS
Tel: 01604 738300

Greater Manchester
(Greater Manchester, Cheshire, Merseyside, Cumbria, Lancashire)
Quay House
Quay Street
Manchester M3 3JB
Tel: 0161 952 8200

London and South East
(all London boroughs)
Rose Court
2 Southwark Bridge Road
London SE1 9HS
Tel: 020 7717 2100

The Marches
(Hereford and Worcester, Shropshire, Staffordshire)
The Marches House
Midway
Newcastle-under-Lyme ST5 1DT
Tel: 01782 602300

North East
(Cleveland, Durham, Northumberland, Tyne and Wear)
Arden House
Regent Centre
Regent Farm Road
Gosforth
Newcastle Upon Tyne NE3 3JN
Tel: 0191 202 6200

North Midlands
(Derbyshire, Lincolnshire, Nottinghamshire)
1st Floor
The Pearson Building
55 Upper Parliament Street
Nottingham NG1 6AU
Tel: 0115 971 2800

Northern Home Counties
(Bedfordshire, Buckinghamshire, Cambridgeshire, Hertfordshire)
14 Cardiff Road
Luton LU1 1PP
Tel: 01582 444200

Scotland East
(Borders, Central, Fife, Grampian, Highland, Lothian, Tayside and
the island areas of Orkney and Sheltland)
Belford House
59 Belford Road
Edinburgh EH4 3UE
Tel: 0131 247 2000

Scotland West
(Dumfries and Galloway, Srathclyde and the Western Isles)
375 West George Street
Glasgow G2 4LW
Tel: 0141 275 3000

South
(Berkshire, Dorset, Hampshire, Isle of Wight, Wiltshire)
Priestly House
Priestly Road
Basingstoke RG24 9NW
Tel: 01256 404000

South West
(Avon, Cornwall, Devon, Gloucestershire, Somerset, Isles of Scilly)
Inter City House
Mitchell Lane
Victoria Street
Bristol BS1 6AN
Tel: 0117 988 6000

South Yorkshire and Humberside
(Humberside, South Yorkshire)
Sovereign House
110 Queen Street
Sheffield S1 2ES
Tel: 0114 291 2300

Wales
(Clwyd, Dyfed, Gwent, Gwynedd, Mid Glamorgan, Powys, South Glamorgan, West Glamorgan)
Brunel House
2 Fitzalan Road
Cardiff CF2 1SH
Tel: 029 2026 3000

West and North Yorkshire
(North Yorkshire, West Yorkshire)
8 St Paul's Street
Leeds LS1 2LE
Tel: 0113 283 4200

West Midlands
(West Midlands)
McLaren Building
35 Dale End
Birmingham B4 7NP
Tel: 0121 607 6200

Institute of Insurance Brokers
Higham Business Centre
Midland Road
Higham Ferrers NN10 8DW
Tel: 01933 410 003
Fax: 01933 410 020
Email: inst.ins.brokers@iib-uk.com
Website: www.iib-uk.com

The Institute of Risk Management
Lloyds Avenue House
6 Lloyds Avenue
London EC3N 3AX
Tel: 020 7709 9808
Fax: 020 7709 0716
Email: enquiries@theIRM.org
Website: www.theirm.org

Institution for Electrical Engineers
Savoy Place
London WC2R 0BL
Tel: 020 7240 1871
Fax: 020 7240 7735
Website: www.iee.org.uk

Institution of Occupational Safety and Health
The Grange
Highfield Drive
Wigton
Leicestershire LE18 1NN
Tel: 0116 257 3100
Fax: 0116 257 3101
Website: www.iosh.co.uk

Insurance Brokers Registration Council
Higham Business Centre
Midland Road
Higham Ferrers NN10 8DW
Tel: 01933 359083
Fax: 01933 359077

Motoring Uninsured Loss Recoveries Association
Tamesis House
35 St Phillips Avenue
Worcester Park KT4 8JA

Royal Society for the Prevention of Accidents
RoSPA House
353 Bristol Road
Birmingham B5 7ST
Tel: 0121 248 2000
Fax: 0121 248 2001
Website: www.rospa.co.uk

The Stationery Office
Tel: 0870 6005522
Fax: 0870 6005533
Website: www.itsofficial.co.uk

Index

D

L